Richard T. ⸺

27/8/90.

THE ENGLISH
READER

THE ENGLISH READER

An Anthology edited by
Godfrey Smith

PAVILION
MICHAEL JOSEPH

for
David Hughes
who made the valley ring

First published in Great Britain in 1988 by
PAVILION BOOKS LIMITED
196 Shaftesbury Avenue, London WC2H 8JL
in association with Michael Joseph Limited
27 Wrights Lane, Kensington, London W8 5TZ

Compilation, introduction and commentary copyright
© Godfrey Smith 1988. Copyright information for individual
extracts is given on pp. 301–2

Designed by Tom Sawyer

A CIP catalogue record for this book is
available from the British Library

ISBN 185145 250 4

Typeset by Wyvern Typesetting Limited, Bristol
Printed and bound by Billing and Sons Limited, Worcester

CONTENTS

THE MYSTERIOUS ENGLISH

DAMN YOU ENGLAND!

ANGLO-SAXON ATTITUDES

SOME ENGLISH FACES

OH BERNARD, THIS IS SO SUDDEN

A RIGHT LITTLE, TIGHT LITTLE CLINIC

DUFFLE COATS AND SPOTTED DICK

YOUR LORDSHIPS' MOST HUMBLE SERVANT

FORTY YEARS ON

STANDING OVATION

JOLLY BOATING WEATHER

GENTLEMEN MAY PRANCE BUT NOT DANCE

BROWN STREETS WITH LIGHTS OF GOLD

THE WAY THROUGH THE WOODS

CONTENTS

CONSIDER WHAT NATION THIS IS

NOT WAVING BUT DROWNING

ALL WHAT JAZZ

INTRODUCTION

Anyone hoping to find here a summer idyll about hearts at peace under an English heaven had best look elsewhere. This is not that kind of book. It lays no claim to encapsulate or encompass England or the English; any such claim would clearly be absurd. It is not meant to teach or edify. It is not intended to open new avenues or shed fresh light. It is meant entirely to divert.

It is about a curiously mysterious, elusive, and little understood people. It tries to show them warts and all, and will undoubtedly give offence to all those who see England as the best of all possible worlds. It is about a country that is changing fast; so fast that there has been little enough time for the English to understand what has been happening; let alone for anyone else to get a clear picture.

Yet it is not meant to be a downbeat or depressing story. On the contrary, I think England has an enormous amount going for it; but not always in the way people believe.

Partly still feudal, partly innovative, casual yet broadly caring, tolerant yet often uncomprehending, England is now a province of Europe and is unlikely ever to be anything else. It is one of the most inscrutable yet unquestionably civilised places on earth. It has given birth to a great literature, devised codes of law that have been adopted world-wide, evolved a legislature that creaks under the strains imposed on it, yet still has not been superseded by better. It is a land as quirkily ugly as it is breathtakingly beautiful, at once philistine and cultivated, reasonable and illogical, turbulent and peaceful, beset by saints and sinners, yobs and yuppies. It is changing very fast, and no-one quite knows how its story will end.

This is a partisan ragbag of gewgaws; of snapshots and snatches of prose and song; an unassuming kaleidoscope of sights and sounds and scents; one man's England. May it give as much pleasure to read as it did to assemble.

Godfrey Smith
Malmesbury, Summer 1988

THE MYSTERIOUS
ENGLISH

First, three solid and, on the whole, traditional views of England and the English from three celebrated pens. George Orwell, with whom we open the book, is perhaps the most sensible and middle-of-the-road; he notes English gentleness, snobbishness, and xenophobia. Next, Stanley Baldwin who, though now out of fashion, probably had a command of received English style given to only a few prime ministers, on what we might almost call the Worthington view of England: the tinkle of the hammer on the anvil, the sound of the scythe against the whetstone. He hopes that the English tradition will live on ten thousand centuries after the English Empire has gone. It is a long shot, but who knows? He might be right. E.M. Forster has perhaps the most subtle perception of English character. His contrast between the emotions of his Indian friend and himself on parting company after a week's holiday is as engaging as it is comic. The Indian wants a large emotional scene; Forster, the Englishman, a small one. Forster notes too that, in an emergency, the Frenchman panics, while the Englishman remains calm. The Englishman, however, has a nervous breakdown later. He compares the English character to the sea: it looks blue and level; it is only when we look closely into it that we see it has a dozen colours, and depth below depth, and fish swimming in them. And, to continue his metaphor, the fish are English emotions, which are always trying to get up to the surface, but don't quite know how.

THE ENGLISH PEOPLE

GEORGE ORWELL

Our imaginary foreign observer would certainly be struck by our gentleness: by the orderly behaviour of English crowds, the lack of pushing and quarrelling, the willingness to form queues, the good temper of harassed, overworked people like bus conductors. The manners of the English working class are not always very graceful, but they are extremely considerate. Great care is taken in showing a stranger the way, blind people can travel across London with the certainty that they will be helped on and off every bus and across every street. In war-time a few of the policemen carry revolvers, but England has nothing corresponding to the *gendarmerie*, the semi-military police living in barracks and armed with rifles (sometimes even with tanks and aeroplanes), who are the guardians of society all the way from Calais to Tokyo. And except for certain well-defined areas in half a dozen big towns there is very little crime or violence. The average of honesty is lower in the big towns than in the country, but even in London the news-vendor can safely leave his pile of pennies on the pavement while he goes for a drink. The prevailing gentleness of manners is a recent thing, however. Well within living memory it was impossible for a smartly dressed person to walk down Ratcliff Highway without being assaulted, and an eminent jurist, asked to name a typically English crime, could answer: 'Kicking your wife to death'.

There is no revolutionary tradition in England, and even in extremist political parties, it is only the middle-class membership that thinks in revolutionary terms. The masses still more or less assume that 'against the law' is a synonym for 'wrong'. It is known that the criminal law is harsh and full of anomalies and that litigation is so expensive as always to favour the rich against the poor: but there is a general feeling that the law, such as it is, will be scrupulously administered, that a judge or magistrate cannot be bribed, that no one will be punished without trial. An Englishman does not believe in his bones, as a Spanish or Italian peasant does, that the law is simply a racket. It is precisely this general confidence in the law that has allowed a good deal of recent tampering with Habeas Corpus to escape public notice. But it also causes some ugly situations to end peacefully. During the worst of the London blitz the authorities tried to prevent the public from using the Tube stations as shelters. The people did not reply by storming the gates, they simply bought themselves penny-halfpenny tickets: they thus had legal status as passengers, and there was no thought of turning them out again.

The traditional English xenophobia is stronger among the working class than the middle class. It was partly the resistance of the trade unions that prevented a really large influx of refugees from the Fascist countries before the war, and when the German refugees were interned in 1940, it was not the working class that protested. The difference in habits, and especially in food and language, makes it very hard for English working people to get on with foreigners. Their diet differs a great deal from that of any European nation, and they are extremely conservative about it. As a rule they will refuse even to sample a foreign dish, they regard such things as garlic and olive oil with disgust, life is unlivable to them unless they have tea and puddings. And the peculiarities of the English language make it almost impossible for anyone who has left school at fourteen to learn a foreign language after he has grown up. In the French Foreign Legion, for instance, the British and American legionaries seldom rise out of the ranks, because they cannot learn French, whereas a German learns French in a few months. English working people, as a rule, think it effeminate even to pronounce a foreign word correctly. This is bound up with the fact that the upper classes learn foreign languages as a regular part of their education. Travelling abroad, speaking foreign tongues, enjoying foreign food, are vaguely felt to be upper-class habits, a species of snobbery, so that xenophobia is reinforced by class jealousy.

Perhaps the most horrible spectacles in England are the Dogs' Cemeteries in Kensington Gardens, at Stoke Poges (it actually adjoins the churchyard where Gray wrote his famous 'Elegy') and at various other places. But there were also the Animals' ARP [Air Raid Precautions] Centres, with miniature stretchers for cats, and in the first year of the war there was the spectacle of Animal Day being celebrated with all its usual pomp in the middle of the Dunkirk evacuation. Although its worst follies are committed by the upper-class women, the animal cult runs right through the nation and is probably bound up with the decay of agriculture and the dwindled birthrate. Several years of stringent rationing have failed to reduce the dog and cat population, and even in poor quarters of big towns the bird-fanciers' shops display canary seed at prices ranging up to twenty-five shillings a pint.

Hypocrisy is so generally accepted as part of the English character that a foreign observer would be prepared to meet with it at every turn, but he would find especially ripe examples in the laws dealing with gambling, drinking, prostitution, and profanity. He would find it difficult to reconcile the anti-imperialistic sentiments which are commonly expressed in England with the size of the British Empire. If he were a continental European he would notice with ironical amusement that the English think it wicked to have a big army but see nothing wrong in having a big navy. This too he would set down as hypocrisy – not altogether fairly, for it is the fact of being an island, and therefore not needing a big army, that has allowed British democratic institutions to grow up, and the mass of the people are fairly well aware of this.

Exaggerated class distinctions have been diminishing over a period of about thirty years, and the war has probably speeded up the process, but newcomers to England are still astonished and sometimes horrified by the blatant differences between class and class. The great majority of the people can still be 'placed' in an instant by their manners, clothes and general appearance. Even the physical type differs considerably, the upper classes being on an average several inches taller than the working class. But the most striking difference of all is in language and accent. The English working class, as Mr Wyndham Lewis has put it, are 'branded on the tongue'. And though class distinctions do not exactly coincide with economic distinctions, the contrast between wealth and poverty is very much more glaring, and more taken for granted, than in most countries.

The English were the inventors of several of the world's most popular games, and have spread them more widely than any other product of their culture. The word 'football' is mispronounced by scores of millions who have never heard of Shakespeare or Magna Carta. The English themselves are not outstandingly good at all games, but they enjoy playing them, and to an extent that strikes foreigners as childish they enjoy reading about them and betting on them. During the between-war years the football pools did more than any other one thing to make life bearable for the unemployed. Professional footballers, boxers, jockeys, and even cricketers enjoy a popularity that no scientist or artist could hope to rival. Nevertheless sport worship is not carried to quite such imbecile lengths as one would imagine from reading the popular press. When the brilliant lightweight boxer, Kid Lewis, stood for Parliament in his native borough, he only scored a hundred and twenty-five votes.

These traits that we have enumerated are probably the ones that would strike an intelligent observer first. Out of them he might feel that he could construct a reliable picture of the English character. But then probably a thought would strike him: is there such a thing as 'the English character'? Can one talk about nations as though they were individuals? And supposing that one can, is there any genuine continuity between the England of today and the England of the past?

As he wandered through the London streets, he would notice the old prints in the bookshop windows, and it would occur to him that if these

18

things are representative, then England must have changed a great deal. It is not much more than a hundred years since the distinguishing mark of English life was its brutality. The common people, to judge by the prints, spent their time in an almost unending round of fighting, whoring, drunkenness and bull-baiting. Moreover, even the physical type appears to have changed. Where are they gone, the hulking draymen and low-browed prize-fighters, the brawny sailors with their buttocks bursting out of their white trousers, and the great overblown beauties with their swelling bosoms, like the figure-heads of Nelson's ships? What had these people in common with the gentle-mannered, undemonstrative, law-abiding English of today? Do such things as 'national cultures' really exist?

This is one of those questions, like the freedom of the will or the identity of the individual, in which all the arguments are on one side and instinctive knowledge is on the other. It is not easy to discover the connecting thread that runs through English life from the sixteenth century onwards, but all English people who bother about such subjects feel that it exists. They feel that they understand the institutions that have come to them out of the past – Parliament, for instance, or sabbatarianism, or the subtle grading of the class system – with an inherited knowledge impossible to a foreigner. Individuals, too, are felt to conform to a national pattern. D. H. Lawrence is felt to be 'very English', but so is Blake; Dr Johnson and G. K. Chesterton are somehow the same kind of person. The belief that we resemble our ancestors – that Shakespeare, say, is more like a modern Englishman than a modern Frenchman or German – may be unreasonable, but by existing it influences conduct. Myths which are believed in tend to become true, because they set up a type, or 'persona', which the average person will do his best to resemble.

During the bad period of 1940 it became clear that in Britain national solidarity is stronger than class antagonism. If it were really true that 'the proletarian has no country', 1940 was the time for him to show it. It was exactly then, however, that class feeling slipped into the background, only reappearing when the immediate danger had passed. Moreover, it is probable that the stolid behaviour of the British town populations under the bombing was partly due to the existence of the national 'persona' – that is, to their preconceived idea of themselves. Traditionally the Englishman is phleg-matic, unimaginative, not easily rattled: and since that is what he thinks he ought to be, that is what he tends to become. Dislike of hysteria and 'fuss', admiration for stubbornness, are all but universal in England, being shared by everyone except the intelligentsia. Millions of English people willingly accept as their national emblem the bulldog, an animal noted for its obstinacy, ugliness, and impenetrable stupidity. They have a remarkable readiness to admit that foreigners are more 'clever' than themselves, and yet they feel that it would be an outrage against the laws of God and Nature for England to be ruled by foreigners. Our imaginary observer would notice, perhaps, that Wordsworth's sonnets during the Napoleonic war might have been written during this one. He would know already that England has produced poets and scientists rather than philosophers, theologians, or pure theorists of any description. And he might end by deciding that a profound, almost unconscious patriotism and an inability to think logically are the abiding features of the English character, traceable in English literature from Shakespeare onwards.

1944

ON ENGLAND

STANLEY BALDWIN

To me, England is the country, and the country is England. And when I ask myself what I mean by England, when I think of England when I am abroad, England comes to me through my various senses – through the ear, through the eye, and through certain imperishable scents. I will tell you what they are, and there may be those among you who feel as I do.

The sounds of England, the tinkle of the hammer on the anvil in the country smithy, the corncrake on a dewy morning, the sound of the scythe against the whetstone, and the sight of a plough team coming over the brow of a hill, the sight that has been seen in England since England was a land, and may be seen in England long after the Empire has perished and every works in England has ceased to function, for centuries the one eternal sight of England. The wild anemones in the woods in April, the last load at night of hay being drawn down a lane as the twilight comes on, when you can scarcely distinguish the figures of the horses as they take it home to the farm, and above all, most subtle, most penetrating and most moving, the smell of wood smoke coming up in an autumn evening, or the smell of the scutch fires: that wood smoke that our ancestors, tens of thousands of years ago, must have caught on the air when they were coming home with the result of the day's forage, when they were still nomads, and when they were still roaming the forests and the plains of the continent of Europe. These things strike down into the very depths of our nature, and touch chords that go back to the beginning of time and the human race, but they are chords that with every year of our life sound a deeper note in our innermost being.

These are the things that make England, and I grieve for it that they are not the childish inheritance of the majority of the people today in our country. They ought to be the inheritance of every child born into this country, but nothing can be more touching than to see how the working man and woman after generations in the towns will have their tiny bit of garden if they can, will go to gardens if they can, to look at something they have never seen as children, but which their ancestors knew and loved. The love of these things is innate and inherent in our people. It makes for that love of home, one of the strongest features of our race, and it is that that makes our race seek its new home in the Dominions overseas, where they have room to see things like this that they can no more see at home. It is that power of making homes, almost peculiar to our people, and it is one of the sources of their greatness. They go overseas, and they take with them what they learned at home: love of justice, love of truth, and the broad humanity that are so characteristic of English people. It may well be that these traits on which we pride ourselves, which we hope to show and try to show in our own lives, may survive – survive among our people so long as they are a people – and I hope and believe this, that just as today more than fifteen centuries since the last of those great Roman legionaries left England, we still speak of the Roman strength, and the Roman work, and the Roman character, so perhaps in the ten thousandth century, long after the Empires of this world as we know them have fallen and others have risen and fallen, and risen and fallen again, the men who are then on this earth may yet speak of those characteristics which we prize as the characteristics of the English, and that long after, maybe, the name of the country has passed away, wherever men are honourable and upright and persevering, lovers of home, of their brethren, of justice and of humanity, the men in the world of that day may say, 'We still have among us the gifts of that great English race.'

1926

NOTES ON THE ENGLISH CHARACTER

E M FORSTER

First Note. I had better let the cat out of the bag at once and record my opinion that the character of the English is essentially middle-class. There is a sound historical reason for this, for, since the end of the eighteenth century, the middle classes have been the dominant force in our community. They gained wealth by the Industrial Revolution, political power by the Reform Bill of 1832; they are connected with the rise and organization of the British Empire; they are responsible for the literature of the nineteenth century. Solidity, caution, integrity, efficiency. Lack of imagination, hypocrisy. These qualities characterize the middle classes in every country, but in England they are national characteristics also, because only in England have the middle classes been in power for one hundred and fifty years. Napoleon, in his rude way, called us 'a nation of shopkeepers'. We prefer to call ourselves 'a great commercial nation' – it sounds more dignified – but the two phrases amount to the same. Of course there are other classes: there is an aristocracy, there are the poor. But it is on the middle classes that the eye of the critic rests – just as it rests on the poor in Russia and on the aristocracy in Japan. Russia is symbolized by the peasant or by the factory worker; Japan by the samurai; the national figure of England is Mr Bull with his top hat, his comfortable clothes, his substantial stomach, and his substantial balance at the bank. Saint George may caper on banners and in the speeches of politicians, but it is John Bull who delivers the goods. And even Saint George – if Gibbon is correct – wore a top hat once; he was an army contractor and supplied indifferent bacon. It all amounts to the same in the end.

Second Note. Just as the heart of England is the middle classes, so the heart of

21

the middle classes is the public-school system. This extraordinary institution is local. It does not even exist all over the British Isles. It is unknown in Ireland, almost unknown in Scotland (countries excluded from my survey), and though it may inspire other great institutions – Aligarh, for example, and some of the schools in the United States – it remains unique, because it was created by the Anglo-Saxon middle classes, and can flourish only where they flourish. How perfectly it expresses their character – far better, for instance, than does the university, into which social and spiritual complexities have already entered. With its boarding-houses, its compulsory games, its system of prefects and fagging, its insistence on good form and on *esprit de corps*, it produces a type whose weight is out of all proportion to its numbers.

On leaving his school, the boy either sets to work at once – goes into the army or into business, or emigrates – or else proceeds to the university, and after three or four years there enters some other profession – becomes a barrister, doctor, civil servant, schoolmaster, or journalist. (If through some mishap he does not become a manual worker or an artist.) In all these careers his education, or the absence of it, influences him. Its memories influence him also. Many men look back on their school days as the happiest of their lives. They remember with regret that golden time when life, though hard, was not yet complex; when they all worked together and played together and thought together, so far as they thought at all: when they were taught that school is the world in miniature and believed that no one can love his country who does not love his school. And they prolong that time as best they can by joining their Old Boys' society; indeed, some of them remain Old Boys and nothing else for the rest of their lives. They attribute all good to the school. They worship it. They quote the remark that 'the battle of Waterloo was won on the playing-fields of Eton'. It is nothing to them that the remark is inapplicable historically and was never made by the Duke of Wellington, and that the Duke of Wellington was an Irishman. They go on quoting it because it expresses their sentiments; they feel that if the Duke of Wellington didn't make it he ought to have, and if he wasn't an Englishman he ought to have been. And they go forth into a world that is not entirely composed of public-school men or even of Anglo-Saxons, but of men who are as various as the sands of the sea; into a world of whose richness and subtlety they have no conception. They go forth into it with well-developed bodies, fairly developed minds, and undeveloped hearts. And it is this undeveloped heart that is largely responsible for the difficulties of Englishmen abroad. An undeveloped heart – not a cold one. The difference is important, and on it my next note will be based.

For it is not that the Englishman can't feel – it is that he is afraid to feel. He has been taught at his public school that feeling is bad form. He must not express great joy or sorrow, or even open his mouth too wide when he talks – his pipe might fall out if he did. He must bottle up his emotions, or let them out only on a very special occasion.

Once upon a time (this is an anecdote) I went for a week's holiday on the Continent with an Indian friend. We both enjoyed ourselves and were sorry when the week was over, but on parting our behaviour was absolutely different. He was plunged in despair. He felt that because the holiday was over all happiness was over until the world ended. He could not express his sorrow too much. But in me the Englishman came out strong. I reflected that we should meet again in a month or two, and could write in the interval if we had anything to say; and under these circumstances I could not see what there was to make a fuss about. It wasn't as if we were parting forever or dying. 'Buck up,' I said, 'do buck up.' He refused to buck up, and I left him plunged in gloom.

The conclusion of the anecdote is even more instructive. For when we met the next month our conversation threw a good deal of light on the English character. I began by scolding my friend. I told him that he had been wrong to feel and display so much emotion upon so slight an occasion; that it was inappropriate. The word 'inappropriate' roused him to fury. 'What?' he cried. 'Do you measure out your emotions as if they were potatoes?' I did not like the simile of the potatoes, but after a moment's reflection I said, 'Yes, I do; and what's more, I think I ought to. A small occasion demands a little emotion, just as a large occasion demands a great one. I would like my emotions to be appropriate. This may be measuring them like potatoes, but it is better than slopping them about like water from a pail, which is what you did.' He did not like the simile of the pail. 'If those are your opinions, they part us forever,' he cried, and left the room. Returning immediately, he added: 'No – but your whole attitude toward emotion is wrong. Emotion has nothing to do with appropriateness. It matters only that it shall be sincere. I happened to feel deeply. I showed it. It doesn't matter whether I ought to have felt deeply or not.'

This remark impressed me very much. Yet I could not agree with it, and said that I valued emotion as much as he did, but used it differently; if I poured it out on small occasions I was afraid of having none left for the great ones, and of being bankrupt at the crises of life. Note the word 'bankrupt'. I spoke as a member of a prudent middle-class nation, always anxious to meet my liabilities. But my friend spoke as an Oriental, and the Oriental has behind him a tradition, not of middle-class prudence, but of kingly munificence and splendour. He feels his resources are endless, just as John Bull feels his are finite. As regards material resources, the Oriental is clearly unwise. Money isn't endless. If we spend or give away all the money we have, we haven't any more, and must take the consequences, which are frequently unpleasant. But, as regards the resources of the spirit, he may be right. The emotions may be endless. The more we express them, the more we may have to express.

> True love in this differs from gold and clay,
> That to divide is not to take away,

says Shelley. Shelley, at all events, believes that the wealth of the spirit is endless; that we may express it copiously, passionately, and always; and that we can never feel sorrow or joy too acutely.

In the above anecdote, I have figured as a typical Englishman. I will now descend from that dizzy and somewhat unfamiliar height, and return to my business of note-taking. A note on the *slowness* of the English character. The Englishman appears to be cold and unemotional because he is really slow. When an event happens, he may understand it quickly enough with his mind, but he takes quite a while to feel it. Once upon a time a coach, containing some Englishmen and some Frenchmen, was driving over the Alps. The horses ran away, and as they were dashing across a bridge the coach caught on the stonework, tottered, and nearly fell into the ravine below. The Frenchmen were frantic with terror: they screamed and gesticulated and flung themselves about, as Frenchmen would. The Englishmen sat quite calm. An hour later the coach drew up at an inn to change horses, and by that time the situations were exactly reversed. The Frenchmen had forgotten all about the danger, and were chattering gaily; the Englishmen had just begun to feel it, and one had a nervous breakdown and was obliged to go to bed. We have here a clear physical difference between the two races – a difference that goes deep into character. The Frenchmen responded at once; the Englishmen responded in time. They were slow and they were also practical. Their instinct forbade them to throw themselves about in the coach, because it was more likely to tip over if they did. They had this extraordinary appreciation of *fact* that we shall notice again and again. When a disaster comes, the English instinct is to do what can be done first, and to postpone the feeling as long as possible. Hence they are splendid at emergencies. No doubt they are brave – no one will deny that – but bravery is partly an affair of the nerves, and the English nervous system is well equipped for meeting a physical emergency. It acts promptly and feels slowly. Such a combination is fruitful, and anyone who possesses it has gone a long way toward being brave. And when the action is over, then the Englishman can feel.

There is one more consideration – a most important one. If the English nature is cold, how is it that it has produced a great literature and a literature that is particularly great in poetry? Judged by its prose, English literature would not stand in the first rank. It is its poetry that raises it to the level of Greek, Persian, or French. And yet the English are supposed to be so unpoetical. How is this? The nation that produced the Elizabethan drama and the Lake Poets cannot be a cold, unpoetical nation. We can't get fire out of ice. Since literature always rests upon national character, there must be in the English nature hidden springs of fire to produce the fire we see. The warm sympathy, the romance, the imagination, that we look for in Englishmen whom we meet, and too often vainly look for, must exist in the nation as a whole, or we could not have this outburst of national song. An undeveloped heart – not a cold one.

The trouble is that the English nature is not at all easy to understand. It has a great air of simplicity, it advertises itself as simple, but the more we consider it, the greater the problems we shall encounter. People talk of the mysterious East, but the West also is mysterious. It has depths that do not reveal themselves at the first gaze. We know what the sea looks like from a distance: it is of one colour, and level, and obviously cannot contain such creatures as fish. But if we look into the sea over the edge of a boat, we see a dozen colours, and depth below depth, and fish swimming in them. That sea is the

English character – apparently imperturbable and even. The depths and the colours are the English romanticism and the English sensitiveness – we do not expect to find such things, but they exist. And – to continue my metaphor – the fish are the English emotions, which are always trying to get up to the surface, but don't quite know how. For the most part we see them moving far below, distorted and obscure. Now and then they succeed and we exclaim, 'Why, the Englishman has emotions! He actually can feel!' And occasionally we see that beautiful creature the flying fish, which rises out of the water altogether into the air and the sunlight. English literature is a flying fish. It is a sample of the life that goes on day after day beneath the surface; it is a proof that beauty and emotion exist in the salt, inhospitable sea.

1936

DAMN YOU ENGLAND!

And now, a sharp change of mood and pace. When John Osborne made his stunning début with Look Back in Anger *in 1956, he changed the English theatre for good. The anodyne comedies of Binkie Beaumont were out; the gritty imperatives of the kitchen sink were in. Osborne brought to his task an exhilarating command of the English language, and a talent for invective seldom equalled this century. His 'Letter to His Fellow Countrymen', published in the Socialist journal* Tribune *in 1961, caused a splendid storm. What few realized at the time was that his hatred was the other side of love. In a speech of his we shall read later, he pilloried the received view of an Edwardian England, all golden sunshine and C Major chords, which he held to be preposterously far-fetched – as no doubt it was. Yet only recently he was urging* Spectator *readers to join him in savouring a new book called* Children of the Souls, *a threnody on the doomed* jeunesse dorée *of Edwardian England which he confessed he had found almost unbearable to read. He hated England for shattering his romantic image of it. Still, the letter is a masterpiece of diatribe.*

Then Alan Bennett gave us his play The Old Country *in which a Philby lookalike who has gone over to the other side sits in his Russian dacha, still wearing his Garrick Club tie, reading* The Times, *and playing Elgar incessantly on his gramophone. He remains English in all but one crucial regard. His analysis – through the viewpoint of his Hilary/Philby character – of E. M. Forster's famous remark about betraying his country rather than betraying his friend is riveting.*

A LETTER TO MY FELLOW COUNTRYMEN

JOHN OSBORNE

This is a letter of hate. It is for you, my countrymen. I mean those men of my country who have defiled it. The men with manic fingers leading the sightless, feeble, betrayed body of my country to its death. You are its murderers, and there's little left in my own brain but the thoughts of murder for you.

I cannot even address you as I began as 'Dear', for that word alone would sin against my hatred. And this, my hatred for you, and those who tolerate you, is about all I have left and all the petty dignity my death may keep.

No, this is not the highly paid 'anger' or the 'rhetoric' you like to smile at (you've tried to mangle my language, too). You'll not pour pennies into my coffin for this; you are *my* object. I am not yours. You are my vessel, you are *my* hatred. That is my final identity. True, it will no doubt die with me in a short time and by your unceasing efforts.

But perhaps it could be preserved, somewhere, in the dead world that you have prepared for us, perhaps the tiny, unbared spark of my human hatred might kindle, just for the briefest moment in time, the life you lost for us.

I fear death. I dread it daily. I cling wretchedly to life, as I have always done. I fear death, but I cannot hate it as I hate you. It is only you I hate, and those who let you live, function and prosper.

My hatred for you is almost the only constant satisfaction you have left me. My favourite fantasy is four minutes or so non-commercial viewing as you fry in your democratically elected hot seats in Westminster, preferably with your condoning democratic constituents.

There is murder in my brain, and I carry a knife in my heart for every one of you. Macmillan, and you, Gaitskell, you particularly. I wish we could hang you all out, with your dirty washing, on your damned Oder-Neisse Line, and those seven out of ten Americans, too. I would willingly watch you all die for the West, if only I could keep my own miniscule portion of it, you could all go ahead and die for Berlin, for Democracy, to keep out the red hordes or whatever you like.

You have instructed me in my hatred for thirty years. You have perfected it, and made it the blunt, obsolete instrument it is now. I only hope it will keep me going. I think it will. I think it may sustain me in the last few months.

Till then, damn you, England. You're rotting now, and quite soon you'll disappear. My hate will outrun you yet, if only for a few seconds. I wish it could be eternal.

I write this from another country, with murder in my brain and a knife carried in my heart for every one of you. I am not alone. If *we* had just the ultimate decency and courage, we would strike at you – now, before you blaspheme against the world in our name. There is nothing I should not give for your blood on my head.

But all I can offer you is my hatred. You will be untouched by that, for you are untouchable. Untouchable, unteachable, impregnable.

If you were offered the heart of Jesus Christ, your Lord and your Saviour – though not mine, alas – you'd sniff at it like sour offal.

For that is the Kind of Men you are.

Believe me,

    In sincere and utter hatred,

    Your Fellow Countryman

1961

THE OLD COUNTRY

ALAN BENNETT

VERONICA: And who was it tipped you off?

HILARY: It could have been anybody.

DUFF: Anybody brought up on Forster. 'If I had to choose between betraying my country and betraying my friend I hope I should have the guts to betray my country.'

VERONICA: The old boy must have had nice friends. I'd plump for the old Union Jack any day.

HILARY: All that's rubbish anyway.

DUFF: Hilary.

HILARY: Nancy rubbish. You only have to substitute 'my wife' for 'my friend' to find it's nothing like as noble. 'If I had to choose between betraying my country and betraying my wife I hope I should have the guts to betray my country.' Well . . . yes. I should hope so too. Wouldn't most people? And put the other way round it's sheer music hall. 'If I had to choose between betraying my country and betraying my wife I should betray my wife.' 'Your wife?' 'My wife.' 'Kindly leave the country.' If I had to choose between betraying my country and betraying my children I hope I should have the guts to betray my country. *Guts?* Or. If I had to choose between betraying my country and betraying . . . my brother-in-law . . . No, you see Duff. Friend is what does it. My friend. That's what brings in the cellos. My friend. Who is my friend? My friend is the memory of the youth half of them were gone on at school. My friend is True Love as it presents itself the one and only time in their stunted, little lives in the shape of some fourteen-year-old tart giving them the glad eye during the service of Nine Lessons and Carols. And then of course they did have a choice, if they had but known it. If only in the matter of a kiss in the long grass behind the sightscreens. A choice between country, which is to say school, headmaster, government club and class; and fidelity, which is to say friendship, honour, compassion and all the other virtues which, if they were going to get anywhere at all in the world they were going to have to betray anyway.

BRON: They? You. Us.

HILARY: No. That is their game and I have never played it.

BRON: But not wives. They never get a look in. Wives are part of the betrayal. Wives are part of the selling-out. Wives are settling for something. Do not go home. Do not settle down. 'Leave for Cape Wrath tonight.'

VERONICA: And your friend, whoever he was?

HILARY: Unknown and unthanked.

DUFF: He certainly did you a good turn.

HILARY: Possibly. Possibly. After all we weren't entirely welcome here either. Like the unlooked for arrival of a distant relative from Australia. Naturally they made the best of it. Kitted us out. Job. Flat. Not unpleasant. But a good turn would you say, Bron? Not entirely.

VERONICA: So come back.

DUFF: Let me come clean. There have been several occasions this last year (so different is the atmosphere nowadays) when one or two of us have been sitting around, powers that be in a mood of relaxation when quite independently your name has come up. And people have suddenly started scratching their heads and saying, 'What are we going to do about old Hilary?' You've been stuck here now for what, thirteen, fourteen years. Fourteen years *in partibus infidelium*, and the upshot is, some of us are now prepared to come out and say enough is enough. Now I can't quite say, 'Come home. All is forgiven.' There are still one or two people who feel quite strongly. Time dwindles their number but the fact remains, there were deaths, disappearances. People . . . died. Some of them first class. And I think you will probably be made to stand in the corner for three or four years,

five at the outside, which with remission means three, which with parole would probably be two and in one of these open places (I'm on the board of a couple) more hydros than houses of correction. Librarian pushing your trolly round. Rather fun, I would have thought. Then once that's out of the way you can get a little place somewhere. Gloucestershire would be nice, handy for Bath. They've got a delightful festival now . . . and Bristol, the Old Vic, restaurants galore; England's changed since your day, all sorts of places now where you can get a really first-class meal. And financially, of course, no more problems. Television, the Sundays, people falling over themselves. You could even write this book you were talking about. Set up your stall in the open market. I guarantee you'll have plenty of customers. Granted some people are going to turn their backs, but we live in a pluralist society and what does that mean: it means somebody somewhere loves you. What do you say?
BRON: You're wasting your time.
VERONICA: Did you know?
BRON: No.
HILARY: She never asked.
BRON: Because I never dreamed. What had it to do with me? You think your husband is in central heating. You find out he is in refrigerators. A commercial traveller toting his cheap little case of samples round the suburbs. Little appointments. Rickmansworth. Ruislip. Dollis Hill.
HILARY: Not Dollis Hill. Never Dollis Hill. I give you Ruislip, Pinner. But not Dollis Hill.
BRON: What does it matter?
HILARY: My wife has no sense of place. To her one spot is very much like another. It matters to me. It was my rendezvous. The top of my week. My epiphany. But hardly a double life. About as double as yours is double, Duff. The inner life of personal relations. The outer life of anagrams and Ongar. I say Ongar. Ruislip. Meetings at line's ending.
DUFF: At the station?
HILARY: Thereabouts. I used to walk from the station. Always walked. I took my umbrella, strode out into the suburbs and really revelled in it. Priestley, Duff. Wells. A little man on the loose. Past the ideal homes and Green Line bus stops. Factory sportsfields lined with poplars. I was so *happy*. Is it still unloved, that landscape? I loved it. Boarding kennels, down-at-heel riding schools, damp bungalows in wizened orchards. The metropolis tailing off into these forlorn enterprises. And not inappropriate. Had my superiors been blessed with irony I might have thought the setting deliberately chosen to point up the folly of individual endeavour. As it was I grew fond of it. And just as well. Shacks, allotments, dead ground. So many places like that now. Here. Africa. Soon, already, Arabia. Well, it suits me. At home in one you can be at home in them all.
DUFF: Forgive me, but am I fanciful if I begin to see your defection, say rather your odyssey in terms almost of a choice of *setting*? The heart of the country. The edge of the city. Two worlds. Past. Future. Not difficult to betray your country in so drab a setting for that setting has already betrayed the country you stood for: the house in the park, the church in the trees. No. Well.

31

Possibly not.

HILARY: Is it a programme note that you want? Extracts from pertinent texts to point you in the right direction. Shots of the Depression, the upper classes at play. Injustice the impetus, the guilt of one's breeding. Neat. Good intentioned. The best motives gone wrong. Would that find favour?

DUFF: It's not unfamiliar. The road many took. Though few went so far.

1978

ANGLO-SAXON ATTITUDES

Although the New Statesman *is not what it was – and which of us is? – one undisputed contribution it has made to the gaiety of the nation has been a brilliant collation of quotations in the public print over the previous week. Run together, they present a hardly credible picture of the island race's knuckle-headed chauvinism, snobbery, and xenophobia. Could these magnificently deranged remarks be authentic – or are they the fruit of midnight labour by some* New Statesman *hack? The answer is hardly more credible than the quotes themselves.*

ANGLO-SAXON ATTITUDES

NEW STATESMAN

MR WOGG AND MR WOPP
It is time English people showed a natural and legitimate pride of race. When foreigners take English names, surely it is not seemly for them to assume good old English surnames. Let certain names be set apart for their purpose. – Letter in *Evening Standard*.

A POSTERIORI
Standing, with his back to a real fireplace, the British father presents to his wife and children a picture of dignity and importance. Standing with his back to a steaming radiator, the American father looks just ordinary. – *Daily Mirror*

SOVEREIGN RITES
The practice of singing the National Anthem in the Stock Exchange on appropriate occasions is to be resumed . . . Singing will be conducted from a seat in the Gilt-edged market. – *Financial Times*

PERFIDIOUS ALIENS
'Don't ever expect anyone but an English person to understand what an agreement means.' – County Court Judge, reported by *Evening Argus*

CHOLERA
If poverty and oppression continue to be the lot of Asiatic peoples, they bring it on themselves by indulging in costly and wicked passions like the hatred of foreigners. – *Tablet*

WRONG DIRECTION
All UNO can do is to pass resolutions. When these are directed at Britain they have no moral force and should be treated with contempt. – Editorial in *Daily Express*

PYRRHIC DEFEAT

The many forces that have suffered defeat at the hands of the British soldier with all his crudities appear to prefer to be defeated by him rather than by any army in the world. – Letter in *The Times*

BLOWING HOT AND COLD

How can the French expect to attract our tourist trade? This year, at five different French hotels, the tap marked 'C' turned out to be 'H'. – Letter in *Evening Chronicle*

FIFTH COLUMN

If general architectural standards in England since the war are considered to be low, the fault may be due to the influence of foreign architects who obtained teaching posts here during the war. – Letter in *The Times*

BULLY BEEF

Mr S. K. Spokes, a Clipston farmer, told Market Harborough NFU members last night that for the sake of peace he did not believe people in the East should be encouraged to eat beef.

Mr Spokes said: 'My experience is that to give men plenty of red meat to eat makes them so fit and well that they become almost violent. I think we have enough trouble with the violent people we already have, and I suggest we leave these people to their rice. Let us not aggravate the situation by wanting them to start eating beef.' – *Leicester Mercury*

MISSING LINK

Having spent many years seeing strange faces of many nations, I believe that this is probably the only country capable of producing faces which carry their pedigree for all to see. – Letter in *Daily Express*

DIRTY FOREIGNERS . . .

When so much is said about dogs being forbidden in food shops, why are foreigners allowed to handle food, and even smell it before purchase? Surely this is even more unhygienic than a well-trained dog walking through a shop? – Letter in *Bedfordshire Times & Standard*

. . . AND CLEAN FOREIGNERS

Indians who use Nuneaton public slipper baths are using so much hot water that Nuneaton Borough Council proposes to charge them a special rate. A Council official said today: 'These Indians do not bath like English people. They first scrub themselves in a bath of hot water and the process is repeated with a second bathful. Then they have it filled a third time to rinse their bodies. All this is running away with the hot water supply. We are going to explain the position to the Indians and will have to charge them for each bathful.' – *Birmingham Mail*

OTHER RANKS
Councillor Wallsgrove commented: 'I have nothing against coloured people personally, but I feel the general public would prefer to be driven by a white man. I know many Indians are perfect gentlemen, but I don't think they should go into an intimate business like the taxi business.' – *Coventry Evening Telegraph*

BILATERAL
Of course we English believe in God. We always have, but what is more to the point He believes in us. How otherwise could we have built a mighty Empire? – Letter in *Manchester Evening News*

LET THERE BE DARK
I cannot help wondering why God created coloured people, seeing all the resultant difficulties caused thereby. – *Church Times*

SOUTH-WEST FRONTIER
And Mr Cyril Rigby, at No. 32, said: 'I am not racially prejudiced but I don't want coloured people in my road. They ought to go to Brixton. They would be happy there.' – *Daily Mail*

OWN MEDICINE
There were four of us in the doctor's waiting room when in walked a Pakistani. He was about to go straight into the surgery when a woman jumped up and grabbed his arm, saying in very deliberate English: 'We are before you. You take your turn. Understand?' The Pakistani, in equally deliberate English, replied: 'No, you are after me. Me doctor. Understand?' – *Daily Mirror*

LIGHTEN OUR DARKNESS
Their collective attitude was perhaps best summed up by the Conservative woman councillor who told us: 'Oh yes, we Tory councillors have done a lot for race relations. I do think it's very important. After all, but for the Grace of God, we'd be black ourselves, wouldn't we?' – *Sunday Times*

PADDY FIELDS
A lance corporal in the Royal Artillery put the problem a little more succinctly: 'We wouldn't have no bother here if the Irish were wogs; if they was wogs we could just get stuck in and sort them out and no one would worry. Instead of that, there's all this talk about us murdering them.' – *Sunday Times*

GOOD IN BED
The first black teddy bear is selling twice as fast as the conventional brown 'teddies', according to the Watford firm which makes them. Children have taken well to them, but many women are buying the black bears which project 'a very powerful virile masculine image'. – *Guardian*

SPORT
Our first parents – Adam and Eve – were white. How then did the coloured races come into existence? This intriguing question baffles me. – Letter in *Daily Mail*

HERRING FOLK
We had made love twice in half an hour and I took £10 from his trousers and then another £20 because I don't like the way Americans dominate everyone in Great Yarmouth. – *News of the World*

PREYED ON
Pakistani Moslems who use the front room of a house in Slough for prayers have been ordered to stop by the council. Mr Mohammed Afzal said: 'The neighbours can't have complained of noise because we prayed silently.' Mr John King the borough engineer, said: 'It is true we have had no complaints, but we are concerned that this should be going on in a residential area.' – *Guardian*

COLD SHOULDER
One employer gave as his reason for not employing a coloured school-leaver: 'Your pigmentation would make you more allergic to frostbite in our frozen food.' – *Daily Telegraph*

KNOCKABOUT FUN
Leaders of immigrant communities in the Hulme and Moss Side districts of Manchester yesterday were urgently checking for any racial links after at least 500 coloured youths injured six police officers, two of them seriously, and damaged nine police vehicles. Chief Supt Ralph Lees, head of the police division covering the area, stressed there had been no racial undertones. 'Relationships between the coloured community and the police are absolutely excellent,' he declared. – *Daily Telegraph*

SLANTED
It was stated that Mr Chan was given exploding cigarettes by workmates, his gold lighter went missing and he was threatened and called a 'yellow bastard' on the factory night shift. The tribunal ruled that Mr Chan, of Ingleborough Drive, Ryton, now a waiter, had not been racially discriminated against. – *Daily Telegraph*

GOING SEPTIC
Peter Hardy, the MP for Rother Valley, has an elderly constituent who had a hospital appointment. 'The person was confused when the staff used the continental seven,' he said. 'I do not believe we should adopt all these continental practices. The French should learn to write numbers far more clearly.' – *Sheffield Star*

1968

SOME
ENGLISH FACES

Now a group of portraits in which the character and skill of the writer is as important as the subject he has chosen. That urbane and insightful political columnist Alan Watkins opens his book Brief Lives *with this beautifully judged picture of Kingsley Amis. W. H. Auden very seldom fails to delight and his essay on Lewis Carroll does not let us down; Virginia Woolf makes us long to get back to Parson Woodforde's Diary again. The two short fragments about Shakespeare are as fascinating as they are tantalizing: Ben Jonson was his friend ('I loved the man and do honour his memory on this side Idolatry as much as any'). If only, alas, he could have given us more than those two hundred and fifty precious words! John Aubrey's testimony is not quite so reliable. He was, after all, born nine years after Shakespeare died, but he knew many people who knew him – notably Ben Jonson himself. This time we get five hundred words and could have done with a hundred times as many.*

Immortal evenings are tolerably rare in our literature; but that night when Wordsworth and Lamb and Keats sat down together with Benjamin Haydon is happily preserved for all time in the painter's fresh-minted prose. Charles seems to have been the life and soul of the party, but then, as Haydon tells us, he went, joking to the last. Still, it is fascinating to be given the lively impression that we were members of that immortal supper party too.

Finally, a personal favourite: Ken Tynan's delicious portrait of the Australian boulevardier Stanley Parker written when Ken was all of twenty-two. Stanley hated it; yet in retrospect there is not a line in it that most of us would not have been proud to have said of us. 'He is the safest person I know,' Ken affirmed, 'in whom to invest the next ten minutes of one's life.'

KINGSLEY AMIS

16 April 1922

ALAN WATKINS

Kingsley Amis was the outstanding English novelist of those who began their writing careers after 1945. He was born and brought up in Clapham, in a standard semi-detached house of the inter-war period – basically two up and two down, with a kitchen and a bathroom. His father, William Robert Amis, was a senior clerk in a mustard firm in the City. W. R. Amis's family came from Norwich, where they had a glass-selling business. He played cricket, tennis and the piano. Kingsley's mother, Rosa Amis, was also musical, having a good singing voice, but resented that her sister had been musically trained, whereas she had not.

This sister went mad. Amis remembered perceiving her then undiagnosed insanity when he was a small boy, and she would take already extinguished matches out of the living room and into the kitchen. But she recovered her reason on the death of her husband. She was asked to stay on in the lunatic asylum to which she had been committed, on account of her competence and helpfulness. She ended her days in charge of the kitchens of a London teaching hospital. This piece of family history was sometimes retailed by Amis.

His parents both came from Denmark Hill, where they had met in the Baptist chapel. His own upbringing, however, was more moral – or moralistic – than religious. Masturbation was a particular cause of conflict; and Amis showed early strength of character in refusing to believe the exaggerated accounts given by his parents of the deleterious consequences of the practice. The wireless set, important in a small house in the 1930s, was another cause of conflict. Amis early developed a taste for classical music, while his father vainly tried to interest him in Gilbert and Sullivan. His father said with some justice that his reflections on Amis senior's musical taste would be more convincing if he could play a musical instrument himself. The house contained some books, though not many, chiefly encyclopaedias and novels from circulating libraries. One of his parents' recreations was singing round the piano with friends and relations.

He was an only child. He was educated first at a local fee-paying school and then, also as a day boy, at the City of London School, which his father and uncles had also attended. His father was determined that he should go there. He failed the scholarship examination to the school when he was eleven but was accepted nonetheless as a fee-payer: he won a scholarship a year later when he was already at the school. He admired the tolerance of the City of London, compared to other boys' schools of the time, and was grateful for the education he received there.

He distinguished himself not only in English and Classics but also in Mathematics. In later life he would sometimes regret – perhaps only half meaning it – that he had not been a scientist or a mathematician. Certainly such mathematical knowledge as he possessed served him well in the Army, in the Royal Corps of Signals; significantly, he was in the 1950s one of the few men of letters who did not heap scorn on the Oxford school of linguistic philosophy because it was 'trivial' or 'did not deal with the real issues'. He enjoyed posing as a philistine because he caused annoyance thereby, but no one could have been more of an intellectual, though his genius was not for the analysis of political concepts.

While he was in the sixth form the school was evacuated to Marlborough College in Wiltshire, where he spent five terms. He was surprised, both then and later, by the inhospitable and aloof attitude of the college's masters and boys; but he was allowed to join the chapel choir, and found that singing in it was – and was to be – one of the most satisfying experiences of his life. He tried for a scholarship at St Catharine's College, Cambridge, but was unsuccessful. He then tried for one available at Christ Church or St John's College, Oxford. The choice of college was narrow because Amis was determined to win a scholarship in English: if he had made Classics his subject, as he could have done, the choice of college would have been wider, and the likelihood of winning a scholarship greater. He put down Christ Church as his first choice but was awarded an exhibition at St John's instead. He went up to Oxford in April 1941 but spent only four terms there before joining the Army. In this earlier period at St John's he first met Philip Larkin, who became a life-long friend.

He joined the Corps of Signals partly because he thought he would like the work – as he did, up to a point – and partly because he did not want to get killed. In this too he was successful, though he had a by no means restful or comfortable war. He was in France after the allied invasion and spent weeks at a time sleeping in a tent. He ended up as a Captain.

He was lucky to be demobilized quickly, and returned to Oxford. He won a first and then embarked on a B.Litt. degree. He was appointed a lecturer in English at University College, Swansea, on the reasonable assumption by the college authorities that he would be duly awarded this degree. In fact he failed, which, Amis later said, was virtually unheard of. He would recall with amusement that he was a B.Litt. (Failed). By this time, however, things had gone too far at Swansea, and the offer stood. Amis, in later years, would become irritated when people asked him: 'What made you choose Swansea?' He would reply: 'Swansea chose me. It was a job, that's all.'

In 1948, while still at St John's, he had married Hilary (Hilly) Bardwell, a fair-haired, beautiful girl who was at the Oxford art school. They quickly had three children, Martin, Philip and Sally. Amis was specially close to his sons – he used to kiss Martin on meeting him, when he was in his fifties, and Martin in his thirties. Both his sons were a source of comfort and strength to him when his second marriage, to the novelist Elizabeth Jane Howard (whom he married in 1965 following an affair begun at the Cheltenham Literary Festival), ended in 1981.

Amis was happy at Swansea. Looking back, he thought it was the best period of his life. He liked to drink with his students, who included John and Mary Morgan, and Geoffrey and Mavis Nicholson (all subsequently journalists of one kind or another). They remained his friends in London from the mid-1960s onwards. It was at Swansea that Amis wrote *Lucky Jim*, *That Uncertain Feeling*, *I Like it Here* and, his favourite novel, *Take a Girl Like You*. The last was his favourite because, though published in 1960, it had been written in the late 1950s, and anticipated with some prescience, so Amis subsequently thought, the dilemma of the 1960s about whether nice girls should sleep with men. (Though there were some reviewers who considered that he was writing about a non-existent dilemma, or one that had been resolved in favour of sexual intercourse, Amis's novel was almost certainly a more accurate reflection of the preoccupations of the time.)

Lucky Jim, which was published in 1954, was a seminal work in that it said: 'No, life isn't like that. It's like this.' The hero of the pre-1939 novels by Anthony Powell and Evelyn Waugh – and of Cyril Connolly's one venture, *The Rock Pool* – was a former public schoolboy who had recently come down from Oxford. His work was unsatisfactory to him but there was money in the background. He was either a homosexual or an incompetent and unlucky heterosexual. He had picaresque adventures either with members of the upper classes or with inhabitants of higher Bohemia. These adventures occurred usually in London, though sometimes in the country or abroad. Amis altered the conventions of this kind of novel with permanent effect.

Though there had been heroes like Jim Dixon before (in the novels of C. P. Snow, for instance), they had been treated differently, with apparent sympathy and seriousness but, in reality, with patronage. Amis changed this way of looking at things (exemplified by *Jude the Obscure*) for ever. He struck a mighty blow for democracy in the English novel.

It was at this time that Amis was included as one of the leading 'angry young men' – among the others were John Osborne, John Wain, Colin Wilson and, through his autobiography *Time and Place*, George Scott. (The phrase was originally the title of Leslie Paul's autobiography, *Angry Young Man*. Paul was an amateur churchman, was little-known and received hardly any credit for the invention of the phrase.) In fact neither Amis nor Jim Dixon was specially angry about anything. Indeed, Amis became much angrier as he grew older. The angry young men were linked in the weekly journals to 'the Movement', that group of Oxford poets whose leading members were Amis, Larkin, Wain and Elizabeth Jennings. One weekly in particular, the *Spectator*, was instrumental. The then literary editor, J. D. Scott, claimed subsequently in a memoir that (aided by Iain Hamilton) he had virtually invented the whole Movement in an article deliberately designed to arouse controversy and interest. However, there is no doubt that the poetic side of the Movement was deliberately reacting against the rhetoric of the 1940s. There is equally no doubt that Amis and Wain were writing different novels from those which had been published before 1939. 'Angry young men' was a foolish phrase but it nevertheless had some meaning.

By 1961 Amis had decided that he could keep himself and his family by writing alone and that he did not have to go on teaching. When he left Swansea in 1961, however, he went not to London but to Peterhouse, Cambridge, as a Fellow and teacher of English. He went to Peterhouse partly because one of his friends, George Gale, had been an undergraduate there, and there was a kind of Peterhouse network or connection in which Amis was involved. But his time at Cambridge was not entirely happy.

What really drove me out was paradoxically what made me most reluctant to leave: teaching. Nobody who has not experienced it can fully imagine the peculiar drain which this activity makes on one's energy, nor its unique rewards. Ten or twelve hours a week, old boy? the businessman or journalist (or educationist) asks incredulously: you don't call that a job of work do you? I do. Leaving out preparation – and I had plenty of that, it never having occurred to me before that the works of Racine or Strindberg were necessary parts of an English course – I found myself fit for nothing much more exacting than playing the gramophone after three supervisions a day.

Then there was the high table company:

The moment when I finally decided it was not for me came when I was dining out at – never mind. Throughout the first course and most of the second, the talk at my end had turned exclusively upon the paintings, drawings, engravings and whatnot my neighbour had been buying. Noticing, presumably, that I had nothing whatever to contribute to this discussion, another guest asked me: 'And what is *your* particular, er, line of, er, country in this, er?' With truly operatic humility of tone and gesture, I said: 'I'm afraid I don't sort of go in for any of that kind of thing.' The other man said: 'H'm' – not a vocable in actual common use, but he used it. Then he said: 'I think that's a dreadful thing to say.' I went on keeping quiet for some time after that, wishing, for perhaps the hundredth time since arriving at Cambridge, that I were Jim Dixon.

From 1965 he lived with his second wife Jane first in Hertfordshire and then in a large, detached Georgian house in Flask Walk, Hampstead. When he and Jane separated he lived with his first wife Hilly and her new husband, Lord Kilmarnock, in Kentish Town. For one of Amis's peculiarities was that he could not bear to be alone, especially at night. He required someone to share not so much his bed as his abode. He was also incapable – or claimed he was incapable – of doing anything for himself of a practical nature. He further had an aversion, not uncommon, to travelling by underground.

He was of medium height, with a tendency to put on weight. But he had never eaten much – he remembered his mother trying to force food on him – and as he grew older he ate even less. Though he wrote an informative book *On Drink*, he was more a beer-and-spirits (mainly the latter) than a wine man. He disliked both the country and abroad. He was a disillusioned heterosexual but never a ladies' man: he liked pubs, clubs (especially the Garrick, of which he was a pillar) and masculine talk.

Having written a Fabian pamphlet in which he said he could not envisage voting anything but Labour, he moved to the right politically from the mid-1960s onwards. But his attack on Lord Robbins's expansionist plans for higher education, with the sentence which summarized his opposition, 'More will mean worse', was written in 1960. The change in his political position came about largely through his distaste for the Soviet Union in both its internal and its external aspects. He was fortified in his attitude by his friendships with Robert Conquest and Tibor Szamuely. The three used to meet once a week (later, once a month) for lunch at Bertorelli's Restaurant in Charlotte Street.

Shortly after his second marriage Amis told the journalist Henry Fairlie, one of his friends, that Fairlie would not be so welcome at Amis's house as he had been in the past because his then new wife insisted on certain standards of decorum which Fairlie did not fulfil. Fairlie regarded this as a bit of a joke but was hurt nonetheless. Certainly Amis made some moves in the direction of a changed mode of life at around this time. For instance, he began to take snuff, though after some years he relinquished the habit, and smoked small cigars instead.

His eyes were slightly protuberant and were apt for simulating astonishment or rage. He was an excellent mimic who did not, however, press his impersonations on his friends. He dressed neatly but informally, in a jacket (often of corduroy), twill trousers, a checked shirt and a woven woollen tie.

He liked to wear quite thick woollen socks. He rarely wore a suit. He was more a natural host than a natural guest, happiest at home with friends and a glass of whisky. His recreations were reading thrillers and listening to music, both classical music and modern jazz. His dislike of writers canonized by the Cambridge English School, such as Jane Austen, Henry James and D. H. Lawrence, and his elevation of other writers, such as Henry Newbolt, Rudyard Kipling and A. Conan Doyle, had about it an element of only doing it to annoy, but was nevertheless an honest expression of his literary judgement.

He was frightened of loneliness but – though death makes several appearances in his novels and poems – denied that he was frightened of death: he was, he said, frightened of the process of dying, a different matter. He was a conscientious writer who, on a good day, would write – or, rather, type – 1,000 words of a novel. He was usually an amusing and sometimes a sad man. To which tribute he would have replied: 'Thanks very bloody much. Bloody marvellous.'

1982

LEWIS CARROLL

W H AUDEN

In the evening of Friday, July 4, 1862, the Reverend Charles Lutwidge Dodgson, lecturer and tutor in mathematics at Christ Church, Oxford, wrote in his diary:

> Atkinson brought over to my rooms some friends of his, a Mrs and Miss Peters, of whom I took photographs, and who afterward looked over my album and stayed to lunch. They then went off to the Museum and Duckworth and I made an expedition *up* the river to Godstow with the three Liddells: we had tea on the bank there, and did not reach Christ Church again till quarter past 8, when we took them on to my rooms to see my collection of micro-photographs, and restored them to the Deanery just before 9.

'The three Liddells' were the daughters of the Dean of Christ Church, one of the authors of the famous Liddell & Scott Greek lexicon. Their names were Lorina Charlotte, Alice, and Edith – nicknamed Matilda. Alice was ten years old.

This was by no means their first expedition together. For some years they had been seeing a lot of one another. In the winter, they would go to Dodgson's rooms and sit on the sofa beside him while he told them stories, which he illustrated by pencil or ink drawings as he went along. Four or five times in the summer term he would take them out on the river, bringing with him a large basket of cakes and a kettle. On such occasions, Dodgson exchanged his clerical suit for white flannel trousers and his black top hat for a hard white straw hat. He always carried himself upright 'as if he had swallowed a poker'.

Outwardly there was nothing to distinguish the Godstow expedition from any other. And nobody today would remember that it ever took place but for what seems almost a pure accident. He had told the children many stories before, to which they had listened with delight, and they begged him to tell them another. This time, perhaps, he was in better storytelling form than usual, for his friend Mr Duckworth was evidently impressed:

> I rowed *stroke* and he rowed *bow* . . . the story was actually composed and spoken *over my shoulder* for the benefit of Alice Liddell, who was acting as 'cox' of our gig. I remember turning round and saying 'Dodgson, is this an extempore romance of yours?' And he replied: 'Yes, I'm inventing as we go along.'

Anyway, this time Alice did what she had never done before – she asked him to write the story down. At first he said he would think about it, but she continued to pester him until, eventually, he gave his promise to do so. In his diary for November 13, he notes: 'Began writing the fairy-tale for Alice – I hope to finish it by Christmas.'

In fact, the text was finished on February 10, 1863. Tenniel's illustrations were not completed until September, 1864, and *Alice in Wonderland* was published by Macmillan in 1865 (which is also, incidentally, the year of the first performance of another masterpiece, Wagner's *Tristan und Isolde*).

These events are memorable because they reveal a kind of human being who is, I believe extremely rare – a man of genius who, in regard to his genius, is without egoism. In other respects, Dodgson was neither selfless nor without vanity. As a member of Senior Common Room, he was a difficult colleague, forever complaining about some minor negligence or inconvenience. He held strong and conservative views upon almost every question affecting the College or the University, and the savagery of his polemical pamphlets, like 'The New Belfry of Christ Church' or 'Twelve Months in a Curatorship', cannot have endeared him to his opponents.

He was proud of his photography, and justly so, for he was one of the best portrait photographers of the century. He had great hopes for his theory of Symbolic Logic, which is, I understand, more highly regarded today than it was at the time. As his diaries show, he also thought well of his little inventions – and he was always inventing something: a *memoria technica* for the logarithms of all primes under 100; a game of arithmetical croquet; a rule for finding the day of the week for any date of the month, a substitute for glue; a system of proportional representation; a method of controlling the carriage traffic at Covent Garden; an apparatus for making notes in the dark; an improved steering gear for a tricycle; and he always sought publication for his light verse. But when it came to the one thing which he did superbly well, where he was without any rival – namely, telling stories to children – the thought of himself, of publication and immortal fame, never seems to have entered his head.

The two *Alice* books were no freak achievements. There are passages in letters to children where the writing is just as good. For example:

> It's so frightfully hot here that I've been almost too weak to hold a pen, and even if I had been able, there was no ink – it had all evaporated into a cloud of black steam, and in that state it has been floating about the room, inking the walls and ceiling till they're hardly fit to be seen: today, it is cooler, and a little has come back into the ink bottle in the form of black snow.

He went on telling impromptu stories to children all his life, which were never written down and, for all we know, may have surpassed the ones that were.

Though no human character can be explained away in terms of his upbringing or environment, it is legitimate to look for influencing factors. In Dodgson's case, one such factor may have been his position as the oldest boy – the son of a clergyman – in a large family: he had seven sisters and three brothers. By the time he was eleven he had made himself the family entertainer. He constructed a train, built out of a wheelbarrow, a barrel, and a small truck, which conveyed passengers from one station in the rectory garden to another, and in the rules he drew up for this game, the Lewis Carroll imagination is already evident:

> All passengers when upset are requested to lie still until picked up – as it is requisite that at least three trains should go over them, to entitle them to the attention of the doctor and assistants.
>
> When a passenger has no money and still wants to go by train, he must stop at whatever station he happens to be at, and earn money – making tea for the stationmaster (who drinks it at all hours of the day and night) and grinding sand for the company (what use they make of it they are not bound to explain.)

Two years later, he became the editor and chief contributor for a succession of family magazines, the last of which, *The Rectory Umbrella*, was still appearing after he had become an Oxford don and first printed the opening quatrain of 'Jabberwocky'.

Thus, at the beginning of his career as a writer, he was writing directly for an audience with which he was intimate and in which he had no literary rival. The average writer, at least today, has a very different experience. When he begins writing, he has no audience except himself; his first audience is likely to be one of rival, as yet unpublished, authors, and his only chance of acquiring an audience of his own is to get published, in little magazines or popular ones; and this audience consists of readers whom he does not know personally.

It seems clear that what, as an imaginative creator, Dodgson valued most was the immediate and intimate response of his audience, and its undivided attention (hence, perhaps, his passion for the theatre). His writings for adults, no less than his children's stories, are for the 'family' – Oxford to him was another and larger rectory. Even in the only company with whom he felt so completely at home that his stammer disappeared, the company of little girls, he preferred to see them singly. As he wrote to one mother:

> Would you kindly tell me if I may reckon your girls as invitable to tea, or dinner, singly. I know of cases where they are invitable in sets only (like the circulating-library novels), and such friendships I don't think worth going on with. I don't think anyone knows what girl-nature *is*, who has only seen them in the presence of their mothers or sisters.

Many guesses, plausible and implausible, have been made as to the historical origins of the characters and events in the *Alice* books, but one may be sure that many allusions which were apparent to the Liddell children are now irrecoverable. When he told a story, it was always for a particular child. One of them, not Alice, records:

> One thing that made his stories particularly charming to a child was that he often took his cue from her remarks – a question would set him off on quite a new trail of ideas, so that one felt one had somehow helped to make the story, and it seemed a personal possession.

Very few writers, I believe, however much they desire fame for their books, enjoy being a public figure who is recognized on the street by strangers, but Dodgson hated publicity more than most. He refused to allow any picture of himself to appear – 'Nothing would be more unpleasant for me than to have my face known to strangers' – and he gave orders that any letters addressed to L. Carroll, Christ Church, Oxford, were to be returned to the sender with the endorsement 'not known'.

But thanks to Alice Liddell's importunity, and luckily for us, the intimate narrator became a world-famous author. As usually happens with a masterpiece, the initial critical reception of *Alice in Wonderland* was mixed. The *Illustrated London News* and the *Pall Mall Gazette* liked it; the *Spectator*, though generally approving, condemned the Mad Hatter's tea-party; the *Athenaeum* thought it a 'stiff, overwrought story', and the *Illustrated Times*, while conceding that the author possessed a fertile imagination, declared that Alice's adventures 'are too extravagantly absurd to produce more diversion than disappointment and irritation.'

When, seven years later, *Through the Looking-Glass* appeared, the critics knew, from the enormous public success of its predecessor, that it must be good – though I can think of no more unlikely literary comparison than that of Henry Kingsley, who wrote: 'This is the finest thing we have had since *Martin Chuzzlewit.*'

And the book's fame has continued to grow. I have always thought one might learn much about the cultural history of a country by going through the speeches made by its public men over a certain period, in legislatures, in law courts, and at official banquets, and making a list of the books quoted from without attribution. So far as Great Britain is concerned, I strongly suspect that, for the past fifty years, the two *Alice* books and *The Hunting of the Snark* have headed it.

How do American readers react? Though nearly all the Americans I know personally loved Lewis Carroll as children, they may not be representative of American taste in general. Certainly, in every American book read by children – from *Huckleberry Finn* to the *Oz* books – which I have come across, nothing could be more remote from their worlds than the world of Alice.

The American child-hero – are there any American child-heroines? – is a Noble Savage, an anarchist, and, even when he reflects, predominantly concerned with movement and action. He may do almost anything except sit still. His heroic virtue – that is to say, his superiority to adults – lies in his freedom from conventional ways of thinking and acting: *all* social habits, from manners to creeds, are regarded as false or hypocritical or both. All emperors are really naked. Alice, surely, must come to the average American as a shock.

To begin with, she is a 'lady'. When, puzzled by the novelty of Wonderland, she asks herself if she could have changed into some other child, she is quite certain what sort of child she does *not* want to be:

> 'I'm sure I can't be Mabel, for I know all sorts of things, and she, oh, she knows such a very little . . . I must be Mabel after all, and I shall have to go and live in that poky little house, and have next to no toys to play with . . . No, I've made up my mind about it: if I'm Mabel, I'll stay down here.'

Among grown-ups, she knows the difference between servants and mistresses:

> 'He took me for his house-maid,' she said to herself as she ran. 'How surprised he'll be when he finds out who I am. . . .'
> 'The governess would never think of excusing my lessons for that. If she couldn't remember my name, she'd call me "Miss" as the servants do.'

And when the Red Queen advises her: 'Speak in French when you can't think of the English for a thing – turn out your toes as you walk – and remember who you are!' – she knows that the answer to the question, 'Who am I?' is really: 'I am Alice Liddell, daughter of the Dean of Christ Church.'

What is most likely to bewilder an American child, however, is not Alice's class-consciousness, which is easy to miss, but the peculiar relation of children and grown-ups to law and social manners. It is the child-heroine Alice who is invariably reasonable, self-controlled, and polite, while all the other inhabitants, human or animal, of Wonderland and the Looking-Glass are unsocial eccentrics – at the mercy of their passions and extremely bad-mannered, like the Queen of Hearts, the Duchess, the Hatter, and Humpty Dumpty, or grotesquely incompetent, like the White Queen and the White Knight.

What Alice finds so extraordinary about the people and events in these worlds is the anarchy which she is forever trying to make sense and order out of. In both books, games play an important role. The whole structure of *Through the Looking-Glass* is based on chess, and the Queen of Hearts' favourite pastime is croquet – both of them games which Alice knows how to play. To play a game, it is essential that the players know and obey its rules, and are skilful enough to do the right or reasonable thing at least half the time. Anarchy and incompetence are incompatible with play.

Croquet played with hedgehogs, flamingos, and soldiers instead of the conventional balls, mallets, and hoops is conceivable, provided that they are willing to imitate the behaviour of these inanimate objects, but, in Wonderland, they behave as they choose and the game is impossible to play.

In the Looking-Glass world, the problem is different. It is not, like Wonderland, a place of complete anarchy where everybody says and does whatever comes into his head, but a completely determined world without choice. Tweedledum and Tweedledee, the Lion and the Unicorn, the Red Knight and the White, must fight at regular intervals, irrespective of their feelings. In Wonderland, Alice has to adjust herself to a life without laws; in Looking-Glass Land, to one governed by laws to which she is unaccustomed. She has to learn, for example, to walk away from a place in order to reach it, or to run fast in order to remain where she is. In Wonderland, she is the only person with self-control; in Looking-Glass Land, the only competent one. But for the way she plays a pawn, one feels that the game of chess would never be completed.

In both worlds, one of the most important and powerful characters is not a person but the English language. Alice, who had hitherto supposed that words were passive objects, discovers that they have a life and will of their own. When she tries to remember poems she has learned, new lines come into her head unbidden, and, when she thinks she knows what a word means, it turns out to mean something else.

> 'And so these three little sisters – they were learning to draw, you know –
> 'What did they draw?' . . .
> 'Treacle – *from a treacle well*. . . .'
> 'But they were in the well.'
> 'Of course they were: well in.' . . .

> 'How old did you say you were?'
> 'Seven years and six months.'
> 'Wrong! You never said a word like it!' . . .

> 'You take some flour.'
> 'Where do you pick the flower? In a garden or in the hedges?'
> 'Well, it isn't *picked* at all: it's *ground*.'
> 'How many acres of ground?'

Nothing, surely, could be more remote from the American image of the pioneering, hunting, prepolitical hero than this preoccupation with language. It is the concern of the solitary thinker, for language is the mother of thought, and of the politician – in the Greek sense – for speech is the medium by which we disclose ourselves to others. The American hero is neither.

Both of Alice's 'dreams' end in a state of developing chaos from which she wakes just in time before they can become nightmares:

> At this the whole pack rose up in the air, and came flying down upon her; she gave a little scream, half of fright and half of anger, and tried to beat them off, and found herself lying on the bank with her head in the lap of her sister. . . .

> Already several of the guests were lying down in the dishes, and the soup ladle was walking up the table towards Alice's chair, and beckoning to her impatiently to get out of its way.
> 'I can't stand this any longer!' she cried, as she jumped up and seized the table-cloth with both hands: one good pull, and plates, dishes, guests and candles came crashing down together in a heap on the floor.

Wonderland and Looking-Glass Land are fun to visit but no places to live in. Even when she is there, Alice can ask herself with some nostalgia 'if anything would ever happen in a natural way again,' and by 'natural' she means the opposite of what Rousseau would mean. She means peaceful, civilized society.

There are good books which are only for adults, because their comprehension presupposes adult experiences, but there are no good books which are only for children. A child who enjoys the *Alice* books will continue to enjoy them when he or she is grown up, though his 'reading' of what they mean will probably change. In assessing their value, there are two questions one can ask: first, what insight do they provide as to how the world appears to a child?; and, second, to what extent is the world really like that?

According to Lewis Carroll, what a child desires before anything else is that the world in which he finds himself should make sense. It is not the commands and prohibitions, as such, which adults impose that the child resents, but rather that he cannot perceive any law linking one command to another in a consistent pattern.

The child is told, for example, that he must not do such-and-such, and then sees adults doing precisely that. This occurs especially often in the realm of social manners. In well-bred society, people treat each other with courtesy but, in trying to teach their children to be polite, their method of instruction is often that of a drill sergeant. Without realizing it, adults can be rude to children in ways which, if they were dealing with one of their own kind, would get them knocked down. How many children, when they are silenced with the command, 'Speak when you're spoken to!' must have longed to retort as Alice does:

'But if everybody obeyed that rule, and if you only spoke when you were spoken to, and the other person always waited for *you* to begin, you see that nobody would ever say anything.'

It would be an exaggeration to say that children see adults as they really are, but, like servants, they see them at moments when they are not concerned with making a favourable impression.

As everybody knows, Dodgson's Muse was incarnated in a succession of girls between the ages of eight and eleven. Little boys he feared and disliked: they were grubby and noisy and broke things. Most adults he found insensitive. At the age of twenty-four, he wrote in his diary:

I think that the character of most that I meet is merely refined animal. How few seem to care for the only subjects of real interest in life!

Naturally, most of his 'child-friends' came from middle- or upper-middle class English homes. He mentions having met one American child and the encounter was not a success:

Lily Alice Godfrey, from New York: aged 8; but talked like a girl of 15 or 16, and declined to be kissed on wishing good-by, on the ground that she 'never kissed gentlemen'. . . . I fear it is true that there are no children in America.

And the children he understood best were the quiet and imaginative ones. Thus Irene Vanbrugh, who must have been going through a tomboy phase when she met him, says:

He had a deep love for children, though I am inclined to think not such a great understanding of them. . . . His great delight was to teach me his Game of Logic. Dare I say this made the evening rather long, when the band was playing outside on the parade, and the moon shining on the sea?

The question for an adult reader of Lewis Carroll, however, is not the author's psychological peculiarities, but the validity of his heroine. Is Alice, that is to say, an adequate symbol for what every human being should try to be like?

I am inclined to answer yes. A girl of eleven (or a boy of twelve) who comes from a good home – a home, that is, where she has known both love and discipline and where the life of the mind is taken seriously but not solemnly – can be a most remarkable creature. No longer a baby, she has learned self-control, acquired a sense of her identity, and can think logically without ceasing to be imaginative. She does not know, of course, that her sense of identity has been too easily won – the gift of her parents rather than her own doing – and that she is soon going to lose it, first in the *Sturm und Drang* of adolescence and then, when she enters the adult social world, in anxieties over money and status.

But one cannot meet a girl or a boy of this kind without feeling that what she or he is – by luck and momentarily – is what, after many years and countless follies and errors, one would like, in the end, to become.

1943

JAMES WOODFORDE

VIRGINIA WOOLF

One could wish that the psycho-analysts would go into the question of diary-keeping. For often it is the one mysterious fact in a life otherwise as clear as the sky and as candid as the dawn. Parson Woodforde is a case in point – his diary is the only mystery about him. For forty-three years he sat down almost daily to record what he did on Monday and what he had for dinner on Tuesday; but for whom he wrote or why he wrote it is impossible to say. He does not unburden his soul in his diary; yet it is no mere record of engagements and expenses. As for literary fame, there is no sign that he ever thought of it, and finally, though the man himself is peaceable above all things, there are little indiscretions and criticisms which would have got him into trouble and hurt the feelings of his friends had they read them. What purpose, then, did the sixty-eight little books fulfil? Perhaps it was the desire for intimacy. When James Woodforde opened one of his neat manuscript books he entered into conversation with a second James Woodforde, who was not quite the same as the reverend gentleman who visited the poor and preached in the church. These two friends said much that all the world might hear; but they had a few secrets which they shared with each other only. It was a great comfort, for example, that Christmas when Nancy, Betsy and Mr Walker seemed to be in conspiracy against him, to exclaim in the diary, 'The treatment I meet with for my Civility this Christmas is to me abominable.' The second James Woodforde sympathized and agreed. Again, when a stranger abused his hospitality it was a relief to inform the other self who lived in the little book that he had put him to sleep in the attic story, 'and I treated him as one that would be too free if treated kindly'. It is easy to understand why, in the quiet life of a country parish, these two bachelor friends became in time inseparable. An essential part of him would have died had he been forbidden to keep his diary. When indeed he thought himself in the grip of death he still wrote on and on. And as we read – if reading is the word for it – we seem to be listening to someone who is murmuring over the events of the day to himself in the quiet space which precedes sleep. It is not writing, and, to speak of the truth, it is not reading. It is slipping through half a dozen pages and strolling to the window and looking out. It is going on thinking about the Woodfordes while we watch the people in the street below. It is taking a walk and making up the life and character of James Woodforde as we go. It is not reading any more than it is writing – what to call it we scarcely know.

James Woodforde, then, was one of those smooth-cheeked, steady-eyed men, demure to look at, whom we can never imagine except in the prime of life. He was of an equable temper, with only such acerbities and touchinesses as are generally to be found in those who have had a love affair in their youth and remained, as they fancy, unwed because of it. The Parson's love affair, however, was nothing very tremendous. Once when he was a young man in Somerset he liked to walk over to Shepton and to visit a certain 'sweet tempered' Betsy White who lived there. He had a great mind 'to make a bold stroke' and ask her to marry him. He went so far, indeed, as to propose marriage 'when opportunity served', and Betsy was willing. But he delayed; time passed; four years passed indeed, and Betsy went to Devonshire, met a Mr Webster, who had five hundred pounds a year, and married him. When James Woodforde met them in the turnpike road he could say little, 'being shy', but to his diary he remarked – and this no doubt was his private version of the affair ever after – 'she has proved herself to me a mere jilt'.

But he was a young man then, and as time went on we cannot help suspecting that he was glad to consider the question of marriage shelved once and for all so that he might settle down with his niece Nancy at Weston Longueville, and give himself simply and solely, every day and all day, to the great business of living. Again, what else to call it we do not know.

For James Woodforde was nothing in particular. Life had it all her own way with him. He had no special gift; he had no oddity or infirmity. It is idle to pretend that he was a zealous priest. God in Heaven was much the same to him as King George upon the throne – a kindly Monarch, that is to say, whose festivals one kept by preaching a sermon on Sunday much as one kept the Royal birthday by firing a blunderbuss and drinking a toast at dinner. Should anything untoward happen, like the death of a boy who was dragged and killed by a horse, he would instantly, but rather perfunctorily, exclaim, 'I hope to God the Poor Boy is happy', and add, 'We all came home singing'; just as when Justice Creed's peacock spread its tail – 'and most noble it is' – he could exclaim, 'How wonderful are Thy Works O God in every Being'. But there was no fanaticism, no enthusiasm, no lyric impulse about James Woodforde. In all these pages, indeed, each so neatly divided into compartments, and each of those again filled, as the days themselves were filled, quietly and fully in a hand steady as the pacing of a well-tempered nag, one can only call to mind a single poetic phrase about the transit of Venus. 'It appeared as a black patch upon a fair Lady's face,' he says. The words themselves are mild enough, but they hang over the undulating expanse of the Parson's prose with the resplendence of the star itself. So in the Fen country a barn or a tree appears twice its natural size against the surrounding flats. But what led him to this palpable excess that summer's night we cannot tell. It cannot have been that he was drunk. He spoke out too roundly against such failings in his brother Jack to be guilty himself. Temperamentally he was among the eaters of meat and not among the drinkers of wine. When we think of the Woodfordes, uncle and niece, we think of them as often as not waiting with some impatience for their dinner. Gravely they watch the joint as it is set upon the table; swiftly they get their knives to work upon the succulent leg or loin; without much comment, unless a word is passed about the gravy or the stuffing, they go on eating. So they munch, day after day, year in, year out, until between them they must have devoured herds of sheep and oxen, flocks of poultry, an odd dozen or so of swans and cygnets, bushels of apples and plums, while the pastries and the jellies crumble and squash beneath their spoons in mountains, in pyramids, in pagodas. Never was there a book so stuffed with food as this one is. To read the bill of fare respectfully and punctually set forth gives one a sense of repletion. Trout and chicken, mutton and peas, pork and apple sauce – so the joints succeed each other at dinner, and there is supper with more joints still to come, all, no doubt, home grown, and of the juiciest and sweetest; all cooked, often by the mistress herself, in the plainest English way, save when the dinner was at Weston Hall and Mrs Custance surprised them with a London dainty – a pyramid of jelly, that is to say, with a 'landscape appearing through it'. After dinner sometimes, Mrs Custance, for whom James Woodforde had a chivalrous devotion, would play the 'Sticcardo Pastorale', and make 'very soft music indeed'; or would get out her work-box and show them how neatly contrived it was, unless indeed she were giving birth to another child upstairs. These infants the Parson would baptize and very frequently he would bury them. They died almost as frequently as they were born. The Parson had a deep respect for the Custances. They were all that country gentry should be – a little given to the habit of keeping mistresses, perhaps, but that peccadillo could be forgiven them in view of their generosity to the poor, the kindness they showed to Nancy, and their condescension in asking the Parson to dinner when they had great people staying with them. Yet great people were not much to James's liking. Deeply though he respected the nobility, 'one must confess,' he said, 'that being with our equals is much more agreeable.'

Not only did Parson Woodforde know what was agreeable; that rare gift was by the bounty of Nature supplemented by another equally rare – he could have what he wanted. The age was propitious. Monday, Tuesday, Wednesday – they follow each other and each little compartment seems filled with content. The days were not crowded, but they were enviably varied. Fellow of New College though he was, he did things with his own hands, not merely with his own head. He lived in every room of the house – in the study he wrote sermons, in the dining-room he ate copiously; he cooked in the kitchen, he played cards in the parlour. And then he took his coat and stick and went coursing his greyhounds in the fields. Year in, year out, the provisioning of the house and its defence against the cold of winter and the drought of summer fell upon him. Like a general he surveyed the seasons and took steps to make his own little camp safe with coal and wood and beef and beer against the enemy. His day thus had to accommodate a jumble of incongruous occupations. There is religion to be served, and the pig to be killed; the sick to be visited and dinner to be eaten; the dead to be buried and beer to be brewed; Convocation to be attended and the cow to be bolused. Life and death, mortality and immortality, jostle in his pages and make a good mixed marriage of it: '. . . found the old gentleman almost at his last gasp. Totally senseless with rattlings in his Throat. Dinner today boiled beef and Rabbit rosted.' All is as it should be; life is like that.

Surely, surely, then, here is one of the breathing-spaces in human affairs – here in Norfolk at the end of the eighteenth century at the Parsonage. For once man is content with his lot; harmony is achieved; his house fits him; a tree is a tree; a chair is a chair; each knows its office and fulfils it. Looking through the eyes of Parson Woodforde, the different lives of men seem orderly and settled. Far away guns roar; a King falls; but the sound is not loud enough to scare the rooks here in Norfolk. The proportions of things are different. The Continent is so distant that it looks a mere blur; America scarcely exists; Australia is unknown. But a magnifying glass is laid upon the fields of Norfolk. Every blade of grass is visible there. We see every lane and every field; the ruts on the roads and the peasants' faces. Each house stands in its own breadth of meadow isolated and independent. No wires link village to village. No voices thread the air. The body also is more present and more real. It suffers more acutely. No anaesthetic deadens physical pain. The surgeon's knife hovers real and sharp above the limb. Cold strikes unmitigated upon the house. The milk freezes in the pans; the water is thick with ice in the basins. One can scarcely walk from one room to another in the Parsonage in winter. Poor men and women are frozen to death upon the roads. Often no letters come and there are no visitors and no newspapers. The Parsonage stands alone in the midst of the frost-bound fields. At last, Heaven be praised, life circulates again; a man comes to the door with a Madagascar monkey, another brings a box containing a child with two distinct perfect heads; there is a rumour that a balloon is going to rise at Norwich. Every little incident stands out sharp and clear. The drive to Norwich even is something of an adventure. One must trundle every step of the way behind a horse. But look how distinct the trees stand in the hedges; how slowly the cattle move their heads as the carriage trots by; how gradually the spires of Norwich raise themselves above the hill. And then how clear-cut and familiar are the faces of the few people who are our friends – the Custances, Mr du Quesne. Friendship has time to solidify, to become a lasting, a valuable possession.

True, Nancy of the younger generation is visited now and then by a flighty notion that she is missing something, that she wants something. One day she complained to her uncle that life was very dull: she complained 'of the dismal situation of my house, nothing to be seen, and little or no visiting or being visited, &c.', and made him very uneasy. We could read Nancy a little lecture upon the folly of wanting that 'et cetera'. Look what your 'et cetera' has brought to pass, we might say; half the countries of Europe are bankrupt; there is a red line of villas on every green hill-side; your Norfolk roads are black as tar; there is no end to 'visiting or being visited'. But Nancy has an answer to make us, to the effect that our past is her present. You, she says, think it a great privilege to be born in the eighteenth century, because one called cowslips pagles and rode in a curricle instead of driving in a car. But you are utterly wrong, you fanatical lovers of memoirs, she goes on. I can assure you, my life was often intolerably dull. I did not laugh at the things that make you laugh. It did not amuse me when my uncle dreamt of a hat or saw bubbles in the beer, and said that meant a death in the family; I thought so too. Betsy Davy mourned young Walker with all her heart in spite of dressing in sprigged paduasoy. There is a great deal of humbug talked of the eighteenth century. Your delight in old times and old diaries is half impure. You make up something that never had any existence. Our sober reality is only a dream to you – so Nancy grieves and complains, living through the eighteenth century day by day, hour by hour.

Still, if it is a dream, let us indulge it a moment longer. Let us believe that some things last, and some places and some people are not touched by change. On a fine May morning, with the rooks rising and the hares scampering and the plover calling among the long grass, there is much to encourage the illusion. It is we who change and perish. Parson Woodforde lives on. It is the kings and queens who lie in prison. It is the great towns that are ravaged with anarchy and confusion. But the river Wensum still flows; Mrs Custance is brought to bed of yet another baby; there is the first swallow of the year. The spring comes, and summer with its hay and strawberries; then autumn, when the walnuts are exceptionally fine though the pears are poor; so we lapse into winter, which is indeed boisterous, but the house, thank God, withstands the storm; and then again there is the first swallow, and Parson Woodforde takes his greyhounds out a–coursing.

1932

OF OUR FELLOW COUNTRYMAN
SHAKESPEARE

BEN JONSON

I remember, the Players have often mentioned it as an honour to *Shakespeare*, that in his writing (whatsoever he penned) he never blotted out line. My answer hath been, would he had blotted a thousand. Which they thought a malevolent speech. I had not told posterity this, but for their ignorance, who choose that circumstance to commend their friend by, wherein he most faulted; And to justify mine own candour (for I loved the man, and do honour his memory (on this side Idolatry) as much as any). He was (indeed) honest, and of an open and free nature: had an excellent *Phantsie*; brave notions, and gentle expressions: wherein he flowed with that facility, that sometime it was necessary he should be stopped: *Sufflaminandus erat*; as *Augustus* said of *Haterius*. His wit was in his own power; would the rule of it had been so too. Many times he fell into those things, could not escape laughter: As when he said in the person of *Caesar*, one speaking to him; *Caesar thou dost me wrong*. He replied: *Caesar did never wrong, but with just cause*: and such like; which were ridiculous. But he redeemed his vices with his virtues. There was ever more in him to be praised than to be pardoned.

1640

MR WILLIAM SHAKESPEARE

JOHN AUBREY

Mr William Shakespeare was borne at Stratford upon Avon in the County of Warwick. His father was a Butcher, and I have been told heretofore by some of the neighbours, that when he was a boy he exercised his father's Trade, but when he kill'd a Calfe he would doe it in a high style, and make a Speech. There was at this time another Butcher's son in this Towne that was held not at all inferior to him for a naturall witt, his acquaintance and coetanean, byt dyed young.

This William, being inclined naturally to Poetry and acting, came to London, I guesse about 18: and was an Actor at one of the Play-houses, and did acte exceedingly well: now B. Johnson was never a good Actor but an excellent Instructor.

He began early to make essayes at Dramatique Poetry, which at that time was very lowe; and his Playes tooke well.

He was a handsome, well-shap't man: very good company, and of a very readie and pleasant smoothe Witt.

The humour of the Constable in Midsomernight's Dreame, he happened to take at Grendon, in Bucks (I thinke it was Midsomer night that he happened to lye there) which is the roade from London to Stratford, and there was living that Constable about 1642, when I first came to Oxon. Ben Johnson and he did gather Humours of men dayly where ever they came. One time as he was at the Tavern at Stratford super Avon, one Combes, an old rich Usurer, was to be buryed. He makes there this extemporary Epitaph:

> Ten in the Hundred the Devill allowes,
> But Combes will have twelve he sweares and vowes:
> If anyone askes who lies in this Tombe,
> Hoh! quoth the Devill, 'Tis my John o' Combe.

He was wont to goe to his native Countrey once a yeare. I thinke I have been told that he left 2 or 300 pounds per annum there and thereabout to a sister.

I have heard Sir William Davenant and Mr Thomas Shadwell (who is counted the best Comoedian we have now) say that he had a most prodigious Witt, and did admire his naturall parts beyond all other Dramaticall writers.

His Comoedies will remaine witt as long as the English tongue is understood, for that he handles *mores hominum* [the ways of mankind]. Now our present writers reflect so much on particular persons and coxcombeities that twenty yeares hence they will not be understood.

Though, as Ben Johnson sayes of him, that he had little Latine and lesse Greek, he understood Latine pretty well: for he had been in his younger yeares a schoolmaster in the countrey.

He was wont to say that he never blotted out a line in his life. Sayd Ben Johnson, I wish he had blotted-out a thousand.

1693

A PARTY: WORDSWORTH, LAMB, KEATS

B R HAYDON

In December Wordsworth was in town, and as Keats wished to know him I made up a party to dinner of Charles Lamb, Wordsworth, Keats and Monkhouse, his friend; and a very pleasant party we had.

I wrote to Lamb, and told him the address was '22 Lisson Grove, North, at Rossi's, half way up, right hand corner.' I received his characteristic reply.

My dear Haydon,

I will come with pleasure to 22 Lisson Grove, North, at Rossi's, half way up, right hand side, if I can find it.

Yours,

C. LAMB.

20, Russel Court,
   Covent Garden East,
      half way up, next the corner,
         left hand side.

On December 28th the immortal dinner came off in my painting-room, with Jerusalem towering up behind us as a background. Wordsworth was in fine cue, and we had a glorious set-to – on Homer, Shakespeare, Milton and Virgil. Lamb got exceedingly merry and exquisitely witty; and his fun in the midst of Wordsworth's solemn intonations of oratory was like the sarcasm and wit of the fool in the intervals of Lear's passion. He made a speech and voted me absent, and made them drink my health. 'Now,' said Lamb, 'you old lake poet, you rascally poet, why do you call Voltaire dull?' We all defended Wordsworth, and affirmed there was a state of mind when Voltaire would be dull. 'Well,' said Lamb, 'here's Voltaire – the Messiah of the French nation, and a very proper one too.'

He then, in a strain of humour beyond description, abused me for putting Newton's head into my picture; 'a fellow,' said he, 'who believed nothing unless it was as clear as the three sides of a triangle.' And then he and Keats agreed he had destroyed all the poetry of the rainbow by reducing it to the prismatic colours. It was impossible to resist him, and we all drank 'Newton's health, and confusion to mathematics.' It was delightful to see the good humour of Wordsworth in giving in to all our frolics without affectation and laughing as heartily as the best of us.

By this time other friends joined, amongst them poor Ritchie who was going to penetrate by Fezzan to Timbuctoo. I introduced him to all as 'a gentleman going to Africa'. Lamb seemed to take no notice; but all of a sudden he roared out: 'Which is the gentleman we are going to lose?' We then drank the victim's health, in which Ritchie joined.

In the morning of this delightful day, a gentleman, a perfect stranger, had called on me. He said he knew my friends, had an enthusiasm for Wordsworth, and begged I would procure him the happiness of an introduction. He told me he was a comptroller of stamps, and often had correspondence with the poet. I thought it a liberty; but still, as he seemed a gentleman, I told him he might come.

When we retired to tea we found the comptroller. In introducing him to Wordsworth I forgot to say who he was. After a little time the comptroller looked down, looked up and said to Wordsworth: 'Don't you think, sir, Milton was a great genius?' Keats looked at me, Wordsworth looked at the comptroller. Lamb who was dozing by the fire turned round and said: 'Pray, sir, did you say Milton was a great genius?' 'No, sir; I asked Mr Wordsworth if he were not.' 'Oh,' said Lamb, 'then you are a silly fellow.' 'Charles! my dear Charles!' said Wordsworth; but Lamb, perfectly innocent of the confusion he had created, was off again by the fire.

After an awful pause the comptroller said: 'Don't you think Newton a great genius?' I could not stand it any longer. Keats put his head into my books. Ritchie squeezed in a laugh. Wordsworth seemed asking himself: 'Who is this?' Lamb got up, and taking a candle, said: 'Sir, will you allow me to look at your phrenological development?' He then turned his back on the poor man, and at every question of the comptroller he chaunted:

> Diddle diddle dumpling, my son John
> Went to bed with his breeches on.

The man in office, finding Wordsworth did not know who he was, said in a spasmodic and half-chuckling anticipation of assured victory: 'I have had the honour of some correspondence with you, Mr Wordsworth.' 'With me, sir?' said Wordsworth, 'not that I remember.' 'Don't you, sir? I am a comptroller of stamps.' There was a dead silence, the comptroller evidently thinking that was enough. While we were waiting for Wordsworth's reply, Lamb sung out:

> Hey diddle diddle
> The cat and the fiddle.

'My dear Charles!', said Wordsworth.

> Diddle diddle dumpling, my son John,

chaunted Lamb, and then rising, exclaimed: 'Do let me have another look at that gentleman's organs.' Keats and I hurried Lamb into the painting-room, shut the door and gave way to inextinguishable laughter. Monkhouse followed and tried to get Lamb away. We went back, but the comptroller was irreconcilable. We soothed and smiled and asked him to supper. He stayed though his dignity was sorely affected. However, being a good-natured man, we parted all in good humour, and no ill effects followed.

All the while, until Monkhouse succeeded, we could hear Lamb struggling in the painting-room and calling at intervals: 'Who is that fellow? Allow me to see his organs once more.'

It was indeed an immortal evening. Wordsworth's fine intonation as he quoted Milton and Virgil, Keats' eager inspired look, Lamb's quaint sparkle of lambent humour, so speeded the stream of conversation, that in my life I never passed a more delightful time. All our fun was within bounds. Not a word passed that an apostle might not have listened to. It was a night worthy of the Elizabethan age, and my solemn Jerusalem flashing up by the flame of the fire, with Christ hanging over us like a vision, all made up a picture which will long glow upon

> that inward eye
> Which is the bliss of solitude.

Keats made Ritchie promise he would carry his *Endymion* to the great desert of Sahara and fling it in the midst.

Poor Ritchie went to Africa, and died, as Lamb foresaw, in 1819. Keats died in 1821, at Rome. C. Lamb is gone, joking to the last. Monkhouse is dead, and Wordsworth and I are the only two now living (1841) of that glorious party.

1853

STANLEY PARKER

KENNETH TYNAN

I deserve, I think, a little space now for a clown so intimately bound up with a sky-rocketingly delightful part of my life that his image is magnified for me beyond all reasonable proportions. He is not a professional humorist; his audiences must never exceed half a dozen, and those preferably tipsy; and it may be that in writing about him I am being as blind as the people in Thurber's savage little story, who thought Jack Klohman the funniest man they had ever seen. Nevertheless, I want to write about Stanley Parker, because it is quite possible that nobody else ever will. And a personal note closes a chapter so neatly.

This is a sane thanksgiving and a farewell to Stanley, and I write it because he is centrally tangled and embedded in what I like to remember of Oxford, and because I have laughed with him more clamorously, more forgetfully of time and station, more recklessly, than with anyone else. I hope the years are so generous and joy-spawning to him as he has been to me.

Stanley Parker came to Oxford in 1942 to goad the sleeping demons of gaiety from their frozen dens in a grey and warlike city. He brought with him his mother, his brother, a flossy and glossy journalistic reputation in Australia and London, and the buoyancy of twenty-eight spendthrift years. It was rather like letting a rogue elephant loose in a mausoleum. Stanley's

61

friendship with Oxford began, like many of his attachments, by unpremeditated assault. He was never very good at premeditation; I see him rather as an impulsive explorer of sunny moments, which he can inflate into big gleaming bubbles, and deck his day withal, as if they were so many Chinese lanterns. In Stanley's company motives and means and ends and all things aforethought seem tiny and squalid, fit only for page three of the *Oxford Mail*. He is the safest person I know in whom to invest the next ten minutes of one's life; you will be gladdened, if not enriched. He will be a sort of Ronald Searle schoolboy, yet jocund, and plumply droll, and his laughter will be the heart's laughter, which is ease.

I met him some years ago at a party in Trinity College; we sat on the lawn drinking wine, and I thought, here is a fat lizard. I now propose to give up fifteen hundred words to explaining how wrong I was.

Stanley is the Vulgar One, the Big Imp, a laughing buddha sculpted in lava; a Savoy Grill Falstaff; a sophisticated Billy Bunter, a demoniacal and uproarious Owl of the Remove who flies hooting by night. In the same way as Noël Coward looks like an Oriental butler, Stanley looks like a Filipino houseboy. Observe the quick fastidious step, hips held high, shoulders almost in flight: he moves with all the wobble and purpose of a blancmange disdainfully deserting Lyons for Claridges, high tea for theatre supper. 'It's no good your saying a *word*,' his face tells us, 'I will *not* be eaten with plastic spoons.' The forehead, wryly bulging, betokens determination. His sandals fussily brush the pavement; just as fussily, words brush against his lips as he speaks. It is not a juicy voice, but dry and florid, save when it swoops down to emphasize and point a phrase, and is bolstered up again with a rose-red intestinal chuckle. Then the whole body becomes a madcap jelly, thunderously quaking, and the voice a squelching roar. There is an epic quality about Stanley's smallest mischief, an animal capering; in Oxford he has the loony unexpectedness of a giant panda at the Algonquin. Rococo black finger-curls crowd over a merry sleazy face; in his bustling mock-pomp he sees every party as a gladiatorial arena, and if there is not blood and sand on the floor there ought to be. Yet I would not call him flamboyant; by comparison with his own Lupercalian standards of gaiety he works with a splendid economy and is almost a miniaturist. He rarely makes huge gestures, but when he does, he will probably knock a table over, so tremendous and unlooked-for is his physical strength. He dances with amazing lightness and deftness, bouncing like a rubber puppet and never missing a beat; at parties he has the authority and agility of an oriental nabob in whose body the soul of a marmoset has found temporary refuge.

He lives a life of exuberant exclamation marks, vast eyebrow-raising question-marks, and curiously inverted commas; he sees everything heavily italicized, and has no time for anything as half-hearted as a semi-colon. I doubt whether he believes in the existence of full stops. If the things around him are not on a gargantuan scale, he will strive to make them so. Introduce him to a man with a strong laugh, and a moment later you will find him telling everyone that the man has not stopped laughing in fifteen years, that he has been laughing at the sheer absurdity of living, with tears streaming down his face. (Stanley once came within an ace of holding a Laughing Party for all the professional laughers in the University.) Everything Stanley cherishes is anti-realistic; his world is peopled with that which is against or beyond reality. This is his compensation for the fruitlessness of everyday; with wild verbal felicity he spends his time retouching the dull succession of blurred half-tone prints which add up to being alive. Like a lightning telescope, his mind exaggerates drab fact; and all words, fair or foul, are his legitimate meat.

Yet he never swears, not even to say 'hell' or 'damn'. It has been suggested that his profound belief in the existence of evil is akin to that of the provincial spinster; it is probably nearer to that of the Catholic martyr. He explained one bout of self-mortification by telling me sombrely: 'I don't think I could survive a sudden death.' Once he refused point-blank to go to a party, because he heard that a hypnotist was to be present; he said he was appalled that such men should be fêted and encouraged. Even in their most frenzied lubricities, the men of the High Renaissance kept their awe of God, and so does Stanley. As Shaw said of Stalin: 'You might guess him to be the illegitimate soldier-son of a cardinal.' In his most elastic party-moods, he retains a certain perspiring holiness, like a Papal bull in a blue china shop; and, like most pontiffs, in addition to knowing good from evil, he knows instinctively which of two photographers represents *The Tatler*, and which the *Daily Mirror*.

He has drawn and written about nearly everybody who *is* everybody; but he will agree that his finest gift is talk. He is the funniest talker I have ever heard, and yet his conversation springs largely from two sources – one, a marvellous eye for physiognomical peculiarity, and two, a marvellous ear for verbal bric-à-brac. He dips, swallow-like, into a sea of words, and comes up dripping and diffuse. His methods are those of snowball accumulation; it is thus that he creates legends where no legend was. The Curator of a zoo once gave him an owl for a birthday present; it was beautifully stuffed, he thought, and he had it put on the mantelpiece beside the stuffed canary. Later, as the party raged into the night, he returned to admire it. It immediately screamed in his face TOO WOOO TOO WOOO and 'began flapping round the room, drinking all the drink, making love to everybody . . .'. It was too much. Ashen, Stanley gathered his shaken dignity about him. 'Either the owl goes, or I go,' he said steadily; '*The owl must leave.*' The owl left.

Stanley is the great escapist; he will never admit that reality is anything more than the unfinished sketch of a careless and indolent creator. It is Stanley's mission to finish the job; he will be the *reductor ad absurdum* of the commonplace. Show him a smallish nose, and he will describe it as 'just two holes in the face', and finally, by almost skull-splitting extension, it will become *concave*. The extremeness of his vision reminds me of a passage in Max Beerbohm:

> The jester must be able to grapple his theme and hang on to it, twisting it this way and that, and making it yield magically all manner of strange and precious things, one after another, without pause. He must have invention

keeping pace with utterance. He must be inexhaustible. Only so can he exhaust us.

A favourite theme has to do with a headline which he saw years ago in an Australian daily. 'BEAR IN COURT' it said; and Stanley can still relive the joy of the first image that occurred to him – could it be that 'the bruin in question' had swept into the throne-room with three feathers on its head, and curtsied? The page proved to be the story of a Mrs Bear, whose psychiatrist reported on her in a sentence which Stanley has never quite got over: 'She was quite normal, *except* that whenever the phrase "point of pin" was mentioned, she thought the word "toe" was indicated.' It is upon such baffled blind alleys of meaning as this that Stanley really lets go. When his brother dreamt of an apocryphal best-seller called *The Whist Between Us*, Stanley spent a morning explaining exactly how it was going to be turned into a film with Anna Neagle and Michael Wilding; he can devote hours of orgiastic talk to deciding just what sort of a woman would have a name like Enid Sharp-Bolster or Didi de Pledge. And you would have to know Stanley very well to understand why the mere mention of concrete floors nowadays gives me hysterics. Set him dithyrambing on a malleable theme, and its changing lights will lure him on into visions in which frogs, frigates, fire hydrants and incantations to the moon will all have a perfectly reasonable place. He never tells jokes or laughs when they are told him. 'Jokes *happen*,' he will say: and his business is to make them happen near him, not to collect them at second hand.

Sometimes ecstasy ties his tongue; as when he thrice insisted to a sloe-eyed Piccadilly bus conductress that he wanted a ticket to 'H-H-Hard Pike – H-H-H-Hard Pike Corner'. Even more attractively confused was his gauche farewell, many years ago, to Athene Seyler. 'Well,' he said, shifting from foot to foot, 'better be get alonging.'

He can be a very hard worker when the fit seizes him; when I first knew him, he could talk of nothing but his new pictures of Gigli and T. S. Eliot. His very holidays and truancies from work are athletic and prostrating; I can think of no one who can better communicate the glow of knowing (in the words that open *The Lost Weekend*) that 'the barometer of his emotional nature is set for a spell of riot'. I do not think he writes particularly well, and his drawings, though Shaw called them 'dramatic criticisms', are very much of the thirties – nearly all represent a left profile staring glumly and intently into mist. But as a *boulevardier* he is unique in Oxford, perhaps in England; and to stoke up that indomitable personality is a full-time job, involving endless night-shifts. Oddly, he is full of love; Max Beerbohm's phrase for him was 'potent in pencil as in pen, but not, I think, in poison'. He still takes his mother to every first-night he attends, and he loves his friends with the pertinacity of an anaconda. I once asked him for an epithet to sum up his whole being, and he proudly replied: 'Wholesome.' He likes piggy pleasures ('I adore food and bacon and things'); and I have often reflected that his existence might be divided into three parts – pork, apple sauce, and stuffing. His most beloved book is *Zuleika Dobson*; he reads the Greeks and the Decadents avidly, and sometimes wonders idly what happened to literature between the death of Pindar and the birth of Whistler. The best acting he has ever seen was Sybil Thorndike's Medea, which he saw sixteen times; and the most humbling genius he ever met was, he says, Pavlova. His proudest recent memory is of a letter Frances Day wrote him addressed to 'Stanley Parker, Oxford'. It was instantly delivered.

For Stanley, laughter is god-like, and despair the ultimate evil. I have heard him say, after a bright evening at the theatre: 'God was with me all evening; he was on my knee.' He detests solitude and cannot remember being alone; except voluntarily, once a week, when he goes to church in mid-afternoon and meditates wasted days. It is 'a very un-smart church' and if interrupted, he pretends to be an ikon.

He especially warms to Mae West and all that drapes itself about her – sequins, ostrich feathers, pink spotlights; all that is deliberately artificial, faintly funny, and nostalgic of the middle thirties. One of his favourite lines comes from a minor triumph of Miss West's in which, cocooned in silk and lace, she turned to her coloured maid and said with almost feudal scorn: 'Beulah – peel me a grape.' This is the life Stanley thirsts after, and it is a sad truth that he has never even aspired to a recognizable pair of shoes.

Never, while you live, permit him to be serious; the brow wrinkles, the lips purse up with affected boredom, and he will talk endlessly in a flurry of furtive platitude. But when a fat woman enters a room, garish under a pumpkin hat, Stanley's face will collapse into a comic mask and you can relax again. He may be going to fall in love with her, or to make outrageous suggestions about her; it matters little; he will be funny. His humorous reflexes are hair-triggered: one afternoon, by sheer loquacity, he persuaded me that Woodstock Road (which telescopes away northwards to the suburbs of hell) was Europe's playground. And he can make the Randolph bar at midday seem as innocent and sunlit and sensual as Hieronymus Bosch's Garden of Delights. Neurosis in his presence becomes a laughable fiction; he is Edward Lear and Lewis Carroll stripped of frailty and whimsey and dipped thoroughly in beer and bacon-fat. There is an almost Chinese imperturbability about him ('I worship everything that is Ping'): often he reminds me of a dissolute old mandarin with a gourmet's love of peacock's tongues and a hatchet up either sleeve.

Sometimes I decide he is a pernicious rascal, a wicked vagabond, and I argue hotly against him, and call him a pantaloon Micawber. It is easy to despise, easier still to pity him: the frightful thing is that he remains full of laughter, knowing your motives better than you do yourself. We do not always see eye to eye. But we invariably see ego to ego.

1950

WHY DID GOD MAKE YOU SO BLOODY LOVELY?

On 14 February the island race goes collectively mad. Some eight and a half million Valentine's Cards are dispatched, and newspapers groan under the weight of bizarre, arcane, and often unashamedly erotic messages. As Noël Coward nearly said: the French wouldn't care to, the Americans wouldn't dare to, but the allegedly po-faced English have no inhibitions about declaring their love at all; as one anonymous swain memorably puts it: 'all those other wet sloppy things.'

VALENTINE'S DAY MESSAGES

THE *OBSERVER*

FAT ARSE Let's find the first sweet fruit of spring and never look back. Love you ZUESS.

BIG BUM Love every scrap of you. Hugs and kisses. SOFTPAWS LIMPOPO.

CAN I CARESS Your thighs with my tongue? Love you always APOLLO.

CAPTAIN I'm your man. Cad as I am you're the girl who fits the slipper, please always be my skipper. I LOVE YOU.

CAROL, hugs, cuddles and all those other wet sloppy things. LOVE YOU FOREVER.

CHERYL you make all my stitches hurt. All my love always ALASTAIR.

I LOVE YOU. I love you. I love you. I love you. I love you. I love you. I love you. I love you. TEAPOT.

I LOVE YOUR squiggy bottom. Love No 2 SQUIGGY BOTTOM.

MY LITTLE MUSTARD SEED. You can share my king size duvet, if I can yours. LOVE SNUFFLES.

STEAL MY SHEETS, Snore and Fart, Simon, forever, in my Heart. HILLA.

THE *SUNDAY TIMES*

CORNFLAKE – I want you for breakfast for ever.

J.S.S. Why did God make you so bloody lovely? Lotsa love AO.T.L.

PHILIP, small, old, grey, wrinkled and snoozy: I love you.

1988

FUNNY THING
WAR

Rupert Brooke's centenary has just been celebrated and his mythology is now effectively demolished. It was Winston Churchill's over-the-top obituary in The Times which set the legend rolling and which, interestingly, drew protests within a few months of his death from his Cambridge friends that this was not the man they knew. If Brooke had lived, I think he would have ended up in the BBC, perhaps producing plays a little left of the centre for the Third Programme (as it then was). One or two of his poems are not at all bad (Philip Larkin gives us no fewer than six in his Oxford Book of Twentieth Century English Verse – as many as he allows himself). However, he is most under-rated as a travel writer. His Letters from America end with an essay on the outbreak of the 1914–18 war which has been pilloried by Cyril Connolly for its sentimentality; but it was probably an honest evocation of the chaos that went through his mind at the news. Had he lived to see any action the romance would no doubt have been knocked out of his prose, as it certainly was out of Sassoon's poetry in short, bitter pieces like Attack ('O Jesus, make it stop!').

Noël Coward has been criticized for condescension in This Happy Breed; in plain truth, his account of lower middle class family life between two world wars and then in war itself has the ring of verisimilitude. Frank's final speech at the end of Act 1 may sound a touch embarrassing now; but a lot of fathers talked like that in those days.

Leslie Baily's BBC Scrapbooks are one of the most effective tools we have for the recreation of inter-war England. Snow White and the Seven Dwarfs is packing them in while German tanks mass on the frontiers of Austria. The Queen Elizabeth is launched by the Queen at Clydebank while the King, who should have done it, is in London signing a State of Emergency. Churchill walks out of the Commons when Chamberlain brings back peace in our time; Flanagan and Allen are singing 'The Umbrella Man'. And so on.

The process by which the English transform the horror of war into the stuff of comedy is clearly evinced by the next set of pieces. First, we have The White Cliffs by Alice Duer Miller which, frankly, was not taken altogether seriously at the time. Its story is trite, and its sugary cast of stock English characters out-minivers Mrs Miniver. Yet its last lines somehow manage to end up in all the quotation books: 'I have seen much to hate here – much to forgive/ But in a world where England is finished and dead/ I do not wish to live'. The poem was turned down by several publishers and only given a very small initial printing, but had 200,000 copies by April 1942.

Richard Hillary was another wartime bestseller. He was one of the last of the long-haired boys, the student pilots who took to the skies in 1940 to play romantic gladiators in the Battle of Britain. He had five kills to his credit before he was shot down and rescued badly burned. His book, The Last Enemy, has sold 300,000 copies in English and been translated into every European language. It was his first and last book. He managed to inveigle himself back into flying and was killed at the age of twenty-three. No wonder his book was such a hit. How much he would have enjoyed the brilliant parody of it in Beyond the Fringe a quarter of a century later. In exactly the same way H. V. Morton's square and solemn account of Home Guard duties during the Battle of Britain was taken seriously at the time: Dad's Army still lay in the womb of the irreverent future. Still, fine reporting still has clout, and Mollie Panter-Downes, who covered London for many years for the New Yorker, gives us a pin-sharp record of the scene in London on VE Night: 'The floodlighted face of Big Ben loomed like a kind moon.'

AN UNUSUAL YOUNG MAN

RUPERT BROOKE

Some say the Declaration of War threw us into a primitive abyss of hatred and the lust for blood. Others declare that we behaved very well. I do not know. I only know the thoughts that flowed through the mind of a friend of mine when he heard the news. My friend – I shall make no endeavour to excuse him – is a normal, even ordinary man, wholly English, twenty-four years old, active and given to music. By a chance he was ignorant of the events of the world during the last days of July. He was camping with some friends in a remote part of Cornwall, and had gone on, with a companion, for a four-days' sail. So it wasn't till they beached her again that they heard. A youth ran down to them with a telegram: 'We're at war with Germany. We've joined France and Russia.'

My friend ate and drank, and then climbed a hill of gorse, and sat alone, looking at the sea. His mind was full of confused images, and the sense of strain. In answer to the word 'Germany', a train of vague thoughts dragged across his brain. The pompous middle-class vulgarity of the building of Berlin; the wide and restful beauty of Munich; the taste of beer; innumerable quiet, glittering *cafés*; the *Ring*; the swish of evening air in the face, as one *skis* down past the pines; a certain angle of the eyes in the face; long nights of drinking, and singing and laughter; the admirable beauty of German wives and mothers; certain friends; some tunes; the quiet length of evening over the Starnberger-See. Between him and the Cornish sea he saw quite clearly an April morning on a lake south of Berlin, the grey water slipping past his little boat, and a peasant-woman, suddenly revealed against apple-blossom, hanging up blue and scarlet garments to dry in the sun. Children played about her; and she sang as she worked. And he remembered a night in Munich spent with a students' *Kneipe*. From eight to one they had continually emptied immense jugs of beer, and smoked, and sung English and German songs in profound chorus. And when the party broke up he found himself arm-in-arm with the president, who was a vast Jew, and with an Apollonian youth called Leo Diringer, who said he was a poet. There was also a fourth man, of whom he could remember no detail. Together, walking with ferocious care down the middle of the street, they had swayed through Schwabing seeking an open *café*. Café Benz was closed, but further up there was a little place still lighted, inhabited by one waiter, innumerable chairs and tables piled on each other for the night, and a row of chess-boards, in front of which sat a little bald, bearded man in dress-clothes, waiting. The little man seemed to them infinitely pathetic. Four against one, they played him at chess, and were beaten. They bowed, and passed into the night. Leo Diringer recited a sonnet, and slept suddenly at the foot of a lamp-post. The Jew's heavy-lidded eyes shone with a final flicker of caution, and he turned homeward resolutely, to the last not wholly drunk. My friend had wandered to his lodgings, in an infinite peace. He could not remember what had happened to the fourth man. . . .

A thousand little figures tumbled through his mind. But they no longer brought with them that air of comfortable kindliness which Germany had always signified for him. Something in him kept urging, 'You must hate these things, find evil in them.' There was that half-conscious agony of breaking a mental habit, painting out a mass of associations, which he had felt in ceasing to believe in a religion, or, more acutely, after quarrelling with a friend. He knew that was absurd. The picture came to him of encountering the Jew, or Diringer, or old Wolf, or little Streckmann, the pianist, in a raid on the East Coast, or on the Continent, slashing at them in a stagey, dimly-imagined battle. Ridiculous. He vaguely imagined a series of heroic feats, vast enterprise, and the applause of crowds. . . .

From that egotism he was awakened to a different one, by the thought that this day meant war and the change of all things he knew. He realized, with increasing resentment, that music would be neglected. And he wouldn't be able, for example, to camp out. He might have to volunteer for military training and service. Some of his friends would be killed. The Russian ballet wouldn't return. His own relationship with A——, a girl he intermittently adored, would be changed. Absurd, but inevitable; because – he scarcely worded it to himself – he and she and everyone else were going to be different. His mind fluttered irascibly to escape from this thought, but still came back to it, like a tethered bird. Then he became calmer, and wandered out for a time into fantasy.

A cloud over the sun woke him to consciousness of his own thoughts; and he found, with perplexity, that they were continually recurring to two periods of his life, the days after the death of his mother, and the time of his first deep estrangement from one he loved. After a bit he understood this. Now, as then, his mind had been completely divided into two parts: the upper running about aimlessly from one half-relevant thought to another, the lower unconscious half labouring with some profound and unknowable change. This feeling of ignorant helplessness linked him with those past crises. His consciousness was like the light scurry of waves at full tide, when the deeper waters are pausing and gathering and turning home. Something was growing in his heart, and he couldn't tell what. But as he thought 'England and Germany', the word 'England' seemed to flash like a line of foam. With a sudden tightening of his heart, he realized that there might be a raid on the English coast. He didn't imagine any possibility of it *succeeding*, but only of enemies and warfare on English soil. The idea sickened him. He was immensely surprised to perceive that the actual earth of England held for him a quality which he found in A——, and in a friend's honour, and scarcely anywhere else, a quality which, if he'd ever been sentimental enough to use the word, he'd have called 'holiness'. His astonishment grew as the full flood of 'England' swept him on from thought to thought. He felt the triumphant helplessness of a lover. Grey, uneven little fields, and small, ancient hedges rushed before him, wild flowers, elms and beeches, gentleness, sedate houses of red brick, proudly unassuming, a countryside of rambling hills and friendly copses. He seemed to be raised high, looking down on a landscape compounded of the western view from the Cotswolds, and the Weald, and the high land in Wiltshire, and the Midlands seen from the hills above Princes Risborough. And all this to the accompaniment of tunes heard long ago, an intolerable number of them being hymns. There was, in his mind, a confused multitude of faces, to most of which he could not put a name. At one moment he was on an Atlantic liner, sick for home, making Plymouth at nightfall; and at another, diving into a little rocky pool through which the Teign flows, north of Bovey; and again, waking, stiff with dew, to see the dawn come up over the Royston plain. And continually he seemed to see the set of a mouth which he knew for his mother's, and A——'s face, and, inexplicably, the face of an old man he had once passed in a Warwickshire village. To his great disgust, the most commonplace sentiments found utterance in him. At the same time he was extraordinarily happy. . . .

1916

ATTACK

SIEGFRIED SASSOON

At dawn the ridge emerges massed and dun
In the wild purple of the glow'ring sun,
Smouldering through spouts of drifting smoke that shroud
The menacing scarred slope; and, one by one,
Tanks creep and topple forward to the wire.
The barrage roars and lifts. Then, clumsily bowed
With bombs and guns and shovels and battle-gear,
Men jostle and climb to meet the bristling fire.
Lines of grey, muttering faces, masked with fear,
They leave their trenches, going over the top,
While time ticks blank and busy on their wrists,
And hope, with furtive eyes and grappling fists,
Flounders in mud. O Jesus, make it stop!

THIS HAPPY BREED

NOËL COWARD

At this moment there is a great commotion outside in the garden. FRANK *and* BOB's *voices are heard singing 'Rule Britannia' at the top of their lungs. They come in, grimy but gay.*

FRANK (*striking an attitude in front of* ETHEL): . . . Britons never, never, never shall be slaves!

ETHEL: 'Old your noise, Frank Gibbons, you'll wake up the whole street.

FRANK: Who cares! We have come unscathed, my friend and I, through untold perils, and you grumble about a bit of noise.

ETHEL: You've come unscathed through a few public houses, too, or I'm no judge.

BOB: Well, there's no denying, Mrs G., we had a couple at the Plough with Captain Burchell, who brought us all the way from Baker Street in his car, and then just one more next door with me.

FRANK: That makes three all told, not so bad when you come to think we've saved our country from the 'orrors of bloody revolution.

ETHEL: And don't swear neither. You'd better go and wash while I dish up your supper. You'll stay and have a bite, won't you, Bob?

BOB: No, thanks all the same. Nora's got something for me next door.

FRANK: Have a drink?

ETHEL: You've had quite enough drink, Frank, and well you know it.

BOB: Better not, old man. Ethel's right, the women are always right, that's why we cherish them, isn't it? Queenie?

ETHEL: You'd better cherish yourself next door, Bob Mitchell. Nora'll be having one of her upsets if she's got something hot ready for you and you're not there to eat it.

BOB: All right, all right – I thought I'd just deliver your old man safe and sound into your loving arms – good night, all.

FRANK: That's right, drive my best pal out of the house, that's all the thanks he gets for saving my life.

ETHEL: How d'you mean, saving your life?

FRANK: An old lady at Cricklewood attacked me with an umbrella, and quick as a flash he wrested it from her and hit her on the bottom with it!

VI (*giggling*): Oh, Dad, you are awful!

FRANK: Good night, cock, see you tomorrow.

BOB: Righto, sweet dreams. Toodle-ooo, everybody!

He goes out again, through the French windows.

ETHEL: Go on, Frank. (*She starts cutting some bread.*) Here, Queenie, this bread's like iron, run into the kitchen and make your dad a bit of toast while I get the soup, the toaster's on the dresser.

QUEENIE (*taking the bread and going out*): All right, Mum.

FRANK goes out after her.

VI: I'll get the soup, Mother, you stay here, you're tired.

PHYLLIS: Can I help?

ETHEL: No thank you, dear.

VI goes out.

ETHEL sits down in the armchair by the fireplace.

PHYLLIS: Mr Gibbons and Mr Mitchell were in the war together, weren't they?

ETHEL: Yes, and to hear them talk you'd think they were the only ones that was.

There is the sound of the front door bell.

There's the bell! (*She jumps up.*)

PHYLLIS: I'll go, Mrs Gibbons.

PHYLLIS runs out of the room.

ETHEL stands by the fireplace waiting anxiously. There is the sound of voices in the hall, then SAM comes in holding REG by the arm. PHYLLIS follows them. REG's head is bandaged. ETHEL gives a cry.

ETHEL: Reg! What's happened?

SAM: He's all right, Mrs Gibbons –

ETHEL: Here, Reg, sit down here, dear.

REG (*sitting down*): Don't fuss, Mother, I'm all right.

SAM: There was some trouble in the Whitechapel Road, and he got hit by a stone. That was yesterday.

ETHEL: What was he doing in the Whitechapel Road yesterday or any other time?

REG (*smiling a little*): Hallo, Phyl, what are you doing here?

PHYLLIS: I came over on me bike to find out where you were.

REG: Oh, I see . . . thanks.

ETHEL: I've been worrying my heart out about you, you ought to be ashamed of yourself.

FRANK comes in, followed by VI.

FRANK: Hallo – what's up?

ETHEL: It's Reg, he's been hurt.

SAM: It's nothing serious, I took him to the hospital last night, the doctor said it was only a graze.

VI (*grimly*): This is all your fault, Sam, you know that, don't you?

FRANK (going over to REG): Shut up a minute, Vi . . . feel all right, son?

REG (*sullenly*): Of course I feel all right.

ETHEL: He'd better go up to bed, hadn't he?

FRANK: Leave him where he is a minute.

ETHEL: Don't go for him tonight, Frank, he looks worn out.

FRANK: I'm not going for anybody. I want my supper.

He goes to the table and sits down. ETHEL takes the bowl of soup from VI and serves it to him. She is looking at REG anxiously out of the corner of her eye as she does so. QUEENIE enters with the toast.

VI: You may not be going for anybody, Dad, but I am.

SAM: I think I'll be getting along now.

VI: Not until you've heard what I've got to say, you're not.

REG: Oh, shut up, Vi, what's it got to do with you?

VI: It's all very fine for you to say that nothing serious has happened, Sam, but I should like to remark here and now that it's small thanks to you that it hasn't. You're nothing but a great silly show-off anyhow, and you've been filling Reg up with your rotten ideas till he can't see straight. Reg thinks you're wonderful, he's younger than you and easily led, but I don't think you're wonderful. I'd think more of you if you did a bit more and talked a bit less. And the next time you come here on a Sunday evening and start pawing me about and saying that Love's the most glorious thing in the world for rich and poor alike, you'll get such a smack in the face that'll make you wish you'd never been born. . . .

SAM: Look here, Vi. . . .

VI: You get out of this house once and for all and don't you show your nose in it again until you've changed your way of thinking. I don't want to have anything to do with a man who listens to a lot of dirty foreigners and goes against his own country. There may be a lot of things wrong but it's not a noisy great gasbag like you that's going to set them right.

SAM: If that's the way you feel, there isn't anything more to be said.

VI: You're right, dead right, there isn't. Go on, get out! I don't want ever to see you again as long as I live!

In silence SAM turns and goes out of the room. VI waits until she hears the front door slam and then bursts into tears and rushes out into the garden.

FRANK: Where's the pepper got to?

QUEENIE: In the sideboard – here – (*She gets it.*)

ETHEL: Oh, dear – I'd better go after her.

FRANK: Much better leave her alone.

REG: Vi hasn't any right to go at Sam like that. What does she know about anything anyway?

FRANK: You keep quiet son. I'll talk to you presently.

ETHEL: He really ought to go to bed, Frank, he looks that seedy. . . . (*To REG*) Is your head paining you, dear?

REG (*irritably*): No, Mum, it's all right, just aching a bit, that's all.

PHYLLIS: I think I'd better be getting back now, Mrs Gibbons.

ETHEL: Very well, dear, be careful how you go, there's probably a lot of people about tonight.

PHYLLIS: Good night, Queenie.

QUEENIE: Good night, Phyl.

PHYLLIS: Good night, Mr Gibbons.

FRANK: Good night, Phyllis.

PHYLLIS: I hope your head'll be better in the morning, Reg.

REG: Thanks for coming round.

PHYLLIS: Good night.

REG: See you tomorrow?

PHYLLIS: Oh – all right.

PHYLLIS *goes out.*

FRANK (*lighting a cigarette*): Run out into the garden, Queenie, and fetch Vi in, it's time we was all in bed.

QUEENIE: Righto, Dad.

She goes into the garden.
FRANK: Go on up, Ethel, I'll turn out.
ETHEL: Promise me you won't be hard on him tonight, Frank – look, he's as white as a sheet.
REG (*defiantly*): I feel fine, Mum, don't worry about me.
FRANK: Well, that's good news, anyway.
ETHEL: Come in and say good night to me on your way to bed.
REG: All right.
ETHEL *stands about helplessly for a moment, and then, one more imploring look at* FRANK, *she goes out of the room.*
FRANK *takes a bottle of whisky, a syphon and two glasses out of the sideboard.*
FRANK: Feel like a drink, Reg?
REG (*surprised*): Oh – yes, thanks.
    FRANK *pours two drinks out in silence and takes one over to* REG.
FRANK: Here you are. . . .
    FRANK *stands leaning against the mantelpiece looking down at* REG.
REG: Well, Dad – let's have it and get it over with.
FRANK: Easier said than done, you and me don't quite see things the same way, do we?
REG: No, I suppose not.
FRANK: That's the trouble really, it's a pity, too, and I don't see what there is to be done about it. Got any ideas?
REG: I'm not a kid any more, you know, Dad. I'm grown-up now.
FRANK: Yes, I realize that all right.
REG: I know you think all the things I believe in are wrong. . . .
FRANK: That's where you make a mistake, son, I don't think any such thing. You've got a right to your opinions the same as I've got a right to mine. The only thing that worries me is that you should get it into your head that everybody's against you and what's more that all these ideas you've picked up, from Sam and Sam's friends, are new. They're not new, they're as old as the hills. Anybody with any sense has always known about the injustice of some people having a lot and other people having nothing at all, but where I think you go wrong is to blame it all on systems and governments. You've got to go deeper than that to find out the cause of most of the troubles of this world, and when you've had a good look, you'll see likely as not that good old human nature's at the bottom of the whole thing.
REG: If everybody had the same chance as everybody else, human nature'd be better, wouldn't it?
FRANK: It doesn't seem as though we were ever going to find that out, does it? It looks like a bit of a deadlock to me.
REG: As long as we go on admitting that, the workers of the world will go on being ground down and the capitalists will go on fattening on their blood and sweat.
FRANK: Oh, don't let's start all that now, let's use our own words, not other people's.
REG: I don't know what you mean.
FRANK: Oh, come off it, Reg, a kid of your age to be talking about blood and

sweat and capitalism! When I was rising twenty I had a damn sight more cheerful things to think about than that, I can tell you.

REG: Old people always think that all young people want is to enjoy themselves.

FRANK: Don't you sit there and tell me you 'aven't been enjoying yourself tip-top these last few days running about the streets and throwing stones and yelling your head off. . . .

REG: It's no use talking, Dad, you don't understand, and you never will.

FRANK: No, you're quite right, arguing never got anybody anywhere, I'll just give you one bit of advice, and then we'll call it a day. How does that suit?

REG (*suspiciously*): What is it?

FRANK: It's this son. I belong to a generation of men, most of which aren't here any more, and we all did the same thing for the same reason, no matter what we thought about politics. Now all that's over and we're all going on as best as we can as though nothing had happened. But as a matter of fact several things did happen and one of them was the country suddenly got tired, it's tired now. But the old girl's got stamina and don't you make any mistake about it and it's up to us ordinary people to keep things steady. That's your job, my son, and just you remember it, and the next time you slam out of the house without a word and never let your mother know where you are and worry her to death, I'll lather the living daylight out of you. Now cut along upstairs and get a bit of sleep.

REG (*rising*): All right, Dad.

FRANK: And don't forget to go in and say good night to your mum.

REG: All right, Dad – thanks, Dad.

REG goes out.

FRANK looks round the room, finishes his drink, turns out the lights and follows him as –

THE CURTAIN FALLS.

1943

'WORLD AIN'T WOT IT USED TO BE'

LESLIE BAILY

The demand for gaiety amid 1938's darkness is shown again in the fact that this was Lambeth Walk Year as well as Munich Year. A musical play, *Me and My Girl*, a near-flop when staged at the Victoria Palace at the end of 1937, had its fortune changed by a broadcast from the stage; thereafter it piled up 1,646 performances, the longest theatre run of the Thirties, starring Lupino Lane. In dance halls its hit-tune had all western Europe 'Doing the Lambeth Walk – OI!' The Nazis passed the tune as fit for human consumption once they had checked that composer Noël Gay was not a Jew.

J. B. Priestley, creative and versatile, dominated the stage at this period with plays ranging from a roaring Yorkshire farce, *When We Were Married*, to serious plays like *Time and the Conways* and *I Have Been Here Before* in which his subject was Dunne's much-discussed theory of time, 'the curious feeling which almost everyone has now and then experienced – that sudden, fleeting, disturbing conviction that something which is happening at the moment *happened before*.' The most serious and topical of subjects treated on the stage and in radio was war. It was not entirely funked, as unemployment had been in the London theatre (barring *Love on the Dole*). The tragic dilemma of modern man was voiced in Charles Morgan's play *The Flashing Stream*: 'The misery they want to cure by force is the misery they have created by force – and will create again.' Robert Sherwood's *Idiot's Delight*, starring Raymond Massey, was set in an Alpine country cowering under imminent threat of aerial bombardment, where 'It needs only one spark, set off anywhere by one ego-maniac, to send it all up in one final, fatal explosion,' said one character – and this play was advertised as about to open in London when German troops entered Austria in very real life, on March 11, 1938.

In Vienna alone 76,000 people were arrested, including von Schuschnigg and his government. The stark truth came through from newspaper correspondents such as G. E. R. Gedge of the *Daily Telegraph*: 'You will shrug your comfortable shoulders in England, you'll say "bogey tales" when I tell you of Viennese women whose husbands were arrested without charge receiving a small parcel from the postman with the curt intimation: "To pay, 150 marks for the cremation of your husband – ashes enclosed, from Dachau".'

Now we understood what Nazism meant. I think many people who lived in Britain during the six months from the occupation of Austria to the Munich crisis in September 1938 would agree that this was the most tense and unhappy period in their lives, or at any rate in the nation's life. War, later on, could be perilous and extremely unpleasant but at least we knew which course the nation was taking (especially after Churchill took the helm) and each of us knew where his own part lay, but the long suspense and vacillation in the spring and summer of 1938 was a nightmare. When Mass Observation tested public opinion in the streets they found firstly a widespread resistance to the idea that war was coming; secondly, 'although most people are anxious and would like to know more about the issues . . . they are discouraged and bewildered by the official secrecy and newspaper contradictions.' There were many answers of this kind: 'Don't know what we ought to do – these bloody Fascists – it's the kids I'm thinking of.' We had seen in the papers what air-raids in Spain did to kids. The sound of a plane was not yet a sound of menace to our children. We looked on them with particular tenderness as we stood in the queue for *Snow White and the Seven Dwarfs*, while they bought their jelly babies for tuppence a quarter and gobstoppers at a farthing each. Through the summer of 1938 tension mounted. German tanks now stood on the frontiers of Austria with Czechoslovakia, and Hitler piled pressure on the Czechs for the 'liberation' of the German-speaking Sudeten areas. 'I keep racking my brains to try and devise some means of averting a catastrophe,' wrote Chamberlain.

In the crisis month of September, according to Mass Observation's poll, seventy per cent of the British public approved the Prime Minister's visit to Berchtesgaden for the first of the appeasement negotiations. To and fro the old man flew with his famous umbrella. He was sixty-nine and had never flown before.

Godesberg was the scene of the second meeting, a week after the first. By now Chamberlain-popularity was down to sixty per cent. Typical 'anti' opinion was this from a London bus conductor: 'How the hell's he got the right to go over and do a dirty trick like that on the Czechs? Who'll trust us now?' Chamberlain boarded his plane again, smiling confidently at the movie cameras, and like a dog wagging its tail over a well-recovered bone he placed the settlement at Hitler's feet, only to be told, 'This solution is no longer any use.' The Führer had raised the stakes to the immediate military occupation of the Sudetenland to lines drawn by himself, and no international supervision. Godesberg ended icily. Chamberlain told Hitler he was behaving like a conqueror, not a negotiator.

The Premier flew back; thirty-four London hospitals were cleared for casualties and thousands of unemployed found work at last, digging slit-trenches in London parks. Searchlights were mounted, and a few anti-aircraft guns. Everyone bought electric torches. Public buildings were protected behind sandbags; private windows were criss-crossed with anti-splinter sticky strips; trainloads of children were evacuated with gas-mask boxes slung round their necks. Village cottages were packed with evacuee families. In this last week of September everyone expected war, Guernica magnified a thousand times, plus gas. At Broadcasting House gas-tight doors were fixed, and an announcer had to say this in as mild tones as he could summon: 'The Home Office announces that the designing of gas masks for babies has been difficult but this has been surmounted and production is now in hand; in the meantime a good measure of protection can be afforded by wrapping the baby completely in a blanket when it could with safety be carried through gas to the nearest gas-proof shelter.'

A week of tension was relieved by a sense of humour such as that of an ARP warden fitting gas masks who told a distressed woman who brought her bowl of goldfish to the depot: 'They'll be all right, ma'am, put them in your mask along with you.'

Britain's secret radar system was on twenty-four hours watch in the London area, the Clyde, the Forth, the Tyne and the Wash. The navy was mobilized. On the same day a new liner was due to be launched by King George VI at Clydebank; his Queen went in his place and christened the ship with her own name, *Queen Elizabeth*, while in London the King signed a State of Emergency. He suggested that he should send a personal letter to Hitler 'as one ex-serviceman to another' appealing to him to spare the world's youth from another war, but the Premier thought Hitler might reply insultingly; instead, Chamberlain himself sent a 'last appeal'. Hitler's reply, an invitation to a conference at Munich with Daladier of France and Mussolini of Italy (Czechoslovakia *not* invited) was read in the Commons amid what BBC news called 'scenes perhaps unexampled for enthusiasm and emotion'.

'I hope the House will release me now to go and see what I can make of this last effort,' said Mr Chamberlain. The House rose cheering and waving order papers. Only a few did not join in what Harold Nicolson called 'a lamentable exhibition of mass hysteria'. Churchill, Eden and Amery walked out.

That night the Prime Minister flew off again, and by a complete coincidence a new show called *These Foolish Things* opened at the London Palladium with Flanagan and Allen singing:

> *He'll patch up your troubles then go on his way*
> *Singin' toodle luma luma toodle-ay,*
> * Toodle luma luma toodle-ay,*
> *Any umbrellas to mend today?*

Mr Alan Bullock says: 'At Munich they amputated the Sudetenland, surrendered to Hitler Czechoslovakia's fortifications and many of her industries, severed her railways, retired her undefeated army. This "settlement" was presented to the Czechs as a *fait accompli*, and next day the German tanks rolled in.

How many foresaw this in 1938 as Chamberlain flew back to London? He received 40,000 letters from people who believe he had saved the world from war. The commentator for the BBC Television Service that day at Heston airport was Mr Freddy Grisewood: 'Houses near the aerodrome had put out the flags they'd last flown at the Coronation. It was a wet day. The Premier came out of his plane holding his umbrella, smiling cheerfully. Members of the Cabinet greeted him. He was given a letter of congratulation from the King. He was photographed waving the famous scrap of paper signed by Hitler, promising to resolve all future differences by consultation. I remember a young airman at my side saying "I'll believe that when I see it." But I think doubters were one in a hundred that day. The Premier drove to Buckingham Palace and appeared on the balcony. Then his car had a job getting to Downing Street through the cheering crowds. He appeared at an upper window and made his speech – "I believe it is peace for our time." . . . A few days later I noticed that sweet shops were selling sugar umbrellas.'

The Times said: 'No conqueror returning from victory on the battlefields has come adorned with nobler laurels.' Most newspapers thought Munich better than war. Approval ranged from the *Sunday Dispatch* describing Chamberlain as a Fairy Prince to the Archbishop of Canterbury verifying that the prayers of the nation had been answered. In the next few days people had second thoughts: 'A deep yearning for peace is shot through by dismay at the humiliation of surrender,' said the London *Star*. The Commons voted 366 for the Munich agreement, 144 against. Attlee said that a gallant and democratic people had been 'betrayed and handed over to a ruthless despotism'. Some thirty Conservatives rebelled against the Government, including Duff Cooper (who resigned from the Cabinet), Anthony Eden, Harold Macmillan, Robert Boothby, Duncan Sandys, and Winston Churchill who said: 'We have sustained a total and unmitigated defeat.'

One last scene at the height of the 1938 crisis I remember so well. At a

Promenade Concert the audience cheered as a bust of Sir Henry Wood was unveiled in Queen's Hall to honour, in his presence, half-a-century of service to music at the Proms. Their sentiment was his – as he put it in a *Scrapbook*: 'Music is one of the few elements associated with the progress of civilization which I can heartily endorse.'

We walked out into the night, our hearts filled with thankfulness for that other world, a world of truth and beauty, a world without fear. Above, the searchlights were swinging their arms in their silent saturnalia. Two years later Queen's Hall was blown to blazes.

1937

THE WHITE CLIFFS

ALICE DUER MILLER

I have loved England, dearly and deeply,
Since that first morning, shining and pure,
The white cliffs of Dover I saw rising steeply
Out of the sea that once made her secure.

I had no thought then of husband or lover,
I was a traveller, the guest of a week;
Yet when they pointed 'the white cliffs of Dover',
Startled I found there were tears on my cheek.

I have loved England, and still as a stranger,
Here is my home and I still am alone.
Now in her hour of trial and danger,
Only the English are really her own.

John had one of those English faces
    That always were and will always be
Found in the cream of English places
    Till England herself sink into the sea –
A blond, bowed face with prominent eyes
A little bit bluer than English skies.

You see it in ruffs and suits of armour,
    You see it in wigs of many styles,
Soldier and sailor, judge and farmer –
    That face has governed the British Isles,
By the power, for good or ill bestowed,
Only on those who live by code.

Oh, that inflexible code of living,
    That seems so easy and unconstrained,
The Englishman's code of taking and giving
    Rights and privileges pre-ordained,
Based since English life began
On the prime importance of being a man.

And were they not English, our forefathers, never more
    English than when they shook the dust of her sod
From their feet for ever, angrily seeking a shore
    Where in his own way a man might worship his God.
Never more English than when they dared to be
    Rebels against her – that stern intractable sense
Of that which no man can stomach and still be free,
    Writing: 'When in the course of human events . . .'
Writing it out so all the world could see
    Whence come the powers of all just governments.
The tree of Liberty grew and changed and spread,
    But the seed was English.
                    I am American bred,
I have seen much to hate here – much to forgive,
    But in a world where England is finished and dead,
I do not wish to live.

1941

THE LAST ENEMY

RICHARD HILLARY

At this time the Germans were sending over comparatively few bombers. They were making a determined attempt to wipe out our entire Fighter Force, and from dawn till dusk the sky was filled with Messerschmitt 109's and 110's.

Half a dozen of us always slept over at the Dispersal Hut to be ready for a surprise enemy attack at dawn. This entailed being up by four-thirty and by five o'clock having our machines warmed up and the oxygen, sights, and ammunition tested. The first Hun attack usually came over about breakfast-time and from then until eight o'clock at night we were almost continuously in the air. We ate when we could, baked beans and bacon and eggs being sent over from the Mess.

On the morning after our arrival I walked over with Peter Howes and Broody. Howes was at Hornchurch with another Squadron and worried because he had as yet shot nothing down. Every evening when we came into the Mess he would ask us how many we had got and then go over miserably to his room. His Squadron had had a number of losses and was due for relief. If ever a man needed it, it was Howes. Broody, on the other hand, was in a high state of excitement, his sharp eager face grinning from ear to ear. We left Howes at his Dispersal Hut and walked over to where our machines were being warmed up. The voice of the controller came unhurried over the loud-speaker, telling us to take off, and in a few seconds we were running for our machines. I climbed into the cockpit of my plane and felt an empty sensation of suspense in the pit of my stomach. For one second time seemed to stand still and I stared blankly in front of me. I knew that that morning I was to kill for the first time. That I might be killed or in any way injured did not occur to me. Later, when we were losing pilots regularly, I did consider it in an abstract way when on the ground; but once in the air, never. I knew it could not happen to me. I suppose every pilot knows that, knows it cannot happen to him; even when he is taking off for the last time, when he will not return, he knows that he cannot be killed. I wondered idly what he was like, this man I would kill. Was he young, was he fat, would he die with the Fuehrer's name on his lips, or would he die alone, in that last moment conscious of himself as a man? I would never know. Then I was being strapped in, my mind automatically checking the controls, and we were off.

We ran into them at 18,000 feet, twenty yellow-nosed Messerschmitt 109's, about 500 feet above us. Our Squadron strength was eight, and as they came down on us we went into line astern and turned head on to them. Brian Carbury, who was leading the Section, dropped the nose of his machine, and I could almost feel the leading Nazi pilot push forward on his stick to bring his guns to bear. At the same moment Brian hauled hard back on his own control stick and led us over them in a steep climbing turn to the left. In two vital seconds they lost their advantage. I saw Brian let go a burst of fire at the leading plane, saw the pilot put his machine into a half roll, and knew that he was mine. Automatically, I kicked the rudder to the left to get him at right angles, turned the gun-button to 'Fire', and let go in a four-second burst with full deflection. He came right through my sights and I saw the tracer from all eight guns thud home. For a second he seemed to hang motionless; then a jet of red flame shot upwards and he spun out of sight.

For the next few minutes I was too busy looking after myself to think of anything, but when, after a short while, they turned and made off over the Channel, and we were ordered to our base, my mind began to work again.

It had happened.

My first emotion was one of satisfaction, satisfaction at a job adequately done, at the final logical conclusion of months of specialized training. And then I had a feeling of the essential rightness of it all. He was dead and I was alive; it could so easily have been the other way round; and that would somehow have been right too. I realized in that moment just how lucky a fighter pilot is. He has none of the personalized emotions of the soldier, handed a rifle and bayonet and told to charge. He does not even have to share the dangerous emotions of the bomber pilot who night after night must experience that childhood longing for smashing things. The fighter pilot's emotions are those of the duellist – cool, precise, impersonal. He is privileged to kill well. For if one must either kill or be killed, as now one must, it should, I feel, be done with dignity. Death should be given the setting it deserves; it should never be a pettiness; and for the fighter pilot it never can be.

From this flight Broody Benson did not return.

1942

AFTERMYTH OF WAR

BENNETT, COOK, MILLER AND MOORE

JON: This was war.

Piano: Chopin prelude under next speech.

ALAN: I had a pretty quiet war, really. I was one of the Few. We were stationed down at Biggin Hill. One Sunday we got word that Jerry was coming in – over Hastings, I think it was. We got up there as quickly as we could, and everything was very calm and peaceful. England lay like a green carpet below me, and the war seemed worlds away. I could see Tunbridge Wells, and the sun glinting on the river, and I remembered that last weekend I'd spent there with Celia that summer of '39, and her playing the piano in the cool of the evening. Suddenly, Jerry was coming at me out of a bank of cloud. I let him have it, and I think I must have got him in the wing, because he spiralled past me out of control. As he did so – I will always remember this – I got a glimpse of his face, and, you know – he smiled. Funny thing, war.

There is the sound of hearty singing with the piano: 'Let Him Go, Let Him Tarry' etc. Peter enters.

PETER: Perkins! (*Jon breaks away from the singing.*) Sorry to drag you away from the fun, old boy. War's not going very well, you know.

JON: Oh my God!

PETER: We are two down, and the ball's in the enemy court. War is a psychological thing, Perkins, rather like a game of football. You know how in a game of football ten men often play better than eleven – ?

JON: Yes, sir.

PETER: Perkins, we are asking you to be that one man. I want you to lay down your life, Perkins. We need a futile gesture at this stage. It will raise the whole tone of the war. Get up in a crate, Perkins, pop over to Bremen, take a shufti, don't come back. Goodbye, Perkins. God, I wish I was going too.

JON: Goodbye sir – or is it – *au revoir*?

PETER: *No*, Perkins.

Jon goes off.

1963

I SAW TWO ENGLANDS

H V MORTON

It was a still night. The moon was hidden by high cloud. I stood on the church tower, watching and listening. Pale fields of oats moved in the night wind, gleaming like water.

When I climbed the belfry ladders a few moments ago to keep the second watch, I came out on the lead-covered tower with its breast-high parapet, and there I saw, outlined against the sky, the heroic shape of my companion.

His forage cap might have been a Norman helmet or a medieval casque; and I paused in admiration, telling myself with incredulity that it was only old Tom Burns, the cowman from Brambles.

At the sound of my approach, the figure turned, and a rich, loamy voice said:

'They searchlights be präper busy over Gallows' Hill way tonight.'

Then old Tom turned heavily and, insinuating his bulky frame into the trap-door, vanished into the stone tube of darkness, leaving me alone upon the church tower.

Yes, it is a still night. And now the clouds part and the moon, shining through, casts green shadows so that I can see the little hamlet lying below among haystacks and fields, the lime-washed cottages with front gardens bright with Canterbury Bells, geraniums and poppies; and I think that a more peaceful bit of old England could not be found than this village of ours. Yet in every cottage sleeps an armed man. If I rang the bell now, they would come running out with their rifles, ready to defend their homes. Such a thing has not happened in Britain since the Middle Ages.

It would not surprise me to know that a generation to come will look back upon the trials and anxieties which now beset us as the most dramatic and adventurous incident in the whole of England's history. I think one is peculiarly conscious of this in a country district full of old farm-houses which have been standing for centuries: buildings whose panelling conceals secret rooms, whose wide chimneys lead to 'priests' holes', whose windows have known the tap of a secret code in the night, whose barns and outhouses have stabled many a strange horse and have concealed many a mysterious rider.

As I look down upon the sleeping village, and away over the dark woodlands to such places as Brackett's Farm – a notorious hiding-place for Cavaliers during the Civil War – I think that the awareness of these once sleepy old villages is merely a return of their youth. Danger has skipped us for a century or two; and now we are back in Danger, with a gun under the bed and an ear cocked for the sound of a signal.

Nothing I have known in English life has approached the eagerness with which ordinary men have run to arms in order to defend their homes. My own point of view, and, indeed, it is that of all the farmers, the farm labourers and the cowmen who compose our Home Guard, is that should the rest of

England fall, our own parish would hold out to the last man. The responsibility of defending our own village has given to that village a gigantic significance in our eyes. To us it seems the main objective of any invader. When I look at the map, I am sometimes amazed to see how small and unimportant it must appear to anyone not in our Platoon. But if all villages throughout England think as we do, what a hedge of opposition they present to anyone who dares to set an invader's foot upon this island.

Standing up there like some baron's man brooding on these parish matters, it comes to me that one of the most remarkable things about this war is the quiet way England has ceased to be a country or even a county for many of us, and has become a parish. All over our land, villages once proclaimed dead and done for have awakened to arms. People scarcely on speaking terms have come together to organize defence. Cross roads, ditches, hedges and old tumble-down barns have achieved an unsuspected importance after survey by the slightly myopic eyes of those of us who were soldiers twenty odd years ago.

I, who once thought of England as a whole, and was in the habit of going to Cornwall or Cumberland on the spur of the moment, have not left my parish for months. Neither do I wish to do so; my parish has become England. This is a wonderful thing, and I never get tired of thinking about it. Since France collapsed and flung us all back into the early Nineteenth Century, with 'Boney' on the doorstep, life in the country districts of England has become romantic and realistic. Danger has given us a common purpose. It has given us a meeting-place. It has accomplished for the villages of England what musical young men from Oxford, with bells at their knees, and earnest women in Liberty silk gowns hoped to do a decade ago: it has made England almost 'merrie' again.

It has blown to a flame smouldering local loyalties and traditions. It has roused the English genius for improvisation. It has brought us face to face with the fact that we love our country well enough to die for her.

1942

LONDON WAR NOTES

MOLLIE PANTER-DOWNES

May 7, VE Day; the war ends in Europe.

The big day started off here with a coincidence. In the last hours of peace, in September, 1939, a violent thunderstorm broke over the city, making a lot of people think for a moment that the first air raid had begun. Early Tuesday morning, VE day, nature tidily brought the war to an end with an imitation of a blitz so realistic that many Londoners started awake and reached blurrily for the bedside torch. Then they remembered, and, sighing with relief, fell asleep again as the thunder rolled over the capital, already waiting with its flags. The decorations had blossomed on the streets Monday afternoon. By six that night, Piccadilly Circus and all the city's other focal points were jammed with a cheerful, expectant crowd waiting for an official statement from Downing Street. Movie cameramen crouched patiently on the roof-tops. When a brewer's van rattled by and the driver leaned out and yelled 'It's all over,' the crowd cheered, then went on waiting. Presently, word spread that the announcement would be delayed, and the day, which had started off like a rocket, began to fizzle slowly and damply out.

When the day finally came, it was like no other day that anyone can remember. It had a flavour of its own, an extemporaneousness which gave it something of the quality of a vast, happy village fête as people wandered about, sat, sang, and slept against a summer background of trees, grass, flowers, and water. It was not, people said, like the 1918 Armistice Day, for at no time was the reaction hysterical. It was not like the Coronation, for the crowds were larger and their gaiety, which held up all through the night, was obviously not picked up in a pub. The day also surprised the prophets who had said that only the young would be resilient enough to celebrate in a big way. Apparently, the desire to assist in London's celebration combusted spontaneously in the bosom of every member of every family, from the smallest babies, with their hair done up in red-white-and-blue ribbons, to beaming elderly couples who, utterly without self-consciousness, strolled up and down the streets arm in arm in red-white-and-blue paper hats. Even the dogs wore immense tricolored bows. Rosettes sprouted from the slabs of pork in the butcher shops, which, like other food stores, were open for a couple of hours in the morning. With their customary practicality, house-wives put bread before circuses. They waited in the long bakery queues, the string bags of the common round in one hand and the Union Jack of the glad occasion in the other. Even queues seemed tolerable that morning. The bells had begun to peal and, after the storm, London was having that perfect, hot, English summer's day which, one sometimes feels, is to be found only in the imaginations of the lyric poets.

The girls in their thin, bright dresses heightened the impression that the city had been taken over by an enormous family picnic. The number of extraordinarily pretty young girls, who presumably are hidden on working days inside the factories and government offices, was astonishing. They streamed out into the parks and streets like flocks of twittering, gaily plumaged cockney birds. In their freshly curled hair were cornflowers and poppies, and they wore red-white-and-blue ribbons around their narrow waists. Some of them even tied ribbons around their bare ankles. Strolling with their uniformed boys, arms candidly about each other, they provided a constant, gay, simple marginal decoration to the big, solemn moments of the day. The crowds milled back and forth between the Palace, Westminster, Trafalgar Square, and Piccadilly Circus, and when they got tired they simply sat down wherever they happened to be – on the grass, on doorsteps, or on the curb – and watched the other people or spread handkerchiefs over their faces and took a nap. Everybody appeared determined to see the King and Queen and Mr Churchill at least once, and few could have been disappointed.

One small boy, holding on to his father's hand, wanted to see the trench shelters in Green Park too. 'You don't want to see shelters today,' his father said. 'You'll never have to use them again, son.' 'Never?' the child asked doubtfully. 'Never!' the man cried, almost angrily. '*Never!* Understand?' In the open space before the Palace, one of the places where the Prime Minister's speech was to be relayed by loudspeaker at three o'clock, the crowds seemed a little intimidated by the nearness of that symbolic block of grey stone. The people who chose to open their lunch baskets and munch sandwiches there among the flowerbeds of tulips were rather subdued. Piccadilly Circus attracted the more demonstrative spirits.

By lunchtime, in the Circus, the buses had to slow to a crawl in order to get through the tightly packed, laughing people. A lad in the black beret of the Tank Corps was the first to climb the little pyramidal Angkor Vat of scaffolding and sandbags which was erected early in the war to protect the pedestal of the Eros statue after the figure had been removed to safekeeping. The boy shinnied up to the top and took a tiptoe Eros pose, aiming an imaginary bow, while the crowd roared. He was followed by a paratrooper in a maroon beret, who, after getting up to the top, reached down and hauled up a blond young woman in a very tight pair of green slacks. When she got to the top, the Tank Corps soldier promptly grabbed her in his arms and, encouraged by ecstatic cheers from the whole Circus, seemed about to enact the classic rôle of Eros right on the top of the monument. Nothing came of it, because a moment later a couple of GIs joined them and before long the pyramid was covered with boys and girls. They sat jammed together in an affectionate mass, swinging their legs over the sides, wearing each other's uniform caps, and calling down wisecracks to the crowd. 'My God,' someone said, 'think of a flying bomb coming down on this!' When a firecracker went off, a hawker with a tray of tin brooches of Monty's head happily yelled that comforting, sometimes fallacious phrase of the blitz nights, 'All right, mates, it's one of ours!'

All day long, the deadly past was for most people only just under the surface of the beautiful, safe present – so much so that the government decided against sounding the sirens in a triumphant 'all clear' for fear that the noise would revive too many painful memories. For the same reason, there were no salutes of guns – only the pealing of the bells and the whistles of tugs on the Thames sounding the doot, doot, doot, dooooot of the V, and the roar of the planes, which swooped back and forth over the city, dropping red and green signals toward the blur of smiling, upturned faces.

It was without doubt Churchill's day. Thousands of King George's subjects wedged themselves in front of the Palace throughout the day, chanting ceaselessly 'We want the King' and cheering themselves hoarse when he and the Queen and their daughters appeared, but when the crowd saw Churchill, there was a deep, full-throated, almost reverent roar. He was at the head of a procession of Members of Parliament, walking back to the House of Commons from the traditional St Margaret's Thanksgiving Service. Instantly, he was surrounded by people – people running, standing on tiptoe, holding up babies so that they could be told later they had seen him, and shouting affectionately the absurd little nurserymaid name, 'Winnie, Winnie!' One of two happily sozzled, very old, and incredibly dirty cockneys who had been engaged in a slow, shuffling dance, like a couple of Shakespearean clowns, bellowed, 'That's 'im, that's 'is little old lovely bald 'ead!' The crowds saw Churchill again later, when he emerged from Commons and was driven off in the back of a small open car, rosy, smiling, and looking immensely happy. Ernest Bevin, following in another car, got a cheer, too. Herbert Morrison, sitting unobtrusively in a corner of a third car, was hardly recognized, and the other Cabinet Ministers did no better. The crowd had ears, eyes, and throats for no one but Churchill, and for him everyone in it seemed to have the hearing, sight, and lungs of fifty men. His slightly formal official broadcast, which was followed by buglers sounding the 'cease firing' call, did not strike the emotional note that had been expected, but he hit it perfectly in his subsequent informal speech ('My dear friends, this is your victory. . . .') from a Whitehall balcony.

All day long, little extra celebrations started up. In the Mall, a model of a Gallic cock waltzed on a pole over the heads of the singing people. 'It's the Free French,' said someone. The Belgians in the crowd tagged along after a Belgian flag that marched by, its bearer invisible. A procession of students raced through Green Park, among exploding squibs, clashing dustbin lids like cymbals and waving an immense Jeyes Disinfectant poster as a banner. American sailors and laughing girls formed a conga line down the middle of Piccadilly, and cockneys linked arms in the Lambeth Walk. It was a day and night of no fixed plan and no organized merriment. Each group danced its own dance, sang its own song, and went its own way as the spirit moved it. The most tolerant, self-effacing people in London on VE Day were the police, who simply stood by, smiling benignly, while soldiers swung by one arm from lamp standards and laughing groups tore down hoardings to build the evening's bonfires. Actually, the police were not unduly strained. The extraordinary thing about the crowds was that they were almost all sober. The number of drunks one saw in that whole day and night could have been counted on two hands – possibly because the pubs were sold out so early. The young service men and women who swung arm in arm down the middle of every street, singing and swarming over the few cars rash enough to come out, were simply happy with an immense holiday happiness. Just before the King's speech, at nine Tuesday night, the big lamps outside the Palace came on and there were cheers and ohs from children who had never seen anything of that kind in their short, blacked-out lives. As the evening wore on, most of the public buildings were floodlighted. The night was as warm as midsummer, and London, its shabbiness now hidden and its domes and remaining Wren spires warmed by lights and bonfires, was suddenly magnificent. The handsomest building of all was the National Gallery, standing out honey-coloured near a ghostly, blue-shadowed St Martin's and the Charles I bit of Whitehall. The floodlighted face of Big Ben loomed like a kind moon.

1972

MURDER
YOUR DARLINGS

Now for four views on English style. First, short and sweet Quiller-Couch's admirable advice: murder your darlings. In style, if not in life, this is sound sense. Then, a long and discursive, but always riveting speech by Dorothy L. Sayers on 'The Mysterious English', in which she develops her thesis that the strength of the English language lies in its mixed roots; as she splendidly puts it: 'It is the thunder of the Latin polysyllables that makes the Saxon monosyllables so ominous and so terrific.' Orwell picks her up on the double roots of English, Anglo-Saxon and Norman-French, and then develops his theory that the language is going through a temporary decadence because the educated are out of touch with the working class. He was certainly right in his prediction that the educated English accent would be abandoned; it is very nearly extinct. There is a standard English which has taken its place, but that is by no means the same thing.

What all these writers have in common is a vast respect for plain English and William Rees-Mogg takes it as the theme in his Presidential Address to the English Association – a speech which is, in itself, an object lesson in the plain style.

And next, a group of pieces which all illustrate traditional English style at its best. First, the familiar and deeply satisfying words of the 1662 Book of Morning Prayer. It is now increasingly rarely heard in our churches, and I print it here both for the pleasure of seeing it again and because I suspect that there will be some young readers not even aware of it. Next, the haunting verdict of Francis Bacon on Great Place. 'It is a strange desire,' he says, 'to seek Power, and to lose Liberty'. How true. Then John Evelyn's sizzling dispatch from the Great Fire of London; we can almost feel the ground still hot under the soles of his shoes.

For Chesterton, it is an English perversity to pretend to be bad speakers: eighteenth-century England, he says, blazed with brilliant speakers. And not just the eighteenth. Where else could you have heard a speech to equal Beaverbrook's last, delivered on his 85th birthday, a few days before his death? Certainly no one who heard it will ever forget it.

'To see the golden sun,' William Hazlitt begins in his essay on the 'Feeling of Immortality in Youth'; and goes on to give us one of the greatest sentences in the language. Finally, Cyril Connolly memorably transfixes the home sickness induced by opening the pages of Country Life – even when ensconced enviably by the October Mediterranean.

ON STYLE

SIR ARTHUR QUILLER-COUCH

To begin with, let me plead that you have been told of one or two things which Style is *not*; which have little or nothing to do with Style, though sometimes vulgarly mistaken for it. Style, for example, is not – can never be – extraneous Ornament. You remember, may be, the Persian lover whom I quoted to you out of Newman: how to convey his passion he sought a professional letter-writer and purchased a vocabulary charged with ornament, wherewith to attract the fair one as with a basket of jewels. Well, in this extraneous, professional, purchased ornamentation, you have something which Style *is not*: and if you here require a practical rule of me, I will present you with this: 'Whenever you feel an impulse to perpetrate a piece of exceptionally fine writing, obey it – whole-heartedly – and delete it before sending your manuscript to press. *Murder your darlings.*'

1917

THE MYSTERIOUS ENGLISH

A Speech delivered in London, 1940

DOROTHY L SAYERS

The first, most important thing to notice, and the one which gives the clue to all the rest, is that the English are mongrels; and that, alone of all nations upon earth, they pride themselves upon being mongrels. If ever you hear a man boast of his pure English blood, he may be a Bostonian, he may be a Jew; but whatever he is, he is not English. When Queen Elizabeth said that she was 'mere English', she meant that she had a Welsh surname, though she was a Londoner on the distaff side; when I say I am English, I mean that my mother's family came from Hampshire, and that I have one Scotch and one Irish grandparent.

Ask a man of real English descent whether his people came over with William the Conqueror, and he will probably reply: 'Good Heavens, no! We're Saxon; there were Budgeries in the Manor of Budge when Billy the Conk arrived. Of course,' he will add, and all his subsequent qualifications will begin with 'of course' – 'of course, a good deal of Norman blood came into the family afterwards. We're a pretty mixed lot, really. There's a legend that old Sir Gilbert brought back a Saracen bride after the third Crusade. And there was Captain John Budgery, the one that sailed with Hawkins – he married a Red Indian – sort of Pocahontas business, you know. And, of course, there's a lot of Scotch and Irish in me, though my mother's grandfather was pure Huguenot. And I've sometimes fancied there might be a dash of the tar-brush somewhere – there was Robert Budgery who turned up as the missing heir from South America in the eighteenth century, nobody ever knew where his mother came from. The Cornish branch, of course, have a strong Spanish streak in them; the Armada, you know, and all that.' So he rambles on, unrolling the history of England along with his family tree, and getting more and more mongrel, and more and more pleased with himself, at every word.

We may disbelieve the legend about old Sir Gilbert and the Pocahontas romance; the important thing is that that is what the Englishman likes to believe about himself. And one thing we must remember: that before the Conquest there was no such thing as an Englishman. There were Angles and

93

Saxons, Danes, various kinds of British Celt, and probably some people with traces of Roman descent, but the strange compound we call an Englishman had not yet appeared, any more than the English language. The basic Englishman is the compound of Anglo-Saxon and Norman-French; and though he contains elements from both those main sources, his characteristic Englishry is neither of them, but the blend of the two.

In this, he is exactly like his own English language. The Anglo-Saxon Chronicle is not written in English: it is written in Anglo-Saxon; the *Tristan* of Thomas is not written in English: it is written in Anglo-French. But the romances written in England in the twelfth and thirteenth centuries are written in what, though antiquated and difficult, is quite definitely and increasingly recognizable as the English speech of today; and by the time we get to Chaucer, we are reading something that cannot possibly be called a variety of French or of Anglo-Saxon. It is English; a language in its own right, with its roots in two civilizations, and the most various, flexible, rich and expressive instrument of human speech since the days of Pericles. The well-meaning people who used to implore us to 'return to our native Anglo-Saxon tongue' – to call an omnibus a folk-wain and remorse of conscience the againbite of inwit – were really asking us to abandon our English heritage altogether. English is rich and flexible because it is double-rooted; the whole business of the English writer is to know when to use his Saxon and when to use his French, and therefore his Latin, vocabulary; for the Latin runs readily along with the Saxon because the French words are there to give it passage. Look at this:

> This my hand will rather
> The multitudinous seas incarnadine,
> Making the green one red.

It is the thunder of the Latin polysyllables that makes the Saxon monosyllables so ominous and so terrific. As the language, so the nation. The strength of the English, their adaptibility, their strange talent for improvisation, their disconcerting mixture of the practical and the visionary are the virtues of their mongrel breeding. It is not surprising that the English are dubious about Nordic blood and racial purity. In small and peaceable peoples they consider claims to purity of blood to be harmless and pretty, but rather childish and absurd; in large and ferocious peoples they consider them to be ugly and dangerous, but none the less childish and absurd. (For you will notice that the English, with their misguided and frivolous sense of humour, which is the despair of all earnest peoples, think a thing none the less funny because it may be dangerous; this is one of the things about them which earnest foreigners find misleading and tiresome.)

A direct result of the mongrel nature of the English, and a thing very noticeable about them, is that they have never in their lives been what the Germans still are, that is a *Volk*. From the first beginnings of their Englishry, they have been, not a race, but a nation. The comparative absence of folk-music and folk-customs from England is remarkable, compared with their energetic survival in, say, the Highlands of Scotland; and the English have never had a folk-costume at all. The thing that ties them together is not a consciousness of common blood so much as a common law, a common culture, and a very long memory of national consciousness. The law, generally speaking, is Saxon; the culture, generally speaking, is continental.

This at once makes a distinction between us and, say, the Scots, whose law is, generally speaking, Roman, while their culture was, for a long time, largely racial. The English, on the whole, got their constitutional teething over remarkably early. They were already nationally conscious when, in Henry II's reign, they objected to interference by the Pope, not on religious grounds, but because he was a foreign sovereign putting his finger in the English political pie. The Englishman's offensive feeling of superiority over aliens is largely due to the recollection that England was a nation before other peoples had grown out of being tribes, or clans, or bits and pieces of the Roman Empire. The fact that, only the other day, an arrested man was required to be produced under Habeas Corpus, on the ground that his detention was 'contrary to the Great Charter', is the sort of thing that reminds the Englishman just how far his rights as a national go back. England is a nation; in essentials she has never, since the time that she could properly be called England, been anything else.

As a result of this, the arrogance and insolence of English people became proverbial at a surprisingly early date. Already somewhere about the fourteenth century, visiting observers are heard to remark plaintively that the English 'do not like foreigners'; and somewhere about Queen Elizabeth's time we hear the characteristic English compliment that so-and-so is 'almost like an Englishman'. The national consciousness is fully established. I doubt whether any other nation uses the word 'foreigner' and 'alien' with such offensive intonations as the English. As a French observer has remarked: in France, the most thriving hotel in a town is often called: 'Hôtel des Étrangers'. What English establishment could hope to do business under the title: 'Aliens' Hotel'?

Another result of this is the focusing of the political life of the Three Kingdoms about England. It is perfectly true that, ever since the Union, and, indeed, long before that, great posts in the executive and in the services have frequently been held by Scots, Irishmen, Welshmen and Jews. The Celtic members of the community continually point this out, and with very great justice. But the framework in which these men function is the English framework. Foreigners, especially enemy foreigners, make no mistake about this. '*Gott strafe* England,' they say, and the legendary Scotsman who laboriously altered this to '*Gott strafe* Britain' correctly recognized the compliment implied. It is England who is the object of hymns of hate: 'Wir fahren gegen England.' The real enemy is England, and that peculiar English conception of the State which the rest of Britain has assimilated, and to which it so magnificently works.

1946

THE ENGLISH LANGUAGE

GEORGE ORWELL

The English language has two outstanding characteristics to which most of its minor oddities can be finally traced. These characteristics are a very large vocabulary and simplicity of grammar.

If it is not the largest in the world, the English vocabulary is certainly among the largest. English is really two languages, Anglo–Saxon and Norman-French, and during the last three centuries it has been reinforced on an enormous scale by new words deliberately created from Latin and Greek roots. But in addition the vocabulary is made much larger than it appears by the practice of turning one part of speech into another. For example, almost any noun can be used as a verb: this in effect gives an extra range of verbs, so that you have *knife* as well as *stab*, *school* as well as *teach*, *fire* as well as *burn*, and so on. Then again, certain verbs can be given as many as twenty different meanings simply by adding prepositions to them. (Examples are *get out of*, *get up*, *give out*, *take over*.) Verbs can also change into nouns with considerable freedom, and by the use of affixes such as *-y*, *-ful*, *-like*, any noun can be turned into an adjective. More freely than in most languages, verbs and adjectives can be turned into their opposites by means of the prefix *un-*. And adjectives can be made more emphatic or given a new twist by tying a noun to them; for example, *lily-white*, *sky-blue*, *coal-black*, *iron-hard*, etc.

But English is also, and to an unnecessary extent, a borrowing language. It readily takes over any foreign word that seems to fill a need, often altering the meaning in doing so. A recent example is the word *blitz*. As a verb this word did not appear in print till late in 1940, but it has already become part of the language. Other examples from the vast armoury of borrowed words are *garage*, *charabanc*, *alias*, *alibi*, *steppe*, *thug*, *role*, *menu*, *lasso*, *rendezvous*, *chemise*. It will be noticed that in most cases an English equivalent exists already, so that borrowing adds to the already large stock of synonyms.

English grammar is simple. The language is almost completely uninflected, a peculiarity which marks it off from almost all languages west of China. Any regular English verb has only three inflections, the third person singular, the present participle, and the past participle. Thus, for instance, the verb *to kill* consists of *kill*, *kills*, *killing*, *killed*, and that is all. There is, of course, a great wealth of tenses, very much subtilized in meaning, but these are made by the use of auxiliaries which themselves barely inflect. *May*, *might*, *shall*, *will*, *should*, *would* do not inflect at all, except in the obsolete second person singular. The upshot is that every person in every tense of such a verb as *to kill* can be expressed in only about thirty words including the pronouns, or about forty if one includes the second person singular. The corresponding number in, for instance, French would be somewhere near two hundred. And in English there is the added advantage that the auxiliaries which are used to make the tenses are the same in every case.

There is no such thing in English as declension of nouns, and there is no gender. Nor are there many irregular plurals or comparatives. Moreover, the tendency is always towards greater simplicity, both in grammar and syntax. Long sentences with dependent clauses grow more and more unpopular, irregular but time-saving formations such as the 'American subjunctive' (*it is necessary that you go* instead of *it is necessary that you should go*) gain ground, and difficult rules, such as the difference between *shall* and *will*, or *that* and *which*, are more and more ignored. If it continues to develop along its present lines English will ultimately have more in common with the uninflected languages of East Asia than with the languages of Europe.

The greatest quality of English is its enormous range not only of meaning but of *tone*. It is capable of endless subtleties, and of everything from the most high-flown rhetoric to the most brutal coarseness. On the other hand, its lack of grammar makes it easily compressible. It is the language of lyric poetry, and also of headlines. On its lower levels it is very easy to learn, in spite of its irrational spelling. It can also for international purposes be reduced to very simple pidgin dialects, ranging from Basic to the 'Bêche-de-mer' English used in the South Pacific. It is therefore well suited to be a world lingua franca, and it has in fact spread more widely than any other language.

But there are also great disadvantages, or at least great dangers, in speaking English as one's native tongue. To begin with, as was pointed out earlier in this essay, the English are very poor linguists. Their own language is grammatically so simple that unless they have gone through the discipline of learning a foreign language in childhood, they are often quite unable to grasp what is meant by gender, person, and case. A completely illiterate Indian will pick up English far faster than a British soldier will pick up Hindustani. Nearly five million Indians are literate in English and millions more speak it in a debased form. There are some tens of thousands of Indians who speak English as nearly as possible perfectly; yet the number of Englishmen speaking any Indian language perfectly would not amount to more than a few scores. But the great weakness of English is its capacity for debasement. Just because it is so easy to use, it is easy to use *badly*.

To write or even to speak English is not a science but an art. There are no reliable rules: there is only the general principle that concrete words are better than abstract ones, and that the shortest way of saying anything is always the best. Mere correctness is no guarantee whatever of good writing. A sentence like 'an enjoyable time was had by all present' is perfectly correct English, and so is the unintelligible mess of words on an income-tax return. Whoever writes English is involved in a struggle that never lets up even for a sentence. He is struggling against vagueness, against obscurity, against the lure of the decorative adjective, against the encroachment of Latin and Greek, and, above all, against the worn-out phrases and dead metaphors with which the language is cluttered up. In speaking, these dangers are more easily avoided, but spoken English differs from written English more sharply than is the case in most languages. In the spoken tongue every word that can be omitted is omitted, every possible abbreviation is used. Meaning is conveyed quite largely by emphasis, though curiously enough the English do not gesticulate, as one might reasonably expect them to do. A sentence like *No, I don't mean that one, I mean that one* is perfectly intelligible when spoken aloud, even without a gesture. But spoken English, when it tries to be dignified and logical, usually takes on the vices of written English, as you can see by spending half an hour either in the House of Commons or at the Marble Arch.

English is peculiarly subject to jargons. Doctors, scientists, businessmen, officials, sportsmen, economists, and political theorists all have their characteristic perversion of the language, which can be studied in the appropriate magazines from the *Lancet* to the *Labour Monthly*. But probably the deadliest enemy of good English is what is called 'standard English'. This dreary dialect, the language of leading articles, White Papers, political speeches, and BBC news bulletins, is undoubtedly spreading: it is spreading downwards in the social scale, and outwards into the spoken language. Its characteristic is its reliance on ready-made phrases – *in due course, take the earliest opportunity, warm appreciation, deepest regret, explore every avenue, ring the changes, take up the cudgels, legitimate assumption, the answer is in the affirmative,* etc etc – which may once have been fresh and vivid, but have now become mere thought-saving devices, having the same relation to living English as a crutch has to a leg. Anyone preparing a broadcast or writing to *The Times* adopts this kind of language almost instinctively, and it infects the spoken tongue as well. So much has our language been weakened that the imbecile chatter in Swift's essay on polite conversation (a satire on the upper-class talk of Swift's own day) would actually be rather a good conversation by modern standards.

The temporary decadence of the English language is due, like so much else, to our anachronistic class system. 'Educated' English has grown anaemic because for long past it has not been reinvigorated from below. The people likeliest to use simple concrete language, and to think of metaphors that really call up a visual image, are those who are in contact with physical reality. A useful word like *bottleneck*, for instance, would be most likely to occur to someone used to dealing with conveyor belts: or again, the expressive military phrase *to winkle out* implies acquaintance both with winkles and with machine-gun nests. And the vitality of English depends on a steady supply of images of this kind. It follows that language, at any rate the English language, suffers when the educated classes lose touch with the manual workers. As things are at present, nearly every Englishman, whatever his origins, feels the working-class manner of speech, and even working-class idioms, to be inferior. Cockney, the most widespread dialect, is the most despised of all. Any word or usage that is supposedly cockney is looked on as vulgar, even when, as is sometimes the case, it is merely an archaism. An example is *ain't*, which is now abandoned in favour of the much weaker form *aren't*. But *ain't* was good enough English eighty years ago, and Queen Victoria would have said *ain't*.

During the past forty years, and especially the past dozen years, English has borrowed largely from American, while American has shown no tendency to borrow from English. The reason for this is partly political. Anti-British feeling in the United States is far stronger than anti-American feeling in England, and most Americans dislike using a word or phrase which they know to be British. But American has gained a footing in England partly because of the vivid, almost poetic quality of its slang, partly because certain American usages (for instance, the formation of verbs by adding *ize* to a noun) save time, and most of all because one can adopt an American word without crossing a class barrier. From the English point of view American words have no class label. This applies even to thieves' slang. Words like *stooge* and *stool-pigeon* are considered much less vulgar than words like *nark* and *split*. Even a very snobbish English person would probably not mind calling a policeman a *cop*, which is American, but he would object to calling him a *copper*, which is working-class English. To the working classes, on the other hand, the use of Americanisms is a way of escaping from cockney without adopting the BBC dialect, which they instinctively dislike and cannot easily master. Hence, especially in the big towns, working-class children now use American slang from the moment that they learn to talk. And there is a noticeable tendency to use American words even when they are not slang and when an English equivalent already exists: for instance *car* for *tram*, *escalator* for *moving staircase*, *automobile* for *motor car*.

This process will probably continue for some time. One cannot check it simply by protesting against it, and in any case many American words and expressions are well worth adopting. Some are necessary neologisms, others (for instance, *fall* for *autumn*) are old words which we ought never to have dropped. But it ought to be realized that on the whole American is a bad influence and has already had a debasing effect.

To begin with, American has some of the vices of English in an exaggerated form. The interchangeability of different parts of speech has been carried further, the distinction between transitive and intransitive verbs tends to break down, and many words are used which have no meaning whatever. For example, whereas English alters the meaning of a verb by tacking a preposition on to it, the American tendency is to burden every verb with a preposition that adds nothing to its meaning (*win out*, *lose out*, *face up to*, etc). On the other hand, American has broken more completely than English with the past and with literary traditions. It not only produces words like *beautician*, *moronic*, and *sexualize*, but often replaces strong primary words by feeble euphemisms. For instance, many Americans seem to regard the word *death* and various words that go with it (*corpse*, *coffin*, *shroud*) as almost unmentionable. But above all, to adopt the American language whole-heartedly would probably mean a huge loss of vocabulary. For though American produces vivid and witty turns of speech, it is terribly poor in names for natural objects and localities. Even the streets in American cities are usually known by numbers instead of names. If we really intended to model our language upon American we should have, for instance, to lump the lady-bird, the daddy-long-legs, the saw-fly, the water-boatman, the cockchafer, the cricket, the death-watch beetle and scores of other insects all together under the inexpressive name of *bug*. We should lose the poetic names of our wild flowers, and also, probably, our habit of giving individual names to every street, pub, field, lane, and hillock. In so far as American is adopted, that is the tendency. Those who take their language from the films, or from papers such as *Life* and *Time*, always prefer the slick time-saving word to the one with a history behind it. As to accent, it is doubtful whether the American accent has the superiority which it is now fashionable to claim for it. The 'educated' English accent, a product of the last thirty years, is undoubtedly very bad and is likely to be abandoned, but the average English person probably speaks as clearly as the average American. Most English people blur their vowel sounds, but most Americans swallow their con-sonants. Many Americans pronounce, for instance, *water* as though it had no T in it, or even as though it had no consonant in it at all, except the W. On the whole we are justified in regarding the American language with suspicion. We ought to be ready to borrow its best words, but we ought not to let it modify the actual structure of our language.

However, there is no chance of resisting the American influence unless we can put new life into English itself. And it is difficult to do this while words and idioms are prevented from circulating freely among all sections of the population. English people of all classes now find it natural to express incredulity by the American slang phrase *sez you*. Many would even tell you in good faith that *sez you* has no English equivalent. Actually it has a whole string of them – for instance, *not half, I don't think, come off it, less of it, and then you wake up*, or simply *garn*. But most of these would be considered vulgar: you would never find an expression like *not half* in a *Times* leader, for instance. And on the other hand many necessary abstract words, especially words of Latin origin, are rejected by the working class because they sound public-schoolish, 'tony' and effeminate. Language ought to be the joint creation of poets and manual workers, and in modern England it is difficult for these two classes to meet. When they can do so again – as, in a different way, they could in the feudal past – English may show more clearly than at present its kinship with the language of Shakespeare and Defoe.

1946

THE PLAIN STYLE IN ENGLISH PROSE

WILLIAM REES-MOGG

I think that every editor must regard the ability to write straightforward English prose as the talent of whose shortage he is most conscious. I am certainly not, this morning, going to make a discrimination which has sometimes been made between the plain style in English prose and more ornamented or rhetorical styles, on the basis that one is good and the other is not. I believe that both have their part in the use of English prose.

Certainly as Mr Bernard Levin's editor for ten years and as Chairman of the Johnson Society, for me to be critical of what one might term rhetorical English prose would be extremely ungrateful. However, for every column of rhetorical prose that one publishes in a newspaper, one has to publish at least fifty columns of non-rhetorical prose, and it is, therefore, the plain style which I would like to examine.

The plain style goes back deep into English history. Pepys in 1661 said he went to church, and heard a good plain sermon. I am not quite sure that 'plain' in that sentence is entirely flattering to the cleric who was delivering the sermon, but it seems to me to be broadly favourable.

The plain style is not always at its best. When it is not at its best, it can certainly lapse into a certain dullness and a certain monotony, but when it is at its best I have noted a few adjectives which might be applied to the plain style in English prose.

It is humble, and that is certainly a virtue. It is clear, and that is a great virtue in prose. It is often clinical, and has an element of precision in it, as it lends itself particularly well to the writings of doctors, who need to write English precisely. It is direct; it is detailed; it is relatively little ornamented, though it is not without its own relatively subtle elements of ornament. It is essentially logical. It is craftsmanlike. It has in it often an English irony. It is natural – a word which is applied to this style of English prose almost as often as 'plain' itself. It is sometimes sceptical. It has been the natural prose of sceptical philosophers, of those who wish to trim the fat off ideology. It is moderate; it does not go into extremes of usage. It is pragmatic, and it is truthful.

These are a description of a particular part of the whole English culture. It is the quiet Englishman that we are describing, and the attraction that the quiet in aesthetics has always had for the Englishman. It is a quality, of course, which one finds well outside the range of prose, or even the range of literature. There is a passage – a rather well-known passage – in Evelyn Waugh's *Brideshead Revisited* in which he is talking about architecture. Evelyn Waugh was himself when he wanted to be, a master of the plain style in English prose.

> More even than the work of the great architects, I loved buildings that grew silently with the centuries, catching and keeping the best of each generation, while time curbed the artist's pride and philistine's vulgarity and repaired the clumsiness of the dull workman.

We can see this not only in architecture, for the same thing appears in English furniture design, particularly perhaps in the eighteenth century. If one calls to one's mind the idea of a piece of French furniture of the mid-eighteenth century, it would be perhaps a bombé commode made for Versailles, with a lot of movement in the wood and a lot of brass objects attached to it, a piece which to the English eye has always seemed too luxurious and too ostentatious, and indeed is only preserved by the extraordinarily high quality of its craftsmanship from downright vulgarity. If one considers the typical English piece of furniture of the same period, it would not first come to one's mind, to think of the height of William Kent or even one of the more eccentric pieces in Chippendale's book of design, but some piece of plain mahogany furniture, solidly made, not very highly ornamented, absolutely simple to its purpose, strong, and with a capacity to survive.

101

When we are talking about this particular style of English prose, the first point to note about it is how deep it is in the national psychology. Yet not in the psychology of the English alone.

Many of the masters of the plain style in English prose are in fact Scottish. The directness, the precision, the liking for the definite and the ordinary which were a part of the Scottish Enlightenment result in the clearest prose. The clarity of Hume or of Adam Smith is characteristic of the plain style at its very best.

If one looks at the history of this style, there is, I think, no doubt who is the first of the masters of it, certainly the most influential, and the one whose character and interests most foreshadow the uses to which this style was going to be put. The first master is Francis Bacon. I have to quote from an edition of Francis Bacon which was printed in 1787 at the Logographic Press, which you will remember was the press set up by John Walter, who had in 1785, founded *The Times*; I feel that it is attractive to be able to read from print so closely associated with the foundation of *The Times* the views of Bacon on how English ought to be written. I will first read a passage from [the preface] . . . on how Bacon himself wrote:

> In the composing of his books, he principally drove at strength and perspicuity of expression; not elegance, or spruceness of language. And in writing or dictating, would often ask, if the meaning were expressed 'clearly and plainly enough:' As knowing it fit, that words should be subservient to matter, not matter to words.

That is, I think, the essence of the style we are discussing, and when Bacon himself is writing about the distempers of learning, he writes:

> Here then we see the first corruption of learning, when men study words, and not matter; of which though I have brought late examples only, yet such false taste prevailed more or less in times past, and will again hereafter. Now, it is not possible, but this very circumstance should tend much to the discredit of learning, even with the ignorant vulgar, when they see learned men's writings, like the first letter of a patent, which, though it be drawn out with various turns and flourishes of the pen, yet is but a single letter.

He does go on to say, and this is a very important qualification:

> It is a thing not hastily to be condemned for a man to illustrate and smooth the obscurities and roughness of philosophy, with the splendor of words. . . .

He was not, therefore, wholly opposed to the high style, but he was wholly committed to the view that language is there to reveal meaning, and meaning must never be subordinated to language.

If we look behind Bacon, then I do not think we can find fully-fledged examples of the English plain style, but I think we can find many important influences on its development. The century before Bacon is a century of important religious argument, and the group who seem to me to foreshadow in their philosophy and in their psychology the English plain style, are the group of the English Renaissance rather than the English Reformation; that is More rather than Cranmer.

Certainly Thomas More, with his sense of irony and his sense of brevity, is psychologically attuned to the English plain style. So also, though he was not an English writer, was Erasmus, and so was their friend – a far more important figure in the development of the English language than he is commonly recognized as being – Sir Thomas Elyot. Sir Thomas Elyot's *Governor* has been said to be the first book written in English which is readily accessible to the modern reader. His *Dictionary*, though it is a Latin–English dictionary, is the first dictionary which gives a codification for the English language, and it gives it in direct and simple terms.

On the other hand, there is the religious influence. In the period of the reign of King Edward VI the intellectuals who worked with Cranmer had a very strong influence on the English language as they did on every other aspect of English life. But their influence was not plain. When one reads their writings, they are very highly charged. Their language is very beautiful, and it is often very moving, but it does not choose, as one might think from the fact that they were Protestants, and that they were the forerunners of the Puritans, the simple level at which religious writing is perhaps at its best.

Nevertheless, there is no doubt a large religious content in the formation of the plain style. The injunction of St Paul 'let your yea be yea, and your nay be nay' had a strong influence on the Puritans who were interpreting in literal terms the injunctions of the Bible, and who were partially under the influence of St Paul. The Puritan influence resented the rococo language of the Court, and we therefore get a feeling on the Puritan side that language ought to be simple and direct. But it is not a Puritan whom I would instance as the second master of the plain style.

The second master to my mind is George Herbert. George Herbert's prose is perhaps undervalued because his poetry is valued so highly. *A Priest to the Temple* is one of the supreme examples of English at its most simple and its most beautiful; I shall quote a passage which I would regard as the quintessential example of the plain style in English at its most effective. In *A Priest to the Temple*, which he wrote for himself, and was only published after his death, he wrote short chapters on the various functions that the priest had to carry out, and Chapter XIII is The Parson's Church:

> The Country Parson hath a special care of his Church, that all things there be decent, and befitting his Name, by which it is called. Therefore, First, he takes order that all things be in good repair; as walls plastered, windows glazed, floor paved, seats whole, firm and uniform, especially that the Pulpit, and Desk, and Communion Table, and Font be as they ought, for those great duties that are performed in them. Secondly, That the Church be swept, and kept clean without dust, or Cobwebs, and at great Festivals

strewed, and stuck with boughs, and perfumed with incense. Thirdly, That there be fit and proper Texts of Scripture everywhere painted, and that all the painting be grave, and reverend, not with light colours or foolish antics. Fourthly, That all the Books appointed by Authority be there, and those not torn or fouled, but whole and clean, and well bound; and that there be a fitting and sightly Communion Cloth of fine linen, with a handsome, and seemly Carpet of good and costly Stuff, or Cloth, and all kept sweet and clean, in a strong and decent Chest, with a Chalice, and Cover, and a Stoop or Flagon: and a Basin for Alms and Offerings; besides which, he hath a Poor-man's Box conveniently seated, to receive the Charity of well-minded people, and to lay up treasure for the sick and needy.

That has all the virtues of the style. It has its precision, it has its sense of detail, it has its avoidance of rhetoric – indeed specifically disclaims rhetoric in the ornamentation of the church itself, and its meaning is instantly and directly conveyed.

The third master whom I am going to propose, and this would give a somewhat different picture of the development of English prose from the picture that is most often presented, would be John Locke.

John Locke is the father of almost every development of thought in this country. He is not only the father of English philosophy, of English psychology, of English educational theory, but also the father of English economic theory, of English political theory – he is a philosopher of the widest possible range who, if he were not an Englishman, would perhaps be even more famous in the world than he already is.

His own style has at first a certain ruggedness about it. He had, I think, probably not a perfect ear for the music of the English language, but it is written with the most powerful intelligence concentrated on the meaning of the language. The views I thought I would quote are his views about the way in which English should be taught – views which he expressed in 'Some Thoughts on Education' in which he suggested that teaching people to write elaborate Latin theses was something of a waste of time.

When they understand how to write English with due Connexion, Propriety, and Order, and are pretty well Masters of a tolerable Narrative Stile . . .

(and I must say that the number of people who are pretty well masters of a tolerable narrative style could be counted on the fingers of one hand, nowadays and perhaps at any other time)

. . . they may be advanced to writing of Letters, wherein they should not be put upon any strains of Wit or Complement; but taught to express their own plain easie sence, without any incoherence, confusion or roughness.

And if only we could all express our plain easy sense without any incoherence, confusion or roughness, how much better this world would be.

Locke, I think, is particularly important because this is a style which has been used in English outside imaginative literature as well as inside; it is the style of the English scientists; it is the style of the English doctors; it is the style of the English philosophers; it is the style of the English economists. We are not, on the whole, accustomed to read such works with a high consciousness of style. Just occasionally one will get a comment such as one gets about Maynard Keynes, that he wrote in a more perspicuous style, in a more interesting style, in a style with better pacing than the majority of the imaginative authors of his own period. Purely as a stylist, Maynard Keynes is the equal, in my judgement, of any of the members of the Bloomsbury group to which he belonged. It is the subject matter which makes him of less interest to people who are primarily interested in imaginative literature, and not any difference in pure stylistic ability or quality between, say, Maynard Keynes and Virginia Woolf.

If we carry on looking at what use the style was put to, in the eighteenth century it develops in many ways. You get the use of it for journalism by Defoe, the father of English journalism and the man who invented almost every device that as journalists we use. He invented the leading article, the use of short paragraphs as in Lord Beaverbrook's *Daily Express*. Here is an example of the plain style which you will probably recognize:

> I was born in the year 1632 in the city of York, of a good family, though not of that county, my father being a foreigner of Bremen who settled first at Hull.

and I shall not award any prizes for anybody to say to which book those are the introductory words, or to what desert island they lead.

It was used also for literature. Addison is a master of the plain style – with perhaps a little bit too much sugar on it. Goldsmith was also somewhat sweet in his use, but *The Vicar of Wakefield* is a novel written with a beautiful and limpid quality of style, now oddly enough much out of fashion. The quotation I might perhaps make from *The Vicar of Wakefield*, since it bears on this very view. The Vicar himself says –

> I chose my wife as she did her wedding gown – not for a fine, glossy surface, but for such qualities as would wear well.

A compliment which I think few vicars' wives would now actually relish.

Swift used the plain style for satire. Johnson attacked Swift for not being willing to risk a metaphor, but Swift drew his style tautly. It is one of those sharp styles which is like a succession of dagger blows.

In the eighteenth century the plain style was used very much in medicine. The eighteenth century doctors write extremely good English – Cheyne, Meade, Arbuthnot (Arbuthnot who was also a satirist with Swift) – and the English medical literature of the eighteenth century is, as a result, perfectly clear, perfectly understandable, except when they are writing in medical

Latin, which is totally unintelligible.

The classical British school of economists largely originated in Scotland. It is notable that good theoretical economics must be precisely written. The classical school of English economics contains a great deal of English writing of the highest quality.

The first member – the grandfather in effect – of that School was John Locke himself. The next to develop the theory was David Hume. It was the Scottish Enlightenment which took economics from where it had been left by Locke, and started to develop it as a modern scientific subject of serious study. Hume was succeeded by Adam Smith; they worked closely together. Both Hume's writings on economics and Adam Smith's writings are written with no ornament, no attempt to impress, but with a clarity, a naturalness, which grows from the clarity of their thinking itself.

Of the later English writers on economics, Ricardo is undoubtedly difficult – and one would not recommend Ricardo as an agreeable light evening's reading. Malthus, on the other hand, wrote again with great purity and simplicity of style, and one can follow Malthus's economic arguments, whether they are right or wrong (some of them are both right and important), with the greatest ease and facility.

Too much neglected is the religious prose of the eighteenth century. There is the great Bishop Berkeley, and there is also that other great Bishop, Bishop Butler, and his most famous quotation, which contains a truth of life expressed in the most direct way – 'Things and actions are what they are, and the consequences of them will be what they will be. Why then should we desire to be deceived?' and why then should we desire to be deceived is perhaps the question that this style itself asks.

In the nineteenth century there is a greater diversity between the culture of natural sciences and the imaginative culture. But if one looks at the nineteenth century novelists, there is one who is outstanding for his use of the plain style as his medium of expression; one sees what an effect it has on his novels, on his account of the world, and how it relates to his view of the world itself. When I was young it was thought that there were three Victorian novelists, though more have since been discovered, and that they were Thackeray, Dickens and Trollope. In fact, when I was very young, it was thought that there were only two Victorian novelists, and that they were Thackeray and Dickens.

Thackeray is a whimsical writer, and this whimsicality goes against the simplicity and directness of speech. Dickens is a rhetorical writer. One may like his rhetoric or not like it. It is, at times, morbid, but it is always rhetoric, it is the language of an excited mind, designed to excite other minds also. Dickens is always on the verge of brain fever. It is Trollope who speaks in the direct English voice, and it was interesting during the war that it was Trollope's fame that returned; people who wanted to have a calm, a moderate, a realistic voice to listen to, and wanted to be reminded of an England which had seemed particularly to possess those qualities, read Trollope with renewed pleasure; one of the natural things is that the taste for Trollope, having been revived, has never again departed.

In political writing, I suppose that the Victorian master of this style is Bagehot. Bagehot wrote everything he wrote well. Norman St John Stevas's edition is spreading out year by year (if the Prime Minister dismissed Norman from office in order to allow him to complete his edition of Bagehot, that is the only possible good reason for her having taken that unusual step) and one cannot open it without coming across, in relation to some quite unexpected subject, a clarity of language which is moving to the point of being beautiful. He was writing for the *Economist* a note on what to buy on the Stock Exchange. What subject could one think more likely to destroy the virtues of style, yet one finds the sentence:

> It is quite right to take counsel, to hear what is to be said, and to use it as ground for a decision, but it must be used to aid the intellect, not to supersede the discretion.

But for the nineteenth century one would probably look to the scientists. Darwin is not only obviously a scientist of the very first rank, he is also an English prose writer of the first rank. Indeed, the impact that *The Origin of Species* had owed almost as much to the fact that everybody could perfectly understand what Darwin was saying as to the revolutionary theories which he was in fact expounding. Those theories had existed, at least in scattered form, in other men's writings and in other men's ideas before Darwin published his work.

The exposition enormously strengthened the theory, and certainly increased its impact; and when one reads *The Origin of Species* one finds a clarity of exposition, straightforward words used in a straightforward way, that makes it extremely powerful. I would like if I might to read you a passage where he is discussing the theories of Malthus as applied to the animal world:

> There is no exception to the rule that every organic being naturally increases at so high a rate, that if not destroyed, the earth would soon be covered by the progeny of a single pair. Even slow-breeding man has doubled in twenty-five years, and at this rate, in a few thousand years, there would literally not be standing room for his progeny. Linnaeus has calculated that if an annual plant produced only two seeds – and there is no plant so unproductive as this – and their seedlings next year produced two, and so on, then in twenty years there would be a million plants. The elephant is reckoned the slowest breeder of all known animals, and I have taken some pains to estimate its probably minimum rate of natural increase: it will be under the mark to assume that it breeds when thirty years old, and goes on breeding till ninety years old, bringing forth three pair of young in this interval; if this be so, at the end of the fifth century there would be alive fifteen million elephants, descended from the first pair.

We come on into the early twentieth century. We have so many possible examples to explore but I would like to turn to an American philosopher – to

107

William James. There is a fascinating contrast between not only the mind, but also the style, of William James and his brother Henry. Henry, the supreme example of his period, of a style which is mannered, personal, refined, intriguing; William a master not only in his ideas, but also in his language, of the plain and direct mode of writing prose. As a philosopher he is in the line of Locke and Hume and, I suppose, is a predecessor of some of the most influential philosophers in England in the twentieth century. His theory, pragmatism, he defined as the doctrine that the whole meaning of a conception expresses itself in practical consequences. He had this to say about the frame of mind of Hume, and I think it bears on the subject which we have been discussing:

> Loyalty to clearness and integrity of perception, dislike of blurred outlines, of vague identifications are its characteristics. It loves to recognize particulars in their full completeness, and the more of them it can carry, the happier it is.

This is, therefore, a style which is something more than a style. Just as when one is reading French, one is conscious that a particular, rather heightened type of clarity, the clarity which finds its supreme expression in Voltaire, is the most French of all the French styles and tells one most about the way in which that nation thinks, so I believe the plain style in English relates to a number of characteristics which are innate in the national culture.

It relates to the pragmatic quality, both of English philosophy, and of English life. It relates to the sense of moderation; it relates to the English dislike, or distrust, of extremism of all kinds; it relates to an English distrust of display; it relates to the high value and virtue which the English believe is derived from naturalness – the desire to have a moderate form of nature, not nature red in tooth and claw, but nature modified, controlled, restrained. These writers often produce language which is of great beauty, but it is beauty of a subtle kind; it is beauty which arrives not out of emphasis, let alone out of false emphasis, but out of soft and gentle modulations designed to increase the precision of meaning. It is, I believe, one of the great themes of the life of the English nation, that we have had so many writers on such a wide variety of subjects, who have been able to use the English language in so natural, and so plain a way.

1984

THE BOOK OF COMMON PRAYER

Dearly beloved brethren, the Scripture moveth us in sundry places to acknowledge and confess our manifold sins and wickedness; and that we should not dissemble nor cloke them before the face of Almighty God our heavenly Father; but confess them with an humble, lowly, penitent, and obedient heart; to the end that we may obtain forgiveness of the same, by his infinite goodness and mercy. And although we ought at all times humbly to acknowledge our sins before God; yet ought we most chiefly so to do, when we assemble and meet together to render thanks for the great benefits that we have received at his hands, to set forth his most worthy praise, to hear his most holy Word, and to ask those things which are requisite and necessary, as well for the body as the soul. Wherefore I pray and beseech you, as many as are here present, to accompany me with a pure heart, and humble voice, unto the throne of the heavenly grace, saying after me;

A general Confession

To be said of the whole Congregation after the Minister, all kneeling.

Almighty and most merciful Father; We have erred, and strayed from thy ways like lost sheep. We have followed too much the devices and desires of our own hearts. We have offended against thy holy laws. We have left undone those things which we ought to have done; And we have done those things which we ought not to have done; And there is no health in us. But thou, O Lord, have mercy upon us, miserable offenders. Spare thou them, O God, which confess their faults. Restore thou them that are penitent; According to thy promises declared unto mankind in Christ Jesu our Lord. And grant, O most merciful Father, for his sake; That we may hereafter live a godly, righteous, and sober life, To the glory of thy holy Name. Amen.

The Absolution, or Remission of sins,

To be pronounced by the Priest alone, standing; the people still kneeling.

Almighty God, the Father of our Lord Jesus Christ, who desireth not the death of a sinner, but rather that he may turn from his wickedness, and live; and hath given power, and commandment, to his Ministers, to declare and pronounce to his people, being penitent, the Absolution and Remission of their sins: He pardoneth and absolveth all them that truly repent, and unfeignedly believe his holy Gospel. Wherefore let us beseech him to grant us true repentance, and his holy Spirit, that those things may please him, which we do at this present; and that the rest of our life hereafter may be pure, and holy; so that at the last we may come to his eternal joy; through Jesus Christ our Lord.

The people shall answer here, and at the end of all other prayers, Amen.

1662

109

OF GREAT PLACE

FRANCIS BACON

Men in *Great Place* are thrice *Servants*: Servants of the Sovereign or State; Servants of Fame; and Servants of Business. So as they have no Freedom; neither in their Persons, nor in their Actions, nor in their Times. It is a strange desire, to seek Power, and to lose Liberty; or to seek Power over others, and to lose Power over a Man's Self. The Rising unto *Place* is laborious; and by Pains Men come to greater Pains: and it is sometimes base; and by Indignities, Men come to Dignities. The Standing is slippery, and the Regress is either a downfall, or at least an Eclipse, which is a Melancholy Thing.

1612

THE GREAT FIRE

JOHN EVELYN

Sept 7. I went this morning on foot from *Whitehall* as far as *London Bridge*, through the late *Fleet Street, Ludgate Hill,* by *St Paul's, Cheapside, Exchange, Bishopsgate, Aldersgate,* and out to *Moorfields,* thence through *Cornhill,* &c., with extraordinary difficulty, clambering over heaps of yet smoking rubbish, and frequently mistaking where I was. The ground under my feet so hot, that it even burnt the soles of my shoes. In the meantime his Majesty got to the *Tower* by water, to demolish the houses about the graff [wharf], which being built entirely about it, had they taken fire and attacked the *White Tower* where the magazine of powder lay, would undoubtedly not only have beaten down and destroyed all the bridge, but sunk and torn the vessels in the river, and rendered the demolition beyond all expression for several miles about the country.

At my return I was infinitely concerned to find that goodly Church *St Paul's* now a sad ruin, and that beautiful portico (for structure comparable to any in Europe, as not long before repaired by the late King) now rent in pieces, flakes of vast stone split asunder, and nothing remaining entire but the inscription in the architrave, showing by whom it was built, which had not one letter of it defaced. It was astonishing to see what immense stones the heat had in a manner calcined, so that all the ornaments, columns, freizes, capitals, and projectures of massy *Portland* stone flew off, even to the very roof, where a sheet of lead covering a great space (no less than six acres by measure) was totally melted; the ruins of the vaulted roof falling broke into *St Faith's,* which being filled with the magazines of books belonging to the *Stationers,* and carried thither for safety, they were all consumed, burning for a week following. It is also observable that the lead over the altar at the East end was untouched, and among the divers monuments, the body of one Bishop remained entire.

Thus lay in ashes that most venerable Church, one of the most ancient pieces of early piety in the Christian world, besides near 100 more. The lead, iron-work, bells, plate, &c., melted; the exquisitely wrought *Mercers' Chapel*, the sumptuous *Exchange*, the august fabric of *Christ Church*, all the rest of the *Companies' Halls*, splendid buildings, arches, entries, all in dust; the fountains dried up and ruined, whilst the very waters remained boiling; the voragos of subterranean cellars, wells, and dungeons, formerly warehouses, still burning in stench and dark clouds of smoke, so that in five or six miles traversing about, I did not see one load of timber unconsumed, nor many stones but what were calcined white as snow. The people who now walked about the ruins appeared like men in some dismal desert, or rather in some great City laid waste by a cruel enemy; to which was added the stench that came from some poor creatures' bodies, beds, and other combustible goods. Sir *Tho. Gressham's* statue, though fallen from its nich in the *Royal Exchange*, remained entire, when all those of the Kings since the Conquest were broken to pieces; also the standard in *Cornhill*, and *Queen Elizabeth's* effigies, with some arms on *Ludgate*, continued with but little detriment, whilst the vast iron chains of the *City* streets, hinges, bars and gates of prisons were many of them melted and reduced to cinders by the vehement heat.

Nor was I yet able to pass through any of the narrower streets, but kept the widest; the ground and air, smoke and fiery vapour, continued so intense that my hair was almost singed, and my feet unsufferably surbated [made sore]. The by-lanes and narrower streets were quite filled up with rubbish, nor could one have possibly known where he was, but by the ruins of some Church or Hall, that had some remarkable tower or pinnacle remaining. I then went towards Islington and *Highgate*, where one might have seen 200,000 people of all ranks and degrees dispersed and lying along by their heaps of what they could save from the fire, deploring their loss, and though ready to perish for hunger and destitution, yet not asking one penny for relief, which to me appeared a stranger sight than any I had yet beheld. His Majesty and Council indeed took all imaginable care for their relief by proclamation for the country to come in and refresh them with provisions.

1666

THE WAR WITH THE GREAT REPUBLICS

G K CHESTERTON

We cannot understand the eighteenth century so long as we suppose that rhetoric is artificial because it is artistic. We do not fall into this folly about any of the other arts. We talk of a man picking out notes arranged in ivory on a wooden piano 'with much feeling', or of his pouring out his soul by scraping on cat-gut after a training as careful as an acrobat's. But we are still haunted with a prejudice that verbal form and verbal effect must somehow be hypocritical when they are the link between things so living as a man and a mob. We doubt the feeling of the old-fashioned orator, because his periods are so rounded and pointed as to convey his feeling. Now before any criticism of the eighteenth-century worthies must be put the proviso of their perfect artistic sincerity. Their oratory was unrhymed poetry, and it had the humanity of poetry. It was not even unmetrical poetry; that century is full of great phrases, often spoken on the spur of great moments, which have in them the throb and recurrence of song, as of a man thinking to a tune. Nelson's 'In honour I gained them, in honour I will die with them' has more rhythm than much that is called *vers libres*. Patrick Henry's 'Give me liberty or give me death' might be a great line in Walt Whitman.

It is one of the many quaint perversities of the English to pretend to be bad speakers; but in fact the most English eighteenth-century epoch blazed with brilliant speakers. There may have been finer writing in France; there was no such fine speaking as in England. The Parliament had faults enough, but it was sincere enough to be rhetorical. The Parliament was corrupt, as it is now; though the examples of corruption were then often really made examples, in the sense of warnings, where they are now examples only in the sense of patterns. The Parliament was indifferent to the constituencies, as it is now; though perhaps the constituencies were less indifferent to the Parliament. The Parliament was snobbish, as it is now, though perhaps more respectful to mere rank and less to mere wealth. But the Parliament was a Parliament; it did fulfil its name and duty by talking, and trying to talk well. It did not merely do things because they do not bear talking about – as it does now. It was then, to the eternal glory of our country, a great 'talking-shop', not a mere buying and selling shop for financial tips and official places. And as with any other artist, the care the eighteenth-century man expended on oratory is a proof of his sincerity, not a disproof of it. An enthusiastic eulogium by Burke is as rich and elaborate as a lover's sonnet; but it is because Burke is really enthusiastic, like the lover. An angry sentence by Junius is as carefully compounded as a Renascence poison; but it is because Junius is really angry – like the poisoner. Now, nobody who has realized this psychological truth can doubt for a moment that many of the English aristocrats of the eighteenth century had a real enthusiasm for liberty; their voices lift like trumpets upon the very word. Whatever their immediate forebears may have meant, these men meant what they said when they talked of the high memory of Hampden or the majesty of Magna Carta. Those Patriots whom Walpole called the Boys included many who really were patriots – or better still, who really were boys. If we prefer to put it so, among the Whig aristocrats were many who really were Whigs; Whigs by all the ideal definitions which identified the party with a defence of law against tyrants and courtiers. But if anybody deduces, from the fact that the Whig aristocrats were Whigs, any doubt about whether the Whig aristocrats were aristocrats, there is one practical test and reply. It might be tested in many ways: by the game laws and enclosure laws they passed, or by the strict code of the duel and the definition of honour on which they all insisted. But if it be really questioned whether I am right in calling their whole world an aristocracy, and the very reverse of it a democracy, the true historical test is this: that when republicanism really entered the world, they instantly waged two great wars with it – or (if the view be preferred) it instantly waged two great wars with them. America and France revealed the real nature of the English Parliament. Ice may sparkle, but a real spark will show it is only ice. So when the red fire of the Revolution touched the frosty splendours of the Whigs, there was instantly a hissing and a strife; a strife of the flame to melt the ice, of the water to quench the flame.

It has been noted that one of the virtues of the aristocrats was liberty, especially liberty among themselves. It might even be said that one of the virtues of the aristocrats was cynicism. They were not stuffed with our fashionable fiction, with its stiff and wooden figures of a good man named Washington and a bad man named Boney. They at least were aware that Washington's cause was not so obviously white nor Napoleon's so obviously black as most books in general circulation would indicate. They had a natural admiration for the military genius of Washington and Napoleon; they had the most unmixed contempt for the German Royal Family. But they were, as a class, not only against both Washington and Napoleon, but against them both for the same reason. And it was that they both stood for democracy.

Great injustice is done to the English aristocratic government of the time through a failure to realize this fundamental difference, especially in the case of America. There is a wrong-headed humour about the English which appears especially in this, that while they often (as in the case of Ireland) make themselves out right where they were entirely wrong, they are easily persuaded (as in the case of America) to make themselves out entirely wrong where there is at least a case for their having been more or less right. George III's Government laid certain taxes on the colonial community on the eastern seaboard of America. It was certainly not self-evident, in the sense of law and precedent, that the imperial government could not lay taxes on such colonists. Nor were the taxes themselves of that practically oppressive sort which rightly raise everywhere the common casuistry of revolution. The Whig oligarchs had their faults, but utter lack of sympathy with liberty, especially local liberty, and with their adventurous kindred beyond the seas, was by no means one of their faults. Chatham, the great chief of the new and very national *noblesse*, was typical of them in being free from the faintest illiberality and irritation against the colonies as such. He would have made them free and even favoured colonies, if only he could have kept them as colonies. Burke, who was then the eloquent voice of Whiggism, and was destined later to show how wholly it was a voice of aristocracy, went of course even further. Even North compromised; and though George III, being a fool, might himself have refused to compromise, he had already failed to effect the Bolingbroke scheme of the restitution of the royal power. The case for the Americans, the real reason for calling them right in the quarrel, was something much deeper than the quarrel. They were at issue, not with a dead monarchy, but with a living aristocracy; they declared war on something much finer and more formidable than poor old George. Nevertheless, the popular tradition, especially in America, has pictured it primarily as a duel of George III and George Washington; and, as we have noticed more than

113

once, such pictures though figurative are seldom false. King George's head was not much more useful on the throne than it was on the sign-board of a tavern; nevertheless, the sign-board was really a sign, and a sign of the times. It stood for a tavern that sold not English but German beer. It stood for that side of the Whig policy which Chatham showed when he was tolerant to America alone, but intolerant of America when allied with France. That very wooden sign stood, in short, for the same thing as the juncture with Frederick the Great; it stood for that Anglo-German alliance which, at a very much later time in history, was to turn into the world-old Teutonic Race.

Roughly and frankly speaking, we may say that America forced the quarrel. She wished to be separate, which was to her but another phrase for wishing to be free. She was not thinking of her wrongs as a colony, but already of her rights as a republic. The negative effect of so small a difference could never have changed the world, without the positive effect of a great ideal, one may say of a great new religion. The real case for the colonists is that they felt they could be something, which they also felt, and justly, that England would not help them to be. England would probably have allowed the colonists all sorts of concessions and constitutional privileges; but England could not allow the colonists equality: I do not mean equality with her, but even with each other. Chatham might have compromised with Washington, because Washington was a gentleman; but Chatham could hardly have conceived a country not governed by gentlemen. Burke was apparently ready to grant everything to America; but he would not have been ready to grant what America eventually gained. If he had seen American democracy, he would have been as much appalled by it as he was by French democracy, and would always have been by any democracy. In a word, the Whigs were liberal and even generous aristocrats, but they were aristocrats; that is why their concessions were as vain as their conquests. We talk, with a humiliation too rare with us, about our dubious part in the secession of America. Whether it increase or decrease the humiliation I do not know; but I strongly suspect that we had very little to do with it. I believe we counted for uncommonly little in the case. We did not really drive away the American colonists, nor were they driven. They were led on by a light that went before.

That light came from France, like the armies of Lafayette that came to the help of Washington. France was already in travail with the tremendous spiritual revolution which was soon to reshape the world. Her doctrine, disruptive and creative, was widely misunderstood at the time, and is much misunderstood still, despite the splendid clarity of style in which it was stated by Rousseau in the 'Contrat Social', and by Jefferson in The Declaration of Independence. Say the very word 'equality' in many modern countries, and four hundred fools will leap to their feet at once to explain that some men can be found, on careful examination, to be taller or handsomer than others. As if Danton had not noticed that he was taller than Robespierre, or as if Washington was not well aware that he was handsomer than Franklin. This is no place to expound a philosophy; it will be enough to say in passing, by way of a parable, that when we say that all pennies are equal, we do not mean that they all look exactly the same. We mean that they are absolutely equal in their one absolute character, in the most important thing about them. It may be put practically by saying that they are coins of a certain value, twelve of which go to a shilling. It may be put symbolically, and even mystically, by saying that they all bear the image of the King. And, though the most mystical, it is also the most practical summary of equality that all men bear the image of the King of Kings. Indeed, it is of course true that this idea had long underlain all Christianity, even in institutions less popular in form than were, for instance, the mob of medieval republics in Italy. A dogma of equal duties implies that of equal rights. I know of no Christian authority that would not admit that it is as wicked to murder a poor man as a rich man, or as bad to burgle an inelegantly furnished house as a tastefully furnished one. But the world had wandered further and further from these truisms, and nobody in the world was further from them than the group of the great English aristocrats. The idea of the equality of men is in substance simply the idea of the importance of man. But it was precisely the notion of the importance of a mere man which seemed startling and indecent to a society whose whole romance and religion now consisted of the importance of a gentleman. It was as if a man had walked naked into Parliament. There is not space here to develop the moral issue in full, but this will suffice to show that the critics concerned about the difference in human types or talents are considerably wasting their time. If they can understand how two coins can count the same though one is bright and the other brown, they might perhaps understand how two men can vote the same though one is bright and the other dull. If, however, they are still satisfied with their solid objection that some men are dull, I can only gravely agree with them, that some men are very dull.

But a few years after Lafayette had returned from helping to found a republic in America he was flung over his own frontiers for resisting the foundation of a republic in France. So furious was the onward stride of this new spirit that the republican of the new world lived to be the reactionary of the old. For when France passed from theory to practice, the question was put to the world in a way not thinkable in connection with the prefatory experiment of a thin population on a colonial coast. The mightiest of human monarchies, like some monstrous immeasurable idol of iron, was melted down in a furnace barely bigger than itself, and recast in a size equally colossal, but in a shape men could not understand. Many, at least, could not understand it, and least of all the liberal aristocracy of England. There were, of course, practical reasons for a continuous foreign policy against France, whether royal or republican. There was primarily the desire to keep any foreigner from menacing us from the Flemish coast; there was, to a much lesser extent, the colonial rivalry in which so much English glory had been gained by the statesmanship of Chatham and the arms of Wolfe and of Clive. The former reason has returned on us with a singular irony; for in order to keep the French out of Flanders we flung ourselves with increasing enthusiasm into a fraternity with the Germans. We purposely fed and pampered the power which was destined in the future to devour Belgium as France would never have devoured it, and threaten us across the sea with terrors of which no Frenchman would ever dream. But indeed much deeper things unified our attitude towards France before and after the Revolution. It is but one stride from despotism to democracy, in logic as well as in history; and oligarchy is equally remote from both. The Bastille fell, and it seemed to an Englishman merely that a despot had turned into a demos. The young Bonaparte rose, and it seemed to an Englishman merely that a demos had once more turned into a despot. He was not wrong in thinking these allotropic forms of the same alien thing; and that thing was equality. For when millions are equally subject to one law, it makes little difference if they are also subject to one lawgiver; the general social life is a level. The one thing that the English have never understood about Napoleon, in all their myriad studies of his mysterious personality, is how impersonal he was. I had almost said how unimportant he was. He said himself, 'I shall go down to history with my code in my hand'; but in practical effects, as distinct from mere name and renown, it would be even truer to say that his code will go down to history with his hand set to it in signature – somewhat illegibly. Thus his testamentary law has broken up big estates and encouraged contented peasants in places where his name is cursed, in places where his name is almost unknown. In his lifetime, of course, it was natural that the annihilating splendour of his military strokes should rivet the eye like flashes of lightning; but his rain fell more silently, and its refreshment remained. It is needless to repeat here that after bursting one world-coalition after another by battles that are the masterpieces of the military art, he was finally worn down by two comparatively popular causes, the resistance of Russia and the resistance of Spain. The former was largely, like so much that is Russian, religious; but in the latter appeared most conspicuously that which concerns us here, the valour, vigilance and high national spirit of England in the eighteenth century. The long Spanish campaign tried and made triumphant the great Irish soldier, afterwards known as Wellington; who has become all the more symbolic since he was finally confronted with Napoleon in the last defeat of the latter at Waterloo. Wellington, though too logical to be at all English, was in many ways typical of the aristocracy; he had irony and independence of mind. But if we wish to realize how rigidly such men remained limited by their class, how little they really knew what was happening in their time, it is enough to note that Wellington seems to have thought he had dismissed Napoleon by saying he was not really a gentleman. If an acute and experienced Chinaman were to say of Chinese Gordon, 'He is not actually a Mandarin', we should think that the Chinese system deserved its reputation for being both rigid and remote.

But the very name of Wellington is enough to suggest another, and with it the reminder that this, though true, is inadequate. There was some truth in the idea that the Englishman was never so English as when he was outside England, and never smacked so much of the soil as when he was on the sea. There has run through the national psychology something that has never had a name except the eccentric and indeed extraordinary name of Robinson Crusoe; which is all the more English for being quite undiscoverable in England. It may be doubted if a French or German boy especially wishes that his cornland or vineland were a desert; but many an English boy has wished that his island were a desert island. But we might even say that the Englishman was too insular for an island. He awoke most to life when his island was sundered from the foundations of the world, when it hung like a planet and flew like a bird. And, by a contradiction, the real British army was in the navy; the boldest of the islanders were scattered over the moving archipelago of a great fleet. There still lay on it, like an increasing light, the legend of the Armada; it was a great fleet full of the glory of having once been a small one. Long before Wellington ever saw Waterloo the ships had done their work, and shattered the French navy in the Spanish seas, leaving like a light upon the sea the life and death of Nelson, who died with his stars on his bosom and his heart upon his sleeve. There is no word for the memory of Nelson except to call him mythical. The very hour of his death, the very name of his ship, are touched with that epic completeness which critics call the long arm of coincidence and prophets the hand of God. His very faults and failures were heroic, not in a loose but in a classic sense; in that he fell only like the legendary heroes, weakened by a woman, not foiled by any foe among men. And he remains the incarnation of a spirit in the English that is purely poetic; so poetic that it fancies itself a thousand things, and sometimes even fancies itself prosaic. At a recent date, in an age of reason, in a country already calling itself dull and business-like, with top-hats and factory chimneys already beginning to rise like towers of funereal efficiency, this country clergyman's son moved to the last in a luminous cloud, and acted a fairy tale. He shall remain as a lesson to those who do not understand England, and a mystery to those who think they do. In outward action he led his ships to victory and died upon a foreign sea; but symbolically he established something indescribable and intimate, something that sounds like a native proverb; he was the man who burnt his ships, and who for ever set the Thames on fire.

1917

LORD BEAVERBROOK'S SPEECH

LORD BEAVERBROOK

My Lord Thomson of Fleet, Viscount Rothermere, my Lords and gentlemen: – I am deeply moved by the wonderful reception you have given me tonight. Also I am grateful for this present which I will esteem and value always.

It is quite true that I am old bones, my legs are very weak, but I still have something in the way of a head. I am still headstrong, and self-willed at that.

I will try to make you a speech tonight. But at 85 years of age, don't expect much. I cannot speak with the eloquence of Sir John Macdonald, born in Scotland, Canada's greatest orator and also Canada's greatest Prime Minister. He was my ideal. I hoped to follow his teaching.

I heard him once. He was speaking from the platform of the last car of his private railway train. He fired me with enthusiasm for the British Empire. And I have been an Imperialist ever since. But not too successful, as you know.

In any case, in my eighty-sixth year, I must speak tonight. And it will be very easy indeed, for me to make a better speech than Sir John could have delivered at the age of 85. And I will tell you why. Because he died at 76.

Many shrewd observers will say that I have not had any pattern, or continuous theme, in my long life. Certainly I have. But I have never been a successful leader. I have always been an apprentice, and never a master, and that has been a weakness in my political activities.

First I was an apprentice to finance in Canada. That was a life of daring adventure. In search of personal fortune and financial independence I promoted eleven companies. And may I say with humble gratitude that each of those eleven is a living example of leadership in commerce or industry in Canada at this very hour. But, of course, the leadership was not provided by me, but by those who came after me.

It was J. H. Thomas who said on the platform at the Albert Hall: 'When Max Aitken was a boy, he lived in a New Brunswick village with fifteen hundred other souls. It was too small for him, and he left for Halifax, a city of fifty thousand. It was too small for him, so he went to Montreal, where there are a quarter-of-a-million people. It was too small for him, so he left for London. He is here. One day London will be too small for him. And he will go to Hell. What then?' said Jim Thomas. 'I'll tell you – it won't be big enough for him.'

Well, I did go to London. And there I decided to become an apprentice in politics. After settling this grave issue about making a political career, I disposed of my Canadian business to my principal lieutenant, Killam. I took out my meagre share. And after fifty years Killam died worth a hundred and fifty millions. Perhaps I might have done more harm if I had stayed in Canada with all that money. However, I was by this time an apprentice to politics. And I sat six or seven years in the House of Commons, saying very little, but possibly learning a great deal.

War. And I served Lloyd George. It was a nerve-racking duty and it was hard to keep in step with that great Prime Minister. But I managed.

After war I became an apprentice in Fleet Street. And that was a real exciting experience.

At last, I thought, I will be a Master. Fancy free. Instead, I became the slave of the Black Art. I did not know freedom again for many a year.

I took over a bankrupt newspaper and lost plenty of money. I had dared to set up in rivalry to Northcliffe – the greatest journalist in the history of Fleet Street.

I was encouraged by the well-known lines:

> He either fears his fate too much,
>   Or his deserts are small
> That dares not put it to the touch
>   To gain or lose it all.

And I very nearly lost it all. Northcliffe had a Sunday paper. So I must have a Sunday paper, too. The *Sunday Express* added enormously to my losses. For several years I wondered: what will it be?

I began, of course, under the mistaken notion that I knew everything about the making of a good paper. Indeed, the curious and interesting thing about journalism is that everybody always knows far more about it than the journalist knows himself. You are subject to criticism – you receive some praise, I admit – but that praise is sometimes suspect. You are not entirely free from the influence of the sycophant – he is about you everywhere and always. But there is an extraordinary notion in the mind of mankind, a universal idea, that each and every one of us could run a newspaper, if we only had the chance, far better than the journalist could do it himself.

Well, I got the chance – I soon learned that I was a know-nothing. And after years of anxiety and much misery our papers began the slow but steady upward climb.

In learning about journalism I had to learn about journalists. Most of the guests here tonight are prominent in the vitally important and bitterly maligned profession of journalism.

No other profession is so heavily criticized. No other is preached at so much and told so often to mend its ways. Some of the loudest critics have a very simple code for us. It is this: 'Don't ever print anything about me that I wouldn't want people to read.'

I am not much impressed by all the talk about standards and codes. The code of a good journalist should be written within himself. It should not be written on parchment but written on his heart. First, he must be true to himself. The man who is not true to himself is no journalist. He must show courage, independence and initiative. He must also, I believe, be a man of optimism. He has no business to be a peddler of gloom and despondency. He must be a respecter of persons, but able to deal with the highest and the lowest on the same basis, which is regard for the public interest and a determination to get at the facts.

The demands made on a journalist's character and sense of duty are heavy. Not every journalist meets the demands in full, but I am proud to say that in my long experience the vast majority of our journalists are an honour to their calling, and that the nation would be much poorer if these men, and women too, were not there to protect the nation from hidden scandals and secret misuse of power. I take more pride in my experience as a journalist than in any other experience I have had in a long and varied life.

Journalism and Politics are closely allied. My political faith was always strong, and many of you will say, also wayward.

For many years I talked and wrote about the Empire. My campaign was welcomed with enthusiasm. Much support and triumphant results in the Constituencies were followed by indifference and finally rejection. Opponents would say: 'Well, if the Empire means so much to you, why don't you go back home again?'

My campaign dwindled. Public attention was focused on world panic and my plans were overwhelmed by failure and my movement was extinguished.

Comfort there was none. I took refuge in reflecting on the fate of my Scottish hero James Graham, first Marquis of Montrose. His campaign failed. And you all know what happened to him. In the merry month of May in 1650, almost to this day, they hanged him in the Grass Market in Edinburgh.

I am not for a moment comparing myself with the great general and poet. Even on the contemporary scene I have been a minor figure, while Montrose's name will live forever. I am only comparing our fates. Both of us came to failure after initial success, and both of us were let down. Montrose was let down, strange to say, by the Earl of Home, and I was let down by the present Earl of Home's predecessor. You know who I mean. I am happy to say that the comparison stops there. Unlike Montrose, I was not let down at the end of a rope.

The Second World War, and once more an apprentice. This time to Industrial Production, under Churchill's guidance, and he sustained me. Without his support I would have failed completely in my task. I didn't stand a chance without his backing.

We were so ill-prepared. Our peril was beyond comprehension. Churchill, after taking office, said to me: 'We will come through in triumph but we may lose our tail feathers.' In that belief in victory he remained steadfast through three years of incredible misfortunes. He never wavered, always steadily looking forward to the day of victory.

What was the genius of this great leader? Many have tried to analyse it. It was incomparable greatness in two spheres. There are men with a magnificent command of words but with a very poor command of events. There are formidable men of action who lack the gift of inspiration. With Churchill, the thought, the word and the deed were one. His war speeches were like Nelson's signal at Trafalgar. They were action in themselves. Confident, defiant and immortal, they strengthened the heart and the hand of all engaged in the deadly struggle. Churchill's speeches mobilized the best that was in us.

Until I became Minister of Aircraft Production in Churchill's Government, I had always associated 'bottlenecks' with pleasure. But the Aircraft Ministry was the biggest bottleneck that was ever known.

The air frames could be produced. But where was the harness? A bottleneck. Where were the power plants? Another bottleneck. And the guns – .303 and 20 mm.? None of it: the air frames were but skeletons.

The very word 'bottleneck' meant gloom and misery to me.

But the bottlenecks were overcome and also the enemy.

What about the new world?

What about the prophecies of what the world would be like after the war?

The greatest foresight was that of a murderer – a man condemned to die. He escaped because he was crazy. His name was Hess, Deputy Chancellor of Germany. He came to Scotland in 1941, on a one-way journey.

I was sent by Churchill to interview him. And I tried to make out just why he came. Was he in flight from Germany? Was he a refugee? He said not. He came to negotiate peace with Britain on any terms providing Britain would join Germany in attacking our ally, Russia.

'A victory for England,' he said, 'will be a victory for the Bolsheviks. A Bolshevik victory will sooner or later mean Russian occupation of Germany and the rest of Europe. England would be as incapable of hindering it as any other nation.'

Shortly after Hess made these remarkable predictions, I left under the direction of Churchill for Russia to make a treaty – not for peace, but war.

In Moscow, Stalin said to me: 'Britain means to make peace with Germany, leaving Russia to fight alone.'

I asked him: 'What make you think that?'

'Hess is your line of communication with Hitler,' he said.

'Oh, no,' I said.

'Why then do you not shoot him?'

'He must be tried,' I answered.

'Why did he come to Britain?'

That was the question I was waiting for. I produced the transcript of my conversation with Hess, and also a memo he sent me in his own hand, proposing that Britain should make peace with Germany on our terms providing we would join in a German–British attack on Russia. I told him that Churchill had rejected the plan with contempt.

A word of advice to our friend Lord Thomson of Fleet. He praised my achievements in journalism. Well, I am going to praise his triumphs in television.

What a fine title – Lord Thomson of Fleet! How did Northcliffe and Rothermere, Riddell and Lord Dalziel, and I and some others give him an opportunity of taking that title? I cannot make out. We could have been in before him. But I have a piece of advice to give him, from the very depths of my heart. It is this. That he should be guided by my wisdom and gain benefit by my experience. He should begin a new career at once – become an apprentice as quickly as possible. Give up these newspapers of his and take to politics, or philanthropy, or something or other, so long as he ceases to trouble our little group of newspaper proprietors.

We were so agreeably placed until he came along to disturb the waters of tranquillity.

Here I must say, in my eighty-sixth year, I do not feel greatly different from when I was 85. This is my final word. It is time for me to become an apprentice once more. I have not settled in which direction. But somewhere, sometime soon.

1964

FEELING OF IMMORTALITY IN YOUTH

WILLIAM HAZLITT

Life is indeed a strange gift, and its privileges are most mysterious. No wonder when it is first granted to us, that our gratitude, our admiration, and our delight should prevent us from reflecting on our own nothingness, or from thinking it will ever be recalled. Our first and strongest impressions are borrowed from the mighty scene that is opened to us, and we unconsciously transfer its durability as well as its splendour to ourselves. So newly found, we cannot think of parting with it yet, or at least put off that consideration *sine die*. Like a rustic at a fair, we are full of amazement and rapture, and have no thought of going home, or that it will soon be night. We know our existence only by ourselves, and confound our knowledge with the objects of it. We and Nature are therefore one. Otherwise the illusion, the 'feast of reason and the flow of soul', to which we are invited, is a mockery and a cruel insult. We do not go from a play till the last act is ended, and the lights are about to be extinguished. But the fairy face of Nature still shines on: shall we be called away before the curtain falls, or ere we have scarce had a glimpse of what is going on? Like children, our step-mother Nature holds us up to see the raree-show of the universe, and then, as if we were a burden to her to support, lets us fall down again. Yet what brave sublunary things does not this pageant present, like a ball or *fête* of the universe!

To see the golden sun, the azure sky, the outstretched ocean; to walk upon the green earth, and be lord of a thousand creatures; to look down yawning precipices or over distant sunny vales; to see the world spread out under one's feet on a map; to bring the stars near; to view the smallest insects through a microscope; to read history, and consider the revolutions of empire and the successions of generations; to hear of the glory of Tyre, of Sidon, of Babylon, and of Susa, and to say all these were before me and are now nothing; to say I exist in such a point of time, and in such a point of place; to be a spectator and a part of its ever-moving scene; to witness the change of season, of spring and autumn, of winter and summer; to feel hot and cold, pleasure and pain, beauty and deformity, right and wrong; to be sensible to the accidents of nature; to consider the mighty world of eye and ear; to listen to the stock-dove's notes amid the forest deep; to journey over moor and mountain; to hear the midnight sainted choir; to visit lighted halls, or the cathedral's gloom, or sit in crowded theatres and see life itself mocked; to study the works of art and refine the sense of beauty to agony; to worship fame, and to dream of immortality; to look upon the Vatican, and to read Shakspeare; to gather up the wisdom of the ancients, and to pry into the future; to listen to the trump of war, the shout of victory; to question history as to the movements of the human heart; to seek for truth; to plead the cause of humanity; to overlook the world as if time and nature poured their treasures at our feet – to be and to do all this, and then in a moment to be nothing – to have it all snatched from us as by a juggler's trick, or a phantasmagoria! There is something in this transition from all to nothing that shocks us and damps the enthusiasm of youth new flushed with hope and pleasure, and we cast the comfortless thought as far from us as we can. In the first enjoyment of the state of life we discard the fear of debts and duns, and never think of the final payment of our great debt to Nature. Art we know is long; life, we flatter ourselves, should be so too. We see no end of the difficulties and delays we have to encounter: perfection is slow of attainment, and we must have time to accomplish it in. The fame of the great names we look up to is immortal: and shall not we who contemplate it imbibe a portion of ethereal fire, the *divinae particula aurae*, which nothing can extinguish? A wrinkle in Rembrandt or in Nature takes whole days to resolve itself into its component parts, its softenings and its sharpnesses; we refine upon our perfections, and unfold the intricacies of nature. What a prospect for the future! What a task have we not begun! And shall we be arrested in the middle of it? We do not count our time thus employed lost, or our pains thrown away; we do not flag or grow tired, but gain new vigour at our endless task. Shall Time, then, grudge us to finish what we have begun, and have formed a compact with Nature to do? Why not fill up the blank that is left us in this manner? I have looked for hours at a Rembrandt without being conscious of the flight of time, but with ever new wonder and delight, have thought that not only my own but another existence I could pass in the same manner. This rarefied, refined existence seemed to have no end, nor stint, nor principle of decay in it. The print would remain long after I who looked on it had become the prey of worms. The thing seems in itself out of all reason: health, strength, appetite are opposed to the idea of death, and we are not ready to credit it till we have found our illusions vanished, and our hopes grown cold. Objects in youth, from novelty, etc, are stamped upon the brain with such force and integrity that one thinks nothing can remove or obliterate them. They are riveted there, and appear to us as an element of our nature. It must be a mere violence that destroys them, not a natural decay. In the very strength of this persuasion we seem to enjoy an age by anticipation. We melt down years into a single moment of intense sympathy, and by anticipating the fruits defy the ravages of time. If, then, a single moment of our lives is worth years, shall we set any limits to its total value and extent? Again, does it not happen that so secure do we think ourselves of an indefinite period of existence, that at times, when left to ourselves, and impatient of novelty, we feel annoyed at what seems to us the slow and creeping progress of time, and argue that if it always moves at this tedious snail's pace it will never come to an end? How ready are we to sacrifice any space of time which separates us from a favourite object, little thinking that before long we shall find it move too fast.

1837

THE TIME MACHINE

H G WELLS

The Time Traveller (for so it will be convenient to speak of him) was expounding a recondite matter to us. His grey eyes shone and twinkled, and his usually pale face was flushed and animated. The fire burnt brightly, and the soft radiance of the incandescent lights in the lilies of silver caught the bubbles that flashed and passed in our glasses. Our chairs, being his patents, embraced and caressed us rather than submitted to be sat upon, and there was that luxurious after–dinner atmosphere, when thought runs gracefully free of the trammels of precision. And he put it to us in this way – marking the points with a lean forefinger – as we sat and lazily admired his earnestness over this new paradox (as we thought it) and his fecundity.

'You must follow me carefully. I shall have to controvert one or two ideas that are almost universally accepted. The geometry, for instance, they taught you at school is founded on a misconception.'

'Is not that rather a large thing to expect us to begin upon?' said Filby, an argumentative person with red hair.

'I do not mean to ask you to accept anything without reasonable ground for it. You will soon admit as much as I need from you. You know of course that a mathematical line, a line of thickness *nil*, has no real existence. They taught you that? Neither has a mathematical plane. These things are mere abstractions.'

'That is all right,' said the Psychologist.

'Nor, having only length, breadth, and thickness, can a cube have a real existence.'

'There I object,' said Filby. 'Of course a solid body may exist. All real things –'

'So most people think. But wait a moment. Can an *instantaneous* cube exist?'

'Don't follow you,' said Filby.

'Can a cube that does not last for any time at all, have a real existence?'

Filby became pensive. 'Clearly,' the Time Traveller proceeded, 'any real body must have extension in *four* directions: it must have Length, Breadth, Thickness, and – Duration. But through a natural infirmity of the flesh, which I will explain to you in a moment, we incline to overlook this fact. There are really four dimensions, three which we call the three planes of Space, and a fourth, Time. There is, however, a tendency to draw an unreal distinction between the former three dimensions and the latter, because it happens that our consciousness moves intermittently in one direction along the latter from the beginning to the end of our lives.'

'That,' said a very young man, making spasmodic efforts to relight his cigar over the lamp; 'that . . . very clear indeed.'

'Now, it is very remarkable that this is so extensively overlooked,' continued the Time Traveller, with a slight accession of cheerfulness. 'Really this is what is meant by the Fourth Dimension, though some people who talk about the Fourth Dimension do not know they mean it. It is only another way of looking at Time. *There is no difference between Time and any of the three dimensions of Space except that our consciousness moves along it.* But some foolish people have got hold of the wrong side of that idea. You have all heard what they have to say about this Fourth Dimension?'

'*I* have not,' said the Provincial Mayor.

'It is simply this. That Space, as our mathematicians have it, is spoken of as having three dimensions, which one may call Length, Breadth, and Thickness, and is always definable by reference to three planes, each at right angles to the others. But some philosophical people have been asking why *three* dimensions particularly – why not another direction at right angles to the other three? – and have even tried to construct a Four-Dimensional geometry. Professor Simon Newcomb was expounding this to the New York Mathematical Society only a month or so ago. You know how on a flat surface, which has only two dimensions, we can represent a figure of a three-dimensional solid, and similarly they think that by models of three dimensions they could represent one of four – if they could master the perspective of the thing. See?'

'I think so,' murmured the Provincial Mayor; and, knitting his brows, he lapsed into an introspective state, his lips moving as one who repeats mystic words. 'Yes, I think I see it now,' he said after some time, brightening in a quite transitory manner.

'Well, I do not mind telling you I have been at work upon this geometry of Four Dimensions for some time. Some of my results are curious. For instance, here is a portrait of a man at eight years old, another at fifteen, another at seventeen, another at twenty-three, and so on. All these are evidently sections, as it were, Three-Dimensional representations of his Four-Dimensioned being, which is a fixed and unalterable thing.'

'Scientific people,' proceeded the Time Traveller, after the pause required for the proper assimilation of this, 'know very well that Time is only a kind of Space. Here is a popular scientific diagram, a weather record. This line I trace with my finger shows the movement of the barometer. Yesterday it was so high, yesterday night it fell, then this morning it rose again, and so gently upward to here. Surely the mercury did not trace this line in any of the dimensions of Space generally recognized? But certainly it traced such a line, and that line, therefore, we must conclude was along the Time-Dimension.'

'But,' said the Medical Man, staring hard at a coal in the fire, 'if Time is really only a fourth dimension of Space, why is it, and why has it always been, regarded as something different? And why cannot we move about in Time as we move about in the other dimensions of Space?'

The Time Traveller smiled. 'Are you so sure we can move freely in Space? Right and left we can go, backward and forward freely enough, and men always have done so. I admit we move freely in two dimensions. But how about up and down? Gravitation limits us there.'

'Not exactly,' said the Medical Man. 'There are balloons.'

'But before the balloons, save for spasmodic jumping and the inequalities of the surface, man had no freedom of vertical movement.'

'Still they could move a little up and down,' said the Medical Man.

'Easier, far easier down than up.'

'And you cannot move at all in Time, you cannot get away from the present moment.'

'My dear sir, that is just where you are wrong. That is just where the whole world has gone wrong. We are always getting away from the present moment. Our mental existences, which are immaterial and have no dimensions, are passing along the Time-Dimension with a uniform velocity from the cradle to the grave. Just as we should travel *down* if we began our existence fifty miles above the earth's surface.'

'But the great difficulty is this,' interrupted the Psychologist. 'You *can* move about in all directions of Space, but you cannot move about in Time.'

'That is the germ of my great discovery. But you are wrong to say that we cannot move about in Time. For instance, if I am recalling an incident very vividly I go back to the instant of its occurrence: I become absent-minded, as you say. I jump back for a moment. Of course we have no means of staying back for any length of Time, any more than a savage or an animal has of staying six feet above the ground. But a civilized man is better off than the savage in this respect. He can go up against gravitation in a balloon, and why should he not hope that ultimately he may be able to stop or accelerate his drift along the Time-Dimension, or even turn about and travel the other way?'

'Oh, *this*,' began Filby, 'is all –'

'Why not?' said the Time Traveller.

'It's against reason,' said Filby.

'What reason?' said the Time Traveller.

'You can show black is white by argument,' said Filby, 'but you will never convince me.'

'Possibly not,' said the Time Traveller. 'But now you begin to see the object of my investigations into the geometry of Four Dimensions. Long ago I had a vague inkling of a machine –'

'To travel through Time!' exclaimed the Very Young Man.

'That shall travel indifferently in any direction of Space and Time, as the driver determines.'

Filby contented himself with laughter.

'But I have experimental verification,' said the Time Traveller.

'It would be remarkably convenient for the historian,' the Psychologist suggested. 'One might travel back and verify the accepted account of the Battle of Hastings, for instance!'

'Don't you think you would attract attention?' said the Medical Man. 'Our ancestors had no great tolerance for anachronisms.'

'One might get one's Greek from the very lips of Homer and Plato,' the Very Young Man thought.

'In which case they would certainly plough you for the Little-go. The German scholars have improved Greek so much.'

'Then there is the future,' said the Very Young Man. 'Just think! One might invest all one's money, leave it to accumulate at interest, and hurry on ahead!'

'To discover a society,' said I, 'erected on a strictly communistic basis.'

'Of all the wild extravagant theories!' began the Psychologist.

'Yes, so it seemed to me, and so I never talked of it until –'

'Experimental verification!' cried I. 'You are going to verify *that*?'

'The experiment!' cried Filby, who was getting brain-weary.

'Let's see your experiment anyhow,' said the Psychologist, 'though it's all humbug, you know.'

The Time Traveller smiled round at us. Then, still smiling faintly, and with his hands deep in his trousers pockets, he walked slowly out of the room, and we heard his slippers shuffling down the long passage to his laboratory.

The Psychologist looked at us. 'I wonder what he's got?'

'Some sleight-of-hand trick or other,' said the Medical Man, and Filby tried to tell us about a conjuror he had seen at Burslem, but before he had finished his preface the Time Traveller came back, and Filby's anecdote collapsed.

1895

LA CLÉ DES CHANTS

CYRIL CONNOLLY

'Living for beauty' – October on the Mediterranean; blue sky scoured by the mistral, red and golden vine branches, wind-fretted waves chopping round the empty yachts; plane-trees peeling; palms rearing up their dingy under-linen; mud in the streets and from doorways at night the smell of burning oil. Through the dark evening I used to bicycle in to fetch our dinner, past the harbour with its bobbing launches and the cafés with their signs banging. At the local restaurant there would be one or two 'plats à emporter', to which I would add some wine, sausage and Gruyère cheese, a couple of 'Diplomates' to smoke and a new 'Détective' or 'Chasseur Français'; then I would bowl back heavy-laden with the mistral behind me, a lemur buttoned up inside my jacket with his head sticking out. Up the steep drive it was easy to be blown off into the rosemary, then dinner would be spoilt. We ate it with our fingers beside the fire – true beauty lovers – then plunged into the advertisements in *Country Life*, dreaming of that Priory at Wareham where we would end our days. 'Living for Beauty' entailed a busy life of answering advertisements, writing for prospectuses, for information about cottages in Hampstead, small manors in the West – or else for portable canoes, converted Dutch barges 'that could go through the Canals', second-hand yachts, caravans and cars. Homesick, we liked best the detective stories, because they reeked of whisky, beefsteaks, expresses from Paddington, winter landscapes, old inns and Georgian houses that screen large gardens off the main street of country towns. There live the solicitors and doctors and clever spinsters who brew home-made poison and who come into their own in these exacting tales, there arrive for summer the artist from London and the much-consulted military man. At last we would go to bed, bolting the doors while the lemurs cried in the moonlight, house-ghosts bounding from the mulberries to the palms, from the palms to the tall pines whose cones the dormice nibble, from the pines to the roof, and so to our bedroom window where they would press their eager faces to the pane. In the bathroom one of us would be washing while the other crammed fir-cones in the stove. The stove roars, the water is heated and the room fills with steamy fragrance. The two lemurs are admitted and worm their way down to sleep in the bottom of the bed. In the early morning, while we dream of Wareham, they will creep out round our feet, seize the aromatic toothpaste in their long black gloves, jump through the window and spring with it down to the sunny earth.

1944

OH BERNARD, THIS IS SO SUDDEN

Although the English do not like to swank they still rather fancy themselves as comedians. Certainly their literature is rich in laughter and, thank heaven, the spring does not seem to be drying up. Our first piece in this section arose from a dinner party one day in 1967 when I sat next to a particularly charming and funny girl. She was at that time writing blurbs for Collins' dust jackets. At that time I was Editor of the Sunday Times Magazine and we were just preparing a big issue on marriage. I thought this girl so amusing that I asked her, on an impulse, to send me her own thoughts on the subject. Next Monday morning 'The Young Wife's Tale' landed on my desk. She seemed as funny in print as in person, so I sent her £100 and printed it. This was the beginning of Jilly Cooper's career as miniaturist of the middle class. It's a delight to find her first piece as funny as it was then.

The Daisy Ashford story is one of those pieces of English lore where fact elides imperceptively into fiction. She wrote her masterpiece, The Young Visiters, when she was nine. It remained in a box until it was cleared out in 1917, at which time she was thirty-six. A friend showed it to the novelist Frank Swinnerton, then a reader and editor at Chatto and Windus. While working at the British Legation in Berne Daisy learned that Chatto wanted to publish it. Although some reviewers questioned its authenticity, most gave it a standing ovation. It was an immediate best-seller, a play in 1920, a musical in 1968, and a film in 1984. To the end of her long life – she died only in 1972 – Daisy maintained that the charming preface by Sir James Barrie had underwritten the book's success, but her words speak for themselves.

The vast and sophisticated oeuvre of Aldous Huxley is a little out of fashion now. His polymath sophistication does not weather well; but is shown at its glittering best in one of his early poems, Second Philosopher's Song.

Nathaniel Gubbins was a star Sunday Express columnist for twenty-three years. Improbably, Gubbins was his real name. He created an entire alternative world in his column, peopled by such long-running stars as the Worm, a symbolic suburban man, Sally the Cat and a homespun philosopher called the Sweep. It also included a series of brilliant threnodies of dyspepsia in which his stomach miraculously found tongue as Tum and entered into accusing dialectics with his proprietor. How do we manage without Gubbins nowadays?

In the vast output of P. G. Wodehouse sustained over seventy glorious years, nothing is finer than the account of the Great Sermon Handicap. It belongs properly to another world, where time has stood still since the summer of 1914. Of course, Edwardian England was not really like that. It was just that Wodehouse took what suited him from the golden days between the leaden ones. Could anyone run a Great Sermon Handicap today? England remains the kind of baffling place where the possibility could not be altogether ruled out.

When the BBC ran a series in which famous people were asked to give a favourite piece of prose and verse Dame Celia Johnson named 'How Long, O Lord', but was unable to name the source. Perhaps, she said, it had come from a parish magazine. In a sense, it had. It was written by that marvellously fecund scrivener Keith Waterhouse in his Daily Mirror column and has rightly become a modern classic.

And finally, to give this section a fitting coda, here is one of Noël Coward's greatest songs. It was sung by President Roosevelt and Winston Churchill as light relief from one of their great wartime parleys, and what better?

THE YOUNG WIFE'S TALE

JILLY COOPER

You see her down the market in the lunch hour, battling through the crowds, scuttling from barrow to barrow to find the cheapest cauliflowers or peppers, weighed down by carrier bags and responsibilities.

Last month she was the dolly who blued her wages on clothes and make-up and took her washing home to Mother every week-end – now, in one stride, she is the newly married working wife who must be housekeeper, cook, hostess, laundress, seamstress, beguiling companion, glamour girl, assistant breadwinner and willing bedfellow rolled into one.

Looking back on the first fraught year of my marriage I realize we lived in total screaming chaos. I spent most of my time in tears – not tears of misery, but exhaustion. I couldn't cook, I couldn't sew, I had no idea about running a house, my knowledge of sex was limited to Eustace Chesser and Lady Chatterley – yet suddenly I was on trial: sexually, domestically, commercially, socially, and aware that I was inadequate on every count.

My husband's remarks like: 'Do you really think the book case is the right place for a mouldy apple?' would wound me to the quick – or that despairing 'Let's start as we mean to go on' as he looked at the flotsam of clothes strewn over the bedroom, and resented the fact that I had already appropriated five and three-quarters of the six drawers and three out of four of the coat hangers.

As we made love most of the night, I found it impossible to get up in the morning, cook breakfast, do my face and get out of the house by 8.15. Then followed an exhausting day at the office, only punctuated by one of those scurrying, shopping lunches. I was seldom home – due to the caprice of London Transport – before 7 o'clock. Then there was the bed to be made, breakfast to be washed up, the cat to be fed and chatted up, the day to be discussed and supper to be cooked. This was a proper supper (garlic, aubergines and all). The way to a man's heart was supposed to be through his stomach, so there was no getting away with pork pie or scrambled eggs. When I cooked Moussaka for the first time we didn't eat until one o'clock in the morning.

We were very gregarious and were asked out a great deal. My husband also played cricket and rugger at week-ends, so as a besotted newlywed I was only too happy to abandon the housework and watch him score tries and centuries.

As a result the flat became dirtier and more chaotic. The only time we ever really cleaned it up was when in-laws or relations came to stay, and my husband would then say that it was just like a barracks before the annual general inspection. 'How pretty those dead flowers look,' said a kindly aunt. 'Have they become fashionable in London?'

The only other possible moment to clean the flat was on my husband's occasional TA nights. Then I would hare around like a maniac, dusting and polishing; hoping, for once, to welcome him home scented and beautiful in a negligée with a faint smell of onions drifting from the kitchen. It never worked. Invariably he would let himself in unnoticed to find me tackling a mountain of dust under the bed with my bottom sticking out.

It was only after nine months, when the ice compartment wouldn't shut, that I learnt for the first time about defrosting the fridge. Things in the fridge were another headache. There were always those nine reproachful bowls of dripping, the tins of blackening tomato purée, the fish stock that never graduated into soup and the lettuce liquidizing in the vegetable compartment.

Laundry was another nightmare. It took me months to master the mysteries of the launderette. Very early on in our marriage, a red silk handkerchief found its way into the machine with the rest of the washing. My husband's seven shirts came out streaked crimson like the dawn, and for days he wore cyclamen underpants and claimed he was the only member of the fifteen with a rose-pink jock-strap. Once the washing was done it lay around in pillow cases for ages waiting to be ironed. My mother-in-law once slept peacefully and unknowingly on a pillow case full of wet clothes.

In fact my ironing was so disastrous that for a while we tried the laundry. This presented insuperable problems. One week we were too poor to get it out, the next week-end we'd be away, the next they'd shut by the time we got there, then finally we found they'd lost all our sheets. One laundry, we discovered afterwards from the butcher next door, was notorious for 'losing' sheets.

Our own dinner parties were not without incident. The first time my mother came to dinner the blanquette of veal was flavoured with Vim, and the chocolate mousse, left in the fridge all night, was impregnated with garlic and Kit-e-Kat. The cat once ate his way through two large packets of frozen scampi and, the night my husband's boss came to dinner, stripped the salad niçoise of its tunny fish and anchovies.

The flat, as I have said, got grimier and grimier, and the same week that a fungus began to grow under the sink I overheard someone say at a cocktail party that we lived in 'engaging squalor'. It was the last straw, and we hired a daily woman. It was not a success. I spent far more time than before cleaning up before she came, and after the first few weeks the standard went down. Then my husband came back one lunch hour and found her in our bed with the electric blanket and the wireless on.

The cats – we soon acquired a second – did not add to the ease of our married life. Whenever the doorbell rang I used to drench myself in scent to cover the smell of tomcat, and in summer there were fleas. The landlord forbade pets in the house, so the day he came to look over the flat the cats were locked in the wardrobe.

In spite of the 'engaging squalor', our spare room was permanently occupied; girls who had left their lovers or husbands who had left their wives, people who came from abroad or up from the country, all found a fleabitten home there. The hall was always full of carrier bags full of knickers or the cornucopian suitcases of birds of passage. One man came for two days and stayed for four months. One drunken Irishman who started rampaging lustfully round the flat in the still watches of the night was locked in his bedroom. Next morning we found him in the kitchen making coffee, and the imprint of his huge sleeping body remained outside on the long grass we called our lawn.

'When I was first married,' said a friend wistfully, 'I could never make mayonnaise. Humphrey kept kissing me and the oil would go in great dollops instead of drips, and the whole thing curdled. Now we've been married five years and can afford a mixer, and I make perfect mayonnaise every time now – it's my marriage that has curdled.'

We have been married seven years now – I still can't make mayonnaise – but we're not itching, and our marriage hasn't curdled. Even so I asked my husband to name, after seven years, the things that irritated him most about me.

His answers came out pat and immediate: using his razor on my legs and not washing it out; not putting tops back on tonic or soda water, or the ice tray back in the fridge; those little balls of Kleenex everywhere; the eighteen odd socks in his top drawer; the red rings of indelible lipstick on his handkerchief; running out of loo paper/soap/toothpaste; forgetting to turn off lights/fires/the oven; and, of course, my friends.

OK, OK, I said crossly. Then I remembered a poem by an American, which my husband had sent me when I was feeling suicidal early on in our marriage, which had suddenly made everything all right:

> My clumsiest dear, whose hands shipwreck vases,
> At whose quick touch all glasses chip and ring . . .
> Forgetting your coffee spreading on our flannel,
> Your lipstick grinning on our coat.
> So gaily in love's unbreakable heaven
> Our souls on glory of spilt Bourbon float.
> Be with me, darling, early or late, smash glasses,
> I will study wry music for your sake,
> For should your hands drop white and empty
> All the toys of the world would break.

1971

THE YOUNG VISITERS

DAISY ASHFORD

She looked very beautifull with some red roses in her hat and the dainty red ruge in her cheeks looked quite the thing. Bernard heaved a sigh and his eyes flashed as he beheld her and Ethel thorght to herself what a fine type of manhood he reprisented with his nice thin legs in pale broun trousers and well fitting spats and a red rose in his button hole and rarther a sporting cap which gave him a great air with its quaint check and little flaps to pull down if necessary. Off they started the envy of all the waiters.

They arrived at Windsor very hot from the jorney and Bernard at once hired a boat to row his beloved up the river. Ethel could not row but she much enjoyed seeing the tough sunburnt arms of Bernard tugging at the oars as she lay among the rich cushons of the dainty boat. She had a rarther lazy nature but Bernard did not know of this. However he soon got dog tired and sugested lunch by the mossy bank.

O yes said Ethel quickly opening the sparkling champaigne.

Dont spill any cried Bernard as he carved some chicken.

They eat and drank deeply of the charming viands ending up with merangs and choclates.

Let us now bask under the spreading trees said Bernard in a passiunate tone.

Oh yes lets said Ethel and she opened her dainty parasole and sank down upon the long green grass. She closed her eyes but she was far from asleep. Bernard sat beside her in profound silence gazing at her pink face and long wavy eye lashes. He puffed at his pipe for some moments while the larks gaily caroled in the blue sky. Then he edged a trifle closer to Ethels form.

Ethel he murmured in a trembly voice.

Oh what is it said Ethel hastily sitting up.

Words fail me ejaculated Bernard horsly my passion for you is intense he added fervently. It has grown day and night since I first beheld you.

Oh said Ethel in supprise I am not prepared for this and she lent back against the trunk of the tree.

Bernard placed one arm tightly round her. When will you marry me Ethel he uttered you must be my wife it has come to that I love you so intensly that if you say no I shall perforce dash my body to the brink of yon muddy river he panted wildly.

Oh dont do that implored Ethel breathing rarther hard.

Then say you love me he cried.

Oh Bernard she sighed fervently I certinly love you madly you are to me like a Heathen god she cried looking at his manly form and handsome flashing face I will indeed marry you.

How soon gasped Bernard gazing at her intensly.

As soon as possible said Ethel gently closing her eyes.

My Darling whispered Bernard and he seized her in his arms we will be marrid next week.

Oh Bernard muttered Ethel this is so sudden.

1919

SECOND PHILOSOPHER'S SONG

ALDOUS HUXLEY

If, O my Lesbia, I should commit,
Not fornication, dear, but suicide,
My Thames-blown body (Pliny vouches it)
Would drift face upwards on the oily tide
With the other garbage, till it putrefied.

But you, if all your lovers' frozen hearts
Conspired to send you, desperate, to drown –
Your maiden modesty would float face down,
And men would weep upon your hinder parts.

'Tis the Lord's doing. Marvellous is the plan
By which this best of worlds is wisely planned.
One law He made for woman, one for man:
We bow the head and do not understand.

1920

TUM'S COLUMN

NATHANIEL GUBBINS

Memo to a Stomach: As I am not feeling very fit after being entertained by the Army, will you kindly carry on with the column, please?

(Signed) *N. Gubbins.*

Memo to N. Gubbins: If you don't feel very fit how do you suppose I feel? And what am I to write about?
Further to Memo to Tum: Any damn thing you like.
Further Memo to N. Gubbins: But what?
Further Memo to Tum: Get on with the job and stop arguing.

TUM'S COLUMN

It is my birthday today, May 31, and according to the astrologers I was born in the sign of Gemini the Twins, which means that I have a mercurial disposition, a dual personality, superficial knowledge of many things, but no real knowledge of anything. I am also unreliable, fickle, incapable of concentration, full of new enthusiasms but easily bored. I am likeable and popular, and can argue about any subject on earth without knowing a single thing about it.

All this goes for Mr Gubbins, too, who, of course, was born on the same

135

day as myself.

So far as Mr Gubbins is concerned anything less like winged-footed Mercury could hardly be imagined.

As a matter of fact Mr Gubbins is rather flat-footed and moves slowly and with great reluctance. He is indolent and hates any kind of exertion either physical or mental. But the astrologers are certainly right when they say he is unreliable (I have never had regular meals since I was a baby) and they are not far wrong when they say he will argue about things without knowing anything about them (how many times have I been obliged to listen to sheer nonsense expounded hour after hour with nothing coming down but double Scotches?).

To say that he is popular is right in a way, but I know from bitter experience that this popularity has been bought at a great price in taverns and has nothing to do with sterling qualities or charm of manner. On mornings like this Mr Gubbins's manners are anything but charming and his sterling qualities appear to be confined to one – a certain honesty of opinion about people and things which frequently amounts to rudeness.

Mr Gubbins's present plight (and my own) has been brought about by a tommy gun.

Probably because his shooting has been so bad lately, the Home Guard has taken away his rifle and armed him with this gangster's weapon, hoping, no doubt, that he will be able to hit something when the balloon goes up.

But the new enthusiasm (here the astrologers are right again) has completely gone to his head.

Army officers stationed in the district have been invited to inspect the gun (as if they had never seen one before), and these inspections have developed into parties which have continued into the small hours. Rounds have been fired, ammunition wasted and the local population terrorized.

Then, of course, the Army felt obliged to return the hospitality. And so it has gone on, day after day, night after night, with Mr Gubbins neglecting his work and fancying himself as a sort of middle-aged Commando.

He even invited the Army to fire live rounds at us, but fortunately this arrangement was cancelled. Instead he spent the afternoon throwing grenades and causing me to turn over when I might have been resting.

Of course, I have no control over Mr Gubbins's actions. But I have warned him again and again that I cannot go on like this. I am no longer a young stomach and all this excitement means that even when some food is thrown down at me I am too tired and nervous to deal with it.

Then there was the farewell party given by the Army, and today, I suppose, our birthday party.

Memo to N. Gubbins: In view of what I have suffered during the past few days, do you think we could go without a birthday party just for once?

Memo to Tum: Certainly not.

Memo to N. Gubbins: I think if we cancelled the party it would not only improve our health but please Sir Kingsley Wood.

Memo to Tum: I have no desire to please Sir Kingsley Wood. Stand by for birthday party.

Being the diary of Goody-Goody Gubbins, whose stomach is taking revenge for past ill-treatment and who is making a virtue of necessity by trying to live a clean, wholesome life.

Monday

Rise early, drink glass of hot water, and write note to stomach.
Dear Tum,

As you have thought fit to take petty reprisals for what, after all, were not serious indiscretions, I have decided to turn over a new leaf. Fewer cigarettes will be smoked, fewer (if any) drinks will come down, and you shall have regular meals, such as they are these days. You have already had hot water instead of tea, and you are now about to have the doctor's medicine. What would you like for breakfast?

Reply from Tum:
Dear Sir,

If I have caused you distress and sleeplessness it was not done in the spirit of revenge. I am but an instrument in a scheme of things over which I have no control. Punishment, as you ought to know, is automatic. What you sow, so shall you reap. I don't want any breakfast.

Goody-Goody Gubbins goes for early morning walk in rain, returns and forces breakfast down on Tum. Tum reels under hammer blow, recovers for a moment and starts pincer movement which is later checked by tablespoon-ful of medicine.

G.G.G. goes for another walk, head averted past local, returns and forces lunch down on cringing Tum. This time Tum replies with wedge movement which appears to be advancing upwards but is again checked by medicine.

During afternoon try to read good book while Tum does mopping-up operations with lunch. At six p.m. smoke cigarette and dial T.U.M.

'Hullo. Is that my stomach?'
'Your stomach speaking.'
'How are you getting along?'
'You ought to know.'
'Don't you like the austere life?'
'I find it difficult to adjust myself so quickly.'
'I suppose you'd like a drink?'
'I would.'
'Well, you won't get it. Dinner will be coming down at seven.'
'I haven't dealt with our lunch yet.'
'You wanted regular meals and you're going to have regular meals.'
'Can't you do this thing gradually?'
'T.N.T. Today not Tomorrow. Medicine will be coming down now. Dinner will come down at seven.'
'I am accustomed to bread and cheese and raw onions at eleven.'
'Stand by for dinner at seven. Goodbye to you.'

1978

THE GREAT SERMON HANDICAP

P G WODEHOUSE

I read the letter again. It was from Eustace. Claude and Eustace are twins, and more or less generally admitted to be the curse of the human race.

> The Vicarage,
> Twing, Glos.

> Dear Bertie – Do you want to make a bit of money? I hear you had a bad Goodwood, so you probably do. Well, come down here quick and get in on the biggest sporting event of the season. I'll explain when I see you, but you can take it from me it's all right.

> Claude and I are with a reading party at old Heppenstall's. There are nine of us, not counting your pal Bingo Little, who is tutoring the kid up at the Hall.

> Don't miss this golden opportunity, which may never occur again. Come and join us.

> Yours,
> Eustace

I handed this to Jeeves. He studied it thoughtfully.

'What do you make of it? A rummy communication, what?'

'Very high-spirited young gentlemen, sir, Mr Claude and Mr Eustace. Up to some game, I should be disposed to imagine.'

'Yes. But what game, do you think?'

'It is impossible to say, sir. Did you observe that the letter continues over the page?'

'Eh, what?' I grabbed the thing. This was what was on the other side of the last page:

SERMON HANDICAP
RUNNERS AND BETTING
PROBABLE STARTERS

Rev. Joseph Tucker (Badgwick), scratch.
Rev. Leonard Starkie (Stapleton), scratch.
Rev. Alexander Jones (Upper Bingley), receives three minutes.
Rev. W. Dix (Little Clickton-in-the-Wold), receives five minutes.
Rev. Francis Heppenstall (Twing), receives eight minutes.
Rev. Cuthbert Dibble (Boustead Parva), receives nine minutes.
Rev. Orlo Hough (Boustead Magna), receives nine minutes.
Rev. J. J. Roberts (Fale-by-the-Water), receives ten minutes.
Rev. G. Hayward (Lower Bingley), receives twelve minutes.
Rev. James Bates (Gandle-by-the-Hill), receives fifteen minutes.
(The above have arrived)

PRICES – 5–2, Tucker, Starkie; 3–1, Jones; 9–2, Dix; 6–1, Heppenstall, Dibble, Hough; 100–8 any other.

It baffled me.

'Do you understand it, Jeeves?'

'No, sir.'

'Well, I think we ought to have a look into it, anyway, what?'

'Undoubtedly, sir.'

'Right-o, then. Pack our spare dickey and a toothbrush in a neat brown-paper parcel, send a wire to Lord Wickhammersley to say we're coming, and buy two tickets on the five-ten at Paddington tomorrow.' . . .

Not being one of the official stewards, I had my choice of churches next morning, and naturally I didn't hesitate. The only drawback to going to Lower Bingley was that it was ten miles away, which meant an early start, but I borrowed a bicycle from one of the grooms and tooled off. I had only Eustace's word for it that G. Hayward was such a stayer, and it might have been that he had showed too flattering form at that wedding where the twins had heard him preach; but any misgivings I may have had disappeared the moment he got into the pulpit. Eustace had been right. The man was a trier. He was a tall, rangy-looking greybeard, and he went off from the start with a nice, easy action, pausing and clearing his throat at the end of each sentence, and it wasn't five minutes before I realized that here was the winner. His habit of stopping dead and looking round the church at intervals was worth minutes to us, and in the home stretch we gained no little advantage owing to his dropping his pince-nez and having to grope for them. At the twenty-minute mark he had merely settled down. Twenty-five minutes saw him going strong. And when he finally finished with a good burst, the clock showed thirty-five minutes fourteen seconds. With the handicap which he had been given, this seemed to me to make the event easy for him, and it was with much bonhomie and goodwill to all men that I hopped on to the old bike and started back to the Hall for lunch.

Bingo was talking on the phone when I arrived.

'Fine! Splendid! Topping!' he was saying. 'Eh? Oh, we needn't worry about him. Right-o, I'll tell Bertie.' He hung up the receiver and caught sight of me. 'Oh, hallo, Bertie; I was just talking to Eustace. It's all right, old man. The report from Lower Bingley has just got in. G. Hayward romps home.'

'I knew he would. I've just come from there.'

'Oh, were you there? I went to Badgwick. Tucker ran a splendid race, but the handicap was too much for him. Starkie had a sore throat and was nowhere. Roberts, of Fale-by-the-Water, ran third. Good old G. Hayward!' said Bingo affectionately, and we strolled out on to the terrace.

'Are all the returns in, then?' I asked.

'All except Gandle-by-the-Hill. But we needn't worry about Bates. He never had a chance. By the way, poor old Jeeves loses his tenner. Silly ass!'

'Jeeves! How do you mean?'

'He came to me this morning, just after you had left, and asked me to put a tenner on Bates for him. I told him he was a chump and begged him not to throw his money away, but he would do it.'

'I beg your pardon, sir. This note arrived for you just after you had left the house this morning.'

Jeeves had materialized from nowhere, and was standing at my elbow. 'Eh? What? Note?'

'The Reverend Mr Heppenstall's butler brought it over from the Vicarage, sir. It came too late to be delivered to you at the moment.'

Young Bingo was talking to Jeeves like a father on the subject of betting against the form-book. The yell I gave made him bite his tongue in the middle of a sentence.

'What the dickens is the matter?' he asked, not a little peeved.

'We're dished! Listen to this!'

I read him the note:

> The Vicarage,
> Twing, Glos.
>
> My dear Wooster, – As you may have heard, circumstances over which I have no control will prevent my preaching the sermon on Brotherly Love for which you made such a flattering request. I am unwilling, however, that you shall be disappointed, so, if you will attend divine service at Gandle-by-the-Hill this morning, you will hear my sermon preached by young Bates, my nephew. I have lent him the manuscript at his urgent desire, for between ourselves, there are wheels within wheels. My nephew is one of the candidates for the headmastership of a well-known public school, and the choice has narrowed down between him and one rival.
>
> Late yesterday evening James received private information that the head of the Board of Governors of the school proposed to sit under him this Sunday in order to judge of the merits of his preaching, a most important item in swaying the Board's choice. I acceded to his plea that I lend him my sermon on Brotherly Love, of which, like you, he apparently retains a vivid recollection. It would have been too late for him to compose a sermon of suitable length in place of the brief address which – mistakenly, in my opinion – he had designed to deliver to his rustic flock, and I wished to help the boy.
>
> Trusting that his preaching of the sermon will supply you with as pleasant memories as you say you have of mine, I remain,
>
> Cordially yours,
> F. Heppenstall
>
> PS – The hay-fever has rendered my eyes unpleasantly weak for the time being, so I am dictating this letter to my butler, Brookfield, who will convey it to you.

I don't know when I've experienced a more massive silence than the one that followed my reading of this cheery epistle. Young Bingo gulped once or twice, and practically every known emotion came and went on his face.

Jeeves coughed one soft, low, gentle cough like a sheep with a blade of grass stuck in its throat, and then stood gazing serenely at the landscape. Finally young Bingo spoke.

'Great Scott!' he whispered hoarsely. 'An S.P. job!'

'I believe that is the technical term, sir,' said Jeeves.

'So you had inside information, dash it!' said young Bingo.

'Why, yes, sir,' said Jeeves. 'Brookfield happened to mention the contents of the note to me when he brought it. We are old friends.'

Bingo registered grief, anguish, rage, despair and resentment.

'Well, all I can say,' he cried, 'is that it's a bit thick! Preaching another man's sermon! Do you call that honest? Do you call that playing the game?'

'Well, my dear old thing,' I said, 'be fair. It's quite within the rules. Clergymen do it all the time. They aren't expected always to make up the sermons they preach.'

Jeeves coughed again, and fixed me with an expressionless eye.

'And in the present case, sir, if I may be permitted to take the liberty of making the observation, I think we should make allowances. We should remember that the securing of this headmastership meant everything to the young couple.'

'Young couple! What young couple?'

'The Reverend James Bates, sir, and Lady Cynthia. I am informed by her ladyship's maid that they have been engaged to be married for some weeks – provisionally, so to speak; and his lordship made his consent conditional on Mr Bates securing a really important and remunerative position.'

Young Bingo turned a light green.

'Engaged to be married!'

'Yes, sir.'

There was a silence.

'I think I'll go for a walk,' said Bingo.

'But, my dear old thing,' I said, 'it's just lunch-time. The gong will be going any minute now.'

'I don't want any lunch!' said Bingo.

1924

HOW LONG, O LORD

KEITH WATERHOUSE

And God said unto Noah, Make thee an ark of gopher wood; rooms shalt thou make in the ark, and the length of the ark shall be three hundred cubits.

And of every living thing of all flesh, two of every sort shalt thou bring into the ark, to keep them alive with thee.

And Noah said, Sign here, and leavest Thou a deposit.

And the Lord signed there, and left He a deposit.

And Noah was six hundred years old when the flood of waters was upon

141

the Earth.

And the Lord said unto Noah, Where is the ark, which I commanded thee to build?

And Noah said unto the Lord, Verily, I have had three carpenters off ill.

The gopher wood supplier hath let me down – yea even though the gopher wood hath been on order for nigh upon twelve months. The damp-course specialist hath not turned up. What can I do, O Lord?

And God said unto Noah, I want that ark finished even after seven days and seven nights.

And Noah said, It will be so.

And it was not so.

And the Lord said unto Noah, What seemeth to be the trouble this time?

And Noah said unto the Lord, Mine sub-contractor hath gone bankrupt. The pitch which Thou commandest me to put on the outside and on the inside of the ark hath not arrived. The plumber hath gone on strike.

Noah rent his garments and said, The glazier departeth on holiday to Majorca – yea, even though I offerest him double time. Shem, my son, who helpeth me on the ark side of the business, hath formed a pop group with his brothers Ham and Japheth. Lord I am undone.

And God said in his wrath, Noah, do not thou mucketh Me about.

The end of all flesh is come before me for the Earth is filled with violence through them; and behold, I will destroy them with the Earth. How can I destroy them with the Earth if thou art incapable of completing the job that thou was contracted to do?

And Noah said, Lo, the contract will be fulfilled.

And Lo, it was not fulfilled.

And Noah said unto the Lord, The gopher wood is definitely in the warehouse. Verily, and the gopher wood supplier waiteth only upon his servant to find the invoices before he delivereth the gopher wood unto me.

And the Lord grew angry and said, Scrubbeth thou round the gopher wood. What about the animals?

Of fowls after their kind, and of cattle after their kind, of every creeping thing of the Earth after his kind, two of every sort have I ordered to come unto thee, to keep them alive.

Where for example are the giraffes?

And Noah said unto the Lord, They are expected today.

And the Lord said unto Noah, And where are the clean beasts, the male and the female; to keep their seed alive upon the face of all the Earth?

And Noah said, The van cometh on Tuesday; yea and yea, it will be so.

And the Lord said unto Noah, How about the unicorns?

And Noah wrung his hands and wept, saying, Lord, Lord, they are a discontinued line. Thou canst not get unicorns for love nor money.

And God said, Come thou, Noah, I have left with thee a deposit, and thou hast signed a contract.

Where are the monkeys, and the bears, and the hippopotami, and the elephants, and the zebras and the hartebeests, two of each kind, and of fowls also of the air by sevens, the male and the female?

And Noah said unto the Lord, They have been delivered unto the wrong address, but should arrive on Friday; all save the fowls of the air by sevens, for it hath just been told unto me that fowls of the air are sold only in half-dozens.

And God said unto Noah, Thou hast not made an ark of gopher wood, nor hast thou lined it with pitch within and without; and of every living thing of all flesh, two of every sort hast thou failed to bring into the ark. What sayest thou, Noah?

And Noah kissed the Earth and said, Lord, thou knowest in thy wisdom what it is like with delivery dates.

And the Lord in his wisdom said, Noah, my son, I knowest. Why else dost thou think I have caused a flood to descend upon the Earth?

1986

MAD DOGS AND ENGLISHMEN

NOËL COWARD

In tropical climes there are certain times of day
When all the citizens retire
To tear their clothes off and perspire,
It's one of those rules that the greatest fools obey,
Because the sun is much too sultry
And one must avoid its ultry-violet ray.

Papalaka papalaka papalaka boo,
Papalaka papalaka papalaka boo,
Digariga digariga digariga doo,
Digariga digariga digariga doo!

The natives grieve when the white men leave their huts,
Because they're obviously, definitely nuts!

Mad dogs and Englishmen
Go out in the midday sun,
The Japanese don't care to,
The Chinese wouldn't dare to,
Hindoos and Argentines sleep firmly from twelve to one,
But Englishmen detest a siesta.
In the Philippines
There are lovely screens
To protect you from the glare,
In the Malay States
There are hats like plates
Which the Britishers won't wear.

143

At twelve noon
The natives swoon
And no further work is done,
But mad dogs and Englishmen
Go out in the midday sun.

It's such a surprise for the Eastern eyes to see
That though the English are effete
They're quite impervious to heat,
When the white man rides every native hides in glee,
Because the simple creatures hope he
Will impale his solar topee on a tree.

    Bolyboly bolyboly bolyboly baa,
    Bolyboly bolyboly bolyboly baa,
    Habaninny habaninny habaninny haa,
    Habaninny habaninny habaninny haa.

It seems such a shame
When the English claim
The earth
That they give rise to such hilarity and mirth.

Mad dogs and Englishmen
Go out in the midday sun.
The toughest Burmese bandit
Can never understand it.
In Rangoon the heat of noon
Is just what the natives shun,
They put their Scotch or rye down
And lie down.
In a jungle town
Where the sun beats down
To the rage of man and beast
The English garb
Of the English sahib
Merely gets a bit more creased.
In Bangkok
At twelve o'clock
They foam at the mouth and run,
But mad dogs and Englishmen
Go out in the midday sun.

Mad dogs and Englishmen
Go out in the midday sun.
The smallest Malay rabbit
Deplores this stupid habit.

In Hongkong
They strike a gong
And fire off a noonday gun
To reprimand each inmate
Who's in late.

In the mangrove swamps
Where the python romps
There is peace from twelve to two,
Even caribous
Lie around and snooze
For there's nothing else to do.
In Bengal
To move at all
Is seldom, if ever, done,
But mad dogs and Englishmen
Go out in the midday sun.

1931

145

A RIGHT LITTLE,
TIGHT LITTLE
CLINIC

The condition of England has been well reported over the years. The conversation with a farm lad at Abingdon in 1843 still makes harrowing reading. Things were not much better in London sixty years later when George R. Sims wrote his account of 'Sweated London'. Sims was a celebrated Edwardian journalist, who is perhaps better known as the author of Christmas Day in the Workhouse. He was a playwright, social reformer, criminologist and, slightly surprisingly, bon viveur. He was also, as this piece shows, a first-class reporter.

The English have traditionally been better at drinking than eating. To try to understand the English pub and the people who frequented it an old Harrovian called Tom Harrisson infiltrated himself into Bolton nearly fifty years ago and, with a group of helpers, published a report on what he found. He had previously spent some years exploring some of the most primitive parts of the world in Borneo and the Pacific. It is rather as if he has done the same in Bolton. It is sometimes difficult to gauge the level of sophistication at which his book is to be engaged. Sometimes he seems to be writing tongue in cheek. Is the percentage of references to coughing, swearing, and sniffing to be taken seriously? We may be uncertain; but not when we get to the analysis of subjects discussed in the vault of one pub on the evening of 6 July. It sounds as if Dickens's Mr Jingle has been given a second innings.

Then, a robust defence of English cooking from George Orwell. He was writing in 1945, when some defence was necessary; but his litany of great English dishes seizes the mind, if not the tongue; kippers, muffins, crumpets; bread sauce, mint sauce, apple sauce; Stilton and Wensleydale; and the magnificent Cox's Orange Pippin. Raymond Postgate, historian, socialist, wine-lover, and founder of the Good Food Guide, agreed about the innate excellence of English food but thought it had fallen into the wrong hands. Hence, the tart ten rules he offers in the preface to his very first guide in 1951.

Class is the English pox: but just as the incidence of pox in England has fallen virtually to zero, so has the prevalence of class. We can still see its outlines, as an aerial picture of a Roman village under the fields. Yet Orwell was right, forty years ago, in noting the arrival of a new kind of man, middle-class in income but not much interested in his own social status. With typical shrewdness he noticed that the formation of an enormous airforce meant thousands of working-class young men graduated into the technical middle class by way of the RAF. That process has speeded up in the last half century and it would be fascinating to read Orwell today on English class. Alas, we can only guess what he would say.

We can, however, perhaps sense the way his mind would have moved if we read three critiques of post-war England. The problem now is not poverty or unemployment, Betjeman argues; it is the monochrome face of plenty; the suburbanization of all England: the coming of Tizer and light ale, Izal and Weetabix, the Fifty Shilling Tailor and the Co-op. Very well then, let's move up a notch, and see what the upper middle class can do with their new affluence. Not much better, says Michael Frayn. They've bought a country cottage, and installed a Supa-Heata, and a Victorian pedestal and cistern, and painted the woodwork Melanesian Blue. The blacksmith in Ronald Blythe's modern classic notes the same phenomenon: he wants to do genuine modern work; his customers want everything quaint and curly.

A CONVERSATION, MAY 1843

ALEXANDER SOMERVILLE

Two shillings a-week for lads twelve and fourteen years old. From two and sixpence to three and sixpence a-week for lads fourteen to sixteen years old. Four shillings and five shillings a-week for young men seventeen, eighteen, nineteen, and twenty years old! And by those youths and young men two-thirds of all the ploughing and carting of the farm is done. They are hired from a distance in almost all cases; are hired by the year; provide themselves with food and clothing out of their wages; sleep in a stable-loft or barn, having no fireside to go to; no hot dinners, but everlasting bread and lard, bread and lard, bread and lard!

Here is a conversation with one of them on a large farm near Abingdon:
'You hold the plough, you say; how old are you?'
'I bees sixteen a'most.'
'What wages have you?'
'Three shillin' a-week.'
'Three shillings! Have you nothing else? Don't you get victuals, or part of them, from your master?'
'No, I buys them all.'
'All out of three shillings?'
'Ees, and buys my clothes out of that.'
'And what do you buy to eat?'
'Buy to eat! Why, I buys bread and lard.'
'Do you eat bread and lard always? What have you for breakfast?'
'What have I for breakfast? Why, bread and lard.'
'And what for dinner?'
'Bread and lard.'
'What for supper, the same?'
'Ees, the same for supper – bread and lard.'
'It seems to be always bread and lard; have you no boiled bacon and vegetables?'
'No, there be no place to boil 'em; no time to boil 'em; none to boil.'
'Have you never a hot dinner nor supper; don't you get potatoes?'
'Ees, potatoes, an we pay for 'em. Master lets us boil 'em once a-week an we like.'
'And what do you eat to them; bacon?'
'No.'
'What then?'
'Lard; never has nothing but lard.'
'Can't you boil or cook your victuals any day you choose?'
'No; has no fire.'
'Have you no fire to warm you in cold weather?'
'No, we never has fire.'
'Where do you go in the winter evenings?'

'To bed, when it be time; an it ben't time, we goes to some of the housen as be round about.'

'To the firesides of some of the cottagers, I suppose?'

'Ees, an we can get.'

'What if you cannot get; do you go into the farmhouse?'

'No, mustn't; never goes anywhere but to bed an it be very cold.'

'Where is your bed?'

'In the *tollit*,' [stable loft.]

'How many of you sleep there?'

'All on us as be hired.'

'How many are hired?'

'Four last year, five this.'

'Does any one make the beds for you?'

'No, we make 'em ourselves.'

'Who washes your sheets?'

'Who washes 'em?'

'Yes; they are washed, I suppose?'

'No, they ben't.'

'What, never washed? Do you mean to say you don't have your sheets washed?'

'No, never since I comed.'

'When did you come?'

'Last Michaelmas.'

'Were your bedclothes clean then?'

'I dare say they was.'

'And don't you know how long they are to serve until they are changed again?'

'To Michaelmas, I hear tell.'

'So one change of bedclothes serves a year! Don't you find your bed disagreeable?'

'Do I! I bees too sleepy. I never knows nought of it, only that I has to get up afore I be awake, and never get into it afore I be a'most asleep. I be up at four, and ben't done work afore eight at night.'

'You don't go so long at the plough as that?'

'No; but master be always having summat for we to do as be hired; we be always at summat.'

1852

SWEATED LONDON

GEORGE R SIMS

One would have thought that the meaning of the word 'sweating' as applied to work was sufficiently obvious. But when 'the Sweating System' was inquired into by the Committee of the House of Lords, the meaning became

150

suddenly involved. As a matter of fact the sweater was originally a man who kept his people at work for long hours. A schoolboy who 'sweats' for his examination studies for many hours beyond his usual working day. The schoolboy meaning of the word was originally the trade meaning.

But of late years the sweating system has come to mean an unhappy combination of long hours and low pay. 'The sweater's den' is a workshop – often a dwelling room as well – in which, under the most unhealthy conditions, men and women toil for from sixteen to eighteen hours a day for a wage barely sufficient to keep body and soul together.

The sweating system, as far as London is concerned, exists chiefly at the East End, but it flourishes also in the West, notably in Soho, where the principal 'sweating trade', tailoring, is now largely carried on. Let us visit the East End first, for here we can see the class which has largely contributed to the evil – the destitute foreign Jew – place his alien foot for the first time upon the free soil of England.

Some of the steamers arrive in St Katharine's Docks, and the immigrants – principally, Russian, Polish, and Roumanian Jews – have the advantage of stepping straight from the ship in which they have been cooped up for two days and two nights under conditions which, if it be rough weather, cannot be conducive to comfort.

Many of them, especially those who have come from Russia, have already been despoiled of the little money they had. At the frontier they are sometimes detained for two or even three days, in order that they may be robbed by harpies in collusion with certain subordinate officials. In some cases a man when he asks for a ticket at the frontier railway station is refused by the booking clerk. He is told that tickets can only be issued to emigrants through an agent. The agent then introduces himself, and on one plea or another succeeds in involving the immigrant in expenses which leave him with scarcely a rouble in his pocket at the journey's end.

If he escapes the foreign harpies the immigrant is not even safe when he has reached London. Men, frequently of his own faith and country, wait for him outside the docks, and because he is ignorant and friendless in a strange land, and speaks only his own language, seize upon him and convey him to a shark's boarding house, and keep him there on some pretence or other until he is penniless. Then the 'shark' lends him a few shillings on his luggage, and when that is gone turns him into the street with only the clothes he stands up in. That is how hundreds of Jewish immigrants commence their career as units in the densely-packed population of East London and begin 'to look for work' destitute.

The Jewish community, fully aware of these evils, does its best to guard against them. They have agents who meet every boat, and, addressing the poor aliens in their own language, help them to get their scanty belongings from the docks, and advise and direct them as to lodgings and homes and shelters where they will be honestly dealt with.

Let us meet a ship from Hamburg, laden with men and women who will presently be working in the dens of the sweaters.

It is a pouring wet day. The rain is coming down in torrents, and one has to wade through small lakes and rivulets of mud to reach the narrow pathway leading to Irongate Stairs, where the immigrant passengers of the vessel lying at anchor in the Thames are to land. This is a river steamer, and so the wretched immigrants are taken off in small boats and rowed to the steps. Look at them, the men thin and hungry-eyed, the women with their heads bare and only a thin shawl over their shoulders, the children terrified by the swaying of the boat that lies off waiting to land when the other boats have discharged their load!

What must these people feel as they get their first glimpse of London? All they can see is a blurred and blotted line of wharves and grim buildings, and when at last they land it is in a dark archway crowded with loafers and touts all busily trying to confuse them, to seize their luggage, almost fighting to get possession of it.

Fortunately Mr Somper, the Superintendent of the Poor Jews' Temporary Shelter, is here also. As the scared and shivering foreigners step ashore he speaks to them either in Yiddish or Lettish, and finds out if they have an address to go to. Most of them have something written on a piece of paper which they produce creased and soiled from a pocket. It is the address of a friend or relative, or of a boarding-house. Others have no idea where they are going. Many, asked what money they have, confess to twenty or thirty shillings as their entire fortune. Others at once begin to unfold a tale of robbery at the frontier, and moan that they have scarcely anything. These are at once taken charge of and housed in the shelter until their friends can be found for them. For most of them have friends 'somewhere'. It may be a brother, it may be only a fellow townsman or fellow villager, who came to London years ago. In the shelter they are taken care of with their money and their 'baggage' until their friends can be communicated with or employment obtained.

Here, stepping from the boat, are two young Germans. They are going on to America. Here are two Russians in long coats, high boots, and peaked caps. These also are for America. But the rest of the pale, anxious, and dishevelled crowd are for London. This Russian lad, still wearing the red embroidered shirt of his Fatherland, has been sent for by his brother, a tailor. This young fellow with a wife and two children has nowhere to go. He has come to escape military service and to look for work. Under the dark archway, wet and miserable, there is a crowd of sixty-four men, women, and children huddled together gesticulating and shrieking, and always in mortal terror that some unauthorized person is going to lay hands on the little bundles and sacks which contain their all.

The nervous hysteria of a downtrodden people escaped from bondage is writ large in the high-pitched voices. Some of the women speak in a scream. Some of the men, disputing as to the payment of the sixpence demanded by the boatman, yell and shout as though they were lunatics in a padded cell.

Two English policemen, stolid and self-possessed, listen to the complaints poured into their ears in half a dozen languages and say nothing. When I explain to one that a gesticulating Pole wants to give the boatman into custody for refusing to give up his bundle without the sixpence is paid, the policeman grins and says, 'Lor now, does he?' A young Roumanian Jewess, with two crying children clinging to her skirts, asks me a question in a voice that sounds as though she was calling down the vengeance of Heaven upon me. But Mr Somper comes to the rescue. She is asking me if I know somebody with an impossible name. He is her cousin and came to London last June with 172 other Roumanian Jews driven out by the action of the Government.

But presently the shouting and gesticulating cease. A covered cart is driven up to the entrance of the archway. In this the aliens, directed by an agent, proceed to pile their scanty luggage. A few will not trust their bundles out of their own hands, and carry them. The cart starts, the men, women and children fall into procession, and then move slowly off, tramping in the mud and slush of the roadway through the pouring rain. I forget that I am in London. This melancholy file of men and women carries me to Siberia. With their faces woe-begone, their heads bent, they appear more like a gang of convicts marching to the mines than free men and women making their first acquaintance with the capital of the British Empire, in which they are henceforward to dwell and earn their living. For the bulk of the people I have introduced you to, these scantily-clad, almost penniless Russians, Poles, and Roumanians, will presently be working as tailors and bootmakers in the den of the sweater. Some of the men have handicrafts, but the majority will be taken on as 'greeners', or beginners.

It is the Sunday morning following the arrival of the immigrants at whose disembarkation we assisted. We are in Goulston Street, Whitechapel. To the man of the West the scene is like a weekday fair. Everywhere are stalls and hawkers, and business at the shops is in full swing. Even the money changer's close at hand is open, and the clerks sit at their open ledgers. Half way down Goulston Street stands a group of shabby, careworn, silent men. Foreigners every one of them, you can see at a glance. They are mostly tailors who want a change of masters, but among them are several of their 'friends', new arrivals who have as yet failed to find work. Presently a man approaches. He has a little book in his hand. Some of the men recognize him, and the group falls into an attitude of expectancy. The alien slaves of labour have assembled in the slave market to pass into bondage. The man with the book is the slave dealer. He looks the group over, then calls out in Yiddish the special kind of workers that he is in need of. As he calls the men who answer his requirements hold up their hands. He says a few words to them and enters their names in his book. They will follow him presently to his 'den'. If he wants 'greeners' he turns to the new arrivals. He selects three or four. Then he tells one of the men who know his place to take the 'gang' with him. The slaves fall in and slouch away silently to their new bondage.

We have seen the sweater engaging his hands in the slave market. Let us follow them to the den. But first it will be as well to remove a false impression with regard to the sweater himself. He is not always the wealthy spider sucking the life-blood from the flies he has caught in his web. He is not a gorgeous Hebrew with diamond rings and a big cigar. He is frequently a worker also, a man sweating because he is himself sweated. His one advantage is that he generally knows the whole of his trade. That is to say he can, if he is a tailor, make the whole of a garment; if he is a bootmaker, a complete pair of boots. The foreigners who come to be sweated generally make *one part* only of the article they work at. They learn that one portion of the process and no other. In this they differ from an Englishman, who, if he does tailoring, *is* a tailor. The foreign tailors represent not trained labour but unskilled labour; very few of them could make a complete article. There are, according to a witness before the House of Lords Committee, twenty-five subdivisions of labour in the sweating trade in making a suit of clothes.

There are more than two thousand sweaters in the East of London. Some have workshops, others use their own dwelling rooms. Let us enter a 'dwelling' workshop. It is a room nine feet square. In it fourteen people are at work. There is a coke fire, and seven or eight gas jets are burning. Ventilation there is none. The sweater is at work himself. Hollow-eyed, gaunt-visaged men and women are toiling in various ways. Some have a sewing machine, others are doing handwork. It is evening when we enter. The poor wretches have been at work since six o'clock in the morning. They will go on probably till midnight, for it is the season, and the sweater has his hands full. The wages these poor foreigners can earn by their ceaseless toil will perhaps be eighteen shillings at the week's end. For that they will work on Sunday also. All the gold of the Rothschilds could not tempt *us* to stay an hour in this place, for life is sweeter than gold. Let us hurry out into the air.

Here is another den. In this bootmaking is going on. The men are mostly 'greeners' who have been hired in the slave market. It is a double room knocked into one. In this ten men, and a man and his wife and six children work and sleep.

The Russian 'greener' lives on next to nothing. A cup of tea and a herring are frequently all the food he will have in the twenty-four hours. How can he afford more on the starvation wages he receives from the sweater? Not long ago a Russian who appeared before the Sweating Committee said he had that week worked from 6.30 a.m. to 2.30 a.m. on the following day with only one hour for dinner. He worked harder in London than in Warsaw and made less. But the emigration agent had painted London as a land of gold and tempted him to invest all he had in the world in a ticket.

The struggle is sometimes even too terrible for a Russian Jew. Recently a young 'greener' hanged himself. He had brought his newly-wedded wife from Russia to London, thinking he would get a living. He learnt boot finishing and earned 12s. to 15s. a week. To earn £1 a week he would have to work twenty-two hours out of the twenty-four. At the inquest it was proved that he had tried to do this and his brain had given way. In a fit of madness and despair he hanged himself in the room he occupied with his young wife.

There are various other sweating trades carried on East and West, such as furriery, shirtmaking, mantle-making, and dressmaking. In the West tailoring and dressmaking are the sweated trades. Here the work is irregular. Half the year the men and girls are unemployed, the other half they are working night and day.

English girls are occasionally sweated at the West in the dressmaking and millinery by wealthy Christian employers. With the blinds drawn and the workrooms apparently closed for the day dressmakers work on long beyond the hours allowed by the Factory Acts during the season. Sometimes the inspector gets wind of what is going on and makes a sudden descent on the premises. Then all is consternation. Madame is summoned, and puts the blame on duchesses who want the dresses in a hurry. The Factory Act applies to these workrooms, and consequently the condition of things is far better than in the East End dens. There the Factory Inspector can only enter on a warrant, because the bulk of the dens are in dwelling-houses. The sanitary inspector can enter, but the only result of his occasional interference is that the sweater makes promises which he never performs. Many of the crying evils of the sweating system would be redressed if the Factory and the Sanitary Inspectors had greater powers and worked more harmoniously together.

In the West End the laundry women are 'sweated', and in the small or hand laundries the conditions and the hours are as bad as can be. The cabinet trade has its own sweaters' dens in the homes of the 'garret masters', and here again the sweaters and the victims are largely aliens.

This is but a brief glance at Sweated London. But it may suffice to bring home to the reader one of the pressing problems of the day. Is it right that in our England we should permit a trade which is little better than the importation of foreign slaves? For you must remember that though some of these people come with a fair chance of bettering themselves, and do in many cases succeed, and in process of time become owners of property and employers of labour – generally the property is bad and the labour is sweated – yet a vast number are lured to this country by the misrepresentations of interested parties.

Arguments are constantly adduced on both sides of the question. Parliamentary Committees have gathered evidence on 'Sweating'; the friends of the alien worker have come forward to proclaim his usefulness to the State and to the community. Between friend and foe Time will eventually pronounce judgement.

1904

THE PUB AND THE PEOPLE

TOM HARRISSON

TALKING
The social activity common to almost all drinkers, while drinking, and when drunk, is talking.

What is pub talk about?

Writes a barman:

Conversation. Typical – what's in the news, sensational, sport main topic among men. Work and past events, good old days reminiscencing.

155

Among women their troubles, especially Marital, but of course children, mainly pride in their own Kith and Kin, gossip, scandal, in fact nothing dissimilar to what women talk about in any other place where two or three are gathered together.

During the course of our observations in May and June, one observer took ten minute sample counts of the subjects of conversations in all the pubs that he visited. Only definite *conversations* on the subjects were counted, not isolated references; at least three consecutive statements on a subject were necessary before the subject was counted as a 'conversation'.

Of 157 conversations that were classified under our ten heads the relative proportions were as follows:

Pubs and Drinking	18	per cent
Betting	16	,, ,,
Personal-topo graphical	15	,, ,,
Sport (not betting)	13	,, ,,
Jobs	12	,, ,,
Money	9	,, ,,
Politics	8	,, ,,
Weather	6	,, ,,
Films	2	,, ,,
War	1	,, ,,

. . . Here is a more detailed account, written by the barmen, of the topics of conversation in a vault one evening (July 6):

Power of earth as source of life – Indestructability of matter – Transfer of a player from the Town team – Food and its adulteration as a cause of national decadence – Power of Dictators, comparisons with Britain – England as a self-sufficing nation – Privileges of the land-owning classes – Allotments, and regulations concerning same – Economics of market gardening – Neither pub or pawnshop in Bradford's part of Great Lever, ground landlords objection, or not? – Model pub now in Green Lane.

1943

IN DEFENCE OF ENGLISH COOKING

GEORGE ORWELL
(EVENING STANDARD)

We have heard a good deal of talk in recent years about the desirability of attracting foreign tourists to this country. It is well known that England's two worst faults, from a foreign visitor's point of view, are the gloom of our Sundays and the difficulty of buying a drink.

Both of these are due to fanatical minorities who will need a lot of quelling, including extensive legislation. But there is one point on which public opinion could bring about a rapid change for the better: I mean cooking.

It is commonly said, even by the English themselves, that English cooking is the worst in the world. It is supposed to be not merely incompetent, but also imitative, and I even read quite recently, in a book by a French writer, the remark: 'The best English cooking is, of course, simply French cooking.'

Now that is simply not true. As anyone who has lived long abroad will know, there is a whole host of delicacies which it is quite impossible to obtain outside the English-speaking countries. No doubt the list could be added to, but here are some of the things that I myself have sought for in foreign countries and failed to find.

First of all, kippers, Yorkshire pudding, Devonshire cream, muffins and crumpets. Then a list of puddings that would be interminable if I gave it in full: I will pick out for special mention Christmas pudding, treacle tart and apple dumplings. Then an almost equally long list of cakes: for instance, dark plum cake (such as you used to get at Buzzard's before the war), short-bread and saffron buns. Also innumerable kinds of biscuit, which exist, of course, elsewhere, but are generally admitted to be better and crisper in England.

Then there are the various ways of cooking potatoes that are peculiar to our own country. Where else do you see potatoes roasted under the joint, which is far and away the best way of cooking them? Or the delicious potato cakes that you get in the north of England? And it is far better to cook new potatoes in the English way – that is, boiled with mint and then served with a little melted butter or margarine – than to fry them as is done in most countries.

Then there are the various sauces peculiar to England. For instance, bread sauce, horse-radish sauce, mint sauce and apple sauce; not to mention redcurrant jelly, which is excellent with mutton as well as with hare, and various kinds of sweet pickle, which we seem to have in greater profusion than most countries.

What else? Outside these islands I have never seen a haggis, except one that came out of a tin, nor Dublin prawns, nor Oxford marmalade, nor several other kinds of jam (marrow jam and bramble jelly, for instance), nor sausages of quite the same kind as ours.

Then there are the English cheeses. There are not many of them but I fancy that Stilton is the best cheese of its type in the world, with Wensleydale not far behind. English apples are also outstandingly good, particularly the Cox's Orange Pippin.

And finally, I would like to put in a word for English bread. All the bread is good, from the enormous Jewish loaves flavoured with caraway seeds to the Russian rye bread which is the colour of black treacle. Still, if there is anything quite as good as the soft part of the crust from an English cottage loaf (how soon shall we be seeing cottage loaves again?) I do not know of it.

No doubt some of the things I have named above could be obtained in continental Europe, just as it is possible in London to obtain vodka or bird's nest soup. But they are all native to our shores, and over huge areas they are literally unheard of.

South of, say, Brussels, I do not imagine that you would succeed in getting hold of a suet pudding. In French there is not even a word that exactly translates 'suet'. The French, also, never use mint in cookery and do not use blackcurrants except as a basis of a drink.

It will be seen that we have no cause to be ashamed of our cookery, so far as originality goes or so far as the ingredients go. And yet it must be admitted that there is a serious snag from the foreign visitor's point of view. This is, that you practically don't find good English cooking outside a private house. If you want, say, a good, rich slice of Yorkshire pudding you are more likely to get it in the poorest English home than in a restaurant, which is where the visitor necessarily eats most of his meals.

It is a fact that restaurants which are distinctively English and which also sell good food are very hard to find. Pubs, as a rule, sell no food at all, other than potato crisps and tasteless sandwiches. The expensive restaurants and hotels almost all imitate French cookery and write their menus in French, while if you want a good cheap meal you gravitate naturally towards a Greek, Italian or Chinese restaurant. We are not likely to succeed in attracting tourists while England is thought of as a country of bad food and unintelligible by-laws. At present one cannot do much about it, but sooner or later rationing will come to an end, and then will be the moment for our national cookery to revive. It is not a law of nature that every restaurant in England should be either foreign or bad, and the first step towards an improvement will be a less long-suffering attitude in the British public itself.

1945

THE ENGLISH CLASS SYSTEM

GEORGE ORWELL

In time of war the English class system is the enemy propagandist's best argument. To Dr Goebbels's charge that England is still 'two nations', the only truthful answer would have been that she is in fact three nations. But the peculiarity of English class distinctions is not that they are unjust – for after all, wealth and poverty exist side by side in almost all countries – but that they are anachronistic. They do not exactly correspond to economic distinctions, and what is essentially an industrial and capitalist country is haunted by the ghost of a caste system.

It is usual to classify modern society under three headings: the upper class, or bourgeoisie, the middle class, or petty bourgeoisie, and the working class, or proletariat. This roughly fits the facts, but one can draw no useful inference from it unless one takes account of the subdivisions within the various classes and realizes how deeply the whole English outlook is coloured by romanticism and sheer snobbishness.

England is one of the last remaining countries to cling to the outward forms of feudalism. Titles are maintained and new ones are constantly created, and the House of Lords, consisting mainly of hereditary peers, has real powers. At the same time England has no real aristocracy. The race difference on which aristocratic rule is usually founded was disappearing by the end of the Middle Ages, and the famous medieval families have almost completely vanished. The so-called old families are those that grew rich in the sixteenth, seventeenth and eighteenth centuries. Moreover, the notion that nobility exists in its own right, that you can be a nobleman even if you are poor, was already dying out in the age of Elizabeth, a fact commented on by Shakespeare. And yet, curiously enough, the English ruling class has never developed into a bourgeoisie plain and simple. It has never become purely urban or frankly commercial. The ambition to be a country gentleman, to own and administer land and draw at least a part of your income from rent, has survived every change. So it comes that each new wave of parvenus, instead of simply replacing the existing ruling class, has adopted its habits, intermarried with it, and, after a generation or two, become indistinguishable from it.

The basic reason for this may perhaps be that England is very small and has an equable climate and pleasantly varied scenery. It is almost impossible in England, and not easy even in Scotland, to be more than twenty miles from a town. Rural life is less inherently boorish than it is in bigger countries with colder winters. And the comparative integrity of the British ruling class – for when all is said and done they have not behaved so contemptibly as their European opposite numbers – is probably bound up with their idea of themselves as feudal landowners. This outlook is shared by considerable sections of the middle class. Nearly everyone who can afford to do so sets up as a country gentleman, or at least makes some effort in that direction. The manor house with its park and its walled gardens reappears in reduced form in the stockbroker's week-end cottage, in the suburban villa with its lawn and herbaceous border, perhaps even in the potted nasturtiums on the window-sill of the Bayswater flat. This widespread day-dream is undoubtedly snobbish, it has tended to stabilize class distinctions and has helped to prevent the modernization of English agriculture: but it is mixed up with a kind of idealism, a feeling that style and tradition are more important than money.

Within the middle class there is a sharp division, cultural and not financial, between those who aim at gentility and those who do not. According to the usual classification, everyone between the capitalist and the weekly wage-earner can be lumped together as 'petty bourgeoisie'. This means that the Harley Street physician, the army officer, the grocer, the farmer, the senior civil servant, the solicitor, the clergyman, the schoolmaster, the bank manager, the speculative builder, and the fisherman who owns his own boat, are all in the same class. But no one in England feels them to belong to the same class, and the distinction between them is not a distinction of income but of accent, manners and, to some extent, outlook. Anyone who pays any attention to class differences at all would regard an army officer with £1,000 a year as socially superior to a shopkeeper with £2,000 a year. Even within the upper class a similar distinction holds good, the titled person being almost always more deferred to than an untitled person of larger income. Middle-class people are really graded according to their degree of resemblance to the aristocracy: professional men, senior officials, officers in the fighting services, university lecturers, clergymen, even the literary and scientific intelligentsia, rank higher than businessmen, though on the whole they earn less. It is a peculiarity of this class that their largest item of expenditure is education. Whereas a successful tradesman will send his son to the local grammar school, a clergyman with half his income will underfeed himself for years in order to send his son to a public school, although he knows that he will get no direct return for the money he spends.

There is, however, another noticeable division in the middle class. The old distinction was between the man who is 'a gentleman' and the man who is 'not a gentleman'. In the last thirty years, however, the demands of modern industry, and the technical schools and provincial universities, have brought into being a new kind of man, middle class in income and to some extent in habits, but not much interested in his own social status. People like radio engineers and industrial chemists, whose education has not been of a kind to give them any reverence for the past, and who tend to live in blocks of flats or housing estates where the old social pattern has broken down, are the most nearly classless beings that England possesses. They are an important section of society, because their numbers are constantly growing. The war, for instance, made necessary the formation of an enormous air force, and so you got thousands of young men of working-class origin graduating into the technical middle class by way of the RAF. Any serious reorganization of industry now will have similar effects. And the characteristic outlook of the technicians is already spreading among the older strata of the middle class. One symptom of this is that intermarriage within the middle class is freer than it used to be. Another is the increasing unwillingness of people below the £2,000 a year level to bankrupt themselves in the name of education.

Another series of changes, probably dating from the Education Act of 1870, is occurring in the working class. One cannot altogether acquit the English working class either of snobbishness or of servility. To begin with there is a fairly sharp distinction between the better-paid working class and the very poor. Even in Socialist literature it is common to find contemptuous references to slum-dwellers (the German word *Lumpenproletariat* is much used), and imported labourers with low standards of living, such as the Irish, are greatly looked down on. There is also, probably, more disposition to accept class distinctions as permanent, and even to accept the upper classes as natural leaders, than survives in most countries. It is significant that in the moment of disaster the man best able to unite the nation was Churchill, a Conservative of aristocratic origins. The word 'Sir' is much used in England, and the man of obviously upper-class appearance can usually get more than his fair share of deference from commissionaires, ticket-collectors, police-men, and the like. It is this aspect of English life that seems most shocking to visitors from America and the Dominions. And the tendency towards servility probably did not decrease in the twenty years between the two wars: it may even have increased, owing chiefly to unemployment.

But snobbishness is never quite separable from idealism. The tendency to give the upper classes more than their due is mixed up with a respect for good manners and something vaguely describable as culture. In the south of England, at any rate, it is unquestionable that most working-class people want to resemble the upper classes in manners and habits. The traditional attitude of looking down on the upper classes as effeminate and 'la-di-dah' survives best in the heavy-industry areas. Hostile nicknames like 'toff' and 'swell' have almost disappeared, and even the *Daily Worker* displays advertisements for 'High-Class Gentleman's Tailor'. Above all, throughout southern England there is almost general uneasiness about the cockney accent. In Scotland and northern England snobbishness about the local accents does exist, but it is not nearly so strong or widespread. Many a Yorkshireman definitely prides himself on his broad U's and narrow A's, and will defend them on linguistic grounds. In London there are still people who say 'fice' instead of 'face', but there is probably no one who regards 'fice' as superior. Even a person who claims to despise the bourgeoisie and all its ways will still take care that his children grow up pronouncing their aitches.

But side by side with this there has gone a considerable growth of political consciousness and an increasing impatience with class privilege. Over a period of twenty or thirty years the working class has grown politically more hostile to the upper class, culturally less hostile. There is nothing incongruous in this: both tendencies are symptoms of the levelling of manners which results from machine civilization and which makes the English class system more and more of an anachronism.

The obvious class differences still surviving in England astonish foreign observers, but they are far less marked, and far less real, than they were thirty years ago. People of different social origins, thrown together during the war in the armed forces, or in factories or offices, or as firewatchers and Home Guards, were able to mingle more easily than they did in the 1914–18 war. It is worth listing the various influences which – mechanically, as it were – tend to make Englishmen of all classes less and less different from one another.

First of all, the improvement in industrial technique. Every year less and less people are engaged in heavy manual labour which keeps them constantly tired and, by hypertrophying certain muscles, gives them a distinctive carriage. Secondly, improvements in housing. Between the two wars rehousing was done mostly by the local authorities, who have produced a type of house (the council house, with its bathroom, garden, separate kitchen, and indoor WC) which is nearer to the stockbroker's villa than it is to the labourer's cottage. Thirdly, the mass production of furniture which in ordinary times can be bought on the hire-purchase system. The effect of this is that the interior of a working-class house resembles that of a middle-class house very much more than it did a generation ago. Fourthly, and perhaps most important of all, the mass production of cheap clothes. Thirty years ago the social status of nearly everyone in England could be determined from his appearance, even at two hundred yards' distance. The working classes all wore ready-made clothes, and the ready-made clothes were not only ill-fitting but usually followed the upper-class fashions of ten or fifteen years earlier. The cloth cap was practically a badge of status. It was universal among the working class, while the upper classes only wore it for golf and shooting. This state of affairs is rapidly changing. Ready-made clothes now follow the fashions closely, they are made in many different fittings to suit every kind of figure, and even when they are of very cheap cloth they are superficially not very different from expensive clothes. The result is that it grows harder every year, especially in the case of women, to determine social status at a glance.

Mass-produced literature and amusements have the same effect. Radio programmes, for instance, are necessarily the same for everybody. Films, though often extremely reactionary in their implied outlook, have to appeal to a public of millions and therefore have to avoid stirring up class antagonisms. So also with some of the big-circulation newspapers. The *Daily Express*, for instance, draws its readers from all strata of the population. So also with some of the periodicals that have appeared in the past dozen years. *Punch* is obviously a middle- and upper-class paper, but *Picture Post* is not aimed at any particular class. And lending libraries and very cheap books, such as the Penguins, popularize the habit of reading and probably have a levelling effect on literary taste. Even taste in food tends to grow more uniform owing to the multiplication of cheap but fairly smart restaurants such as those of Messrs Lyons.

We are not justified in assuming that class distinctions are actually disappearing. The essential structure of England is still almost what it was in the nineteenth century. But real differences between man and man are obviously diminishing, and this fact is grasped and even welcomed by people who only a few years ago were clinging desperately to their social prestige.

Whatever may be the ultimate fate of the very rich, the tendency of the working class and the middle class is evidently to merge. It may happen quickly or slowly, according to circumstances. It has been accelerated by the war, and another ten years of all-round rationing, utility clothes, high income tax, and compulsory national service may finish the process once and for all. The final effects of this we cannot foresee. There are observers, both native and foreign, who believe that the fairly large amount of individual freedom that is enjoyed in England depends on having a well-defined class system. Liberty, according to some, is incompatible with equality. But at least it is certain that the present drift *is* towards greater social equality, and that this is what the great mass of the English people desire.

1944

PREFACE TO THE FIRST GOOD FOOD GUIDE

RAYMOND POSTGATE

First Rule. – If you are in a strange town, without any guidance from a friend or an entry in this list, always prefer a clean and brisk-looking public-house. This for two reasons. The first is that you are more likely to find there than in teashops a survival of the older English tradition of solid eating. In both cases the cooking may well be, at the best, unimaginative, but in a pub, at least, you are not expected to peck like a sparrow. As this Guide will be read by foreign visitors, it should perhaps be added that a clean-looking British public-house with a menu outside is a place where any respectable woman can go for her lunch without any disquiet, and it has no resemblance to a Victorian gin-palace or a pre-Prohibition saloon. She should not go into the Public Bar, which may be rough, but into the Saloon Bar or the Lounge; nor need she drink beer, for lemonade and such are sold equally willingly. She should also, by the way, ignore the statement (made even in the *New Yorker*) that 'British beer should be drunk warm'. British beer should be drunk cool. It should not, it is true, be taken ice-cold like lager. The second reason is that the proprietors of licensed houses are having a difficult time, and deserve the support of all benevolent people. They pay heavily for their licences, and the disproportionate taxes on beer have driven away their customers. If they were to be forced out of business a step would have been made towards prohibition, of which there are advocates even in this country. The crime and misery which prohibition brings have been exemplified from Finland to the United States, and in taking lunch at a public-house a woman can placidly feel she is supporting public order and private virtue.

Second Rule. – Remember, in ordering your food, the particular shortages from which we still suffer. The most serious of these is the shortage of butchers' meat. Unfortunately, roasting and grilling, at which the British used to excel, call specially for butchers' meat, and innkeepers feel obliged to offer roasts and grills when they really have not got the materials. Call for chops, steaks and roast beefs, therefore, only in the country where they are more plentiful, and in towns where the restaurant quite obviously and satisfactorily makes a speciality of them. Never call for them in Soho, or the provincial equivalent. Speaking broadly, a Soho *poulet* done anyway will be good and a Soho pork chop be bad.

In addition, there are certain rules of deportment which are worth observing as follows:

Third Rule. – Read the menu outside. If there is no menu outside, don't go in. A restaurant proprietor who is proud of his bill of fare wants everybody to know about it; he if conceals it, it is for one of two reasons. Either it is so expensive or so unimaginative (or both) that you would not enter if you had read it, or else he 'plays favourites' and reserves the good dishes for his friends, trusting that you will not have the resolution to walk out of his restaurant once you have sat down. If the menu includes something called 'speciality' or 'chef's own choice', walk in. You do not have to eat that particular offering, but the mere listing of it suggests that somebody is giving some attention to the cooking, and knows the difference between one dish and another. That is not a thing which, in Britain, you can take for granted.

Fourth Rule. – On sitting down at your table polish the glasses and cutlery with your napkin. Don't do this ostentatiously or with an annoyed expression, do it casually. You wish to give the impression not that you are angry with this particular restaurant, but that you are suspicious after a lifetime of suffering.

Fifth Rule. – Take a long time reading the bill of fare, and see that your wife decides what she wants first. If the Enemy hears one of you say: 'I'll have whatever you do, dear', he immediately decides he has no serious foes to encounter. What you want to impress on the establishment is that it has to deal with a pair of people who know exactly what they want, and are implacable.

Sixth Rule. – Ask the waiter (or waitress) 'What is good today?' or, if you are in Soho: 'What is the *Specialité de la Maison*?' If he answers the equivalent of 'everything is excellent', then he is a bad waiter and it's probably a bad restaurant. But persist; and he (or she) will probably refer to a seedy-looking man in a boiled shirt (or a cross woman in black silk). That is the person who knows, and from him or her you will find out the one thing that is eatable.

Seventh Rule. – If all these fail, and the food and service is vile, refuse to eat it and refuse to pay. Now, I know this is difficult; and that anger causes indigestion. But consider carefully, which anger is worse, and which causes most indigestion? The anger which exhales itself in open fury, and in the words: 'This food is uneatable; I am going'? Or the anger which simmers throughout the meal, and through the paying of the bill, and rumbles all the way home in the bus or train – frustrated, humiliated, and causing heartburn?

Eighth Rule. – This is for wives and girl friends only. There are two expressions from which you must in all circumstances refrain. Do not say, or indicate by your nose or eyelashes: 'Oh, Henry, you aren't going to make a *scene*!' Do not, on the other hand, go to the other extreme, and indicate: 'Henry, this is intolerable. Deal with these people as they deserve!' Your escort is engaged in delicate and dangerous warfare. You are the reserve battalions; you must give him steady and calm support. You must neither run away nor rush vociferating into the front trenches.

Ninth Rule. – At the end, if all has gone well, read the bill carefully and compare it with the menu. Only fools don't add it up. (If, like myself, you cannot add, frown at it and look as if you were adding it up.) Notice whether 'service' has been added, and, if so, leave either no tip or just the odd money you don't want.

Tenth Rule. – If you have had a good dinner, return thanks. There are three grades of thanks: (1) Simple, for ordinary good service, addressed to the waiter or waitress ('That was very good'). (2) High-grade, delivered to the proprietor ('An excellent dinner, Monsieur Isidore; you have excelled yourself'). (3) Majestic, reserved for very great occasions when you have spent a lot of money: 'That was a remarkable dinner. I should like to thank the chef.'

Observing these rules, you will live to a great age, enjoying your food and never suffering from indigestion; good-looking and well-dressed young women will be anxious to be taken out to dinner by you and waiters will address you by name.

1951

LOVE IS DEAD

JOHN BETJEMAN

England, though not yet so ugly as Northern France and Belgium, is very nearly so. The suburbs which once seemed to me so lovely with their freckled tennis girls and their youths in club blazers have spread so far in the wake of the motor car that there is little but suburb left. We are told that we live in the age of the common man. He would be better described as the suburban man. There is a refinement about him which pervades everything he touches and sees. His books are chosen for him by the librarians, his arguing is done for him by Brains Trusts, his dreams are realized for him in the cinema, his records are played for him by the BBC; the walls of his rooms are in quiet pastel shades, he has cereals for breakfast, and he likes everything in moderation, be it beer, religion or tobacco. He has a wife, a motor car and a child. He is the Borough Engineer, the Listener, the Civil Servant, the Town Clerk, the Librarian, the Art Historian, the Income Tax Inspector. So long as he is not any sort of creative artist he can be assured of an income and a pension at the end. He collects facts as some collect stamps, and he abhors excess in colour, speech or decoration. He is not vulgar. He is not the common man, but the average man, which is far worse.

He is our ruler and he rules by committees. He gives us what most people want, and he believes that what is popular is what is best. He is the explanation of such phenomena as plastic tea-cups, Tizer, light ale, quizzes, mystery tours, cafeterias, discussion groups, Chapels of Unity, station announcers. At his best he is as lovable as Mr Pooter, but he is no leader. He is the Lowest Common Multiple, not even the Highest Common Factor. And we have put him in charge of us, whatever his political party at the moment.

His indifference to the look of things is catching. We discover it in our attitude to the horrors with which the delicate variety of our landscape has been afflicted. We accept without murmur the poles and wires with which the Ministry of Fuel and Power has strangled every village, because they bring electric light and telephones to those who have been without these inestimable benefits. We put up with the foully hideous concrete lamp-standards for which the Borough Engineer and the Ministry of Transport are jointly responsible – each playing off the other – because the corpse-light they spew over road and pavement makes it safer for kiddies to cross and easier for lorries to overtake one another round dangerous corners. We slice off old buildings, fell healthy trees, replace hedges with concrete posts and chain-link fencing, all in the name of 'safety first' which is another phrase for 'hurry past'. We accept the collapse of the fabrics of our old churches, the thieving of lead and objects from them, the commandeering and butchering of our scenery by the services, the despoiling of landscaped parks and the abandonment to a fate worse than the workhouse of our country houses, because we are convinced we must save money. Money is even more important than health or road-widening, so it is obviously infinitely more important than something so indeterminate as beauty. He is a foolish man who in a letter to a paper, or at a local council meeting or in Parliament dares to plead for something because it is good to look at or well made. He is not merely a conservative. He is a crank. He is unpatriotic and prepared to sell the country for an invisible asset. We have ceased to use our eyes because we are so worried about money and illness. Beauty is invisible to us. We live in a right little, tight little clinic.

Oh come, come, Mr Betjeman, aren't you allowing your eloquence to run away with you? Things are not so bad as you imagine. I doubt if there has ever been a time when the desire for culture has been so widespread among our menfolk and womenkind. The interest in ballet, in opera, in chamber music and documentary film is something phenomenal. Museums have never had better seasons, and even picture galleries are widely patronized. Then you must admit that in your field of architecture the government housing schemes, particularly for our rural dwellers, have shewn a taste and reticence unknown in the evil days of private speculation by the jerry builder.

I doubt whether this interest in culture is more than an expression of restlessness. It is reaching for something that cannot be explained in terms of economics. It is a desire for the unworldly. It is a search for religion and it is far smarter than Christianity. As for the taste and reticence of government control, it is certainly easier on the eye than the brutalities of the speculator. By looking only at well-laid out municipal estates and averting one's eyes from the acres of unimaginative modern housing, by forgetting those terrible pipedreams come true of thick-necked brutes with flashy cars, elderly blondes and television sets – those modernistic, Egyptian, beaux-arts and other façades of the new factories outside every large town, by ignoring all these and much more, it is possible to live in a fool's paradise of imagined culture, a sort of Welwyn Garden City of the mind.

But look for a moment at what is really there, and the suburban man is before us again. The old High Street just peeps above the shop façades. The well-known chromium and black gloss, Burton the Tailor of Taste, Hepworth, Halford, Stone, Woolworth & Co., Samuel, Bata, The Fifty Shilling Tailor, the Co-op, have transformed what was once a country town with the characteristics of its county into a home from home for the suburbanite, the concrete standards adding the final touch. When the suburbanite leaves Wembley for Wells he finds that the High Street there is just like home, provided that he does not raise his eyes from the pavement to see the old windows and uneven roofs, or go so far off the beaten track as to wander down a side-alley and see the backs of the houses and their neglected Somerset craftsmanship. Enterprising brewers, backing culture for all they are worth, have turned the old inns into 'pubs' and 'locals'. They have made a virtue of the solemn drinking of their chemicals. They have had Izal and porcelain put in the gents, and made the bar similar to it, save that they have added little tables and a counter. Sawdust and oil lamp or engraved glass and gas light, all the subtle distinction between private, jug and bottle, public and saloon, are being merged into the cleanly classlessness of the road-house. The local crudely-painted inn sign is replaced by the standardized sign with the big brewer's name. And inside, the old photographs of local teams and the framed picture from *Pears' Annual* are put in the dustbin, the walls are painted a light biscuit colour and reproductions of favourite artists of a brewers' publicity board are hung in their place. Nationalized or not yet nationalized, the gradual suburbanization of enterprise continues, the killing of local communities, the stamping out of local rivalries and the supplying of everything by lorry from industrial towns. By luxury coach and local bus the villages are drained of life. Jealous of the misery created by too much road transport, the railways are trying to standardize themselves too. Those colours by which we were wont to know the part of England we were in – red for Midland, brown for Great Western, grained oak for East Anglia, green for Southern – have disappeared. For the convenience of suburbanites who like everything uniform and call it Administration, the trains are one of two colours.

Oh prams on concrete balconies, what will your children see? Oh white and antiseptic life in school and home and clinic, oh soul-destroying job with handy pension, oh loveless life of safe monotony, why were you created?

I see the woman with a scarf twisted round her hair and a cigarette in her mouth. She has put the tea tray down upon the file on which my future depends. I see the man on the chain-belt feeling tired, not screwing the final nuts. In a few months I see the engine falling out of the motor car. I see eight porters, two postmen and an inspector standing dazed for forty minutes on a provincial station, staring into space and waiting for what was once the Great Western which is now forty minutes late. I see those sharp-faced girls behind the buffet and the counter insulting the crowds who come to buy. Too bored to think, too proud to pray, too timid to leave what we are used to doing, we have shut ourselves behind our standard roses; we love ourselves only and our neighbours no longer. As for the Incarnation, that is a fairy story for the children, if we think it healthy for children to be told fairy stories. We prefer facts. They are presented to us by the thousand and we can choose those we like. History must not be written with bias, and both sides must be given, even if there is only one side. We know how many tons of coal are produced per week, how many man-hours there are in a pair of nylons, the exact date and the name of the architect and the style of a building. The Herr-Professor-Doktors are writing everything down for us, sometimes throwing in a little hurried pontificating too, so we need never bother to feel or think or see again. We can eat our Weetabix, catch the 8.48, read the sports column and die; for love is dead.

Oh Lord, who hast taught us that all our doings without charity are nothing worth; Send thy Holy Ghost, and pour into our hearts that most excellent gift of charity, the very bond of peace and of all virtues, without which whosoever liveth is counted dead before thee. Grant this for thine only Son Jesus Christ's sake. [BOOK OF COMMON PRAYER.]

The Mead, Wantage
April, 1952

COTTAGE INDUSTRY

MICHAEL FRAYN

The wonderful thing about having a country cottage, say our good friends Christopher and Lavinia Crumble, is that they can have their good friends (such as us) down for the weekend.

'And the wonderful thing about having our friends down for the weekend,' explains Lavinia, as they take our bags and show us our room, 'is that we really have the chance to *talk* to them down here, away from all the mad rush of town life. Don't we, darling?'

'We like to feel we've created a setting for the sort of relaxed house-party thing that used to be such an important part of the civilized way of life in the past,' says Christopher. 'Plain living and high thinking – that kind of thing. We find ourselves talking like *mad* down here. Don't we, darling?'

Apparently the place was absolutely derelict when they found it. All their friends thought they were *crazy*. But of course they got it for a song, and they did it all up themselves.

'We really have put a tremendous amount of work into it. Haven't we, darling?'

'People think we've been spending our weekends idling about in the countryside. But we've scarcely had time to sit down! You really can't imagine how much we've had to do. Can they, darling?'

Apparently *all* the beams we can now see were covered with plaster and wallpaper when they moved in! The doorway we've just come through didn't *exist*! The floor we're now standing on was *completely* rotten! The whole house *reeked* of mildew! We can't really appreciate its present condition, of course, not having seen it in its original state.

'I mean, Christopher did have a tiny worry when we bought it that we might be doing local people out of a house. You know what Christopher's like! But it was absolutely *derelict*. . . .'

'And of course what these people want is really some neat little two-up-and-two-down semi. Isn't it, darling?'

'And if we hadn't done it up somebody else would have. Wouldn't they, darling?'

'They're not all as tender-hearted as we are. And we have put the most tremendous amount of work into the place.'

Have we admired their view, they ask? Oh, God, the view – no, we haven't. Admire, admire. Only six miles or so beyond that electricity sub-station, apparently is the Vale of Relpham, which Walter Bridmore mentions in one of his novels! The window-frame itself, it appears, is treated with Osterman's 'Windowjoy' polyester window-frame sealer.

They expect we'd like a wash etcetera after our journey. It seems terrible to interrupt our discussion of architecture and literature for anything so mundane as a wash etcetera. But there's plenty for us to admire and meditate upon in the bathroom. Apparently Christopher did most of the plumbing himself, and is rather proud of his handiwork. And we're to help ourselves to hot water as lavishly as we like, because they've installed a Supa-Heata, the literature about which we must remind them to give us before we go.

Over lunch the conversation turns to the world of art.

'Did you admire that old Agricultural Show poster in the loo?' inquires Christopher. 'We're frightfully proud of it. Lavinia got it from a little man over in Market Strayborough. Didn't you, darling?'

'Of course, the loo's our great triumph altogether. I found a little man in Morton Winchevers who built us the septic tank for about half what we'd have had to pay a big firm.'

'And she found another little man practically next door to the little man in Market Strayborough who got hold of that Victorian pedestal and cistern for us. Lavinia's got an absolute genius for getting hold of little men. Haven't you, darling?'

In the afternoon we go for a stroll, so that our hosts can point out various features of the locality of which they're particularly proud, and introduce us to one or two *marvellous* locals we absolutely must meet, now that the Crumbles have succeeded by dint of hard work and perseverance in penetrating their natural rural reserve. The long grass in the meadows and the summery smell of the cow-parsley along the lanes put everyone in a gently reflective mood.

'You can get down here in $4\frac{1}{2}$ hours, you know,' says Christopher, 'if you avoid Snaith, and take that little road through Chocking which comes out just this side of Griever. . . .'

'Or $4\frac{1}{4}$, if you don't get held up by all that terrible weekend traffic to the coast where you cross the main road at Westchamps Peverel. . . .'

'Which is awfully good, you know, when you think about it. It means that we can leave here at half-past four on a Monday morning, and be in our respective offices by nine. . . .'

Tea on the lawn, of course, sparks off an earnest debate on the nature of lawns in general, and of Christopher's efforts upon this one in particular, which we gather are beyond all praise, given the patch of thistles and nettles he had to start with.

Night comes down, obscuring the lawn wrested with such difficulty from the weeds, and the much-discussed patch of earth which Lavinia hasn't yet decided whether to fill with orodigia or flowering pangloss, and the blue paintwork on the doors and windows (Luxibrite's Melanesian Blue, which they think – and we definitely agree – is a much more subtle colour than Housallure's Gulfstream or Goyamel's Stratosphere); making the peripatetic conversationalists on the terrace only shadowy shapes as they murmur on into the dusk.

'I'll put the terrace light on. No, no – no trouble at all. We're rather proud of our electric lighting, as a matter of fact. Aren't we, darling?'

'Honestly, you'd never believe the struggle we had to get this place on the supply. It seems a pity not to use it, now we've got it. Doesn't it, darling?'

Yes, it's wonderful, as the Crumbles say, to get away from the dreadful rat-race in town for a day or two, and take a look at the one in the country for a change.

1966

AKENFIELD

RONALD BLYTHE

I was born in Akenfield. It was in the year 1923. I have spent all my life here. I have the family records back to the eighteenth century and my name is mentioned in Domesday Book. We were at Saxmundham then. Then there was a time when we got lost – right out Dennington way. But we found our path eventually. I have a lot of my grandfather's features, although I'm not so tall as he was. I have his hands. Hands last a long time, you know. A village sees the same hands century after century. It is a marvellous thing but it's true. My grandfather was a most extraordinary man and very headstrong. He'd got a way of his own and I tend to take after him. My father started work when he was ten and I started when I was fourteen.

My family had been Liberal till several years ago, then they changed over to Conservative. I don't know why; it was before my time. They had damn little to conserve so I don't know why they did it. Suffolk people are cagey about politics. It makes me laugh when the Tory women stand outside the voting booths on election day 'just ticking the names off the Electoral Roll', as they say. How on earth do they reckon they'll ever discover a thing about the village politics? All the same, I don't think it should be allowed. It makes people nervous. I have a tendency to be like Charles Bradlaugh, who was a Suffolk man. I am not an atheist but I have strong views about politics and the Church. Bradlaugh wasn't against Church, he was against the set-up. I'm against the set-up. But I think it was an extremely good thing that religion should be accepted as the saviour of civilization. So I think it right that it should be carried on. If you forsake religion, it's back to the savages. This is what is happening now. Whatever you think, this is what makes you. You don't have to tell folk everything you think. I have a lot of personal views about religion, for instance, which I never tell a soul. But I've often been tempted, particularly when I was young. I saw cases of men – grown men – in this village, packing their bait to spend the whole Sunday at chapel. People used to go to chapel at nine in the morning and not come home until eight at night. It is the truth. Most of them behaved shocking during the week. It's a fact. They were nothing but a lot of bloody hypocrites. Suffolk used to worship Sunday, not God. I don't know why they all went to this trouble. Anybody with a mite of common sense could see how useless it was, chapel, chapel, chapel, Sunday, Sunday, Sunday. Best suits. They were Baptists. *What were they trying to do?* There were so many of them they could have set the whole village on its ear had they followed Jesus. But all you heard them say was Sunday. Bugger Sunday, I say, and praise God when you can. People never think why they go to church or chapel, they just go. It is very strange.

I was born during the bad times. My brothers and myself went to school for part of the day and to work for the rest of it. When we left school at half past three we'd go gleaning, picking up beans and all such things as that. We'd most likely work till eight if it stayed light. We biked to school at

Framlingham. It was 1934 time. Things weren't very sharp. Father was making out by killing pigs for Danny Linton at Pettistree so we had to bike from school to home, eat some bread and cheese, or whatever there was – and there wasn't much – get an old sack and then bike on to Danny's farm to collect the pigs' insides. Then we biked home with them and tipped them out on the scullery floor and scraped them. We had to get them as white as a board, scratching out all the filth with the back of an old knife. Then we washed them in salty water and – hey presto! – sausage skins. But it wasn't the end. There were all these pails and pails of muck to be got rid of. We had to bike out of the village and bury it. On Saturdays we used to take a bundle of these skins to old Boot the butcher and he'd give us a three-cornered lump of brisket, all fat and bone, and weighing about a stone, in exchange. But even this is better than what happened in 1930, the big black year. In 1930 we had blackbird pie for Christmas dinner – and we had to catch the blackbirds before we had the pie! It had got to Christmas morning and we were going to make do when my father said, 'Come on, boys, let's try a blackbird!' We knocked a few over quite easy. I could take you to the spot where we did it. We cooked the pie in the brick oven.

This was the year my grandfather had to shut down the forge. He never went back to it. I used to walk by it, eyeing it and thinking. But nothing was rosy wherever you looked. Nearly everybody went out of business. Nothing was sold. People who had left school began to think about the Big House. You realized that it was there, with all the gardeners, grooms and maids and food. You have to face it, the Big House was then an asset to the village. It paid us to raise our hats, which is why we did it. I hear people run the gentry down now but they were better than the farmers in a crisis. Theirs was the only hand which fed us which we could see. So we bowed a bit; it cost nothing, even if it wasn't all courtesy. Nobody left, nobody went away. People were content. However hard up they were, they stayed content. The boys had the arse out of their trousers, no socks and the toes out of their boots. My brothers and myself were like this, yet so happy. I think other families were the same. The village kept close.

The biggest change which I have seen in Akenfield is the growth of discontent. Greed. Nobody ever said, 'Bugger you, Jack, my head is out!' when I was a boy. When you wanted help it was given. It was 'Thank you very much', and that was that. You mustn't pay. It was good enough for a row if you offered to pay. Payment was a crime. This was how things were when I told my parents that I wanted to go into the family business. My grandfather had died and my grandmother was paying a man to open the forge and try and do some trade. My father couldn't afford to pay the apprenticeship fee of half-a-crown a week, so I had to do another job as well. I worked from eight to five at the forge and then three more hours night and morning for a man who kept 160 pigs. I was paid a-penny-a-pig-a-week to feed and clean them out. They weren't the little old things you get today, they were big pigs. Enormous . . . 30–35 stone apiece. The pigman used to pay me when the pigs went to market. It would sometimes come to £5 10s., which was a tidy fortune.

It was all agricultural work at the forge. Mostly shoeing. All the horses were still with us and at seventeen I was shoeing an average of eight horses a day. I remember making my first horseshoe. I started work at the forge on August 2nd and I made this shoe on August 4th. They put you straight into the collar in those days! There was no messing about. When you got a job you began doing it right away. You were expected to catch on quick.

The man my grandmother allowed to run the forge was old and when I was just over seventeen he retired, and I had to carry on alone. I now had to do every mortal thing myself. What I didn't know I had to find out or make up. There was nobody to ask. It was a terrible job, but there, we got over it. It was still all farm work, of course. Mostly shoeing. The horseman would stand at the head while the work was being done, so that was a bit of help. He could hold it like. I was such a thin little lad it was a masterpiece how I could hold anything! There was no thought of what you might call art-and-craft work, only plough-coulters, harrows, door-hinges and such farm things. There was no money about; everybody was bare-poor. I charged 6s. 8d. to put four shoes on a horse. I reckoned that with a quiet horse with good feet the task would take an hour. I hardly made a profit. There are still plenty of horses round here, of course – hunt horses, pony-club horses – it is most unusual for a village to have so many of them around. And I don't mind shoeing them. The trouble is that people who have these kind of horses reckon on you shoeing them for next to nothing. I won't do that. Not now. If people will pay what I charge and won't grumble, then I'll shoe for them, but not otherwise. I am supposed to have served a five-year apprenticeship, and if work isn't worth a little when you've done that, then blast them. I won't mess after it. I remember how hard it was to make myself free, for that is what I was really up to when I was here all alone before the war. I don't know what it is, I can't explain it, but you see I am the only one out of all my family – and there are five of us brothers – who had any intention of coming to the smithy. My brothers couldn't have cared less about the place. I wanted to come, *had* to come. But it is silly to be sentimental. What I sometimes think is that I am my grandfather, an old one. It is the truth when I say that I can sit in the shop of a Sunday, smoking my pipe, and be as happy as if I were sitting in the house. I wasn't born soon enough, that is the trouble. By rights, I should be dead and gone. I think like the old people. I have a tendency to do what I want to do, if the maggot bites. However pressing matters are, I do what I fancy. I think, probably, my attitude could be wrong. We have our pressures now with bills and bank managers and book-keeping, but I say to myself, this is not the highest thing; this is business. You are a tradesman; this is the highest thing. Making, doing. I feel I should have lived during the 1700s. That would have done me. But I am losing my place, aren't I?

Well, the war came, and one or two German prisoners came to help me out. They were pleasant lads. When they went back I had a boy from the army school, after he had finished his training. He had been an army apprentice farrier and I finished him off. When he left, one or two more arrived and for the first time in my life I had a few minutes to spare, so I began to amuse myself by making ornamental things. I entered one or two competitions and won prizes. And then, after the war, this wonderful thing happened, I married. The business was steady now. I had over a hundred horses on my books which had to be shod three times a year, which meant that I was making 1,200 shoes a year. Of course, the horses were passing, but so slowly that it didn't seem possible that they were soon to disappear off the farms for ever. I still saw the things I sent to the crafts section of the Suffolk Show as a hobby. I couldn't imagine living by such work.

Then new people came and bought up the old houses. They'd spend a mint of money 'putting it all back as it was'. They couldn't buy the things they needed for the restoration; they hadn't been made for donkey's years. So I had to start making them again. My wife went round, keeping her eye open for bolts, latches, handles, grates; drawing them and finding out their dates, and I made more of them as exactly as you're not likely to tell the difference. Mind you, it took time. It took all hours. But it was a fine thing for me to have something lying on the bench before me made by one of the old men, and my hands doing again what his had done. The new business grew and grew. The Trust House people had bought the Suffolk coaching-houses and now they were doing them up regardless. They wanted to do everything in the old-fashioned way, all mortise-and-tenon studs and plaster. And, of course, hand-made nails. I made all the nails they used. They were each forged and hammered from the hot spar. And they were expensive, I can tell you. You can buy a pound of ordinary machine-made nails for 9d. but mine cost 4$\frac{1}{2}d$. each. A strange thing happened while I was hammering these nails. They found a great pile of Roman nails in the Scottish mountains, all as bright as if they had been made yesterday. I could quite understand why this was because these nails would have been made from lowmore which doesn't rust. It is steel which rusts. Do you know what I thought when I heard of these great Roman nails? – those would have been like the nails they would have used for the Crucifixion. They would have been made from iron smelted with charcoal. This is why the Swedish iron is so good because they were using charcoal right up to my day. But you can't buy iron now; it is all steel. They will smelt it especially for you if you order ten tons of it, but charge you a ridiculous price.

We have to make do with mild steel for all our work, and this is why you get all this trouble with agricultural things breaking sudden like. These steels are too strong. They cannot give. They just get fatigue and snap. They are too good for rough purposes – if you can call anything too good. Iron would do the job much better. But then you can't electric-weld iron. It has to be fire-welded. That is why they manufacture mild steel to fit in with modern methods of production. It is not easier to work – oh no! It is simply easier to weld because you are using electricity and not fire. But iron is always better for bending and real forging. The various parts of the new agricultural machines are all profiled out in the gas-flame; they are cut out flat, not bent. All this has happened during the last few years, so everything is different. We've got a profile machine which cuts the pattern out in a piece of tin. You screw it in on top, light the gas – propane and oxygen – and work with a cutting-head with an electric motor and a magnet attached to it. This runs around your plate and carves out its shape in the metal below. Ours will cut two inches thick. Before this method was invented everything at the smithy had to be forged and knocked into shape.

I don't have a catalogue. I don't like making two of anything. I find out what people can either afford or mean to pay and do a design in keeping with the price. We like to think that when a customer gets something from the forge it is their individual thing. But how much longer we can stick it, I don't know. Not long, I fancy. The time must come when we shall have to settle down to a standard line. It will be a terrible pity if this should happen. So many smiths are just copying the old designs. And making a poor job of it. It is abusing the old tradesmen. I believe that we should work as they worked; this isn't copying, it is getting back into their ways, into their skins. We should either do this or we should go right ahead, like the Germans, and do something absolutely new. The Germans are streets and streets ahead of us with metal designing. They wouldn't do this pretty scrollwork which all the English people love; they only do beautiful, genuine 1960 designs. I show some books of these modern German patterns to the customers. They hesitate. I try and push them, they back away. The man with money to spend on a village house in England has got to have everything quaint and curly.

I never employ extra men, no matter how big the job. I stay up late – we all five stay up late – we crowd the hours. You can't bring outsiders into a place like this; they wouldn't fit in. They would upset the whole atmosphere. I have the boys. They were born in the village, they went to the village school and then they came to me, and I have taught them how to work. And soon they became part of it. It would be fatal to bring in an outsider to spoil it all. When we do a big job we have to *work*. This is understood. Eventually, we get through it. A big job is a big experience.

We don't do more repairs to farm machines than we are forced to. The farmers get most of their repairs done by some mechanically-minded youngster who drives the tractor and they resent having to pay money to people like me. But we don't turn anybody away because the old business was built up on farm work and it is our moral duty to stay within the farming band. We haven't told the farmers not to come. We never did make ploughshares. This is cast-iron work and has to be done in a foundry. But we used to do the plough-coulters – the cutting knives. It was a swine of a job. You always swear terrible when you are doing it. You'd think you'd welded it on and beaten it out, and then you hadn't. It was best not to come to the forge when the plough-coulters were being mended – not if you were squeamish. My father, who was a butcher by trade, said, 'The Lord sent the meat and the devil sent the cooks'. The devil sent the coulters too.

I think I am a dedicated man. I won't have financial trouble – I mean, to hell with it! I won't have life all spoilt by money. I don't worry about dying, although I am mid-way through, but I dread being old and unable to work. We are all living in the rat-race, however far out in the wilds we are. The village is so quiet now. Nobody walks about in it. You don't say you saw your neighbour, you say you passed his car. People wave and toot where they used to talk. They're all out for what they can get. Nobody goes to look at what somebody else has done and have a chat about it. If you saw somebody ploughing or clearing the marsh, you used to meet up with a neighbour and say, 'Let's go and see what he's up to.'

I talk to the boys. I train them in 'steps'. The oldest is twenty-two now and doesn't want much supervising. But the others are fifteen and seventeen and you have to watch them. I treat them as individuals. There's young Den, if you said something amiss to him it would upset him so much you wouldn't do nothing with him for a week. Big as an ox and soft as a girl. He is a great tradesman already. But Robin, you have to swear at him regular once a month, or you wouldn't do anything with him. If those two boys had been apprenticed together, you would have made a man of one and offended the other – or vice versa. You must never offend a boy. I always look at the parents before I take an apprentice. If you know the home, you already know the son.

I'm against sport. I hate it. If work and sport changed places, this country wouldn't be in a muddle. Sport and holidays have become a mania, an insanity. If anybody wanted a holiday, I wouldn't stop them from taking one, but I hate holidays as much as I hate sport, and that's saying something. These boys won't be like me; they'll never work as I have worked – and perhaps they shouldn't have to. I've been working two pieces of metal together on the anvil with the sledge-hammer, when my vest caught fire and I daren't pause to put it out! When two men were working, hitting the anvil in turn, they would get each other's sparks. You would be open right down the front and they flew against your nakedness. A blacksmith always rolls his shirtsleeves under, so the sparks don't lodge in the folds. Now, with the emery sparks, we have to watch out for eye-trouble.

I am worried about everything getting too big. I have been learning how to pack things up to go to America – when only ten years ago, if an order had been finished it lay in the corner of the shop until somebody in the village felt like picking it up. I sometimes want to be alone again. I'm fond of the boys, and they work well, but they take the private spell out of my shop. They are not to blame. It is because everything is rushing so. I am still young myself, and yet I worked here for years with just a pair of tongs, a couple of hammers and a four-and-a-half-gallon cask of beer under the bench. And an old drinking horn which had never been washed up. Now I am packing these things for the United States. I think life would be fuller if I wasn't, and that's a fact.

DUFFLE COATS AND SPOTTED DICK

What a weird place and what a rum lot England and the English must seem at first sight! Clive James is amazed to find the snow is not some kind of dry powder supplied by the effects department, but very wet; Karel Capek finds that London smells of petrol, burnt grass, and tallow; Najaf Koolee Meerza is so taken with the singing of children in church that he confesses it has nourished his heart; a little Indian girl, on the other hand, is afraid her face will turn black if she goes out in the sun. What struck Simone de Beauvoir when she came for Easter fifty years ago was the women coming down to breakfast in tea gowns, the men in bowler hats, the snobbery of Oxford, and that insipid, synthetic food near Euston station (surely Soho would have been a better bet?).

SOFT LANDING

CLIVE JAMES

When we got off the ship in Southampton in that allegedly mild January of 1962 I had nothing to declare at customs except goose-pimples under my white nylon drip-dry shirt. This was not because I had been prudent in my spending but because I had spent the last of my money in Singapore, plus twenty pounds I had borrowed from one of my cabin mates – and which I still owe him, come to think of it. The money had gone on a new suit which I didn't actually have with me in my luggage. The tailors in Singapore's Change Alley had taken my measurements and promised to send the finished suit after me to London. This had seemed like a sensible arrangement, so I had handed over the cash, thereby depriving myself of any leeway for a spending spree later on in Aden. I thus missed out on the chance, seized by most of the other Australians of my own age on the ship, to be guided by the expertise of Arab salesmen in the purchase of German tape-recorders and Japanese cameras at a fraction of the price – something like five-fourths – prevailing in their countries of origin.

In the crater of Aden, while my compatriots knowingly examined the Arabic guarantee forms for machines whose batteries were mysteriously unavailable, I hovered in the heat-hazed background, sullenly attempting not to catch the remaining eye of a beggar whose face had otherwise been entirely chewed off by a camel. It had been very hot in Aden. In England it was very cold: colder than I had ever known. The customs men did a great deal of heavy-handed chaffing about how you cobbers couldn't really call this a winter, ho ho, and what we would look like if there really was a winter, har har, and so on. Their accents were far funnier than their sense of humour. They all seemed to have stepped out of the feature list of an Ealing comedy for the specific purpose of unpacking our luggage and charging us extra for everything in it. My own luggage consisted mainly of one very large suitcase made of mock leather – i.e., real cardboard. This compendium was forced into rotundity by a valuable collection of tennis shorts, running shorts,

Hawaiian shirts, T-shirts, Hong Kong thong rubber sandals, short socks, sandshoes and other apparel equally appropriate for an English winter. The customs officer sifted through the heap twice, the second time looking at me instead of at it, as if my face would betray the secret of the illicit fortunes to be made by smuggling unsuitable clothing across half the world.

As the people all around me were presented with huge bills, I gave silent thanks for being in possession of nothing assessable for duty. The ship's fool – a pimply, bespectacled British emigrant called Tanner who was now emigrating back the other way – was near tears. In Aden and Port Said he had bought, among other things, two tape recorders, a Japanese camera called something like a Naka-mac with a silver box full of lenses, a portable television set slightly larger than an ordinary domestic model but otherwise no different except that it had a handle, a stuffable leather television pouffe for watching it from, a hi-fi outfit with separate components, and a pair of binoculars so powerful that it frightened you to look through them, especially if you saw Tanner. Most of this gear he had about his person, although some of it was packed in large cardboard boxes, because all this was happening in the days before miniaturization, when an amplifier still had valves. The customs officer calculated the duty owing and confronted him with the total, at which he sat down on his boxed telescope and briefly wept. It was more money than he had in the world, so he just signed away the whole mountain of gear and walked on through a long door in the far side of the shed.

A few minutes afterwards I walked through the same door and emerged in England, where it was gently snowing on to a bus full of Australians. There was a small cloud in front of my face which I quickly deduced to be my breath. The bus was provided by the Overseas Visitors' Club, known for short as the OVC. The journey by ship, the bus ride to London and a week of bed and breakfast in Earls Court were all part of the deal, which a few years later would have been called a Package, but at that time was still known as a Scheme. The general thrust of the Scheme was to absorb some of the culture shock, thus rendering it merely benumbing instead of fatal. As the bus, which strangely insisted on calling itself a coach, headed north – or west or east or wherever it was going, except, presumably, south – I looked out into the English landscape and felt glad that I had not been obliged to find my way through it unassisted.

The cars seemed very small, with no overhang at either end. A green bus had 'Green Line' written on it and could therefore safely be assumed to be a Green Line bus, or coach. The shops at the side of the road looked as if they were finely detailed painted accessories for an unusually elaborate Hornby Dublo model railway table-top layout. Above all, as well as around all and beyond all, was the snow, almost exactly resembling the snow that fell in English films on top of people like Alastair Sim and Margaret Rutherford. What I was seeing was a familiar landscape made strange by being actual instead of transmitted through cultural intermediaries. It was a deeply unsettling sensation, which everybody else in the coach must have shared, because for the first time in twelve thousand miles there was a prolonged silence. Then one of the wits explained that the whole roadside façade would fold down after we had roared by, to reveal factories manufacturing rust-prone chromium trim for the Standard Vanguard. There was some nervous laughter and the odd confident assurance that we were already in the outskirts of London. Since the outskirts of London were well known to embrace pretty well everywhere in the south of England up to the outskirts of Birmingham, this seemed a safe bet.

A few ploughed fields presented themselves so that the girls, still pining for members of the ship's crew, might heave a chorus of long sighs at the bunny rabbits zipping across the pinwhale corduroy snow. After that it was one continuous built-up area turning to streetlight in the gathering darkness of what my watch told me was only mid-afternoon. Enveloped in many layers of clothing, people thronging the footpaths seemed to be black, brown or, if white and male, to have longer hair than the females. High to the left of an arching flyover shone the word WIMPEY, a giant, lost, abstract adjective carved from radioactive ruby.

There was no way of telling, when we arrived, that the place we were getting off at was called Earls Court. In those days it was still nicknamed Kangaroo Valley but there were no obvious signs of Australia except the foyer of the OVC, crowded with young men whose jug ears stuck out unmistakably from their short haircuts on either side of a freckled area of skin which could be distinguished as a face, rather than a neck, only by the presence of a nose and a mouth. Here I was relieved to find out that I had been assigned to the same dormitory room as my cabin mates, at a hostel around the corner. So really we were still on board ship, the journey from the OVC foyer around the corner to the hostel being the equivalent of a brisk turn around the deck, while carrying a large suitcase.

The snow was falling thickly enough to replenish a half-inch layer on the footpath, so that my black Julius Marlowe shoes could sink in slightly and, I was interested to notice, be fairly rapidly made wet. It hadn't occurred to me that snow would have this effect. I had always assumed snow to be some form of solid. In the hostel I counted up my financial resources. They came to just a bit more than ten pounds in English money. Ten pounds bought quite a lot at that time, when eight pounds a week was a labourer's living wage and you could get a bar of chocolate for threepence, a chunky hexagonal coin which I at first took to be some form of washer and then spent a lot of time standing on its edge on the bedside table while figuring out what to do next. Improvising brilliantly, I took some of the small amount of money over and above the ten pounds and invested in an aerogramme, which I converted into a begging letter and addressed to my mother, back there in Sydney with no telephone. Her resources being far from limitless, I did my best not to make the letter too heartrending, but after it was finished, folded and sealed I had to leave it on the radiator for the tears to dry out, after which it was wrinkled and dimpled like an azure poppadum.

Dinner in the hostel made me miss the ship-board menu, which until then I would have sworn nothing ever could. What on earth did a spotted dick look like before the custard drowned it? A glass mug of brown water was provided which we were assured was beer. I sipped fitfully at mine while everybody else watched. When I showed no signs of dengue fever or botulism, they tried theirs. Having rolled inaccurately into my bunk, I discovered, like my two cabin mates, that I couldn't sleep for the silence of the engines.

Next day there was still a tendency to cling together. I was in a three-man expedition that set out to find Piccadilly Circus by following a map of the Underground railway system, starting at Earls Court station. To reach the station we had to travel some way on the surface, keeping a wary eye out for hostile natives. It was a relief to find that in daylight at any rate a sizeable part of the local population was Australian. At that time the Earls Court Australians had not yet taken to carrying twelve-packs of Foster's lager, and the broad-brimmed Akubra hat with corks dangling from the brim was never to be more than a myth, but there was no mistaking those open, freckled, eyeless faces, especially when they were sticking out of the top of navy-blue English duffle-coats religiously acquired as a major concession towards blending into the scenery. My own duffle-coat was bright yellow in colour and would not have helped me blend into anything except a sand dune, but luckily it was hanging in my cupboard back in Kogarah, Sydney. Or unluckily, if you considered how cold I felt in my light-green sports coat with the blue fleck. Or would have felt, if I had been less excited. But we were going down in a lift through a hole in the ground to another hole in the ground which would take us under London to Piccadilly Circus. Piccadilly! I even knew what it meant. It was a tailor's term, something to do with sleeves. No doubt the tailors had started a circus when times got tough.

Knowingness evaporated when the tube train pulled into the station. The train was so small that for a moment I thought it was a toy – another component of the Hornby Dublo table-top layout, except this time under the table. You almost had to bend your head getting into it. The electric trains in Sydney were sensibly provided with four feet of spare headroom in case any visiting American basketballer wanted to hitch a ride without taking off his stilts. He might have stood out because of his colour, but at least he wouldn't be bent over double. In this train he would bent over double, but at least he wouldn't stand out because of his colour. Half the people in the crowded carriage seemed to be black or dark brown. They were dressed just the same as the white people and often conspicuously better. I had entered my first multiracial society, all for the price of a tube ticket. If I had come from an apartheid country, I would have had a kit of reflexes that I could have set about modifying. But coming from a monotone dominion whose Aborigines were still thought of, at that time, as something between a sideshow and an embarrassment, I had nothing to go on except a blank feeling which I hoped was receptivity. A sperm whale feeding on a field of squid – not giant squid, just those little squidlets that form its basic diet – cruises along with its mouth open, taking everything in. That was me, open-mouthed to new experience. The sperm whale looks the same when drowning, of course: going down and down with its gob wide open and the pressure building up and up. By Knightsbridge we were making nervous jokes about a journey to the centre of the earth. The escalators leading to the surface at Piccadilly were like sets from *Things to Come*. Then we popped out of the ground and stood rooted to the mushy pavement by the Sheer Englishness of it all. 'Coca-Cola' said a wall of neon, glowing as if day were night – a fair assessment of the overcast morning.

But Eros was sufficiently evocative all by himself and we set off for Buckingham Palace with high hearts, going by way of Nelson's Column and the Admiralty Arch. The Mall showed pink through the churned slush, St James's Park was a spun–sugar cake-scape with clockwork ducks, and a flag on the Palace indicated that She was at home. The Guard obligingly began to change itself just as we arrived, the Coldstreams handing over to the Grenadiers. Tourism was still under control at that time so it was possible to catch the odd glimpse of the participating soldiers, instead of, as now, seeing nothing except the rear view of Norwegians carrying full camping apparatus and holding up cameras to fire blind over the hulking back-packs of other Norwegians standing in front of them. Needless to say we did not regard ourselves as tourists. Whatever our convictions, we were children of the Commonwealth, not to say the Empire. One of us rather embarrassingly stood to attention. It was not myself, since I was a radical socialist at the time, but I understood. It was something emotional that went back to Chad Valley tin toys, Brock fireworks and the every-second-Christmas box of W. Britain's lead soldiers. I remembered my set of Household Cavalry with the right arms that swivelled and the swords held upright, except for the troop leader whose sabre stuck out in line with his extended arm while his horse pranced. When his arm worked loose and fell off I wodged it back on with a gasket of cigarette paper. I can remember remembering this while the band played 'British Grenadiers', and can remember how wet my eyes were, mainly from the cold that was creeping upward from my feet. At first they had been numb. Now they felt like something Scott of the Antarctic might have made a worried note about in his diary if I had been a member of his expedition. As the officers on parade screamed at each other nose to nose from under their forward-tilting bearskins, it began occurring to me that the climate was going to be a problem.

Or part of a larger problem, that of money. There was more sightseeing in the next few days, with the National Gallery putting everything else in perspective. Indeed it put its own contents into perspective, since here again, even more strikingly, there was a discrepancy between the actual and what had been made familiar in reproduction. The Rokeby Venus, for example, was supposed to be the size of half a page in a quarto art book, not as big as the serving window of Harry's Café de Wheels at Woolloomooloo. She looked a bit murky at that stage – they cleaned her a few years later, and perhaps overdid it – but her subtly dimpled bottom, poised at the height of the viewer's eyes, made you wonder about Velázquez's professional detachment. Though most of the rooms in the gallery were still a mystery to me, I was confident enough, or ignorant enough, to decide that Art with a capital 'A' was going to be a source of sensual gratification on all levels. At the Tate Gallery I was relieved to find that the Paul Klee pictures were roughly the same size as in the books. But just to reach the galleries by tube was costing money, and meanwhile time was running out.

There was a grand total of eight pounds left and it didn't help when I lost the lot, along with my prize yellow pig-skin wallet, at Waldo Laidlaw's wedding party. Arriving out of the sky in his usual grand style – absolutely nobody else you knew could afford to fly – Waldo instantly married one of the girls from my ship. Apparently it had all been arranged back in Australia. The party was in the as-yet-unfurnished shell of a ground-floor flat in that part of Camden Town where you could overlook Regent's Park if you could find your way on to the roof. In Waldo's words, overlooking it was easy, because you couldn't see it. All the Australian advertising types were there, the women unattainably well-groomed and the men sporting Chelsea boots, an elastic-sided form of footwear I had not previously encountered. I was the only one dressed for the Australian summer, with three T-shirts and a pair of running shorts on under my Hawaiian shirt and poplin trousers. Feeling the heat of the crowded room, I took off my jacket, left it in the bedroom on the bed with the overcoats, and prepared to dance.

A hit record called 'Let's Twist Again' was playing over and over. Several people among the sophisticated throng had already reached exhibition standard in dancing the Twist. I think I could have matched them through sheer inspiration, but my shoes were in bad shape and tended to stick where they were, cruelly restricting my rate and radius of swivel. In the kitchen there were big tins of brown water you could open with your thumb. I treated the stuff with the contempt it deserved, pronouncing its alcoholic content to be minimal. Pronouncing its algolic contender be mineral. Pronouncing my own name with difficulty. After kneeling in the toilet for some time with my head resting in the bowl I felt fighting fit again and all set to lie down. It was then that I found my wallet missing and did my best to spoil Waldo's celebration by telling him that one of his guests must have lifted it from my jacket. It was courteous of him to arrange a lift home for me instead of throwing me in the canal. When I sobered up a couple of days later it became evident that the wallet must have first of all dropped through the large hole which had developed in the bottom of my jacket's inner pocket and then fallen through the detached lining into the street before I even got to the party. It was still a good jacket otherwise though, with leather buttons like scout woggles.

So the week at the OVC hostel was all used up. One of my cabin mates, the one who had stood to attention in front of Buckingham Palace, moved out to fulfil his ambition of becoming a British officer who would protrude from the top of a rapidly moving armoured car while wearing a beret. At Sydney University he had been an actor but it was now clear that this training had always had no other purpose except to further the attainment of his real aim in life. Though his hyphenated surname would probably have got him the job anyway, it couldn't have hurt his chances that he wore clothes like Dennis Price and talked like Terry-Thomas. I had little patience with his hunger for military tradition but hated to see him go. My other cabin mate was in London to study music. Having made his arrangements, he now moved off and started doing so. Talking grandly of my intention to take a small flat in Knightsbridge, I managed to get some loose change off him before he left, but not enough, and since he was the very man I had touched in order to finance the Singapore suit I could scarcely dun him for a more substantial contribution. A postal order from home would be another week arriving. The snow in Hyde Park was not deep enough for me to build an igloo and my suitcase, although absurdly large when carried, was too cramped to live in. So I lugged it around another corner and occupied the living-room floor of two girls from Sydney's North Shore who had known me at university. After a year in London they were still in Earls Court. I was in no position to mock their lack of enterprise. They were well brought up, well spoken, well equipped and well organized – too well organized to put up with a permanent hobo camp on their parlour carpet. Curmudgeonly, this reluctance, because each evening after helping to drink their wine I generously offered to sleep with either or both. But they shared their meals with me, stuffed my shoes with paper before drying them in the stove, advised me on the purchase of a blue duffle-coat, and helped me look for somewhere to live.

Gently they discouraged my notions of seeking a maisonette in Bayswater or a mews house in Belgravia. There was a bed and breakfast boarding house in Swiss Cottage that wanted only three pounds ten shillings a week. When my postal order came, the girls very kindly drove me there. It was a long way from Kangaroo Valley and when their Volkswagen Beetle splurged away along the overlapping lines of grey slush I stood in the snow beside my mock leather suitcase and felt that I was ashore at last. My boats were burning and I was too far inland to see the flames. I resolved to grow a beard.

1985

LONDON STREETS

KAREL CAPEK

As regards London itself, it smells of petrol, burnt grass, and tallow, thus differing from Paris, where unto these are added the odour of powder, coffee and cheese. In Prague each street has a different smell; in this respect there is no place to beat Prague. The voices of London are a more complicated matter; the inner districts, such as the Strand or Piccadilly, sound, I assure you, like a spinning-mill with thousands of spindles; it clatters, rattles, whirs, mutters, whizzes and rumbles with thousands of packed motor-lorries, buses, cars and steam tractors; and you sit on the top of a bus which cannot move forward and clatters to no purpose, you are shaken up by its rattling and leap about on your seat like some queer stuffed puppet. Then there are side-streets, gardens, squares, roads and groves and crescents up to the wretched street in Notting hill, where I am writing this: all of them streets of Two Pillars, streets of Similar Railings, streets of Seven Steps In Front of

Each House, and so on; now here, a sort of desperate series of variations on the sound 'i' proclaims the milkman, a woeful 'ieiei' merely denotes fire-wood, 'uó' is the coalman's war-cry, and the ghastly yell of a delirious sailor announces that a youth is hawking five cabbage heads in a perambulator. And by night the cats make love as savagely as on the roofs of Palermo, in spite of all reports about English Puritanism. Only the people here are quieter than elsewhere; they talk to each other half-heartedly, and their aim is to get home with the least possible delay. And that is the strangest thing about the English streets: here you do not see respectable ladies telling each other on the kerb what happened at the Smiths or the Greens, nor courting couples strolling arm-in-arm like sleep-walkers, nor worthy citizens seated on their doorstep with their hands on their knees (by the way, here I have not yet seen a carpenter or a locksmith or a workshop or a journeyman or an apprentice; here are nothing but shops, nothing but shops, nothing but Westminster Bank and Midland Bank, Ltd.), nor men drinking in the street, nor benches in the market-square, nor idlers, nor tramps, nor servant-girls, nor pension-ers – in short, nothing, nothing, nothing; the London streets are just a gulley through which life flows to get home. In the streets people do not live, stare, talk, stand or sit; they merely rush through the streets. Here the street is not the most interesting of places, where a thousandfold spectacle meets your gaze, and where a thousand adventures address themselves to you; a place where people whistle or scuffle, bawl, flirt, rest, poetize or philosophize, and enjoy life and indulge in jokes or politics and band themselves together in twos, in threes, in families, in throngs, or in revolutions. In our country, in Italy, in France, the street is a sort of large tavern or public garden, a village green, a meeting-place, a playground and theatre, an extension of home and doorstep; here it is something which belongs to nobody, and which does not bring anyone closer to his fellows; here you do not meet with people, and things, but merely avoid them.

In our country a man thrusts his head out of the window, and he is right in the street. But the English home is separated from the street not merely by a curtain in the window, but also by a garden and a railing, ivy, a patch of grass, a door-knocker and age-old tradition. The English home must have its own garden, for the street does not provide it with a queer and delightful pleasaunce; in the garden it must have its own swing or playground, because the street does not provide it with a playground or the diversions of a skating-rink. The poetry of the English home exists at the expense of the English street which is devoid of poetry. And here no revolutionary throngs will ever march through the streets, because these streets are too long. And also too dull.

Thank goodness that there are buses here, vessels of the desert, camels bearing you on their backs through the infinity of bricks and mortar which is London. One of the things which puzzle me is that they do not miss the way, although, for the greater part, they do not steer by sun or stars, owing to the cloudy condition of the atmosphere here. I still do not know by what secret signs the driver distinguishes Ladbroke Grove from Great Western Road or Kensington Park Road. I do not know why he should prefer to take a trip to

East Acton, instead of riding to Pimlico or Hammersmith. For all these places are so curiously alike that I cannot imagine why he should have specialized in East Acton. Perhaps he has a house there, one of those with two pillars and seven steps by the door. These houses look rather like family vaults; I tried to make a drawing of them, but do what I would, I was unable to obtain a sufficiently hopeless appearance; besides, I have no grey paint to smear over them.

Before I forget: of course, I went to look at Baker Street, but I came back terribly disappointed. There is not the slightest trace of Sherlock Holmes there: it is a business thoroughfare of unexampled respectability, which serves no higher purpose than to lead to Regent's Park, which, after a long endeavour, it almost manages to achieve. If we also briefly touch upon its underground railway station, we have exhausted everything, including our patience.

1923

THOSE BEAUTIFUL FACES

NAJAF KOOLEE MEERZA

Throughout England, Scotland, and Ireland, there is in every town and village an institution for the education of the poor and orphan children. One day in the year, which is the 7th of June, all these children come from every direction to the city of London, accompanied by their teachers and superintendents. Each party have different coloured dresses, the children march two by two, both male and female, all in perfect order; they are beautifully arranged in their way, like a disciplined army. This great church, where they assemble, is a lofty edifice, magnificently built, the sight of it dazzles the mind; there are in it a number of splendid statues cut in marble, with most beautiful figures of animals and birds; in short, if a man does not see it, he could not believe any description of it. The outside of this church all round, and the inside consists of four quarters; each of them is two hundred feet long, and fifty feet broad; the church is three hundred feet high. Around the four parts of the church there are seats beautifully arranged; from the one end to the other there are forty ranks of seats, and all see alike; all of them are made of fine wood, elegantly worked, and cushioned with rich woollen cloth: besides these, there are other places expensively fitted up with beautiful chairs: these are seats for the royal family and their attendants. All these poor children, in regiments and beautiful order, were seated on benches round the church, each company by itself; the seats raised one above the other from the ground up into the dome, so wonderfully, that it could not be described but by a drawing. When all these children took their seats the visitors came into the church. At the gate stood some priests and persons of their religion, dressed in a strange costume. These priests gave the permission for entrance, and held in their hands plates of gold, and every person, who entered the church, put into the plates some charitable money for the support of these children; every one gave according to his ability and zeal. After all came in and sat down, then the very large organ, which they have in this church, began to play, and the children followed by singing. The high tune of the organ and the singing of the children could not be distinguished; all their hymns were composed with reference to this charity, and what the prophets had ordered for this purpose. Everyone in the church was quite silent while all this was going on. Afterwards, one of their great iskofs, a follower of Christ, went up into the pulpit, which was beautifully dressed with rich woollen cloth; he opened the books of the Gospel and Psalms, and read some chapters relating to charity, and gave a sermon to that effect. When the preaching was over, they began singing again so pleasantly, that it nourished the heart. On the whole, it was a most brilliant sight to see those beautiful faces who attended the feast. There must have been at this day in the streets near this church, about 40,000 carriages, beside many who came on horse-back and on foot. The money which is collected, is regularly distributed for the support and education of the children; these children are kept in the parishes till they arrive at the age of maturity.

1836

SCHOOL LIFE

'Don't you understand English or are you just stupid?'

AMRIT WILSON

But for Asian children, racism is impossible to ignore. School, with its white figures of authority, its totally foreign values and judgements, comes as a shock. After the initial effects of this wear off, children begin to realize their own and their parents' position. The rules of the education system, such as bussing and the reception class system (see later in this chapter), are only implicitly racist, but the way Asian children are actually treated in school is often quite overtly so. When a child gets out of line in assembly and the teacher shouts 'Don't you understand English or are you just stupid?', or when Indian parents who do come to speak to teachers are laughed at or rebuffed, children both black and white learn just how Indians are thought of by people who matter. What these children face is a kind of colonial experience which they are far too young to fight against. The children under eleven I spoke to almost invariably had a sense of inferiority similar to that of a colonized people. They were ashamed of anything Indian. They disowned their food and their language and in some cases even their Indian first names. A few tried to make even their skin as inconscpicuous as possible – as white as possible.

187

Interview with girl of nine from Southall:
Q. Would you like to go to India?
A. No, I wouldn't.
Q. Why not?
A. I don't think it is nice in India because sometimes when you come from India you get black.
Q. You don't want to get black?
A. No.
Q. Why not?
A. (touching her face) Because if someone's black, if you touch them in the face you might think your face might get black. It may be catching.

(Although the caste system in India has led to the attitude that it is more attractive to be light skinned than dark, this extreme fear of getting black does not exist in India or Pakistan.)

This apparent rejection of one's race is often accompanied by a desire not to stand out, not to cause trouble, to tip-toe about hoping nobody will notice you. Why? Because this is not your country, because the British have done you a favour by letting you in.

It is an attitude which is known among adults too. A Sikh Conservative Councillor – Mr Mangat – expressed it quite clearly in 1973: 'The best hope for Sikhs in this country lies in abandoning the turban and making themselves as inconspicuous as possible. It would damage community relations and hinder the process of acceptance and integration if Sikhs looked conspicuous in the street' (quoted by Geeta Amin in her B.Tech.Hons thesis *Asian Women in Southall, Political and Social Situation*). In Southall now, particularly since the murder in summer 1976 of a young man, Gurdeep Singh Chaggar, by racist thugs, few Asian adults even think about integration, let alone want it. But young children continue to absorb these racist opinions and their corrupting values.

Interview with Indian girl of nine who was born here and has never been to India:
Q. Do you think there are too many Indians in Southall?
A. Yes.
Q. Why?
A. Because every time I walk somewhere I see lots of Indians.
Q. Would you prefer to see English people?
A. Yes.
Q. Why?
A. Sometimes I think where I walk is India.

Interview with Indian girl, eight years old:
Q. Are there too many Indians in Southall?
A. Yes.
Q. Why?
A. Suppose there is some shop, right. An English man owns it, an Indian

man comes and buys it, right. With too many Indians all the Indians are getting spoilt, they start to do stealing and all.

Classically racist opinions – from Indian children!

For an Asian child growing up in Britain there is a choice. Either you stand outside your community, see them as non-Indians see them, which means, often enough, identifying with racist opinion, or you learn to hate people who say these things. Many children are caught in between. They lead a double life, on the surface passive, even servile, but inside they suffer.

In spring 1974 I was able to interview about 30 Asian, West Indian and English children between the ages of 8 and 11. They were on an outing from school – a day of activities organized by Scope Southall, an independent community organization. I interviewed them individually and in a separate room. They were happy, relaxed children and seemed keen to talk to me about themselves. But when certain subjects were mentioned the Asian kids became silent, hesitant. One of these subjects was food.

The day's activities included a slide show of photographs taken in and around Southall. When pictures of Indian sweet shops were shown, the English and West Indian children present sneered and made vomiting noises while the Asians watched in silent embarrassment.

That Asian children are teased about their food may not seem very important in itself, but it does rather lead to the thought – if people eat food which is thought of as disgusting and unclean what are these people like? And it provides a cover for racist fantasies such as these comments of primary school teachers – 'Southall stinks of curry' or 'I am always sneezing when I come here. It must be the curry.'

Only a minority of teachers I spoke to were interested in the way of life of their Asian pupils and an even smaller number knew anything about it. This lack of interest goes right through the educational system. In Ealing for example (an area where a high proportion of the population is Asian) not one school had facilities for teaching Asian languages. Of course an Asian child here must learn English, but must she or he forget their own language in order to learn English? A girl of ten told me that children in her school were punished if they spoke in their own language. An Indian teacher said that in his school Asian children's names were almost invariably mispronounced. But when in one class he had taken the register and pronounced their names correctly, there had been some laughter from non-Indian children (who were a minority in the class) but floods of embarrassed giggles from Asian children, who seemed to prefer their names to be mispronounced in school.

Indian language and Indian food are seen by whites as inferior, but religion is slightly different. It is seen not as a racial characteristic but as identical with race. Jesus is seen as British and belonging to the British. One English girl of nine asked me 'Coloured people believe in our God, but do you Indians believe in him or do you have a God of your own?' Religious instruction in most schools is not really conducive to respect for non-Christian religions. Children in primary school are often told stories from the Old Testament.

Whether these are presented as interesting old stories or as moralistic and relevant fables depends on the attitude of the head teacher. Teachers often choose to stress that the 'baddies' in these stories are 'idol-worshippers'. And everyone knows that such 'idol-worshippers' abound in the 'East'.

I spoke to Sikh and Hindu children in Southall and none of them had been withdrawn from religious education lessons. Some children from Hindu families even attended Sunday school, mainly because there was nothing much else to do at weekends. An Indian girl of ten said:

> I used to go to Sunday school but I don't go any more. If you went to Sunday school every week you could go to the seaside free. But if you miss only two or three weeks then you pay a little money – 23p, I think it is. I used to go to Sunday school all the time before and they said I could go free. Then I began to go to the temple and I didn't go to Sunday school any more, because I had been to the seaside lots and lots of times – the same one every time.

'English' prayers were seen by these Asian children (mainly Sikhs and Hindus) as innocuous, even in some cases enjoyable, but not of any emotional significance. They often seemed to feel that 'Indian' prayers didn't belong in the world of school. Only one child, a Sikh girl of ten, had attempted to say non-Christian prayers in school.

> Q. Are you religious? Do you say prayers?
> A. Yes, in assembly while they say it in English I do the other one. We have to say the English one and I hate saying da-da-da so I make my own one, an Indian prayer and say it.
> Q. What do the others say about that?
> A. They don't like it. One day we had a fight and they told Miss. Miss said it was all right for me to say my own prayer. Me and Karin, my friend, we do that.

1978

THE PRIME OF LIFE

SIMONE DE BEAUVOIR

We spent our Easter vacation in London. Here was a city that was bigger than Paris, and quite new to us. We sallied forth into the streets, and walked for hours on end. Piccadilly, the City, Hampstead, Putney, Greenwich: we were determined to see everything. We would clamber up to the top deck of a big red bus, drive out to the suburbs, and make our way back on foot. We would have lunch in a Lyons or a Soho restaurant or one of the old chophouses off the Strand, and set out once more. Sometimes it rained, and we didn't know where to take shelter: the absence of cafés disconcerted us. One afternoon the only refuge we could find was in the Underground.

We amused ourselves by observing the conventions of English life. When women came down to breakfast in our hotel dining room they wore astonishing garments somewhere between a tea gown and evening dress. Men really *did* wear bowler hats and carry umbrellas in the afternoon. Soapbox orators *did* hold forth every evening at Hyde Park Corner. The shabby taxis and peeling posters and teashops and ugly window-dressing all disorientated us. We spent hours in the National Gallery, and stayed behind in the Tate to stare at Van Gogh's yellow chair and sunflowers. In the evenings we went to the cinema. We saw that beautiful creature Kay Francis in *Cynara*: 'I have been faithful to thee, Cynara, in my fashion' – this quotation, screened after the credits, was to become a kind of private password between us for years afterwards. I was enthralled by Maskelyne's little theatre where conjurors and magicians performed the most amazing tricks, with a technical brilliance I never saw the like of anywhere else.

I had to admit that despite our private entente certain slight discrepancies of outlook existed between Sartre and myself. I went to the heart of London looking for traces of Shakespeare and Dickens; I explored the byways of Old Chiswick with a sense of rapturous discovery; I dragged Sartre around all the London parks, to Kew Gardens and even as far as Hampton Court. He lingered in lower-class districts, trying to guess at the lives and thoughts of the thousands of unemployed persons who dwelt in these joyless streets. He told me that on our next visit to England he would visit Manchester, Birmingham, all the big industrial cities. He too had his obsessions. He spent a whole day dragging me around Whitechapel in the pouring rain to find a little cinema where, according to one poster, they were showing *Outward Bound*, with Kay Francis and William Powell. The film turned out to be so good that I felt the time had been well spent. But I was the one most set on concocting schemes and bringing them about. Most of the time Sartre accommodated himself to my ideas with so good a grace that I was convinced that his enthusiasm for them matched my own. Very conveniently I persuaded myself that a foreordained harmony existed between us on every single point. 'We are,' I declared, 'as one.' This absolute certainty meant that I never went against my instinctive desires; and when, on two occasions, our desires clashed, I was completely flabbergasted.

In Canterbury we had both been struck by the beauty of the Cathedral, and spent the whole day in unclouded happiness. When we reached Oxford, Sartre was by no means averse to the streets and parks, but he found the snobbishness of the English undergraduate decidedly irksome, and refused to set foot inside any of the colleges. I went through two or three of them by myself, and reproached him for what seemed to me a mere whim. But at least he had not disturbed my own plans. I was far more put out on the afternoon of our projected visit to the British Museum, when he calmly told me he had not the slightest wish to go – though, he added, there was nothing to stop me making the trip alone. This was what I did. But it was in a very listless mood that I trailed around the bas-reliefs and statues and mummies: it had seemed so important that I should see these things, and now I began to wonder if it mattered after all. I refused to admit that my personal desires could contain any element of caprice: they were founded upon values which I regarded as absolute, and reflected imperatives that I held to be categorical. Since I was less wholly reliant upon literature than Sartre, I had a greater need to introduce necessity into my life. But this meant that I must stick to my decisions as though they were blindingly self-evident truths; otherwise my curiosity, my avidity for experience became mere personal characteristics, perhaps even personal faults. I would no longer be subject to an authoritative mandate.

I was still less able to conceive the possibility of any intellectual dissension between us. I believed in truth, and truth is one and indivisible. We thrashed out our ideas and impressions with indefatigable zeal, and were never satisfied till we had reached some agreement. Generally Sartre would propose a 'theory', which I would criticize and modify; sometimes I rejected it altogether, and prevailed upon him to revise it. I accepted, with some amusement, his comparison between English cooking and Locke's empiricism, both of which, he explained to me, were founded upon the analytical principle of juxtaposition. Walking the Thames Embankment or standing before the pictures in the National Gallery, I agreed with practically everything he told me. But one evening, in a little restaurant near Euston Station, we really quarrelled. We were sitting up on the first floor, eating an insipid, synthetic sort of meal, and watching the red glow on the horizon which meant a fire down near the docks. Sartre, with his usual passion for generalization, was trying to define London's place in his over-all pattern. I found the hypothesis he advanced inadequate, tendentious, and without any real value: even the principle upon which he was working irritated me. We resumed, somewhat more heatedly, the discussion that had divided us two years earlier on the heights of Saint-Cloud, and had cropped up more than once since. I maintained that reality extends beyond anything that can be said about it; that instead of reducing it to symbols capable of verbal expression, we should face it as it is – full of ambiguities, baffling, and impenetrable. Sartre replied that anyone who wished, as we did, to arrange the world in a personal pattern must do something more than observe and react; he must grasp the meaning of phenomena and pin them down in words. What made nonsense of our argument was the fact that Sartre was far from understanding London after twelve days' visit, and his résumé of it omitted countless sides of the total picture: to this extent I was justified in rejecting his theory.

1962

YOUR LORDSHIP'S
MOST HUMBLE
SERVANT

Everyone knows Samuel Johnson's great smack in the eye to Lord Chesterfield. The sonorous roll of his sentences is still tremendous: 'The notice which you have been pleased to take of my labours, had it been early, had been kind' and so on. Yet there seems a real possibility that through some administrative cock-up Chesterfield was unaware of Johnson's application for patronage. Certainly he admired Johnson's monumental rebuff and used to show it to his friends. Nor should we forget that he was himself no mean slouch as a writer, as his letters to his son demonstrate. The one on the art of pleasing (written incidentally just about the time that Johnson began to wait in his outward rooms) is a masterpiece of practical advice, if a touch cynical. Flattering men, he points out, turns on praising them on the points where they wish to excel yet are doubtful that they do. So, Richelieu, the ablest statesman of his time, had the idle vanity of wanting to be thought a poet, and that was where it was shrewdest to flatter him. Women, the old sexist goes on, have in general but one object, which is their beauty: 'Nature has hardly formed a woman ugly enough to be insensible to flattery upon her person.' Dare we say that there is still something in it?

LETTER TO LORD CHESTERFIELD

SAMUEL JOHNSON

To the Right Honourable the Earl of Chesterfield.

My Lord,

February 7, 1755.

I have been lately informed, by the proprietor of the World, that two papers, in which my Dictionary is recommended to the publick, were written by your Lordship. To be so distinguished, is an honour, which, being very little accustomed to favours from the great, I know not well how to receive, or in what terms to acknowledge.

When, upon some slight encouragement, I first visited your Lordship, I was overpowered, like the rest of mankind, by the enchantment of your address; and could not forbear to wish that I might boast myself *Le vainqueur du vainqueur de la terre*; – that I might obtain that regard for which I saw the world contending; but I found my attendance so little encouraged, that neither pride nor modesty would suffer me to continue it. When I had once addressed your Lordship in publick, I had exhausted all the art of pleasing which a retired and uncourtly scholar can possess. I had done all that I could; and no man is well pleased to have his all neglected, be it ever so little.

Seven years, my Lord, have now past, since I waited in your outward rooms, or was repulsed from your door; during which time I have been pushing on my work through difficulties, of which it is useless to complain, and have brought it, at last, to the verge of publication, without one act of assistance, one word of encouragement, or one smile of favour. Such treatment I did not expect, for I never had a Patron before.

The shepherd in Virgil grew at last acquainted with Love, and found him a native of the rocks.

Is not a Patron, my Lord, one who looks with unconcern on a man struggling for life in the water, and, when he has reached ground, encumbers him with help? The notice which you have been pleased to take of my labours, had it been early, had been kind; but it has been delayed till I am indifferent, and cannot enjoy it; till I am solitary, and cannot impart it; till I am known, and do not want it. I hope it is no very cynical asperity not to confess obligations where no benefit has been received, or to be unwilling that the publick should consider me as owing that to a Patron, which Providence has enabled me to do for myself.

Having carried on my work thus far with so little obligation to any favourer of learning, I shall not be disappointed though I should conclude it, if less be possible, with less; for I have been long wakened from that dream of hope, in which I once boasted myself with so much exultation,

My Lord,
Your Lordship's most humble,
Most obedient servant,
SAM. JOHNSON.

TO HIS SON

LORD CHESTERFIELD

Dear Boy,

London, October 16, O.S. 1747.

The art of pleasing is a very necessary one to possess; but a very difficult one to acquire. It can hardly be reduced to rules; and your own good sense and observation will teach you more of it than I can. 'Do as you would be done by,' is the surest method that I know of pleasing. Observe carefully what pleases you in others, and probably the same things in you will please others. If you are pleased with the complaisance and attention of others to your humours, your tastes, or your weaknesses, depend upon it, the same complaisance and attention on your part, to theirs, will equally please them. Take the tone of the company that you are in, and do not pretend to give it; be serious, gay, or even trifling, as you find the present humour of the company: this is an attention due from every individual to the majority. Do not tell stories in company; there is nothing more tedious and disagreeable: if by chance you know a very short story, and exceedingly applicable to the present subject of conversation, tell it in as few words as possible; and even then, throw out that you do not love to tell stories; but that the shortness of it tempted you.

Of all things, banish the egotism out of your conversation, and never think of entertaining people with your own personal concerns or private affairs; though they are interesting to you, they are tedious and impertinent to everybody else: besides that, one cannot keep one's own private affairs too secret. Whatever you think your own excellencies may be, do not affectedly display them in company; nor labour, as many people do, to give that turn to the conversation, which may supply you with an opportunity of exhibiting them. If they are real, they will infallibly be discovered, without your pointing them out yourself, and with much more advantage. Never maintain an argument with heat and clamour, though you think or know yourself to be in the right; but give your opinions modestly and coolly, which is the only way to convince; and, if that does not do, try to change the conversation, by saying, with good-humour, 'We shall hardly convince one another; nor is it necessary that we should, so let us talk of something else.'

Remember that there is a local propriety to be observed in all companies; and that what is extremely proper in one company, may be, and often is, highly improper in another.

The jokes, the *bon-mots*, the little adventures, which may do very well in one company, will seem flat and tedious when related in another. The particular characters, the habits, the cant of one company may give merit to a word, or a gesture, which would have none at all if divested of those accidental circumstances. Here people very commonly err; and fond of something that has entertained them in one company, and in certain circumstances, repeat it with emphasis in another, where it is either insipid, or, it may be, offensive, by being ill-timed or misplaced.

Nay, they often do it with this silly preamble, 'I will tell you an excellent thing,' or, 'I will tell you the best thing in the world.' This raises expectations, which when absolutely disappointed, make the relator of this excellent thing look, very deservedly, like a fool.

If you would particularly gain the affection and friendship of particular people, whether men or women, endeavour to find out their predominant excellency, if they have one, and their prevailing weakness, which everybody has; and do justice to the one, and something more than justice to the other. Men have various objects in which they may excel, or at least would be thought to excel; and though they love to hear justice done to them, where they know that they excel, yet they are most and best flattered upon those points where they wish to excel, and yet are doubtful whether they do or not. As for example: Cardinal Richelieu, who was undoubtedly the ablest statesman of his time, or perhaps of any other, had the idle vanity of being thought the best poet too: he envied the great Corneille his reputation, and ordered a criticism to be written upon the *Cid*. Those, therefore, who flattered skilfully, said little to him of his abilities in state affairs, or at least but *en passant*, and as it might naturally occur. But the incense which they gave him – the smoke of which they knew would turn his head in their favour – was as a *bel esprit* and a poet. Why? – Because he was sure of one excellency, and distrustful as to the other.

You will easily discover every man's prevailing vanity by observing his favourite topic of conversation; for every man talks most of what he has most a mind to be thought to excel in. Touch him but there, and you touch him to the quick. The late Sir Robert Walpole (who was certainly an able man) was little open to flattery upon that head, for he was in no doubt himself about it; but his prevailing weakness was, to be thought to have a polite and happy turn to gallantry – of which he had undoubtedly less than any man living. It was his favourite and frequent subject of conversation, which proved to those who had any penetration that it was his prevailing weakness, and they applied to it with success.

Women have, in general, but one object, which is their beauty; upon which, scarce any flattery is too gross for them to follow. Nature has hardly formed a woman ugly enough to be insensible to flattery upon her person; if her face is so shocking that she must, in some degree, be conscious of it, her figure and air, she trusts, make ample amends for it. If her figure is deformed, her face, she thinks, counterbalances it. If they are both bad, she comforts herself that she has graces; a certain manner; a *je ne sais quoi* still more engaging than beauty. This truth is evident, from the studied and elaborate dress of the ugliest woman in the world. An undoubted, uncontested, conscious beauty is, of all women, the least sensible of flattery upon that head; she knows it is her due, and is therefore obliged to nobody for giving it her. She must be flattered upon her understanding, which, though she may possibly not doubt of herself, yet she suspects that men may distrust.

Do not mistake me, and think that I mean to recommend to you abject and criminal flattery: no; flatter nobody's vices or crimes: on the contrary, abhor and discourage them. But there is no living in the world without a complaisant indulgence for people's weaknesses, and innocent, though ridiculous vanities. If a man has a mind to be thought wiser, and a woman handsomer, than they really are, their error is a comfortable one to themselves, and an innocent one with regard to other people; and I would rather make them my friends by indulging them in it, than my enemies by endeavouring (and that to no purpose) to undeceive them.

There are little attentions, likewise, which are infinitely engaging, and which sensibly affect that degree of pride and self-love, which is inseparable from human nature; as they are unquestionable proofs of the regard and consideration which we have for the persons to whom we pay them. As for example: to observe the little habits, the likings, the antipathies, and the tastes of those whom we would gain; and then take care to provide them with the one, and to secure them from the other; giving them genteelly to understand, that you had observed they liked such a dish or such a room; for which reason you had prepared it: or, on the contrary, that having observed they had an aversion to such a dish, a dislike to such a person, etc, you had taken care to avoid presenting them. Such attention to such trifles flatters self-love much more than greater things, as it makes people think themselves almost the only objects of your thoughts and care.

These are some of the *arcana* necessary for your initiation in the great society of the world. I wish I had known them better at your age; I have paid the price of three-and-fifty years for them, and shall not grudge it if you reap the advantage. Adieu!

FORTY YEARS ON

And now for exercises in nostalgia by two of our best playwrights. We have already noted that John Osborne's great cry of rage in his 'Damn You England' letter had its roots in a yearning for an Arcadian England that no longer exists. The same impulse can be detected in Jimmy Porter's long speech on Edwardian England in Look Back in Anger. *Alan Bennett, on the other hand, constructs the whole of his marvellously entertaining play* Forty Years On *around a longing for the same idealized era. It is the heyday of Edward Horner, Raymond Asquith, Julian and Billy Grenfell, the* jeunesse dorée *who were to be cut down in the slaughter on the Somme – exactly the same lost heroes that rivet John Osborne in* Children of the Souls.

LOOK BACK IN ANGER

JOHN OSBORNE

Alison gives Cliff a cigarette. They both light up, and she goes on with her ironing.
JIMMY: Nobody thinks, nobody cares. No beliefs, no convictions and no enthusiasm. Just another Sunday evening.
Cliff sits down again, in his pullover and shorts.
Perhaps there's a concert on. (*Picks up* Radio Times.)
Ah. (*Nudges Cliff with his foot.*) Make some more tea.
Cliff grunts. He is reading again.
Oh, yes. There's a Vaughan Williams. Well, that's something anyway. Something strong, something simple, something English. I suppose people like me aren't supposed to be very patriotic. Somebody said – what was it – we get our cooking from Paris (that's a laugh), our politics from Moscow, and our morals from Port Said. Something like that, anyway. Who was it? (*Pause.*) Well, you wouldn't know anyway. I hate to admit it, but I think I can understand how her Daddy must have felt when he came back from India, after all those years away. The old Edwardian brigade do make their brief little world look pretty tempting. All home-made cakes and croquet, bright ideas, bright uniforms. Always the same picture: high summer, the long days in the sun, slim volumes of verse, crisp linen, the smell of starch. What a romantic picture. Phoney too, of course. It must have rained sometimes. Still, even I regret it somehow, phoney or not. If you've no world of your own, it's rather pleasant to regret the passing of someone else's. I must be getting sentimental. But I must say it's pretty dreary living in the American Age – unless you're an American of course. Perhaps all our children will be Americans. That's a thought isn't it?
He gives Cliff a kick, and shouts at him.
I said that's a thought!

1956

FORTY YEARS ON

ALAN BENNETT

HEADMASTER: Members of Albion House, past and present. Parents and Old Boys. It does not seem so many years since I stood in this hall on November 11, 1918, to declare a half holiday on the occasion of the Armistice. That was my first term at Albion House as a schoolboy, and now I am headmaster and it is my last term. It is a sad occasion . . .

(A jet aircraft roars overhead temporarily drowning his words, and he waits.)

. . . it is a sad occasion, but it is a proud occasion too. I can see now some of the faces of my school-fellows on that never-to-be-forgotten November morning, many of them the sons of old boys who, proud young trees for the felling, fell in that war. And in many a quiet English village there stands today a cenotaph carved with their names, squire's son rubbing shoulders with blacksmith's boy in the magnificent equality of death. Scarce twenty summers sufficed to weather those names before England must needs take up arms in a Second World War.

(Another aircraft passes.)

(Franklin is visibly impatient during this speech. Occasionally he blows his nose, or stares at the ceiling.)

And now that too has passed into history. None of you boys are old enough to remember that Second War, nor even some of you masters. Yet I remember them both. I can still see myself standing at that window one summer day in 1918 and listening to the rumble of the guns in Flanders.

(Franklin blows his nose loudly.)

I stood at that window again in June 1940 to see a lone Spitfire tackle a squadron of the Luftwaffe. Those times left their mark on Albion House. Some of the older ones among you will remember Bombardier Tiffin, our Corps Commandant and Gym Instructor, lately retired. The more observant ones among you will have noticed that one of Bombardier Tiffin's legs was not his own. The other one, God bless him, was lost in the Great War. Some people lost other things, less tangible perhaps than legs but no less worthwhile – they lost illusions, they lost hope, they lost faith. That is why . . . (chewing, Charteris.) That is why the twenties and thirties were such a muddled and grubby time, for lack of all the hopes and ideals that perished on the fields of France. And don't put it in your handkerchief. Hopes and ideals which, in this school, and in schools like it all over the country we have always striven to keep alive in order to be worthy of those who died. It was Baden-Powell I think –

(Franklin clears his throat.)

– I think it was Baden-Powell who said that a Public Schoolboy must be acceptable at a dance, and invaluable in a shipwreck. But I don't think you'd be much use in either, Skinner, if you were playing with the hair of the boy in front. See me afterwards. A silent prayer.

(Franklin does not close his eyes during the prayer.)

O God, look down upon our bodies which are made in Thine own image. Let us delight in our boy bodies that they may grow day by day into man bodies that our boy thoughts may become man thoughts and on that glorious day when manhood dawns upon us it may dawn upon us as on the clean dewy grass with birds singing in our hearts and innocence looking from our eyes. . . .

CARTWRIGHT: Amen.

HEADMASTER: I haven't finished. I haven't finished. As I was praying . . . so that day by day as our bodies grow more beautiful so too our soul life may grow more beautiful as the soul is the mirror of the body and the body the mirror of the soul.

ALL: Amen.

HEADMASTER: This school, this Albion House, this little huddle of buildings in a fold of the downs, home of a long line of English gentlemen, symbol of all that is most enduring in our hopes and traditions. Thirty years ago today, Tupper, the Germans marched into Poland and you're picking your nose. See me afterwards. We aren't a rich school, we aren't a powerful school, not any more. We don't set much store by cleverness at Albion House so we don't run away with all the prizes. We used to do, of course, in the old days and we must not forget those old days, but what we must remember is that we bequeathed our traditions to other schools, and if now they lead where we follow it is because of that. My successor is well-known to you all, in the person of Mr Franklin. . . .

(Wigglesworth cheers feebly.)

When the Governors want your approval of their appointments, Wigglesworth, I'm sure they will ask for it. Mr Franklin has long been my senior housemaster. Now he is promoted to pride of place. Doubtless the future will see many changes. Well, perhaps that is what the future is for. We cannot stand still, even at the best of times. And now, as has always been the custom on this the last day of Term, staff and boys have come together to put on the Play.

Perhaps here I might say a word about Mr Fairbrother, whose jealously guarded province the play has always been. I recall with particular pleasure that first trail-blazing production of *Dear Octopus*, and last year's brave stab at *Samson Agonistes*. We shall miss him and his Delilah of that production, Miss Glenys Budd who has contrived to delight us on innumerable occasions. Now of course she is Mrs Fairbrother. Long may they flourish amid the fleshpots of Torquay. *Ave atque vale.*

O God, bless all those who leave and take their ways into the high places of the earth that the end of leaving may be the beginning of loving, as the beginning of loving is the end of life, so that at the last seekers may become finders and finders keepers for Thy Name's Sake. Amen.

Mr Franklin has put together this term's production . . . a short fling before he is crippled with the burden of administration. He has recruited a veritable galaxy of talent. Connoisseurs of the drama, could they but spare the time from rummaging in the contents of their neighbours' ears, Jarvis, may be interested to note that I myself am to play some part in this year's production. On the distaff side no expense has been spared in procuring the services of Matron *(cheers)*, Miss Nisbitt *(groans)*, and of course Mr Tempest *(wolf whistles)*. Now if I could just see those boys I had occasion to admonish we will sing the school song together and the play will begin shortly. Skinner, Tupper.

ALL: Forty years on, when afar and asunder
    Parted are those who are singing today
    When you look back and forgetfully wonder
    What you were like in your work and your play.
    Then it may be that there will often come o'er you
    Glimpses of notes, like the catch of a song;
    Visions of boyhood shall float then before you,
    Echoes of dreamland shall bear them along.

Chorus;
    Follow up, follow up,
    Follow up, follow up, follow up
    Till the field rings again and again
    With the tramp of the twenty-two men
    Follow up, follow up.

    Forty years on, growing older and older
    Shorter in wind as in memory long
    Feeble of foot and rheumatic of shoulder
    What will it help you that once you were strong?
    God give us bases to guard or beleaguer,
    Games to play out whether earnest or fun;
    Fights for the fearless and goals for the eager,
    Twenty and thirty and forty years on!

1969

STANDING OVATION

England taught the world to play games, and sport plays a leading role in her literature. Cricket has garnered by far the lion's share, as a morning in the library at Lord's will quickly prove. Here I've chosen Ronald Mason's delicious account of Hammond's great innings in the Lord's Test of 1938; and then, because, though often anthologized, it is impossible to resist, A. G. MacDonnell's incomparable account of the village cricket match in Chapter 7 of England, Their England. It is one of the most reassuring reflections on the state of modern England that this magnificent team still tours the English shires each summer. And, to complete our account of cricket, a short but beautiful poem by Alan Ross – no doubt based on a true incident in the Long Room at Lord's.

Although movements of great beauty can suddenly flower from the apparent chaos of ruck and maul, rugby attracts no such fine writing. It is, however, fortunate to have one comic writer of vast skill in Michael Green, as this extract from The Art of Coarse Rugby *will at once reveal.*

The debate about blood sports rages in England as fiercely as ever. All I would say here is that I challenge anyone with a grain of imagination to feel quite the same about hunting, shooting or fishing after reading the three poems which follow next.

HAMMOND IN COMMAND

RONALD MASON

The Lord's Test of 1938 attracted a vast and absorbed crowd, as it always does when Australia are there; the sun shone gloriously upon the opening overs, the excitement was tensed beyond any that had been felt in that place for four years or more. Perhaps it was screwed a point higher by the obscurely sensed international unrest; Austria had gone down before Hitler in the early spring [. . . and in] the background of many minds must have lurked the doubt, even as the immemorial plane-trees rustled in the June heat and the great ground lay open to the sunshine, packed as it had hardly ever been packed before, whether this might be the last time for years or for ever that the English would be permitted the deep pleasure of this classic rivalry and contest. It was an unvoiced doubt but was not silenced for being buried; it gave the occasion an added edge, awakened the common perceptions to a more than common keenness. Hammond won the toss and expectation quickened.

McCormick began as he began that other time in Brisbane, prancing and fearsomely hostile . . . and at the outset of this Test Match he found a little answering greenness in the wicket and made his slightly short-pitched deliveries whip and sing round the apprehensive ears of Barnett and Hutton. Barnett, a straightforward, true batsman who liked straightforward, true bowling, was prone to fence and swish at this kind of thing, while the Hutton of June 1938 on a sporty pitch was neither the Hutton of August 1938 on a shirt-front nor the Hutton of 1950 on anything that was offered. Accord-

206

ingly, there was a tentative air about the batting, and a dangerous tendency to prod; and the score was only 12 when Hutton prodded once too often and spooned a feeble dolly catch. Edrich, who followed, was defeated almost before he was in, missing a blind scared hook before being devastated trying a blind scared pull; and with the score at no more than 31 Barnett was bullied into giving just such another dolly catch as Hutton's. England 31 for 3 with the game barely forty minutes old and the shine still on the ball. The bottom fell out of all England spectators' hopes; or would have fallen out but for the emergence of the assured cocky figure of Eddie Paynter to assist the calm, detached authority of Hammond, playing the fiery imponderabilities of McCormick with apparently minutes to spare.

In these frightening straits Hammond proceeded to one of the greatest innings of his life: greatly set, greatly prepared for, greatly executed. Before he had been in twenty minutes it was clear, and to nobody was it clearer than to Bradman, who was master in this business. McCormick, in face of this impassive contempt, shrivelled into insignificance in a couple of overs. Fleetwood-Smith came on and was instantly thrashed twice for four in his first over, deadly murderous calculated blows off good-length balls, menacingly certain. The dangerous spinner wavered in his length, and Hammond drove another half-volley straight past his boots for four. Even the great O'Reilly found he could not spin the ball as he wished in face of such aggression. Paynter was every bit as calm, and once hit Fleetwood-Smith for six over fine-leg with engaging impudence. The initiative was taken right away from Australia. Against all probability and out of the unpromising depths of initial disaster, Hammond and Paynter took England's score to 134 for 3 before lunch. Hammond had made 70, beautifully in command, relaxed and serene, untroubled by the early disasters. In the interval he and the rest of the players were lined up and presented to King George VI, with Earl Baldwin in attendance; a gracious if distracting ceremony, but failing, one is happy to remember, to turn Hammond's concentration from the matter urgently in hand.

A man I know saw every ball of this day bowled, and for every ball he stood, packed in the overflowing crowd high at the back of the stands behind long-off as you face the pavilion; he was young then and he had an important examination pending, and he should have devoted his day to his books, but he left them on an impulse and came to Lord's. He stood there on his hot and aching feet all day and focused his gaze on the mastery unfolding before them; out of the fogs and frustrations of middle age he says he would gladly, ever so gladly, go through the whole of that day again, for he has remembered it in peace and war, in alien city and alien continent, through tension and tranquillity all his life. He remembers Hammond coming in with squared grim shoulders to the chaos and by the very force of skill and personality raising the England innings on those shoulders to honourable levels again; how after the first sighting minutes he settled compactly to the central task, how soon he flexed his shoulders in an experimental cover-drive, and how for several overs he would ever and again unship one of his great patent off-drives and tingle the palms of cover or extra-cover or mid-off; how Bradman dropped a man back on the crowd's toes at deep extra-cover and how Hammond off the back foot cracked good-length ball after good-length ball at this man in the deep, great reverberating drives that whistled and thrummed with the power of his wrists and shoulders, drives my friend remembers for their individual beauty and power after nearly a quarter of a century – then how as he came to certainty of timing and found at last his effective direction one drive at last cracked clean through the ringed field out of all possible reach and was followed at once by others like it, until the off-side seemed as full of holes as a colander and though the fielders never abated their energy and courage he seemed at the end able to place the ball, and place it at intimidating speed, precisely where he chose. 'It was a throne-room innings,' said Cardus, watching enraptured. 'He played greatly and deserved better bowling.'

McCormick on his return was as good as useless; Fleetwood-Smith and O'Reilly at least kept a length; but not a ball beat the bat for hours. Paynter's crusading lightfoot impudence well matched the crushing authority that Hammond had once and for all triumphantly assumed; he suddenly burst into brilliance, driving and late-cutting to charm the world. Hammond got to his hundred, one of the outstanding Test centuries of his own and his contemporaries' time, in just under two and a half hours; by this time he was playing at will from anywhere in his own half of the wicket, mobile and well-balanced, on the easy hunt for runs. 'He only gave one chance,' says my friend reminiscently, 'and that broke Chipperfield's finger' – and he stifles a cheerful smile, for he is a kindly and humane man. Paynter was a sudden and unexpectedly LBW for 99, a sad oversight to end a glorious attacking innings and a record stand of 222. Denis Compton, chafing at the long wait, was fatally over-impetuous and underestimated the tiring O'Reilly; and at tea England had lost five wickets for 271 and Hammond, steady as Gibraltar, was 140 not out – 70 before lunch, 70 after, an excellent symmetry.

The last two hours were a duel between him and O'Reilly, bowling great-heartedly in the heat and intensifying his accuracy when he might have been expected to relax it. Never so O'Reilly; he plunged venomously to the crease with formidable aggressive energy never abating; he contained Hammond, though leg-stump tactics did not noticeably daunt him from on-drives and leg-hits. The cool reliability of the well-tried Ames supported him refreshingly for the whole of this session; no chance was given, no risk was taken, the day proceeded gravely to its appointed close. A symmetrical one, too; for in this last period he added precisely one more 70 to the other neat 70s of his day's compiling; it was as if he added to the artist's grace a mathematician's native precision. Hammond faced the last over of this racking day and played it coldly and forcefully as a maiden, laying the ball dead under his nose with uncompromising finality. 'All day he had carried a burden,' said Cardus, 'and with a calm which hid from us the weight and magnitude of it. He came to his 200 as easily and as majestically as a liner coming into port.' My friend on the terraces, resting his throbbing feet and stretching his paralysed muscles, took comfort in the reflection that Hammond was probably more weary than he, and saluted him as he cheered him home with the rest of the packed crowd, for uplifting not only the corporate spirit of all England's supporters but a weary student's flagging morale, and for lightening not only his path to the examination-room but his memory for the rest of his life.

And next day Hammond climbed to greater heights; he began where he had left off. He unloosed on the now indifferent bowling a violent barrage of his finest scoring strokes. Cardus threw all his hand on to the table and reported the last brilliant phase of his innings in terms of music, declaring that when the game is lifted into music by the art of a glorious cricketer he could not deny the habits of a lifetime. He added 30 in twenty magnificent minutes, making his total 240 in all and England's 457, and then played forward at McCormick and was bowled leg-stump. The enormous Saturday crowd began their applause before the bails had even come to rest; the roaring acclamation continued and intensified as he receded from the wicket; and then occurred the rare, spontaneous and extraordinarily moving gesture with which very few are ever honoured and which signs for them the day and their subsequent life alike – the Lord's pavilion rose as one man and gave him the standing ovation that no one dictates but that is simply the instinctive corporate tribute of an admiring company to a performance that their blood has told them is worthy of this very special and distinguished accolade.

1962

ENGLAND, THEIR ENGLAND

A G MACDONELL

The scores were level and there was one wicket to fall. The last man in was the blacksmith, leaning heavily upon the shoulder of the baker, who was going to run for him, and limping as if in great pain. He took guard and looked round savagely. He was clearly still in a great rage.

The first ball he received he lashed at wildly and hit straight up in the air to an enormous height. It went up and up and up, until it became difficult to focus it properly against the deep, cloudless blue of the sky, and it carried with it the hopes and fears of an English village. Up and up it went and then at the top it seemed to hang motionless in the air, poised like a hawk, fighting, as it were, a heroic but forlorn battle against the chief invention of Sir Isaac Newton, and then it began its slow descent.

In the meanwhile things were happening below, on the terrestrial sphere. Indeed, the situation was rapidly becoming what the French call *mouvementé*. In the first place, the blacksmith forgot his sprained ankle and set out at a capital rate for the other end, roaring in a great voice as he went, 'Come on, Joe!' The baker, who was running on behalf of the invalid, also set out, and he also roared 'Come on, Joe!' and side by side, like a pair of high-stepping hackneys, the pair cantered along. From the other end Joe set out on his mission, and he roared 'Come on, Bill!' So all three came on. And everything would have been all right, so far as the running was concerned, had it not

209

been for the fact that Joe, very naturally, ran with his head thrown back and his eyes goggling at the hawk–like cricket-ball. And this in itself would not have mattered if it had not been for the fact that the blacksmith and the baker, also very naturally, ran with their heads turned not only upwards but also backwards as well, so that they too gazed at the ball, with an alarming sort of squint and a truly terrific kink in their necks. Half-way down the pitch the three met with a magnificent clang, reminiscent of early, happy days in the tournament-ring at Ashby-de-la-Zouche, and the hopes of the village fell with the resounding fall of their three champions.

But what of the fielding side? Things were not so well with them. If there was doubt and confusion among the warriors of Fordenden, there was also uncertainty and disorganization among the ranks of the invaders. Their main trouble was the excessive concentration of their forces in the neighbourhood of the wicket. Napoleon laid it down that it was impossible to have too many men upon a battlefield, and he used to do everything in his power to call up every available man for a battle. Mr Hodge, after a swift glance at the ascending ball and a swift glance at the disposition of his troops, disagreed profoundly with the Emperor's dictum. He had too many men, far too many. And all except the youth in the blue silk jumper, and the mighty Boone, were moving towards strategical positions underneath the ball, and not one of them appeared to be aware that any of the others existed. Boone had not moved because he was more or less in the right place, but then Boone was not likely to bring off the catch, especially after the episode of the last ball. Major Hawker, shouting 'Mine, mine!' in a magnificently self-confident voice, was coming up from the bowler's end like a battle-cruiser. Mr Harcourt had obviously lost sight of the ball altogether, if indeed he had ever seen it, for he was running round and round Boone and giggling foolishly. Livingstone and Southcott, the two cracks, were approaching competently. Either of them would catch it easily. Mr Hodge had only to choose between them and, coming to a swift decision, he yelled above the din, 'Yours, Livingstone!' Southcott, disciplined cricketer, stopped dead. Then Mr Hodge made a fatal mistake. He remembered Livingstone's two missed sitters, and he reversed his decision and roared 'Yours, Bobby!' Mr Southcott obediently started again, while Livingstone, who had not heard the second order, went straight on. Captain Hodge had restored the *status quo*.

In the meantime the professor of ballistics had made a lightning calculation of angles, velocities, density of the air, barometer-readings and temperatures, and had arrived at the conclusion that the critical point, the spot which ought to be marked in the photographs with an X, was one yard to the north-east of Boone, and he proceeded to take up station there, colliding on the way with Donald and knocking him over. A moment later Bobby Southcott came racing up and tripped over the recumbent Donald and was shot head first into the Abraham-like bosom of Boone. Boone stepped back a yard under the impact and came down with his spiked boot, surmounted by a good eighteen stone of flesh and blood, upon the professor's toe. Almost simultaneously the portly wicket-keeper, whose movements were a positive triumph of the spirit over the body, bumped the professor from behind. The learned man was thus neatly sandwiched between Tweedledum and Tweedledee, and the sandwich was instantly converted into a ragout by Livingstone, who made up for his lack of extra weight – for he was always in perfect training – by his extra momentum. And all the time Mr Shakespeare Pollock hovered alertly upon the outskirts like a Rugby scrum-half, screaming American University cries in a piercingly high tenor voice.

At last the ball came down. To Mr Hodge it seemed a long time before the invention of Sir Isaac Newton finally triumphed. And it was a striking testimony to the mathematical and ballistical skill of the professor that the ball landed with a sharp report upon the top of his head. Thence it leapt up into the air a foot or so, cannoned on to Boone's head, and then trickled slowly down the colossal expanse of the wicket-keeper's back, bouncing slightly as it reached the massive lower portions. It was only a foot from the ground when Mr Shakespeare Pollock sprang into the vortex with a last ear-splitting howl of victory and grabbed it off the seat of the wicket-keeper's trousers. The match was a tie. And hardly anyone on the field knew it except Mr Hodge, the youth in the blue jumper, and Mr Pollock himself. For the two batsmen and the runner, undaunted to the last, had picked themselves up and were bent on completing the single that was to give Fordenden the crown of victory. Unfortunately, dazed with their falls, with excitement, and with the noise, they all three ran for the same wicket, simultaneously realized their error, and all three turned and ran for the other – the blacksmith, ankle and all, in the centre and leading by a yard, so that they looked like pictures of the Russian *troika*. But their effort was in vain, for Mr Pollock had grabbed the ball and the match was a tie.

And both teams spent the evening at the Three Horseshoes, and Mr Harcourt made a speech in Italian about the glories of England and afterwards fell asleep in a corner, and Donald got home to Royal Avenue at 1 o'clock in the morning, feeling that he had not learnt very much about the English from his experience of their national game.

1933

TEST MATCH AT LORD'S

ALAN ROSS

Bailey bowling, McLean cuts him late for one.
I walk from the Long Room into slanting sun.
Two ramrod ancients halt as Statham starts his run.
Then, elbows linked, but straight as sailors
On a tilting deck, they move. One, square-shouldered as a
    tailor's
Model, leans over, whispering in the other's ear:
'Go easy. Steps here. This end bowling.'

Turning, I watch Barnes guide Rhodes into fresher air,
As if to continue an innings, though Rhodes may only play
   by ear.

1955

THE ART OF COARSE RUGBY

MICHAEL GREEN

'That we may wander o'er this bloody field . . .' Shakespeare (Henry V)

It is a wet, drizzling, bitterly cold Saturday afternoon in February. A group of dismal figures in motley rugby kit are shambling along a rough cinder path between a refuse dump and a field of thistles. Behind them a coach driver who unwisely tried to drive down the path is endeavouring to extricate his vehicle from the ditch.

A player at the back of the group speaks. He is a tall lanky man in his late thirties with receding hair and a pronounced stoop. We shall call him Thinny, and he is the Old Rottinghamians Extra B stand-off. He furtively adjusts his surgical underwear as he speaks.

THINNY: Gosh it's cold. Why the hell does the Extra B pitch have to be so far from the pavilion? I don't know why we play the stupid game. You wouldn't think it was February would you? More like December.

Nobody replies. They trudge moodily along in silence. Thinny tries again.

THINNY *(blowing into cupped hands)*: I said I thought it was too cold to play.

This at last rouses some response in his companion, a gross, waddling creature of about thirty-nine, wearing a tattered scrum cap and a faded, patched jersey. We shall call him Fatty.

FATTY: All right. We heard you. You aren't the only one. My mind may not be the delicate mechanism that yours is, but I can get just as cold as you can. To hear you go on anyone'd think you were the only person in the world who ever got cold. It's all right for you. You don't have to keep going down in the mud like I do.

Thinny does not reply. He is too busy lighting a cigarette from the butt of another. Fatty pursues his theme.

FATTY: I don't know why we go through this stupid torture week after week. My wife and kids think I'm nuts. Why don't we sit at home and watch the telly? That's what I like about watching an international – seeing all those stupid fools running around injuring themselves and getting all uncomfortable in the rain and I'm sitting in the warm, drinking whisky and smoking myself sick.

The pair are joined by a third player, whom we shall call Gloomy. He is a lanky youth of about nineteen who has outgrown his strength and his mental powers.

GLOOMY: It'll be murder in this mud. You know the boiler's furred up and there won't be any water after the first team have had their bath?

Neither of his companions reply. Fatty lights up a butt end.

212

GLOOMY: Cor, don't the other side look huge? See that big bloke – I bet he's the wing forward. I bet when he tackles you he absolutely flattens you. You'd better watch out, Thinny.

Fatty and Thinny purse their lips and plod on in silence.

GLOOMY *(warming to his theme)*: They say that bloke who broke his leg last week may have to have it off. . . .

This produces an instantaneous reaction on Fatty and Thinny, who blench and groan.

THINNY: Shut up, will ya?

GLOOMY: Must be rotten to have your leg off. Did you hear the crack when the bone snapped? I bet he wishes he never played last week. . . .

FATTY: Will you shut up if I give you a fag?

GLOOMY: Ta, very much. I knew a boy at school who died after smoking a fag just before a game. It affected his heart.

THINNY: I'll affect your heart in a minute. It's bad enough having to turn out on a foul afternoon like this without you making it worse.

GLOOMY: You ought to give up if you feel like that. You're old enough . . . you must be about forty-five.

THINNY: That's just it – you give up now and you admit old age. Once you stop at my age you never start again. It's like a woman putting on her first corset. It's an admission you're old.

GLOOMY: They say it's dangerous to play after thirty-five. The valves of the heart won't work properly. . . .

He is interrupted by a clod of wet earth on the back of the neck. The little group trudge on in silence. It is a quarter of an hour before they reach the pitch, which is a sodden, lumpy meadow, bearing strong evidence of having been recently occupied by a herd of cows with loose bowels. They are greeted by their captain, a harassed man of about thirty, who is probably the slowest centre threequarter in Europe.

CAPTAIN: Come on, where do you think you've all been? I wanted you. We've got to rearrange the forwards somehow.

FATTY: How many men have we got?

CAPTAIN: Eleven, not counting Knocker.

FATTY: He's not coming. I saw him in the Royal Oak and he said to tell you he was ill.

CAPTAIN *(bitterly)*: The swine! And I think the others have got thirteen. That means we're two down.

THINNY *(instantly)*: Cancel it. Say the ground's unfit. Look at it, it *is* unfit. I'm sinking in up to my ankles. *(Becoming feverish and hysterical)* I tell you it's unfit to play, I tell you we can't play on this. . . . I tell you it's absurd . . . aaaaaaaaaahhhhh . . . *(he breaks off in a paroxysm of coughing as his cigarette smoke goes the wrong way)*.

GLOOMY: I reckon he'll burst a lung before half-time.

The referee approaches. He is an earnest man, in late middle-age, kind-hearted and slow-witted. He can never understand why he is always allocated Extra B games.

REFEREE: Come along, Old Rottinghamians. It'll be dark soon. We're nearly an hour late already.

CAPTAIN: Coming, sir. OK you chaps, let's get sorted out. Jack, you'll have

213

to be a sort of wing-three and full-back in one, and Fred, you float around generally between the pack and the backs. Use your discretion. We'll pack three-two-zero.

THINNY: Who'll go centre now Knocker's ratted on us?

CAPTAIN *(desperately)*: Oh, George'll have to play centre.

GEORGE *(protesting)*: But I'm a hooker.

CAPTAIN: Well, you're a centre now. Come on, stop this arguing and get stuck into them, Old Rottinghamians.

He says this without much conviction, and privately whispers to those around him, 'Don't hurry too much lads, let the bastards wait.' This is because the longer the start is delayed, the less time there will be for play, which is to the Old Rottinghamians' advantage in their weakened state. In any case, play is delayed because the match ball has landed in a heap of cow dirt, and no one will wipe it clean. Eventually the unpleasant task is performed by the captain of the opposing side, who realizes that as far as the Old Rottinghamians are concerned, it can stay there for ever.

Finally the opposition kick off in gathering gloom and at an hour when most first-class matches are just finishing. The ball is caught by Thinny who drops it. An opposing forward picks it up, knocks on four times and passes forward to a colleague, who puts one foot into touch and then dives over by the corner flag, dropping the ball as he does so.

The referee, who has not moved from the centre line, promptly awards a try.

OLD ROTTINGHAMIANS *(all together)*: Hey ref, he went into touch! Hey, ref, what about the knock-on? Hey, ref, what about the forward pass? Hey, ref, what about the obstruction?

Fatty even goes so far as to stand ostentatiously waiting for the line-out, but the referee is adamant.

CAPTAIN *(self-righteously)*: Stop moaning, Old Rottinghamians. Never mind if the ref's a short-sighted old sheep who doesn't know the rules, it doesn't help moaning.

He realizes he is standing about three feet from the referee and moves hurriedly away. Fortunately, the referee is deaf as well as short-sighted, and in any case he is used to a torrent of abuse from the both sides. Meanwhile about four of the Old Rottinghamians have gathered under the crossbar. Fatty, Thinny and one or two others have flung themselves on the ground panting and grumbling.

The opposition kicker is now placing the ball with infinite pains. He has so far taken four minutes over this. Eventually he carefully marches backwards for about thirty paces and stands rigidly at attention before moving forward into an immense run. This is carried out to an accompaniment of continuous sotto voce jeering, blasphemy, insults and obscenity from the Old Rottinghamians, none of whom, however, can raise the energy to charge.

When the kicker reaches the ball, he aims a terrific lunge and digs his toe deep into the ground about two feet in front of it, leaving it quite undisturbed. With a look of intense agony he sinks slowly to the ground, clutching his shattered leg. Quick to seize this advantage, the Old Rottinghamian skipper leads his men in a belated charge. Ignoring the ball and the objections of the referee they trample all over the prostrate kicker, who recovers with alarming suddenness and fights his way clear, protesting.

Order is at last restored and another kick taken. This time the ball goes bowling along the ground and hits the corner flag. The kicker returns to the jeers of his own team and the Old Rottinghamians prepare to reduce the arrears.

It is now half-time. As the referee blows his whistle Fatty and Thinny collapse in their tracks.

FATTY *(coughing as if his lungs would burst, turning red in the face and retching)*: Uuuuuuuurrrrgggggghhhhh. Aaaahhh. Brrouge. Faaaaaaghh. Ooooyer . . . ooooyer . . . ooyer . . . splurge . . . bless me *(only he doesn't say 'bless')*. Gimme a cigarette someone.

Thinny feels in the pocket of his shorts and brings out a filthy, bent object which might at one time have been a cigarette. Fatty produces a book of matches from his shorts and lights it. Then he immediately doubles up in another paroxysm of coughing.

THINNY *(sitting down in a deep puddle as if it was a feather bed)*: You're in a bad way, mate.

FATTY: You're telling me. Why the hell do we go through this ghastly torture week in, week out? Saturday after Saturday the agony goes on . . . retching . . . vomiting . . . panting for breath . . . in continual pain. . . .

THINNY *(looking round hopefully)*: It's getting pretty dark. With luck the ref may have to abandon it.

The captain approaches. He is a worried man. Having forgotten the lemons for the last two home games, he tied a knot in his handkerchief and remembered them. Instead, he forgot a knife and a plate, and all he can offer the two teams is two whole lemons each.

CAPTAIN: Anyone want a bit of lemon? I forgot the knife, so you'll have to try and tear a bit off.

Between them Fatty and Thinny savage the lemons into an unrecognizable pulp which is rejected contemptuously by everyone else. The other side throw their lemons over the hedge. The referee blows an optimistic chirp on his whistle. There is a faint stir among the players but no one moves. He blows again and this time one or two of the younger ones line up in some sort of order.

CAPTAIN *(making a feeble attempt to rouse his men)*: Now come along, Old Rottinghamians, let's get stuck into it this half. Thirty-six-nil isn't hopeless. If they can score it, so can we. Let's get some punch and life and go . . . go . . . go. . . .

He smacks his fist into his palm with such venom that it is paralysed for the rest of the afternoon. Someone throws a bit of mud at him. Fatty discovers he has lined up with the other team and painfully crosses back to the right side.

Thinny, who is stand-off, places the ball upright for the kick-off. It falls over. With mathematical precision he carefully replaces it and stands back with the air of a master. The ball topples over again. A restive muttering grows among the forwards, who give him advice what to do with the ball. It falls over five times altogether.

Eventually Thinny lays it down sideways on the ground and takes a wild boot at it. It spins like a top and travels two feet. The second half has begun. . . .

The Old Rottinghamians' captain is hoarse with urging his men on – a job which is quite futile. But he sticks to it. 'Come on, Old Rotts,' he shouts, leading an untidy and half-hearted foot rush down the field. 'Now we've got them on the YURRRRP. . . .' This exclamation is forced from him as an opponent fly-kicks the ball with unerring accuracy straight into his navel (point first). He collapses. When he recovers the referee awards a penalty against him.

Now the score is 45-nil against the Old Rottinghamians. Holding on to a post as they line up for a conversion, the captain tries to flog some life into them. 'Old Rottinghamians,' he bleats, 'you mustn't let them come through like that. You must mark your men. Thinny, you must tackle.'

A violent bickering ensues. Everyone turns on Gloomy, who, like a sick sheep, is forced out of the flock and retreats to the corner flag. The skipper appeals for peace.

CAPTAIN: Stop this bickering, Old Rottinghamians. We can still do it. Let's try and get just one before the end.

Nobody pays any attention to him. They are still arguing when the kick is taken. From now on their morale goes to pieces and they are solely concerned with venting their irritation somehow. The climax of this comes when Thinny, having been fairly tackled, kicks his opponent as he gets up.

OPPONENT: You rat, I'll get you for that.

THINNY: Just you make a dirty tackle like that again, and I'll fix you proper.

OPPONENT: Oh yeah?

THINNY: Yeah.

OPPONENT: Yeah?

THINNY: Yeah.

OPPONENT: Yeah?

THINNY *(snarling)*: Yeah.

OPPONENT: You and who else?

THINNY: Just me.

OPPONENT: You wouldn't dare, mate.

THINNY: Wouldn't I?

OPPONENT: No.

THINNY: No?

OPPONENT: No.

Suddenly, without warning, Thinny aims a wild and amateurish swipe at his opponent which catches him harmlessly on the shoulder. He lets out a shout of rage and they rush at each other, pummelling with all their not very considerable strength.

FATTY: Go on, Thinny, show the dirty so-and-so where he gets off!

Nobody shows any signs of stopping the fight. In fact each side encourage their own man. The referee comes puffing up, blowing his whistle wildly and in vain.

REFEREE: Now then you two, come along now and stop this nonsense. This isn't how rugby men should behave.

Neither fighter pays the slightest attention. Eventually they are separated by their captains who drag them apart and hold them while they continue to wave their fists and shout at each other.

THINNY: Let me go, Fred, just let me get that filthy hog. He's not fit to play rugby with decent people. . . .

OPPONENT: I ask you . . . was it or was it not a fair tackle? He kicked me . . . and he bit me. Look at them bite marks. I'll murder him if I get him again.

This rouses Thinny to fury and he thrashes so violently that he breaks free. This is awkward, because he doesn't really want to fight, so he pretends to be restrained with difficulty.

REFEREE: Come along you two . . . shake hands and forget it.

After a moment's hesitation the two players advance and take each other's hands, each of them trying to grip the other in such a way as to hurt him. The result is that they look like a couple of Masons engaged in some remote ritual. Having failed to hurt each other they retire muttering and the match goes on. But not for long. It is now nearly pitch dark and lights can be seen twinkling in nearby suburbs. The referee looks at his watch. The first half lasted thirty-one minutes and the second has now lasted twenty-five minutes. It is good enough for Coarse Rugby. He blows a long blast.

CAPTAIN: Old Rottinghamians, three cheers for Bagford Vipers . . . hip . . . hip . . . hooray!

He is answered by a feeble moaning sound, so faint that it merges with the wind which is now beginning to whistle coldly over the pitch.

OPPOSING CAPTAIN *(quietly)*: Don't cheer them lads. They're the dirtiest crowd we've ever played.

THINNY *(approaching the man he fought with a let's-be-friends smile)*: Jolly well played. Sorry we had that little fight.

All the time he is thinking: 'Filthy swine.'

1960

WINDSOR FOREST

ALEXANDER POPE

See! from the brake the whirring pheasant springs,
And mounts exulting on triumphant wings:
Short is his joy; he feels the fiery wound,
Flutters in blood, and panting beats the ground.
Ah! what avail his glossy, varying dyes,
His purple crest, and scarlet-circled eyes,
The vivid green his shining plumes unfold,
His painted wings and breast that flames with gold?

1713

POEM

JOHN MASEFIELD

The fox was strong, he was full of running,
He could run for an hour and then be cunning,
But the cry behind him made him chill,
They were nearer now and they meant to kill.
They meant to run him until his blood
Clogged on his heart as his brush with mud,
Till his back bent up and his tongue hung flagging,
And his belly and brush were filthed from dragging.
Till he crouched stone-still, dead-beat and dirty,
With nothing but teeth against the thirty.
And all the way to that blinding end
He would meet with men and have none his friend:
Men to holloa and men to run him,
With stones to stagger and yells to stun him;
Men to head him, with whips to beat him,
Teeth to mangle and mouths to eat him.
And all the way, that wild high crying,
To cold his blood with the thought of dying,
The horn and the cheer, and the drum-like thunder
Of the horsehooves stamping the meadow under.
He upped his brush and went with a will
For the Sarsen Stones on Wan Dyke Hill.

1919

DON JUAN, CANTO XIII

LORD BYRON

And angling, too, that solitary vice,
Whatever Izaak Walton sings or says;
The quaint, old, cruel coxcomb, in his gullet
Should have a hook, and a small trout to pull it.

1819

JOLLY WEATHER BOATING

It is an oddity of English life that the plangent melody of the 'Eton Boating Song' can arouse a distinct melancholy in many people who were not educated there. It was written by William Cory (Johnson), the Victorian poet and Eton classics master. Hearing it played one summer's evening at Eton he thought of young men quartered in Indian hill forts 'miserably remembering their last row at Eton, pining and craving for lost youthfulness'. In so far as any single human being can be said to have encapsulated that nostalgia, Cory himself must take the largest share of credit or blame.

But it is heaven or hell to be at Eton? A bit of both for most; mainly hell for Dillibe Onyeama in this bitter account of his Eton days only twenty years ago. Fortunately, his athletic prowess took much of the sting away as the years passed and, would you believe, he got the inevitable lump in his throat when he left like everybody else.

ETON BOATING SONG

WILLIAM CORY

Jolly boating weather
And a hay harvest breeze.
Blade on the feather,
Shade off the trees.
Swing, swing together,
With your backs between your knees,
Swing, swing together,
With your backs between your knees.

Harrow may be more clever,
Rugby may make more row,
But we'll row, row for ever,
Steady from stroke to bow.
And nothing in life shall sever
The chain that is round us now,
And nothing in life shall sever
The chain that is round us now.

Others will fill our places,
Dress'd in the old light blue,
We'll recollect our races,
We'll to the flag be true,
And youth will be still in our faces
When we cheer for an Eton crew,
And youth will be still in our faces
When we cheer for an Eton crew.

Twenty years hence this weather
May tempt us from office stools,
We may be slow on the feather,
And seem to the boys old fools,
But we'll still swing together
And swear by the best of schools,
But we'll still swing together
And swear by the best of schools.

1865

NIGGER AT ETON

DILLIBE ONYEAMA

I still had fagging to contend with, however, and it was, of course, detested by everyone except those senior enough to make use of the fags. Fags were summoned in a house by a long, drawn-out shout for a boy. This was a signal to drop whatever you were doing and run like a demon in the direction of the shout. The last to arrive was given the job. Since the duty could entail a trip as far as Windsor during the daylight hours, it was worth your accelerating as rapidly as possible. Anybody who stayed in his room and 'shirked' a boy-call was beaten. Only members of the Library could deliver boy-calls. The Debate could only go round to a fag's room and quietly give him a job to do. Each member of the Library, as I have already mentioned, had two or three personal fags who were responsible for tidying his room, putting out clean clothes, and making sure that all his creature comforts were at hand. Jobs done by fags incompetently were punishable by either a fine or a beating, the latter requiring the housemaster's permission.

There is nothing much to say about my first few days of fagging, except that, like the other boys, I hated it: most of all because we had to contend with it for four terms. I didn't, fortunately, arrive last for any boy-calls or show any incompetence. But it was only the beginning: the future would tell. It was March and getting milder, and the pain and loneliness of the first few days and nights were behind me.

On one such mild morning I entered a Classics division. No sooner was I inside the room than I was greeted with ape noises and racial names from every side.

'Here comes the big black bastard,' shouted one boy, which immediately won him a good laugh. Quietly, with concealed pain and confusion, I asked what it was all about, but only succeeded in starting off another spate of ape noises. I sat down and quietly arranged my books on the desk, thanking my stars that my blushing was invisible. Next I was approached by a handsome, sleek-haired boy, whose father was a rich banker. He took pride in making remarks to me whenever he could, and seemed to thrive on laughter at other people's expense.

1914

'Do you like this country?' he asked. His permanently blushing face held a taunting smile.

'Yeah, it's okay,' I replied rather cagily.

'Do you like the school uniform?'

'It's not all that bad.'

As we spoke there was almost total silence in the room, for everybody was listening, mischievous smiles on most faces.

'Don't you feel ashamed to wear it?' the boy continued.

'No, why should I?' I answered, wondering what was coming.

'Well,' he said, closing the trap, 'I thought that since all Africans usually wore nothing, wearing this would make you feel ashamed.'

A ripple of laughter went round the room, and I was just explaining, rather unnecessarily, that my people did not go around naked, when a boy in my house turned on him. He was joined by a few others, and the classroom was eventually divided between 'nigger lovers' and 'nigger haters'. Things might have got quite out of hand but for the belated arrival of the master at that moment. After the lesson, several of my tormentor's followers crowded round him as we dismissed, as if expecting me to take some sort of action at his remark outside the confines of the classroom where they would defend him. But nothing further happened on that occasion.

That incident is very vividly branded on my mind. It occurred a few weeks after my arrival: not long after I had started to become confident that my career at Eton would be an enjoyable one. What I had feared most about Eton had started. The incident bit deeply, and caused me much pain. I had the impression that it had obviously been arranged beforehand. Whether it was done to test my reaction or just for the sake of annoying me, I was not sure. It was wounding and unprovoked, and I firmly decided that this was my last attempt at playing the quiet black boy who did nothing. This had been the most hurtful of the racial taunts I had so far experienced in a division room. It was usually ape noises and names, which were not, at least, made directly to my face. Most of the racial abuse I had experienced was in the streets and tuck shops – 'Filthy nigger!', 'Wog', 'Black Bastard', 'Go back to the filth where you belong'. Things were not helped by my not knowing what one or two of the terms meant. To start with I found it all rather puzzling, later sad and annoying and finally embittering. Though I had expected to meet racial abuse at Eton, I used to wonder seriously why these things had to be said. What was so bad about being black-skinned that I should be abused for it? I recalled too that in my early days in Africa, there were many whites living there. Nobody ever abused them for being white, and they never abused us for being black.

Two reasons seemed to me the most likely for the racial abuse: my abusers were simply colour prejudiced, or they merely wanted to impress their friends. In retrospect I believe it was more of the latter, and they may not have been necessarily colour prejudiced. But they undoubtedly meant what they said: by picking me out, the sole black figure, they obviously meant to be discriminatory. I thought that racial abuse was sickening and outrageous! There was something about it which made it much more serious, wounding and loathesome than any other abuse: something which made it seem so different, a cut above the rest. What made it seem like this was the boys' usual reaction when I was abused: the serious expectant stares they used to deliver me; as if they knew that something of unrivalled vileness had been said and were expecting an explosive reaction from me.

Be that as it may, I resolved to start hitting back physically. And that was exactly what I did. More often than most I would resort to violence or at least threaten it. This proved to be a big mistake, and I thus quickly became extremely unpopular with a great number of boys. The immediate result of my strong-arm tactics was an even worse outbreak of quite deliberate, unprovoked and unjustified racial abuse. Rumour flew round that I could only get out of trouble by using physical strength, that I hated all forms of racial abuse and just a few simple jibes thrown at me would be good enough to start a punch-up. What effectively happened then was that many who had nothing better to do, except use foul language, simply taunted me in places where they knew I could not retaliate physically. It was possible to be sacked from Eton for starting a punch-up in the streets, where the world could see, so this became a favourite forum for boys to shout abuse. I then had the choice of either ignoring them, which I found difficult to do, or retaliating with words. Often I did this with phrases like 'filthy white trash' or 'albino bastard', which only seemed to amuse them.

When it came to the punch, though, it was usually on the arm. But on one occasion that, suitably, took place in the gymnasium, it was different. I had been watching an exciting boxing match (which we won) and afterwards was talking to a member of our team, Timothy Fearon. He was a fair boy of medium size, tough and cheerful. Clever and good at games, he was about my age but a year ahead in work. Unfortunately he lost a very close and spectacular fight. Amid the shouts of boys lolling around and the bangs and clangs of the ring being taken down in the main gym, he and I chatted outside in the passage, which led to four other smaller gyms.

After a time, a rather motley collection of boys from one of my divisions came sidling over and made as if they wished to speak to me. Tim Fearon did not know them, so said goodbye and left. I would have liked to have followed, but it would have meant losing face when I knew that the front-runner of the little gang, a scruffy, gum-chewing loud-mouth with tously, dark hair, was sure to be looking for trouble of some sort. He asked a few harmless questions about Nigeria.

'Do you look like your mother?' he enquired, which for some reason I said no to, for I look very much like my mother. He went on: 'Do you live in a house?'

'Of course,' I replied logically. 'What else do you think I live in?'

'Well, you see, I was under the impression that all wogs lived in mud huts and trees and wore nothing. Do correct me if I'm wrong,' he said in sarcastic, self-congratulatory tones.

'Well you are wrong,' I stormed, 'so just try and get your facts right in future!'

'Oh, sorry, I'm very sorry,' he replied with a total lack of sincerity, which almost caused his companions to laugh. 'A few years ago, I saw a film on

Africa and the women had bones through their noses. Has your mother got a bone through her nose?'

That did it! His smirking friends and his grinning, self-satisfied face, like a cat that had just swallowed a canary, blinded me with anger and caused my temper to go completely. I swung a powerful right-hander at his chin and caught him right on the point. He dropped to the wooden floor like an inert sack and lay there crying. The happy faces of his friends distorted with shock, and next they were shouting at me with disapproval. The commotion soon brought boys from every corner of the gym. They appeared quite hostile on learning what had happened, and I quickly left.

That incident took place around the middle of my first term, and one unusual thing about it was that I managed to fell my tormentor with one blow. I wasn't usually so lucky. Of course, the incident reached the ears of many in the school, and inevitably worsened my reputation for being a vicious character, and my popularity further declined.

By the end of the eleven-week Lent term (the shortest), my justified reputation for aggression was fully established throughout the school. And the ceaseless taunting I met in view of that was the greatest problem I had that term. It annoyed and worried me more than anything else. Similar incidents became very common in division rooms before the masters' arrival. Concealing my misery by cynical bitterness I struck out more savagely, until the matter became a vicious circle. The more unpopular I became, the more the taunting grew; the more I struck out, the more they jeered . . . but, I have to admit, they easily used to get the better of me. It was usually a situation of me versus half the division room, and sometimes nearly everybody; that is between seventeen to twenty-two boys. On several occasions, though, a few sympathetic characters shouted at my tormentors to leave me alone. But the latter always used adamantly to refuse, and strongly argue that I shouldn't take things to heart so much, and I shouldn't always resort to violence. Much as I would have liked to, I knew I couldn't really hurt any of my tormentors, for fear of the gravity of the injury and the trouble I would be in as a result. Very few boys attempted hitting me back, for two reasons, I felt: firstly, I was black; and I knew too well that they had this idea that the whites were no match for the blacks in strength. And secondly, at 5ft 10in, I found that I was the biggest boy in all my divisions. (I reached over six feet by the time I was fifteen, and 6ft 2½in by the time I left Eton, and in every division I worked in I found that I was one of the biggest boys.)

Inside my house, too, I had established my unpopularity, mostly with the lower boys. But the abuse began there later than outside the house, and it took time for the boys to follow the example set for them. Also the abuse came from only one small group, a term ahead of me in work. Though nothing like as bad or as continual as outside, it was all just as wounding, and on a few occasions I did resort to violence in the passages. When I was abused in lunch and in boys' rooms, where I couldn't start a punch-up, I took offence, threatened my tormentors with violence or that I would complain to my housemaster. Having shown my feelings, most of the other lower boys showed me that I was not to their tastes by having nothing to do with me if they could help it. They never came into my room for a chat, and usually ignored me when I went to theirs, unless I spoke to them. This did not worry me much, as I was happy just to sit and enjoy their exchange of jokes and stories. This was my relationship, on the whole, with the boys my first term and that was how it continued throughout my first year, getting more and more unbearable. In the holidays I never had the courage to confess to my father and my guardian that they had been right, in fact I even denied that I was experiencing any form of teasing, lying to them that I had a great number of friends, and that I was finding the school really enjoyable in every respect.

And indeed there were, in the swinging life of the school, many enjoyable moments. The privileges and some of the popular traditions, were merits of the school. For a boy in his first year, life was not as good as for others. For, as long as he remained a fag, he was pestered right, left and centre by the boy-calls, living under the predominant fear of the Library. He had to watch his footsteps: he knew the members of the Library were ruthless, that they adored beating and were always looking for a chance to get someone beaten. He also knew that as a fag he was in the best position to make blunders, so he had to be very competent. A few continually blundering fags in my house were beaten during my first year. But fortunately I was never beaten for fagging and having great fear for the self-important Library members, I went out of my way to fag as competently as possible. A few times I was fined for forgetting to collect milk from breakfast for the Library's tea. And these fines were usually only a shilling and never more than a half-crown. They were written in a small book kept inside a little tin box in the House Captain's room, and would be collected from the offender in his room after prayers once a week by a member of the Library.

The only good thing about fagging was that a boy's fagmaster tipped him one pound at the end of term. I can't say how delighted I was when my House Captain told me after my first year that my fagging days were over. Like the other fags, I looked forward to the time when I would get the privilege to fag, little knowing that it was to be abolished in my house when I reached that position.

Thus the life of a first year student differed from the others'; his eligibility for fagging made it tougher for him. But putting aside the fagging and racial problems, fate seemed to hold it that my first year was to be full of unfavourable events. The most serious by far was my failure in Trials my second term. These were the exams held at the end of each term at Eton, obviously to test whether boys had learnt anything during the term. If a boy failed on two consecutive occasions, he would have to leave, unless special permission for him to stay longer was given by the Headmaster, and then he would have to remain in the same divisions the following term and not move up. The pass mark was ridiculously low and if any boy failed, it showed he had made very little effort to do his work during the term. Nonetheless, I and several other boys failed, and the news came as a great shock to me. I was so sure that I had done well in general that I boasted ceaselessly to boys, saying this and how easy I had found the exam papers. I was so impatient to hear the results, which were read out in the school hall by the Lower master (the

Headmaster's assistant who had authority over the five hundred or so Lower boys), that I asked my housemaster when he came into my room the night before the results were announced. Standing in my dressing-gown and pyjamas I faced him, smiling respectfully.

'Yes!' he snarled in his deep voice, 'I do know that you haven't done *at all* well in your Trials!' He then angrily looked at me in silence. His murderous blue eyes seemed to smoulder with cold fire, and I couldn't look into them.

At this shock news, my heart gave a sickening lurch. My legs almost gave way, and for a few seconds the whole world seemed to go black.

'B-B-But –' My throat jammed.

'I don't think you bothered to revise at all, did you?' he went on after some seconds that seemed an eternity. I mildly protested that I had, but he persisted. 'No you didn't. It's all this fishing! You've done nothing but fish all term.'

'Di-Di-Did I get any papers back, sir?' I stuttered feebly.

'Yes, about five or six. And that Latin paper you did this morning you scored practically nothing on. And all because of this fishing. If you fail again next half, there'll be trouble.'

On saying this he left, leaving me to stand there in agony. I felt the utter hopelessness of the situation. I felt dazed. The sounds outside the open window suddenly sounded like rivers of doom pouring in with a gurgle and a rush. The whole room seemed to spin round with a roar of confusion and unreality, and I felt I would collapse if I didn't lie down at once. The light was soon off, and I was lying under the sheets, tears silently streaming. I was particularly ashamed of one thing: most boys entered the school at twelve or thirteen, and so I was a bit older than them to start with. I was the oldest boy by far in every division I worked in. In fact my own age group was a year ahead of me in work. In view of all this I felt it was a disgrace to fail Trials, so easy with such a low pass mark. It was true that I had fished a lot throughout the term. Fishing had always been my hobby and I fished in parts of the river Thames that were within the school boundaries. But my housemaster was wrong. I had revised. I had given a lot of time to revision. I just couldn't believe that I'd failed.

Naturally I did not look forward to 'reading over', late in the afternoon the next day, in the knowledge that I had failed. There were about three hundred boys in my block that term, and School Hall sounded like a football stadium as we all waited for the arrival of the Lower master. He was a grey, double-chinned man of about six feet, well known for his beating power. Utter silence descended on his entry. He began reading out the names, beginning with those with distinctions in their results and working downwards, slowly to the bottom, where I knew my name would be read out.

'Failures!' he finally shouted, an expression of distaste coming to his face. 'In Alpha division there were none. In Beta division . . . Viscount Astor, Barclay, Lord Burgersh, the Hon Mr Keyes, Onyeama, Palmer, Smith-Maxwell and Yorke-Long.'

The others among the failures were not easily picked out in the sea of tail-coats and identical striped trousers. But there was no difficulty in locating where I was standing. All heads turned and I felt very nervous and confused.

There was not much reaction among the boys at my failure, no doubt because everybody was looking forward to the next day, the holidays. Several did come and express their sympathy. There was one particular conversation which summed things up. Lanky Charles Nicholson and two of his friends met me some time after the reading over, halfway down the High Street. And amid the noise of traffic and other things, we had a brief conversation. He was a scruffy, but friendly, fellow, and a sociable ruffian who in years to come became one of the school's tallest boys at 6ft 7in.

'Hard luck, Ony,' he said with deep solemnity, 'it must be bloody difficult for you to pass these exams.'

'Why must it be difficult for me?' I questioned glumly.

'Well, because you're an African, you see,' he explained, as if revealing a universal truth. 'And it's not really your fault.'

'Oh fuck off, you bloody white trash,' was my spontaneous reply and I left them, no doubt in dumb incomprehension as to the reason for my offensive reply.

I meant what I said. He thought he was being polite, but did not realize that the implication of his words was abusive: Africans could not expect to be brainy, after all they had just climbed down from the trees! I continually met with similar implications throughout my time at Eton.

However, I was greatly worried about failing Trials again next term. When my housemaster said there'd be trouble if I failed, I took it to mean that I would be sacked. One cold and cloudy afternoon the next term I had a chance to discuss this. It was on the way back from football on the famous playing fields of Eton, which were as usual littered with footballers. I was walking back with Tim Fearon, the boxer, whom we met earlier. A friend of his was present. I asked Fearon what he thought would happen if I failed again. He was reassuring, saying he didn't think I'd be made to leave.

'Don't worry,' he said. 'Besides they wouldn't dare chuck you out.' His voice was sincere and his words cheered me. 'You'd most likely get beaten by the Lower man. But you definitely wouldn't get chucked out.'

'Why not?' I asked, frowning inquisitively.

'You just wouldn't be.'

'But why should they chuck other boys out and not me?' I persisted.

'Well. . . .'

'Because you're a nigger,' interrupted his friend, hoping for a laugh. But Fearon immediately let fly at him, shouting abuse and telling me to ignore him, which I did; but the point was made.

'What difference does it make about me being chucked out, just because I'm black?' I asked.

'Because if you were thrown out of the school, it would get in the papers and most probably a political row would result,' Fearon explained. 'You see, everybody nowadays is incredibly race conscious and it would all boil down to racial prejudice. That is what the school would be frightened of.'

The point had never occurred to me at all. But in the event I did not fail a second time, so the school was not faced with that problem.

1972

GENTLEMEN MAY PRANCE BUT NOT DANCE

Oxford is loved and loathed not simply because it has ancient buildings, priceless libraries, college autonomy and tutorial teaching, but because it is widely held to be imbued with some kind of magic. Television serials like Brideshead Revisited *do little to dispel the sun-dappled myth in every Englishman's head. But it was not like that for everybody: certainly not for Smithers, the scholarship boy in Compton Mackenzie's* fin de siècle *novel* Sinister Street. *He is a poor boy, a carpenter's son, and is to be ragged for his cockney accent and plebeian bearing. Michael Fane, the book's hero, has the grace to feel ashamed, but it is one of the most rebarbative passages on life at Oxford that we have.*

Of course it was all right for some, notably John Betjeman with his Balkan Sobranies and sherry in the cupboard; and for Evelyn Waugh too, living the life of Riley on £100 a term. Finally in this group, a throwaway joke by James Hilton in Lost Horizon: *a graceful compliment coming from a man educated at the Other Place.*

SINISTER STREET

COMPTON MACKENZIE

It was the time of the midsummer moon; and the freshmen in this last week of their state celebrated the beauty of the season with a good deal of midsummer madness. Bonfires were lit for the slightest justification, and rowdy suppers were eaten in college after they had stayed on the river until midnight, rowdy suppers that demanded a great expense of energy before going to bed, in order perhaps to stave off indigestion.

On one of these merry nights towards one o'clock somebody suggested that the hour was a suitable one for the ragging of a certain Smithers who had made himself obnoxious to the modish majority not from any overt act of contumely, but for his general bearing and plebeian origin. This derided Smithers lived on the ground floor of the Palladian fragment known as New Quad. The back of New Quad looked out on the deer-park, and it was unanimously resolved to invade his rooms from the window, so that surprise and alarm would strike at the heart of Smithers.

Half a dozen freshmen, Avery, Lonsdale, Grainger, Cuffe, Sinclair, and Michael, all rendered insensitive to the emotions of other people by the amount of champagne they had drunk, set out to harry Smithers. Michael alone possibly had a personal slight to repay, since Smithers had been one of the freshmen who had sniggered at his momentary mortification in the rooms of Carben the Rugby secretary during his first week. The others were more vaguely injured by Smithers' hitherto undisturbed existence. Avery disliked his face: Lonsdale took exception to his accent: Grainger wanted to see what he looked like: Cuffe was determined to be offensive to somebody: and Sinclair was anxious to follow the fashion.

Not even the magic of the moonlit park deterred these social avengers from their vendetta. They moved silently indeed over the filmy grass and

230

paused to hearken when in the distance the deer stampeded in alarm before their progress, but the fixed idea of Smithers' reformation kept them to their project, and perhaps only Michael felt a slight sense of guilt in profaning this fairy calm with what he admitted to himself might very easily be regarded as a piece of stupid cruelty. Outside Smithers' open window they all stopped; then after hoisting the first man on to the dewy sill, one by one they climbed noiselessly into the sitting-room of the offensive Smithers. Somebody turned on the electric light, and they all stood half-abashed, surveying one another in the crude glare that in contrast with the velvet depths and silver shadows of the woodland they had traversed seemed to illuminate for one moment an unworthy impulse in every heart.

The invaders looked round in surprise at the photographs of what were evidently Smithers' people, photographs like the groups in the parlours of country inns or the tender decorations of a house-maid's mantelpiece.

'I say, look at that fringe,' gurgled Avery, and forthwith he and Lonsdale collapsed on the sofa in a paroxysm of strangled mirth.

Michael, as he gradually took in the features of Smithers' room, began to feel very much ashamed of himself. He recognized the poverty that stood in the background of this splendid 'college career' of Percy or Clarence or whatever other name of feudal magnificence had been awarded to counter-balance 'Smithers'. No doubt the champagne in gradual reaction was over-charging him with sentiment, but observing in turn each tribute from home that adorned with a pathetic utility this bleak room dedicated for generations to poor scholars, Michael felt much inclined to detach himself from the personal ragging of Smithers and go to bed. What seemed to him in this changed mood so particularly sad was that on the evidence of his books Smithers was not sustained by the ascetic glories of learning for the sake of learning. He was evidently no classical scholar with a future of such dignity as would compensate for the scraping and paring of the past. To judge by his books he was at St Mary's to ward off the criticism of outraged Radicals by competing on behalf of the college and the university in scientific knowledge with newer foundations like Manchester or Birmingham. Smithers was merely an advertisement of Oxford's democratic philanthropy, and would gain from this university only a rather inferior training in chemistry at a considerably greater personal cost but with nothing else that Oxford could and did give so prodigally to others more fortunately born.

At this point in Michael's meditations Smithers woke up, and from the bedroom came a demand in startled cockney to know who was there. The reformers were just thinking about their reply, when Smithers, in a long night-gown and heavy-eyed with sleep, appeared in the doorway between his two rooms.

'Well, I'm jiggered,' he gasped. 'What are you fellows doing in my sitting-room?'

It happened that Cuffe at this moment chose to take down from the wall what was probably an enlarged portrait of Smithers' mother in order to examine it more closely. The son, supposing he meant to play some trick with it, sprang across the room, snatched it from Cuffe's grasp, and shouting an objurgation of his native Hackney or Bermondsey, fled through the open window into the deer-park.

Cuffe's expression of dismay was so absurd that everybody laughed very heartily; and the outburst of laughter turned away their thoughts from damaging Smithers' humble property and even from annoying any more Smithers himself with proposals for his reformation.

'I say, we can't let that poor devil run about all night in the park with that picture,' said Grainger. 'Let's catch him and explain we got into his rooms by mistake.'

'I hope he won't throw himself into the river or anything,' murmured Sinclair, anxious not to be involved in any affair that might spoil his reputation for enjoying every rag without the least reproach ever lighting upon him personally.

'I say, for goodness' sake, let's catch him,' begged Michael, who had visions of being sent to explain to a weeping mother in a mean street that her son had died in defending her enlargement.

Out into the moon-washed park the pursuers tumbled, and through its verdurous deeps of giant elms they hurried in search of the outlaw.

'It's like a scene in *The Merry Wives of Windsor*,' Michael said to Avery, and as he spoke he caught a glimpse of the white-robed Smithers, running like a young druid across a glade where the moonlight was undimmed by boughs.

He called to Smithers to go back to his rooms, but whether he went at once or huddled in some hollow tree half the night Michael never knew, for by this time the unwonted stampeding of the deer and the sound of voices in the Fellows' sacred pleasure-ground had roused the Dean who supported by the nocturnal force of the college servants was advancing against the six dis-turbers of the summer night. The next hour was an entrancing time of hot pursuit and swift evasion, of crackling dead branches and sudden falls in lush grass, of stealthy procedure round tree-trunks, and finally of scaling a high wall, dropping heavily down into the rose-beds of the Warden's garden and by one supreme effort of endurance going to ground in St Cuthbert's Quad.

'By Jove, that was a topping rag,' puffed Lonsdale as he filled six glasses with welcome drink. 'I think old Shadbolt spotted me. He said: "It's no use you putting your coat over your 'ead, sir, because I knows you by your gait".'

'I wonder what happened to Smithers,' said Michael.

'Damned good thing if he fell into the Cher,' Avery asserted. 'I don't know why on earth they want to have a bounder like that at St Mary's.'

'A bounder like what?' asked Castleton, who had sloped into the room during Avery's expression of opinion.

Castleton was greeted with much fervour, and a disjointed account of the evening's rag was provided for his entertainment.

'But why don't you let that poor devil alone?' demanded the listener.

At this time of night nobody was able to adduce any very conclusive reason against letting Smithers alone, although Maurice Avery insisted that men like him were very bad for the college.

Dawn was breaking when Michael strolled round Cloisters with

Castleton, determined to probe through the medium of Castleton's common sense and Wykehamist notions the ethical and aesthetic rights of people like Smithers to obtain the education Oxford was held to bestow impartially.

'After all Oxford wasn't founded to provide an expensive three years of idleness for the purpose of giving a social cachet to people like Cuffe,' Castleton pointed out.

'No, no,' Michael agreed, 'but no institution has ever yet remained true to the principles of its founder. The Franciscans, for instance, or Christianity itself. The point surely is not whether it has evolved into something inherently worthless, but whether, however much it may have departed from original intentions, it still serves a useful purpose in the scheme of social order.'

'Oh, I'm not grumbling at what Oxford is,' Castleton went on. 'I simply suggest that the Smitherses have the right, being in a small minority, to demand courtesy from the majority, and after all, Oxford is serving no purpose at all, if she cannot foster good manners in people who are supposed to be born with a natural tendency towards good manners. I should be the first to regret an Oxford with the Smitherses in the majority, but I think that those Smitherses who have fought their way in with considerable difficulty should not go down with the sense of hatred which that poor solitary creature must surely feel against all of us.'

Michael asked Castleton if he had ever talked to him.

'No, I'm afraid I haven't. I'm afraid I'm too lazy to do much more than deplore theoretically these outbursts of rowdy superiority. Now, as I'm beginning to talk almost as priggishly as a new sub-editor of the *Spectator* might talk, to bed.'

The birds were singing, as Michael walked back from escorting Castleton to his rooms. St Mary's tower against the sky opening like a flower seemed to express for him a sudden aspiration of all life towards immortal beauty. In this delicate hour of daybreak all social distinctions, all prejudices and vulgarities became the base and clogging memories of the night before. He felt a sudden guilt in beholding this tranquil college under this tranquil dawn. It seemed spread out for his solitary vision, too incommunicable a delight. And suddenly it struck him that perhaps Smithers might be standing outside the gate of this dream city, that he, too, might wish to salute the sunrise. He blushed with shame at the thought that he had been of those who rushed to drive him away from his contemplation.

Straightway when Michael reached his own door, he sat down and wrote to invite Smithers to his third terminal dinner, never pausing to reflect that so overwhelming an hospitality after such discourtesy might embarrass Smithers more than ever. Yet, after he had worried himself with this reflection, when the invitation had been accepted, he fancied that Smithers sitting on his right hand next to a Guy Hazlewood more charming than Michael had ever known him seemed to enjoy the experience, and triumphantly he told himself that contrary to the doctrine of cynics quixotry was a very effective device.

1914

SUMMONED BY BELLS

JOHN BETJEMAN

Balkan Sobranies in a wooden box,
The college arms upon the lid; Tokay
And sherry in the cupboard; on the shelves
The University Statutes bound in blue,
Crome Yellow, Prancing Nigger, Blunden, Keats.
My walls were painted Bursar's apple-green;
My wide-sashed windows looked across the grass
To tower and hall and lines of pinnacles.
The wind among the elms, the echoing stairs,
The quarters, chimed across the quiet quad
From Magdalen tower and neighbouring turret-clocks,
Gave eighteenth-century splendour to my state.
Privacy after years of public school;
Dignity after years of none at all –
First college rooms, a kingdom of my own:
What words of mine can tell my gratitude?
. . . Silk-dressing-gowned, to Sunday-morning bells,
Long after breakfast had been cleared in Hall,
I wandered to my lavender-scented bath;
Then, with a loosely knotted shantung tie
And hair well soaked in Delhez' Genêt d'Or,
Strolled to the Eastgate. Oxford marmalade
And a thin volume by Lowes Dickinson
But half-engaged my thoughts till Sunday calm
Led me by crumbling walls and echoing lanes,
Past college chapels with their organ-groan
And churches stacked with bicycles outside,
To worship at High Mass in Pusey House.
   Those were the days when that divine baroque
Transformed our English altars and our ways.
Fiddle-back chasuble in mid-Lent pink
Scandalized Rome and Protestants alike:
'Why do you try to ape the Holy See?'
'Why do you sojourn in a halfway house?'
And if these doubts had ever troubled me
(Praise God, they don't) I would have made the move.
What seemed to me a greater question then
Tugged and still tugs: Is Christ the Son of God?
Despite my frequent lapses into lust,
Despite hypocrisy, revenge and hate,
I learned at Pusey House the Catholic faith.
Friends of those days, now patient parish priests,

By worldly standards you have not 'got on'
Who knelt with me as Oxford sunlight streamed
On some colonial bishop's broidered cope.
Some know for all their lives that Christ is God,
Some start upon that arduous love affair
In clouds of doubt and argument; and some
(My closest friends) seem not to want His love –
And why this is I wish to God I knew.

1960

DRINKING

EVELYN WAUGH

In my childhood wine was a rare treat; an adult privilege to which I was admitted on special occasions. At my school there was no tabu against drinking (as there was against tobacco). Housemasters occasionally made a mild grog or cup for senior boys. I remember being embarrassed when one Ascension Day (a whole holiday) my companion got very drunk on liqueurs at a neighbouring hotel. It was at the university that I took to drink, discovering in a crude way the contrasting pleasures of intoxication and discrimination. Of the two, for many years, I preferred the former.

I think that my generation at Oxford, 1921–24, was the last to preserve more or less intact the social habits of the nineteenth century. The ex-service men of the First War had gone down. Undergraduate motor-cars were very few. Women were not seen except in Eights Week. Oxford was still essentially a market-town surrounded by fields. It was rare for a man to go down for a night during term. The generation after ours cherished closer links with London. Girls drove up; men drove down. Cocktail shakers rattled, gramophones discoursed jazz. The Cowley works enveloped the city. But in my day our lives were bounded by the university. For a brief Indian summer we led lives very much like our fathers'.

In the matter of drink, beer was the staple. I speak of undergraduates of average means. There were a few rich men who drank great quantities of champagne and whisky; a few poor men who were reputed to drink cocoa. The average man, of whom I was one, spent £100 a term and went down £300 in debt. Luncheon was served in our rooms with jugs of beer. Beer was always drunk in Hall. At my college there was the custom of 'sconcing' when a breach of decorum, such as mentioning a woman's name or quoting from a foreign tongue, was fined by the provision of beer for the table. At one time I used to drink a tankard of beer for breakfast, but I was alone in that. It was drawn and served without demur. The Dean of my college drank very heavily and was often to be seen feeling his way round the quad in his transit from Common Room to his rooms. There were occasions such as bump-suppers and 'smokers' when whole colleges were given up to bacchanalia. In

235

my first year there was a 'freshers' blind' when we all got drunk on wines and spirits and most of us were sick. Some white colonials got obstreperous and the custom was given up. All drinks were procurable at the buttery but the bursar scrutinized our weekly battels and was liable to remonstrate with a man whose consumption seemed excessive. My friends and I had accounts with wine merchants in the town, relying on the buttery for beer and excellent mild claret, which was the normal beverage at club meetings held in undergraduate rooms. No one whom I knew ever had a bottle of gin in his rooms. I remember only one man being sent down from my college for drunkenness and that not his own; late at night he hospitably passed tumblers of whisky out of his ground-floor window to a friend in the lane, who was picked up insensible by the police. I always thought it a harsh sentence. The poor fellow had come three thousand miles from the United States to imbibe European culture.

There were six or seven clubs with their own premises; some, like the Grid, highly respectable, others, Hogarthian drinking dens. The most notable of the dens was named the Hypocrites, in picturesque Tudor rooms over a bicycle shop in St Aldates (now of course demolished). There the most popular drink was red Burgundy drunk from earthenware tankards. A standing house rule was: 'Gentlemen may prance but not dance.' The oddest of these clubs with premises was the New Reform at the corner of the Cornmarket on Ship Street. This was subsidized by Lloyd George in the belief that it would be a nursery for earnest young Liberals. It became a happy centre of anarchy and debauch. Habits of extravagance grew and in my last year we drank a good deal of champagne in mid-morning at the New Reform and scoffed from the windows at the gowned figures hurrying from lecture to lecture. There was a vogue for whisky and crumpets at tea-time in the Union. I think it is no exaggeration to say that, in my last year, I and most of my friends were drunk three or four times a week, quite gravely drunk, sometimes requiring to be undressed and put to bed, but more often clowning exuberantly and, it seemed to us, very funnily. We were never pugnacious or seriously destructive. It took very little to inebriate at that age and high spirits made us behave more flamboyantly than our state of intoxication really warranted. Not many of us have become drunkards.

We were not discriminating. In a novel I once gave a description of two undergraduates sampling a cellar of claret. I never had that experience at that age. Indeed I do not think that at twenty I could distinguish with any certainty between claret and burgundy. Port was another matter. The tradition of port drinking lingered. Many of the colleges had ample bins of fine vintages of which undergraduates were allowed a strictly limited share. Port we drank with reverence and learned to appreciate. The 1904s were then at their prime, or, at any rate, in excellent condition. We were not ashamed (nor am I now) to relish sweet wine. Yquem had, of course, a unique reputation. Starting to drink it in a mood of ostentation, I was led to the other white Bordeaux. Tokay was then procurable and much relished. Bristol Milk and a dark sherry named Brown Bang were also favourites. We tried anything we could lay our hands on, but table-wines were the least of our interests. We drank them conventionally at luncheon and dinner parties but waited eagerly for the heavier and headier concomitants of dessert.

Nowadays, I am told, men privately drink milk and, when they entertain, do so to entice girls. It is tedious for the young to be constantly reminded what much finer fellows their fathers were and what a much more enjoyable time we had. But there you are; we were and we did.

1963

LOST HORIZON

JAMES HILTON

At this point the tea-bowls were brought in, and talk became less serious between sips of the scented liquid. It was an apt convention, enabling the verbal flow to acquire a touch of that almost frivolous fragrance, and Conway was responsive. When the High Lama asked him whether Shangri-La was not unique in his experience, and if the Western world could offer anything in the least like it, he answered with a smile: 'Well, yes. To be quite frank, it reminds me very slightly of Oxford, where I used to lecture. The scenery there is not so good, but the subjects of study are often just as impractical, and though even the oldest of the dons is not quite so old, they appear to age in a somewhat similar way.'

'You have a sense of humour, my dear Conway,' replied the High Lama, 'for which we shall all be grateful during the years to come.'

1933

BROWN STREETS
WITH
LIGHTS OF GOLD

London has a vast literature too, all the way from the famous description of fog in Bleak House, *through Carlyle's lively picture of the monstrous Wen, and the regret for rural London evoked by Richard Jefferies (could you still see sturdy milkmaids in London a hundred years ago?). And finally, Cyril Connolly's chromatic recall of autumn in London in 1927: '. . . the lamps just lit and wet with rain, alone along the broad street, brown street with lights of gold.'*

FOG

CHARLES DICKENS

London. Michaelmas Term lately over, and the Lord Chancellor sitting in Lincoln's Inn Hall. Implacable November weather. As much mud in the streets as if the waters had but newly retired from the face of the earth, and it would not be wonderful to meet a Megalosaurus, forty feet long or so, waddling like an elephantine lizard up Holborn Hill. Smoke lowering down from chimney-pots, making a soft black drizzle, with flakes of soot in it as big as full-grown snowflakes – gone into mourning, one might imagine, for the death of the sun. Dogs, undistinguishable in mire. Horses, scarcely better – splashed to their very blinkers. Foot passengers, jostling one another's umbrellas, in a general infection of ill-temper, and losing their foothold at street-corners where tens of thousands of other foot passengers have been slipping and sliding since the day broke (if this day ever broke), adding new deposits to the crust upon crust of mud, sticking at those points tenaciously to the pavement, and accumulating at compound interest.

Fog everywhere. Fog up the river, where it flows among green aits and meadows; fog down the river, where it rolls defiled among the tiers of shipping and the waterside pollutions of a great (and dirty) city. Fog on the Essex marshes, fog on the Kentish heights. Fog creeping into the cabooses of collier-brigs; fog lying out on the yards and hovering in the rigging of great ships; fog drooping on the gunwales of barges and small boats. Fog in the eyes and throats of ancient Greenwich pensioners, wheezing by the firesides of their wards; fog in the stem and bowl of the afternoon pipe of the wrathful skipper, down in his close cabin; fog cruelly pinching the toes and fingers of his shivering little 'prentice boy on deck. Chance people on the bridges peeping over the parapets into a nether sky of fog, with fog all round them, as if they were up in a balloon, and hanging in the misty clouds.

Gas looming through the fog in divers places in the streets, much as the sun may, from the spongy fields, be seen to loom by husbandman and ploughboy. Most of the shops lighted two hours before their time – as the gas seems to know, for it has a haggard and unwilling look.

The raw afternoon is rawest, and the dense fog is densest, and the muddy streets are muddiest, near that leaden-headed old obstruction, appropriate ornament for the threshold of a leaden-headed old corporation – Temple Bar.

And hard by Temple Bar, in Lincoln's Inn Hall, at the very heart of the fog, sits the Lord High Chancellor in his High Court of Chancery.

Never can there be fog too thick, never can there come mud and mire too deep, to assort with the groping and floundering condition which this High Court of Chancery, most pestilential of hoary sinners, holds, this day, in the sight of heaven and earth.

1853

CARLYLE IN LONDON

THOMAS CARLYLE

Of this enormous Babel of a place I can give you no account in writing: it is like the heart of all the universe; and the flood of human effort rolls out of it and into it with a violence that almost appals one's very sense. Paris scarcely occupies a quarter of the ground, and does not seem to have the twentieth part of the business. O that our father sey [*saw*] Holborn in a fog! with the black vapour brooding over it, absolutely like fluid ink; and coaches and wains and sheep and oxen and wild people rushing on with bellowings and shrieks and thundering din, as if the earth in general were gone distracted. Today I chanced to pass thro' Smithfield, when the market was three-fourths over. I mounted the steps of a door, and looked abroad upon the area, an irregular space of perhaps thirty acres in extent, encircled with old dingy brick-built houses, and intersected with wooden pens for the cattle. What a scene! Innumerable herds of fat oxen, tied in long rows, or passing at a trot to their several shambles; and thousands of graziers, drovers, butchers, cattle-brokers with their quilted frocks and long goads pushing on the hapless beasts; hurrying to and fro in confused parties, shouting, jostling, cursing, in the midst of rain and *shairn* [*dung*], and braying discord such as the imagination cannot figure. – Then there are stately streets and squares, and calm green recesses to which nothing of this abomination is permitted to enter. No wonder Cobbett calls the place a Wen. It is a monstrous Wen! The thick smoke of it beclouds a space of thirty square miles; and a million of vehicles, from the dog- or cuddy-barrow to the giant waggon, grind along its streets for ever.

There is an excitement in all this, which is pleasant as a transitory feeling, but much against my taste as a permanent one. I had much rather visit London from time to time, than live in it. There is in fact no *right* life in it that I can find: the people are situated here like plants in a hot-house, to which the quiet influences of sky and earth are never in their unadulterated state admitted. It is the case with all ranks: the carman with his huge slouch-hat hanging half-way down his back, consumes his breakfast of bread and tallow or hog's lard, sometimes as he swags along the streets, always in a hurried and precarious fashion, and supplies the deficit by continual pipes, and pots of beer. The fashionable lady rises at three in the afternoon, and begins to live

241

towards midnight. Between these two extremes, the same false and tumultuous manner of existence more or less infests all ranks. It seems as if you were for ever in 'an inn', the feeling of *home* in our acceptation of the term is not known to one of a thousand. You are packed into paltry shells of brick-houses (calculated to endure for forty years, and then fall); every door that slams to in the street is audible in your most secret chamber; the necessaries of life are hawked about through multitudes of hands, and reach you, frequently adulterated, always at rather more than *twice* their cost elsewhere; people's friends must visit them by rule and measure; and when you issue from your door, you are assailed by vast shoals of quacks, and showmen, and street sweepers, and pick-pockets, and mendicants of every degree and shape, all plying in noise or silent craft their several vocations, all in their hearts like 'lions ravening for their prey'. The blackguard population of the place is the most consummately blackguard of anything I ever saw.

1886

THE ROMANCE HAS DEPARTED

RICHARD JEFFERIES

A rattling, thumping, booming noise, like the beating of their war drums by savages, comes over the hedge where the bees are busy at the bramble flowers. The bees take no heed, they pass from flower to flower, seeking the sweet honey to store at home in the hive, as their bee ancestors did before the Roman legions marched to Cowey Stakes. Their habits have not changed; their 'social' relations are the same; they have not called in the aid of machinery to enlarge their liquid wealth, or to increase the facility of collecting it. There is a low murmur rather than a buzz along the hedgerow; but over it the hot summer breeze brings the thumping, rattling, booming sound of hollow metal striking against the ground or in contact with other metal. These ringing noises, which so little accord with the sweet-scented hay and green hedgerows, are caused by the careless handling of milk tins dragged hither and thither by the men who are getting the afternoon milk ready for transit to the railway station miles away. Each tin bears a brazen badge engraved with the name of the milkman who will retail the contents in distant London.

Sturdy milkmaids may still be seen in London, sweeping the crowded pavement clear before them as they walk with swinging tread, a yoke on their shoulders, from door to door. Some remnants of the traditional dairy thus survives in the stony streets that are separated so widely from the country. But here, beside the hay, the hedgerows, the bees, the flowers that precede the blackberries – here in the heart of the meadows the romance has departed. From the refrigerator that cools the milk, the thermometer that tests its temperature, the lactometer that proves its quality, all is mechanized preci-sion. The tins themselves are metal – wood, the old country material for almost every purpose, is eschewed – and they are swung up into a wagon specially built for the purpose. It is the very antithesis of the jolting and cumbrous wagon used for generations in the hayfields and among the corn. It is light, elegantly proportioned, painted, varnished – the work rather of a coachbuilder than a cartwright. The horse harnessed in it is equally unlike the cart-horse. A quick, wiry horse, that may be driven in a trap or gig, is the style – one that will rattle along and catch the train.

The driver takes his seat and handles the reins with the air of a man driving a tradesman's van, instead of walking, like the true old carter, or sitting on the shaft. The vehicle rattles off to the station, where ten, fifteen, or perhaps twenty such converge at the same hour, and then ensues a scene of bustle, chaff, and rough language. The tins are placed in the van specially reserved for them, the whistle sounds, the passengers – who have been wondering why on earth there was all this noise and delay at a little roadside station without so much as a visible steeple – withdraw their heads from the windows; the wheels revolve, and, gathering speed, the train disappears round a curve, hastening to the metropolis.

1880

PALETTE FOR 1927. AUTUMN

CYRIL CONNOLLY

Palette for 1927. *Autumn.* – Brown and gold – brown curtains and chairs of Yeoman's Row, gold tiles in the fire, the green leaves through the lattice windows, then yellow leaves, then black stems of trees. The lights of Brompton Road, the news-boys outside the tube station as I come back from the *New Statesman* to the gramophone, the warm light, the evening paper and a late tea. Drinking with Patrick on idle Sunday mornings, going to the Film Society, dinners alone at the Ivy, theatres alone in the yellow fog. When I say suddenly, 'autumn', I first see nothing but brown and gold, then I see three pictures rolled into one, the brown fur rug on my sofa, the two gold cushions, R.'s brown dress against them, her golden face and hair, a glimpse of the trees through the drawn curtains, a wild excitement in the air – still brown and gold the picture changes, a cold wet afternoon by Battersea bridge, R., slim, golden, slant-eyed, in boy's felt hat and brown jumper, looking down the road and tapping with one foot on the kerb – the swirl of the grey autumnal river, the wet embankment, the waiting figure against the trees of the park, her marsh-green eyes and yellow hair. Windy twilight in the Fulham Road, the roar of buses, the November dusk, walking away from Elm Park Gardens in the eddy of fast-falling leaves from plane and elm crushed close on the rain-swept pavement: swirl of the Debussy quartet matching the wide curve of the road and the depression in my heart: walking on this windy evening, the lamps just lit and wet with rain, alone along the broad street, brown street with lights of gold.

1958

THE WAY THROUGH THE WOODS

The earth of England has the richest literature of all. It can be a lyrical account of the harvest in the hands of R. D. Blackmore or of night on Norcombe Hill by Thomas Hardy. It can be a mysterious and haunting poem, strangely untypical, by Kipling on the way through the woods, or a marvellously observed passage on earthworms by the incomparable Gilbert White. It can be a vivid account of Keighley on the road to Haworth in Mrs Gaskell's Life of Charlotte Brontë, *or a gorgeous evocation of a Pennine town, lightly disguised as Bruddersford, which launches J. B. Priestley into* The Good Companions. *It can be a fizzing account of the smoke and sweat and sparks in the Swindon Railway Works. Finally, a journey by train across Hampshire and Surrey into London made by Louis MacNeice one day in 1938 and forming the great opening passage of his* Autumn Journal. *Close and slow, summer is ending in Hampshire – and in England too. The war is coming.*

HARVEST

R D BLACKMORE

Then the golden harvest came, waving on the broad hillside, and nestling in the quiet nooks scooped from out the fringe of wood. A wealth of harvest, such as never gladdened all our country-side since my father ceased to reap, and his sickle hung to rust. There had not been a man on Exmoor fit to work that reaping-hook, since the time its owner fell, in the prime of life and strength, before a sterner reaper. But now I took it from the wall, where mother proudly stored it, while she watched me, hardly knowing whether she should smile or cry. All the parish was assembled in our upper courtyard; for we were to open the harvest that year, as had been settled with Farmer Nicholas, and with Jasper Kebby, who held the third or little farm. We started in proper order, therefore, as our practice is: first, the parson, Josiah Bowden, wearing his gown and cassock, with the parish Bible in his hand, and a sickle strapped behind him. As he strode along well and stoutly, being a man of substance, all our family came next, I leading mother with one hand, in the other bearing my father's hook, and with a loaf of our own bread and a keg of cider upon my back. Behind us Annie and Lizzie walked, wearing wreaths of cornflowers, set out very prettily, such as mother would have worn, if she had been a farmer's wife, instead of a farmer's widow. Being as she was, she had no adornment, except that her widow's hood was off, and her hair allowed to flow, as if she had been a maiden; and very rich bright hair it was, in spite of all her troubles.

After us, the maidens came, milkmaids and the rest of them, with Betty Muxworthy at their head, scolding even now, because they would not walk fitly. But they only laughed at her; and she knew it was no good to scold, with all the men behind them.

Then the Snowes came trooping forward; Farmer Nicholas in the middle, walking as if he would rather walk to a wheatfield of his own, yet content to

246

follow lead, because he knew himself the leader; and signing every now and
then to the people here and there, as if I were nobody. But to see his three
great daughters, strong and handsome wenches, making upon either side, as
if somebody would run off with them – this was the very thing that taught me
how to value Lorna, and her pure simplicity. After the Snowes, came Jasper
Kebby, with his wife new-married; and a very honest pair they were, upon
only a hundred acres, and a right of common. After these the men came
hotly, without decent order, trying to spy the girls in front, and make good
jokes about them, at which their wives laughed heartily, being jealous when
alone perhaps. And after these men and their wives came all the children
toddling, picking flowers by the way, and chattering and asking questions, as
the children will. There must have been threescore of us, take one with
another, and the lane was full of people. When we were come to the big field-
gate, where the first sickle was to be, Parson Bowden heaved up the rail with
the sleeves of his gown done green with it; and he said that everybody might
hear him, though his breath was short, 'In the name of the Lord, Amen!'

'Amen! So be it!' cried the clerk, who was far behind, being only a
shoemaker.

Then Parson Bowden read some verses from the parish Bible, telling us to
lift up our eyes, and look upon the fields already white to harvest; and then he
laid the Bible down on the square head of the gate-post, and despite his gown
and cassock, three good swipes he cut of corn, and laid them right end
onwards. All this time the rest were huddling outside the gate, and along the
lane, not daring to interfere with parson, but whispering how well he did it.

When he had stowed the corn like that, mother entered, leaning on me,
and we both said, 'Thank the Lord for all His mercies, and these the first fruits
of His hand!' And then the clerk gave out a psalm verse by verse, done very
well; although he sneezed in the midst of it, from a beard of wheat thrust up
his nose by the rival cobbler at Brendon. And when the psalm was sung, so
strongly that the foxgloves on the bank were shaking, like a chime of bells, at
it, parson took a stoop of cider and we all fell to at reaping.

Of course I mean the men, not women; although I know that up the
country, women are allowed to reap; and right well they reap it, keeping row
for row with men, comely, and in due order; yet, meseems, the men must ill
attend to their own reaping-hooks, in fear lest the other cut themselves, being
the weaker vessel. But in our part, women do what seems their proper
business, following well behind the men, out of harm of the swinging hook,
and stooping with their breasts and arms up they catch the swathes of corn,
where the reapers cast them, and tucking them together tightly with a wisp
laid under them, this they fetch around and twist, with a knee to keep it close;
and lo, there is a goodly sheaf, ready to set up in stooks! After these the
children come, gathering each for his little self, if the farmer be right-minded;
until each hath a bundle made as big as himself and longer, and tumbles now
and again with it, in the deeper part of the stubble.

We, the men, kept marching onwards down the flank of the yellow wall,
with knees bent wide, and left arm bowed, and right arm flashing steel. Each
man in his several place, keeping down the rig or chine, on the right side of

the reaper in front, and the left of the man that followed him; each making further sweep and inroad into the golden breadth and depth, each casting leftwards his rich clearance on his foregoer's double track.

So like half a wedge of wildfowl, to and fro we swept the field; and when to either hedge we came, sickles wanted whetting, and throats required moistening, and backs were in need of easing, and every man had much to say, and women wanted praising. Then all returned to the other end, with reaping hooks beneath our arms, and dogs left to mind jackets.

But now, will you believe me well, or will you only laugh at me? For even in the world of wheat, when deep among the garnished crispness of the jointed stalks, and below the feathered yielding of the graceful heads, even as I gripped the swathes and swept the sickle round them, even as I flung them by to rest on brother stubble, through the whirling yellow world, and eagerness of reaping, came the vision of my love, as with downcast eyes she wondered at my power of passion. And then the sweet remembrance glowed, brighter than the sun through wheat, through my very depth of heart, of how she raised those beaming eyes, and ripened in my breast rich hope. Even now I could descry, like high waves in the distance, the rounded heads and folded shadows of the wood of Bagworthy. Perhaps she was walking in the valley, and softly gazing up at them. Oh, to be a bird just there! I could see a bright mist hanging just above the Doone Glen. Perhaps it was shedding its drizzle upon her. Oh, to be a drop of rain! The very breeze which bowed the harvest to my bosom gently, might have come direct from Lorna, with her sweet voice laden. Ah, the flaws of air that wander where they will around her, fan her bright cheek, play with lashes, even revel in her hair and reveal her beauties – man is but a breath, we know, would I were such breath as that!

But confound it, while I ponder, with delicious dreams suspended, with my right arm hanging frustrate and the giant sickle drooped, with my left arm bowed for clasping something more germane than wheat, and my eyes not minding business, but intent on distant woods – confound it, what are the men about, and why am I left vapouring? They have taken advantage of me, the rogues! They are gone to the hedge for the cider-jars; they have had up the sledd of bread and meat, quite softly over the stubble, and if I can believe my eyes (so dazed with Lorna's image), they are sitting down to an excellent dinner before the church clock has gone eleven!

'John Fry, you big villain!' I cried, with John hanging up in the air by the scruff of his neck-cloth, but holding still by his knife and fork, and a goose-leg in between his lips, 'John Fry, what mean you by this, sir?'

'Latt me dowun, or I can't tell 'e,' John answered, with some difficulty. So I let him come down, and I must confess that he had reason on his side. 'Please your worship' – John called me so ever since I returned from London, firmly believing that the King had made me a magistrate at least; though I was to keep it secret – 'us zeed as how your worship were took with thinkin' of King's business, in the middle of the whate-rigg; and so us zed, "Latt un coom to his zell, us had better save taime, by takking our dinner;" and here us be, plaise your worship, and hopps no offence with thic iron spoon full of vried taties.'

I was glad enough to accept the ladle full of fried batatas, and to make the best of things, which is generally done by letting men have their own way. Therefore I managed to dine with them, although it was so early.

For according to all that I can find, in a long life and a varied one, twelve o'clock is the real time for a man to have his dinner. Then the sun is at his noon, calling halt to look around, and then the plants and leaves are turning, each with a little leisure time, before the work of the afternoon. Then is the balance of east and west, and then the right and left side of a man are in due proportion, and contribute fairly with harmonious fluids. And the health of this mode of life, and its reclaiming virtue are well set forth in our ancient rhyme, –

Sunrise, breakfast; sun high, dinner;
Sundown, sup; makes a saint of a sinner.

Whish, the wheat falls! Whirl again; ye have had good dinners; give your master and mistress plenty to supply another year. And in truth we did reap well and fairly, through the whole of that afternoon, I not only keeping lead, but keeping the men up to it. We got through a matter of ten acres, ere the sun between the shocks, broke his light on wheaten plumes, then hung his red cloak on the clouds, and fell into grey slumber.

Seeing this we wiped our sickles and our breasts and foreheads, and soon were on the homeward road, looking forward to good supper.

Of course all the reapers came at night to the harvest supper, and Parson Bowden to say the grace, as well as to help to carve for us. And some help was needed there, I can well assure you; for the reapers had brave appetites, and most of their wives having babies were forced to eat as a duty. Neither failed they of this duty; cut and come again was the order of the evening, as it had been of the day; and I had no time to ask questions, but help meat and ladle gravy. All the while our darling Annie, with her sleeves tucked up and her comely figure panting, was running about with a bucket of taties mashed with lard and cabbage. Even Lizzie had left her books, and was serving out beer and cider; while mother helped plum-pudding largely on pewter plates with the mutton. And all the time Betty Muxworthy was grunting in and out everywhere, not having space to scold even, but changing the dishes, serving the meat, poking the fire, and cooking more. But John Fry would not stir a peg, except with his knife and fork, having all the airs of a visitor, and his wife to keep him eating, till I thought there would be no end of it.

Then having eaten all they could, they prepared themselves with one accord for the business now of drinking. But first they lifted the neck of corn, dressed with ribbons gaily, and set it upon the mantelpiece, each man with his horn a-froth; and then they sang a song about it, every one shouting in the chorus louder than harvest thunderstorm. Some were in the middle of one verse, and some at the end of the next one; yet somehow all managed to get together in the mighty roar of the burden.

Now we sang this song very well the first time, having the parish choir to lead us, and the clarionet, and the parson to give us the time with his cup; and we sang it again the second time, not so but what you might praise it (if you had been with us all the evening), although the parson was gone then, and the clerk not fit to compare with him in the matter of keeping time. But when that song was in its third singing, I defy any man (however sober) to have made out one verse from the other, or even the burden from the verses, inasmuch as every man present, ay, and woman too, sang as became convenient to them, in utterance both of words and tune.

And in truth there was much excuse for them; because it was a noble harvest, fit to thank the Lord for, without His thinking us hypocrites. For we had more land in wheat that year than ever we had before, and twice the crop to the acre; and I could not help now and then remembering, in the midst of the merriment, how my father in the churchyard yonder would have gloried to behold it.

1869

EVENING AND NIGHT

THOMAS HARDY

A Saturday afternoon in November was approaching the time of twilight, and the vast tract of unenclosed wild known as Egdon Heath embrowned itself moment by moment. Overhead the hollow stretch of whitish cloud shutting out the sky was as a tent which had the whole heath for its floor. The heaven being spread with this pallid screen and the earth with the darkest vegetation, their meeting-line at the horizon was clearly marked. In such contrast the heath wore the appearance of an instalment of night which had taken up its place before its astronomical hour was come: darkness had to a great extent arrived hereon, while day stood distinct in the sky. Looking upwards, a furze-cutter would have been inclined to continue work; looking down, he would have decided to finish his faggot and go home.

The distant rims of the world and of the firmament seemed to be a division in time no less than a division in matter. The face of the heath by its mere complexion added half an hour to evening; it could in like manner retard the dawn, sadden noon, anticipate the frowning of storms scarcely generated, and intensify the opacity of a moonless midnight to a cause of shaking and dread. . . .

1874

THE WAY THROUGH THE WOODS

RUDYARD KIPLING

They shut the road through the woods
Seventy years ago.
Weather and rain have undone it again,
And now you would never know
There was once a road through the woods
Before they planted the trees.
It is underneath the coppice and heath
And the thin anemones.
Only the keeper sees
That, where the ring-dove broods,
And the badgers roll at ease,
There was once a road through the woods.
Yet, if you enter the woods
Of a summer evening late,
When the night-air cools on the trout-ringed pools
Where the otter whistles his mate,
(They fear not men in the woods,
Because they see so few.)
You will hear the beat of a horse's feet,
And the swish of a skirt in the dew,
Steadily cantering through
The misty solitudes,
As though they perfectly knew
The old lost road through the woods. . . .
But there is no road through the woods.

1910

EARTHWORMS

GILBERT WHITE

Lands that are subject to frequent inundations are always poor; and probably the reason may be that the worms are drowned. The most insignificant insects and reptiles are of much more consequence, and have much more influence in the economy of nature, than the incurious are aware of; and are mighty in their effect from their minuteness, which renders them less an object of attention, and from their numbers and fecundity. Earthworms, though in appearance a small and despicable link in the chain of nature, yet, if lost, would make a lamentable chasm. For to say nothing of half the birds, and some quadrupeds, which are almost entirely supported by them, worms

251

seem to be the great promoters of vegetation, which would proceed but lamely without them, by boring, perforating, and loosening the soil, and rendering it pervious to rains and the fibres of plants, by drawing straws and stalks of leaves into it; and most of all, by throwing up such infinite numbers of lumps of earth called worm-casts, which is a fine manure for grain and grass. Worms probably provide new soil for hills and slopes where the rain washes the earth away, and they affect slopes, probably, to avoid being flooded. Gardeners and farmers express their detestation of worms; the former, because they render their walks unsightly and make them much work; and the latter, because, as they think, worms eat their green corn. But these men would find that the earth without worms would soon become cold, hard-bound, and void of fermentation, and consequently sterile; and besides, in favour of worms it should be hinted that green corn, plants, and flowers are not so much injured by them as by many species of *coleoptera* in their larva or grub state, and by unnoticed myriads of small shell-less snails, called slugs, which silently and imperceptibly make amazing havoc in the field and garden.

These hints we think proper to throw out in order to set the inquisitive and discerning to work. A good monography of worms would afford much entertainment, and information at the same time; and would open a large and new field in natural history.

1788

THE ROAD TO HAWORTH, 1857

MRS GASKELL

The Leeds and Skipton railway runs along a deep valley of the Aire; a slow and sluggish stream, compared with the neighbouring river of Wharfe. Keighley station is on this line of railway, about a quarter of a mile from the town of the same name. The number of inhabitants and the importance of Keighley have been very greatly increased during the last twenty years, owing to the rapidly extended market for worsted manufactures, a branch of industry that mainly employs the factory population of this part of Yorkshire, which has Bradford for its centre and metropolis.

Keighley is in process of transformation from a populous old-fashioned village into a still more populous and flourishing town. It is evident to the stranger that, as the gable-ended houses, which obtrude themselves cornerwise on the widening street, fall vacant, they are pulled down to allow of greater space for traffic and a more modern style of architecture. The quaint and narrow shop-windows of fifty years ago are giving way to large panes and plate-glass. Nearly every dwelling seems devoted to some branch of commerce. In passing hastily through the town, one hardly perceives where the necessary lawyer and doctor can live, so little appearance is there of any dwelling of the professional middle-class, such as abound in our old cathedral towns. In fact, nothing can be more opposed than the state of society, the modes of thinking, the standards of reference on all points of morality, manners, and even politics and religion, in such a new manufacturing place as Keighley in the north, and any stately, sleepy, picturesque cathedral town in the south. Yet the aspect of Keighley promises well for future stateliness, if not picturesqueness. Grey stone abounds, and the rows of houses built of it have a kind of solid grandeur connected with their uniform and enduring lines. The framework of the doors and the lintels of the windows, even in the smallest dwellings, are made of blocks of stone. There is no painted wood to require continual beautifying, or else present a shabby aspect; and the stone is kept scrupulously clean by the notable Yorkshire housewives. Such glimpses into the interior as a passer-by obtains reveal a rough abundance of the means of living, and diligent and active habits in the women.

The town of Keighley never quite melts into country on the road to Haworth, although the houses become more sparse as the traveller journeys upwards to the grey round hills that seem to bound his journey in a westerly direction. First come some villas, just sufficiently retired from the road to show that they can scarcely belong to any one liable to be summoned in a hurry, at the call of suffering or danger, from his comfortable fireside; the lawyer, the doctor, and the clergyman live at hand, and hardly in the suburbs, with a screen of shrubs for concealment.

In a town one does not look for vivid colouring; what there may be of this is furnished by the wares in the shops, not by foliage or atmospheric effects; but in the country some brilliancy and vividness seems to be instinctively expected, and there is consequently a slight feeling of disappointment at the grey natural tint of every object, near or far off, on the way from Keighley to Haworth. The distance is about four miles; and, as I have said, what with villas, great worsted factories, rows of workmen's houses, with here and there an old-fashioned farmhouse and outbuildings, it can hardly be called 'country' any part of the way. For two miles the road passes over tolerably level ground; distant hills on the left, a 'beck' flowing through meadows on the right, and furnishing water power, at certain points, to the factories built on its banks. The air is dim and lightless with the smoke from all these habitations and places of business. The soil in the valley (or 'bottom', to use the local term) is rich; but as the road begins to ascend the vegetation becomes poorer; it does not flourish, it merely exists; and instead of trees there are only bushes and shrubs about the dwellings. Stone dykes are everywhere used in place of hedges; and what crops there are, on the patches of arable land, consist of pale, hungry-looking, grey-green oats. Right before the traveller on this road rises Haworth village; he can see it for two miles before he arrives, for it is situated on the side of a pretty steep hill, with a back-ground of dun and purple moors, rising and sweeping away yet higher than the church, which is built at the very summit of the long narrow street. All round the horizon there is this same line of sinuous wave-like hills, the scoops into which they fall only revealing other hills beyond, of similar colour and shape, crowned with wild bleak moors – grand from the ideas of solitude and loneliness which they suggest, or oppressive from the feeling which they give of being pent up by some monotonous and illimitable barrier, according to the mood of mind in which the spectator may be.

1857

MR OAKROYD LEAVES HOME

J B PRIESTLEY

There, far below, is the knobbly backbone of England, the Pennine Range. At first, the whole dark length of it, from the Peak to Cross Fell, is visible. Then the Derbyshire hills and the Cumberland fells disappear, for you are descending, somewhere about the middle of the range, where the high moorland thrusts itself between the woollen mills of Yorkshire and the cotton mills of Lancashire. Great winds blow over miles and miles of ling and bog and black rock, and the curlews still go crying in that empty air as they did before the Romans came. There is a glitter of water here and there, from the moorland tarns that are now called reservoirs. In summer you could wander here all day, listening to the larks, and never meet a soul. In winter you could lose your way in an hour or two and die of exposure perhaps, not a dozen miles from where the Bradford trams end or the Burley trams begin. Here are Bodkin Top and High Greave and Black Moor and Four Gates End, and though these are lonely places, almost unchanged since the Domesday Book was compiled, you cannot understand industrial Yorkshire and Lancashire, the wool trade and the cotton trade and many other things besides, such as the popularity of Handel's *Messiah* or the Northern Union Rugby game, without having seen such places. They hide many secrets. Where the moor thins out are patches of ground called 'Intake', which means that they are land wrested from the grasp of the moor. Over to the right is a long smudge of smoke, beneath which the towns of the West Riding lie buried, and fleeces, tops, noils, yarns, stuffs, come and go, in and out of the mills, down to the railways and canals and lorries. All this too, you may say, is a kind of Intake.

At first the towns only seem a blacker edge to the high moorland, so many fantastic outcroppings of its rock, but now that you are closer you see the host of tall chimneys, the rows and rows of little houses, built of blackening stone, that are like tiny sharp ridges on the hills. These windy moors, these clanging dark valleys, these factories and little stone houses, this business of Intaking, have between them bred a race that has special characteristics. Down there are thousands and thousands of men and women who are stocky and hold themselves very stiffly, who have short upper lips and long chins, who use emphatic consonants and very broad vowels and always sound aggressive, who are afraid of nothing but mysterious codes of etiquette and any display of feeling. If it were night, you would notice strange constellations low down in the sky and little golden beetles climbing up to them. These would be street lamps and lighted tramcars on the hills, for here such things are little outposts

254

in No Man's Land and altogether more adventurous and romantic than ordinary street lamps and tramcars. It is not night, however, but a late September afternoon. Some of its sunshine lights up the nearest of the towns, most of it jammed into a narrow valley running up to the moors. It must be Bruddersford, for there, where so many roads meet, is the Town Hall, and if you know the district at all you must immediately recognize the Bruddersford Town Hall, which has a clock that plays *Tom Bowling* and *The Lass of Richmond Hill*. It has been called 'a noble building in the Italian Renaissance style' and always looks as if it had no right to be there.

1929

THE SWINDON RAILWAY WORKS, SPRING 1867

RICHARD JEFFERIES

This factory is perhaps the largest in the West of England. Here are employed as many as seventeen hundred hands – an army of workmen – drawn from the villages round about. Here are made the engines used upon the Great Western Railway. It is open to visitors upon every Wednesday afternoon, and is a sight well worth seeing. A person is in attendance to show it. The place seems to be built somewhat in the form of a parallelogram. Seven tall chimneys belch forth volumes of smoke. The first thing shown to visitors is an engine room near the entrance. Here are two beams of fifty horse-power working with a smooth, oily motion, almost without noise. The yard beneath is, to a stranger, a vast incongruous museum of iron; iron in every possible shape and form, round and square, crooked and straight. Proteus himself never changed into the likeness of such things. The northern shops are devoted to noise, and the voice of the guide is inaudible. Here is a vast wilderness – an endless vista of forges glaring with blue flames, the men all standing by leaning on their hammers, waiting until you pass, while far ahead sparks fly in showers from the tortured anvils high in the air, looking like minute meteors. This place is a temple of Vulcan. If the old motto '*Laborare est orare*', 'labour is prayer', is correct, here be sturdy worshippers of the fire-god. The first glimpse of the factory affords a view of sparks, sweat, and smoke. Smoke, sweat, and sparks is the last thing that is seen.

Passing between a row of fiery furnaces seven times heated, the visitors enter the rail-mill, where the rails are manufactured. This place is a perfect pandemonium. Vast boilers built up in brick close in every side, with the steam hissing like serpents in its efforts to escape. Enormous fly-wheels spin round and round at a velocity which renders the spokes invisible. Steam hammers shake the ground, where once perhaps crouched the timid hare, and stun the ear. These hammers are a miracle of human manufacture. Though it is possible to strike a blow which shall crush iron like earthenware, to bring down a weight of tons, yet a skilful workman can crack a hazel-nut without injuring the kernel. Gazing upon these wonderful hammers the visitor is suddenly scorched upon one side, and turning, finds that a wheelbarrow load of red-hot iron had been thrown down beside him, upon which a jet of water plays, fizzing off into steam. Springing aside he scarcely escapes collision with a mass of red hot metal wheeled along and placed beneath the steam hammer, where it is thumped and bumped flat. His feet now begin to feel the heat of the iron flooring, which the thickest leather cannot keep out. The workmen wear shoes shod with broad headed iron nails from heel to toe. Their legs are defended by greaves – like an iron cricketing pad; their faces by a gauze metal mask. The clang, the rattle, the roar are indescribable; the confusion seems to increase the longer it is looked upon. Yonder, a glare almost too strong for the eyes shows an open furnace door. Out comes a mass of white-hot metal, it is placed on a truck, and wheeled forward to the revolving rollers, and placed between them. Sparks spurt out like a fountain of fire – slowly it passes through, much thinned and lengthened by the process: which is repeated until at length it emerges in the form of a rail. Here come chips of iron – if such an expression might be used – all red hot, sliding along the iron floor to their destination. Look out for your toes! In the dark winter nights the glare from this place can be seen for miles around; lighting up the clouds with a lurid glow like that from some vast conflagration.

1896

AUTUMN JOURNAL

LOUIS MACNEICE

Close and slow, summer is ending in Hampshire,
    Ebbing away down ramps of shaven lawn where close-
       clipped yew
Insulates the lives of retired generals and admirals
    And the spyglasses hung in the hall and the prayer-books
       ready in the pew
And August going out to the tin trumpets of nasturtiums
    And the sunflowers' Salvation Army blare of brass
And the spinster sitting in a deck-chair picking up stitches
    Not raising her eyes to the noise of the 'planes that pass
Northward from Lee-on-Solent. Macrocarpa and cypress
    And roses on a rustic trellis and mulberry trees
And bacon and eggs in a silver dish for breakfast
    And all the inherited assets of bodily ease
And all the inherited worries, rheumatism and taxes,
    And whether Stella will marry and what to do with Dick
And the branch of the family that lost their money in Hatry
    And the passing of the *Morning Post* and of life's climacteric
And the growth of vulgarity, cars that pass the gate-lodge
    And crowds undressing on the beach

And the hiking cockney lovers with thoughts directed
    Neither to God nor Nation but each to each.
But the home is still a sanctum under the pelmets,
    All quiet on the Family Front,
Farmyard noises across the fields at evening
    While the trucks of the Southern Railway dawdle . . . shunt
Into poppy sidings for the night – night which knows no
        passion
    No assault of hands or tongue
For all is old as flint or chalk or pine-needles
    And the rebels and the young
Have taken the train to town or the two-seater
    Unravelling rails or road,
Losing the thread deliberately behind them –
    Autumnal palinode.
And I am in the train too now and summer is going
    South as I go north
Bound for the dead leaves falling, the burning bonfire,
    The dying that brings forth
The harder life, revealing the trees' girders,
    The frost that kills the germs of *laissez-faire*;
West Meon, Tisted, Farnham, Woking, Weybridge,
    Then London's packed and stale and pregnant air.
My dog, a symbol of the abandoned order,
    Lies on the carriage floor,
Her eyes inept and glamorous as a film star's,
    Who wants to live, i.e. wants more
Presents, jewellery, furs, gadgets, solicitations
    As if to live were not
Following the curve of a planet or controlled water
    But a leap in the dark, a tangent, a stray shot.
It is this we learn after so many failures,
    The building of castles in sand, of queens in snow,
That we cannot make any corner in life or in life's beauty,
    That no river is a river which does not flow.
Surbiton, and a woman gets in, painted
    With dyed hair but a ladder in her stocking and eyes
Patient beneath the calculated lashes,
    Inured for ever to surprise;
And the train's rhythm becomes the *ad nauseam* repetition
    Of every tired aubade and maudlin madrigal,
The faded airs of sexual attraction
    Wandering like dead leaves along a warehouse wall:
'I loved my love with a platform ticket,
    A jazz song,
A handbag, a pair of stockings of Paris Sand –
    I loved her long.

I loved her between the lines and against the clock,
　Not until death
But till life did us part I loved her with paper money
　And with whisky on the breath.
I loved her with peacock's eyes and the wares of Carthage,
　With glass and gloves and gold and a powder puff
With blasphemy, camaraderie, and bravado
　And lots of other stuff.
I loved my love with the wings of angels
　Dipped in henna, unearthly red,
With my office hours, with flowers and sirens,
　With my budget, my latchkey, and my daily bread.'
And so to London and down the ever-moving Stairs
Where a warm wind blows the bodies of men together
　And blows apart their complexes and cares.

1939

CONSIDER WHAT NATION THIS IS

Polemical writing has a long and honourable tradition in England. Rage rides well on the language. It can be controlled and majestic, as in Milton's Areopagitica. *It can be chillingly understated, as in Samuel Bamford's account of the butchery at Peterloo. It can be eloquently bitter, as in the young Rebecca West's short essay on the life of Emily Davison, the suffragette who threw herself in front of the King's horse in the 1913 Derby. It can be gentle and faintly puzzled, as in Arthur Bryant's indictment of Versailles. It can be elegantly ironic, as in Siegfried Sassoon's poem* The Case for the Miners. *It can be the case against modern England put with force, whether you agree or not, by the miners' leader Arthur Scargill. It can be the case against capital punishment, put with passion by the late and great Cassandra in the* Daily Mirror *on the morning Ruth Ellis was hanged. It can be an hysterically comic demolition job, as carried out by Bernard Levin in perhaps his most memorable piece of all: 'How an old Geezer fell on Hard Times'. The North Thames Gas Board Area 5 has never been quite the same since.*

AREOPAGITICA

JOHN MILTON

Lords and Commons of England, consider what Nation it is whereof ye are, and whereof ye are the governors: a Nation not slow and dull, but of a quick, ingenious and piercing spirit, acute to invent, subtle and sinewy to discourse, not beneath the reach of any point, the highest that human capacity can soar to. Therefore the studies of Learning in her deepest sciences have been so ancient and so eminent among us, that writers of good antiquity and ablest judgement have been persuaded that even the school of Pythagoras and the Persian wisdom took beginning from the old philosophy of this island. And that wise and civil Roman, Julius Agricola, who governed once here for Caesar, preferred the natural wits of Britain before the laboured studies of the French. Nor is it for nothing that the grave and frugal Transylvanian sends out yearly from as far as the mountainous borders of Russia, and beyond the Hercynian wilderness, not their youth, but their staid men, to learn our language and our theologic arts.

Yet that which is above all this, the favour and the love of Heaven, we have great argument to think in a peculiar manner propitious and propending towards us. Why else was this Nation chosen before any other, that out of her, as out of Sion, should be proclaimed and sounded forth the first tidings and trumpet of Reformation to all Europe? And had it not been the obstinate perverseness of our prelates against the divine and admirable spirit of Wickliff, to suppress him as a schismatic and innovator, perhaps neither the Bohemian Huss and Jerome, no nor the name of Luther or of Calvin, had been ever known: the glory of reforming all our neighbours had been completely ours. But now, as our obdurate clergy have with violence demeaned the matter, we are become hitherto the latest and backwardest scholars, of whom God offered to have made us the teachers. Now once again by all concurrence of signs, and by the general instinct of holy and devout men, as they daily and solemnly express their thoughts, God is decreeing to begin some new and great period in His Church, even to the reforming of Reformation itself: what does He then but reveal Himself to His servants, and as His manner is, first to His Englishmen? I say, as His manner is, first to us, though we mark not the method of His counsels, and are unworthy.

Behold now this vast City: a city of refuge, the mansion house of liberty, encompassed and surrounded with His protection; the shop of war hath not there more anvils and hammers waking, to fashion out the plates and instruments of armed Justice in defence of beleaguered Truth, than there be pens and heads there, sitting by their studious lamps, musing, searching, revolving new notions and ideas wherewith to present, as with their homage and their fealty, the approaching Reformation: others as fast reading, trying all things, assenting to the force of reason and convincement. What could a man require more from a Nation so pliant and so prone to seek after knowledge? What wants there to such a towardly and pregnant soil, but wise and faithful labourers, to make a knowing people, a Nation of Prophets, of Sages, and of Worthies? We reckon more than five months yet to harvest; there need not be five weeks; had we but eyes to lift up, the fields are white already.

Where there is much desire to learn, there of necessity will be much arguing, much writing, many opinions; for opinion in good men is but knowledge in the making. Under these fantastic terrors of sect and schism, we wrong the earnest and zealous thirst after knowledge and understanding which God hath stirred up in this city. What some lament of, we rather should rejoice at, should rather praise this pious forwardness among men, to reassume the ill-reputed care of their Religion into their own hands again. A little generous prudence, a little forbearance of one another, and some grain of charity might win all these diligences to join, and unite in one general and brotherly search after Truth; could we but forgo this prelatical tradition of crowding free consciences and Christian liberties into canons and precepts of men. I doubt not, if some great and worthy stranger should come among us, wise to discern the mould and temper of a people, and how to govern it, observing the high hopes and aims, the diligent alacrity of our extended thoughts and reasonings in the pursuance of truth and freedom, but that he would cry out as Pyrrhus did, admiring the Roman docility and courage: If such were my Epirots, I would not despair the greatest design that could be attempted, to make a Church or Kingdom happy.

Yet these are the men cried out against for schismatics and sectaries; as if, while the temple of the Lord was building, some cutting, some squaring the marble, others hewing the cedars, there should be a sort of irrational men who could not consider there must be many schisms and many dissections made in the quarry and in the timber, ere the house of God can be built. And when every stone is laid artfully together, it cannot be united into a continuity, it can but be contiguous in this world; neither can every piece of

261

the building be of one form; nay rather the perfection consists in this, that, out of many moderate varieties and brotherly dissimilitudes that are not vastly disproportional, arises the goodly and the graceful symmetry that commends the whole pile and structure.

Let us therefore be more considerate builders, more wise in spiritual architecture, when great reformation is expected. For now the time seems come, wherein Moses the great prophet may sit in heaven rejoicing to see that memorable and glorious wish of his fulfilled, when not only our seventy Elders, but all the Lord's people, are become prophets. No marvel then though some men, and some good men too perhaps, but young in goodness, as Joshua then was, envy them. They fret, and out of their own weakness are in agony, lest these divisions and subdivisions will undo us. The adversary again applauds, and waits the hour: When they have branched themselves out, saith he, small enough into parties and partitions, then will be our time. Fool! he sees not the firm root, out of which we all grow, though into branches: nor will be ware until he see our small divided maniples cutting through at every angle of his ill-united and unwieldy brigade. And that we are to hope better of all these supposed sects and schisms, and that we shall not need that solicitude, honest perhaps though over-timorous of them that vex in this behalf, but shall laugh in the end at those malicious applauders of our differences, I have these reasons to persuade me.

First, when a City shall be as it were besieged and blocked about, her navigable river infested, inroads and incursions round, defiance and battle oft rumoured to be marching up even to her walls and suburb trenches, that then the people, or the greater part, more than at other times, wholly taken up with the study of highest and most important matters to be reformed, should be disputing, reasoning, reading, inventing, discoursing, even to a rarity and admiration, things not before discoursed or written of, argues first a singular goodwill, contentedness and confidence in your prudent foresight and safe government, Lords and Commons; and from thence derives itself to a gallant bravery and well-grounded contempt of their enemies, as if there were no small number of as great spirits among us, as his was, who when Rome was nigh besieged by Hannibal, being in the city, bought that piece of ground at no cheap rate, whereon Hannibal himself encamped his own regiment.

Next, it is a lively and cheerful presage of our happy success and victory. For as in a body, when the blood is fresh, the spirits pure and vigorous, not only to vital but to rational faculties, and those in the acutest and the pertest operations of wit and subtlety, it argues in what good plight and constitution the body is so when the cheerfulness of the people is so sprightly up, as that it has not only wherewith to guard well its own freedom and safety, but to spare, and to bestow upon the solidest and sublimest points of controversy and new invention, it betokens us not degenerated, nor drooping to a fatal decay, but casting off the old and wrinkled skin of corruption to outlive these pangs and wax young again, entering the glorious ways of truth and prosperous virtue, destined to become great and honourable in these latter ages. Methinks I see in my mind a noble and puissant nation rousing herself like a strong man after sleep, and shaking her invincible locks. Methinks I see her as an eagle mewing her mighty youth, and kindling her undazzled eyes at the full midday beam; purging and unscaling her long-abused sight at the fountain itself of heavenly radiance; while the whole noise of timorous and flocking birds, with those also that love the twilight, flutter about, amazed at what she means, and in their envious gabble would prognosticate a year of sects and schisms.

What would ye do then? should ye suppress all this flowery crop of knowledge and new light sprung up and yet springing daily in this city? should ye set an oligarchy of twenty engrossers over it, to bring a famine upon our minds again, when we shall know nothing but what is measured to us by their bushel? Believe it, Lords and Commons, they who counsel ye to such a suppressing do as good as bid ye suppress yourselves; and I will soon show how. If it be desired to know the immediate cause of all this free writing and free speaking, there cannot be assigned a truer than your own mild and free and humane government. It is the liberty, Lords and Commons, which your own valorous and happy counsels have purchased us, liberty which is the nurse of all great wits; this is that which hath rarefied and enlightened our spirits like the influence of heaven; this is that which hath enfranchised, enlarged and lifted up our apprehensions degrees above themselves.

Ye cannot make us now less capable, less knowing, less eagerly pursuing of the truth, unless ye first make yourselves, that made us so, less the lovers, less the founders of our true liberty. We can grow ignorant again, brutish, formal and slavish, as ye found us; but you then must first become that which ye cannot be, oppressive, arbitrary and tyrannous, as they were from whom ye have freed us. That our hearts are now more capacious, our thoughts more erected to the search and expectation of greatest and exactest things, is the issue of your own virtue propagated in us; ye cannot suppress that, unless ye reinforce an abrogated and merciless law, that fathers may despatch at will their own children. And who shall then stick closest to ye, and excite others? not he who takes up arms for coat and conduct, and his four nobles of Danegelt. Although I dispraise not the defence of just immunities, yet love my peace better, if that were all. Give me the liberty to know, to utter, and to argue freely according to conscience, above all liberties.

1644

PETERLOO

SAMUEL BAMFORD

By eight o'clock on the morning of Monday, the 16th August, 1819, the whole town of Middleton might be said to be on the alert: some to go to the meeting, and others to see the procession, the like of which for such a purpose, had never before taken place in that neighbourhood.

First were selected twelve of the most comely and decent-looking youths, who were placed in two rows of six each, with each a branch of laurel presented in his hand, as a token of amity and peace; then followed the men of several districts in fives; then the band of music, an excellent one; then the colours: a blue one of silk, with inscriptions in golden letters, 'Unity and Strength', 'Liberty and Fraternity'; a green one of silk, with golden letters, 'Parliaments Annual', 'Suffrage Universal'; and betwixt them, on a staff, a handsome cap of crimson velvet with a tuft of laurel, and the cap tastefully braided, with the word 'Libertas' in front. Next were placed the remainder of the men of the districts in fives.

Every hundred men had a leader, who was distinguished by a sprig of laurel in his hat; others similarly distinguished were appointed over these, and the whole were to obey the directions of a principal conductor, who took his place at the head of the column, with a bugleman to sound his orders. Such were our dispositions on the ground at Barrowfields. At the sound of the bugle not less than three thousand men formed a hollow square, with probably as many people around them, and, an impressive silence having been obtained, I reminded them that they were going to attend the most important meeting that had ever been held for Parliamentary Reform, and I hoped their conduct would be marked by a steadiness and seriousness befitting the occasion, and such as would cast shame upon their enemies, who had always represented the reformers as a mob–like rabble; but they would see they were not so that day. I requested they would not leave their ranks, nor show carelessness, nor inattention to the orders of their leaders; but that they would walk comfortably and agreeably together. Not to offer any insult or provocation by word or deed; not to notice any persons who might do the same by them, but to keep such persons as quiet as possible; for if they began to retaliate, the least disturbance might serve as a pretext for dispersing the meeting. If the peace officers should come to arrest myself or any other person, they were not to offer any resistance, but suffer them to execute their office peaceably. When at the meeting, they were to keep themselves as select as possible, with their banners in the centre, so that if individuals straggled, or got away from the main body, they would know where to find them again by seeing their banners; and when the meeting was dissolved, they were to get close around their banners and leave the town as soon as possible, lest, should they stay drinking or loitering about the streets, their enemies should take advantage, and send some of them to the New Bailey. I also said that, in conformity with a rule of the committee, no sticks, nor weapons of any description, would be allowed to be carried in the ranks; and those who had such were requested to put them aside, or leave them with some friend until their return. In consequence of this order many sticks were left behind; and a few only of the oldest and most infirm amongst us were allowed to carry their walking staves. I may say with truth that we presented a most respectable assemblage of labouring men; all were decently though humbly attired; and I noticed not even one who did not exhibit a white Sunday's shirt, a neck-cloth, and other apparel in the same clean, though homely condition. My address was received with cheers; it was heartily and unanimously assented to. We opened into column, the music struck up, the banners flashed in the sunlight, other music was heard, it was that of the Rochdale party coming to join us. We met, and a shout from ten thousand startled the echoes of the woods and dingles. Then all was quiet save the breath of music; and with intent seriousness we went on.

Our whole column, with the Rochdale people, would probably consist of six thousand men. At our head were a hundred or two of women, mostly young wives, and mine own was amongst them. A hundred or two of our handsomest girls, sweethearts to the lads who were with us, danced to the music, or sung snatches of popular songs; a score or two children were sent back, though some went forward; whilst on each side of our line walked thousands of stragglers. And thus, accompanied by our friends and our dearest and most tender connections, we went slowly towards Manchester.

At Blackley the accession to our ranks and the crowd in the road had become much greater. At Harpurhey we halted, whilst the band and those who thought proper, refreshed with a cup of prime ale from Sam Ogden's tap. When the bugle sounded every man took his place, and we advanced.

From all that I had heard of the disposition of the authorities, I had scarcely expected that we should be allowed to enter Manchester in a body. I had thought it not improbable that they, or some of them, would meet us with a civil and military escort; would read the Riot Act, if they thought proper, and warn us from proceeding, and that we should then have nothing to do but turn back and hold a meeting in our town. I had even fancied that they would be most likely to stop us at the then toll-gate, where the roads forked towards Collyhurst and Newtown; but when I saw both these roads open, with only a horseman or two prancing before us, I began to think that I had over-estimated the forethought of the authorities, and I felt somewhat assured that we should be allowed to enter the town quietly, when, of course, all probability of interruption would be at an end. . . .

A circumstance interesting to myself now occurred. On the bank of an open field on our left I perceived a gentleman observing us attentively. He beckoned me, and I went to him. He was one of my late employers. He took my hand, and rather concernedly, but kindly, said he hoped no harm was intended by all those people who were coming in. I said, 'I would pledge my life for their entire peaceableness.' I asked him to notice them, 'did they look like persons wishing to outrage the law? were they not, on the contrary, evidently heads of decent working families? or members of such families?' 'No, no,' I said, 'my dear sir, and old respected master, if any wrong or violence take place, they will be committed by men of a very different stamp from these.' He said he was very glad to hear me say so; he was happy he had seen me, and gratified by the manner in which I had expressed myself. I asked, did he think we should be interrupted at the meeting? he said he did not believe we should; 'then', I replied, 'all will be well'; and shaking hands, with mutual good wishes, I left him, and took my station as before.

At Newtown we were welcomed with open arms by the poor Irish weavers, who came out in their best drapery, and uttered blessings and words of endearment, many of which were not understood by our rural patriots. Some of them danced, and others stood with clasped hands and tearful eyes, adoring almost, that banner whose colour was their national one, and the emblem of their green island home. We thanked them by the band striking up, 'Saint Patrick's day in the morning.' They were electrified; and we passed on, leaving those warm-hearted suburbans capering and whooping like mad. . . .

My wife I had not seen for some time; but when last I caught a glimpse of her, she was with some decent married females; and thinking the party quite safe in their own discretion, I felt not much uneasiness on their account, and so had greater liberty in attending to the business of the meeting.

In about half an hour after our arrival the sounds of music and reiterated shouts proclaimed the near approach of Mr Hunt and his party; and in a minute or two they were seen coming from Deansgate, preceded by a band of music and several flags. On the driving seat of a barouche sat a neatly dressed female, supporting a small flag, on which were some emblematical drawings and an inscription. Within the carriage were Mr Hunt, who stood up; Mr Johnson, of Smedley Cottage; Mr Moorhouse, of Stockport; Mr Carlile, of London; Mr John Knight, of Manchester; and Mr Saxton, a sub-editor of the *Manchester Observer*. Their approach was hailed by one universal shout from probably eighty thousand persons. They threaded their way slowly past us and through the crowd, which Hunt eyed, I thought, with almost as much of astonishment as satisfaction. This spectacle could not be otherwise in his view than solemnly impressive. Such a mass of human beings he had not beheld till then. His responsibility must weigh on his mind. Their power for good or evil was irresistible, and who should direct that power? Himself alone who had called it forth. The task was great, and not without its peril. The meeting was a tremendous one. He mounted the hustings; the music ceased; Mr Johnson proposed that Mr Hunt should take the chair; it was seconded, and carried with acclamation; and Mr Hunt, stepping towards the front of the stage, took off his white hat, and addressed the people.

Whilst he was doing so, I proposed to an acquaintance that, as the speeches and resolutions were not likely to contain anything new to us, and as we could see them in the papers, we should retire awhile and get some refreshment, of which I stood much in need, being not in very robust health. He assented, and we had got to nearly the outside of the crowd, when a noise and strange murmur arose towards the church. Some persons said it was the Blackburn people coming, and I stood on tip-toe and looked in the direction whence the noise proceeded, and saw a party of cavalry in blue and white uniform come trotting, sword in hand, round the corner of the garden-wall, and to the front of a row of new houses, where they reined up in a line.

'The soldiers are here,' I said; 'we must go back and see what this means.' 'Oh,' some one made reply, 'they are only come to be ready if there should be any disturbance at the meeting.' 'Well, let us go back,' I said, and we forced our way towards the colours.

On the cavalry drawing up they were received with a shout of good-will, as I understood it. They shouted again, waving their sabres over their heads; and then, slackening rein, and striking spur into their steeds, they dashed forward and began cutting the people.

'Stand fast,' I said, 'they are riding upon us; stand fast.' And there was a general cry in our quarter of 'Stand fast.' The cavalry were in confusion: they evidently could not, with all the weight of man and horse, penetrate that compact mass of human beings; and their sabres were plied to hew a way through naked held-up hands and defenceless heads; and then chopped limbs and wound-gaping skulls were seen; and groans and cries were mingled with the din of that horrid confusion. 'Ah! Ah!' 'for shame! for shame!' was shouted. Then, 'Break! break! they are killing them in front, and they cannot get away'; and there was a general cry of 'break! break!' For a moment the crowd held back as in a pause; then was a rush, heavy and resistless as a headlong sea, and a sound like low thunder, with screams, prayers, and imprecations from the crowd moiled and sabre-doomed who could not escape.

By this time Hunt and his companions had disappeared from the hustings, and some of the yeomanry, perhaps less sanguinarily disposed than others, were busied in cutting down the flag-staves and demolishing the flags at the hustings.

On the breaking of the crowd the yeomanry wheeled, and, dashing whenever there was an opening, they followed, pressing and wounding. Many females appeared as the crowd opened; and striplings or mere youths also were found. Their cries were piteous and heart-rending, and would, one might have supposed, have disarmed any human resentment; but here their appeals were in vain. Women, white-vested maids, and tender youths, were indiscriminately sabred or trampled; and we have reason for believing that few were the instances in which that forbearance was vouchsafed which they so earnestly implored.

In ten minutes from the commencement of the havoc the field was an open and almost deserted space. The sun looked down through a sultry and motionless air. The curtains and blinds of the windows within view were all closed. A gentleman or two might occasionally be seen looking out from one of the new houses before mentioned, near the door of which a group of persons (special constables) were collected, and apparently in conversation; others were assisting the wounded or carrying off the dead. The hustings remained, with a few broken and hewed flag-staves erect, and a torn and gashed banner or two dropping; whilst over the whole field were strewed caps, bonnets, hats, shawls, and shoes, and other parts of male and female dress, trampled, torn, and bloody. The yeomanry had dismounted – some were easing their horses' girths, others adjusting their accoutrements, and some were wiping their sabres. Several mounds of human beings still remained where they had fallen, crushed down and smothered. Some of these still groaning, others with staring eyes, were gasping for breath, and others would never breathe more. All was silent save those low sounds, and the occasional snorting and pawing of steeds. Persons might sometimes be noticed peeping from attics and over the tall ridgings of houses, but they quickly withdrew, as if fearful of being observed, or unable to sustain the full gaze of a scene so hideous and abhorrent.

1844

THE LIFE OF EMILY DAVISON

REBECCA WEST

I never dreamed how terrible the life of Emily Davison must have been. Yet she was to me quite a familiar personality ever since I first met her just after her first imprisonment four years ago. She was a wonderful talker. Her talk was an expression of that generosity which was her master-passion, which she has followed till today she is beggared even of her body; it was as though, delighted by the world, which her fine wits and her moral passion had revealed to her, she could not rest till you had seen it too. So I knew her, though I never spoke to her again. I saw her once more; last summer I saw her standing in some London street collecting for the wives and children of the dockers, her cheerfulness and her pyrotechnic intelligence blazing the brighter through a body worn thin by pain and the exactions of good deeds.

But for her last triumph, when in one moment she, by leaving us, became the governor of our thoughts, she led a very ordinary life for a woman of her type and times. She was imprisoned eight times; she hunger-struck seven times; she was forcibly fed forty-nine times. That is the kind of life to which we dedicate our best and kindest and wittiest women; we take it for granted that they shall spend their kindness and their wits in ugly scuffles in dark cells. And now in the constant contemplation of their pain we have become insensible. When enlightened by her violent death, we try to reckon up the price that Emily Davison paid for wearing a fine character in a mean world, we realize that her whole life since she joined the Women's Social and Political Union in 1906 was a tragedy which we ought not to have permitted. For if, when we walked behind her bier on Saturday, we thought of ourselves as doing a dead comrade honour, we were wrong. We were making a march of penitence behind a victim we allowed the Government to do to death.

Emily Davison was a woman of learning: she had taken honours in both the English schools of Oxford and classics and mathematics in London University. When she became a militant suffragist she turned her back on opportunities of distinction as a journalist and teacher. More than that, she entered into a time of financial insecurity; no comfortable background offered her ease between her battles. And eight times she went to prison. So many women have been brave enough to pass through prison unconsumed that, doubting if our race could furnish so much courage at one time, we have come to wonder whether prison is such a place of horror after all. But it was a hell through which she passed eight times. Once, indeed, the law of the land pursued those who maltreated her in gaol. A more than common ruffianly gang of visiting magistrates, who turned a hose of icy water on to her as she barricaded herself in her cell against forcible feeding, had to answer for their offence in the law courts. But we have her own description of an ordeal when her tormentors kept well within the law:

On Wednesday 19 June, from 10 a.m. onwards, we were kept in

solitary confinement.

On Saturday we decided that most of us would barricade our cells after they had been cleaned out. At ten o'clock on the Saturday a regular siege took place in Holloway. On all sides one heard crowbars, blocks and wedges being used; men battering on doors with all their might. The barricading was always followed by cries of the victims, groans and other horrible sounds. These sounds came nearer and nearer in my direction. My turn came. I fought like a demon at my door, which was forced open with crowbars till at last enough room was made for one of the besiegers to get in. He pulled open the door, and in came wardresses and a doctor. I protested loudly that I would not be fed by a junior doctor, and tried to dart out into the passage; then I was seized by about five wardresses, bound into the chair still protesting; and they accomplished their purpose. They threw me on my bed, and at once locked the door and went off to the next victim.

If we subjected the most infamous woman, expert in murder, to such mental and physical torture, we should make ourselves criminals. And this woman was guiltless of any crime. Such torture, so unprovoked, would have turned most of us to the devising of more bitter violence against the Government; but there was a generous twist even to her rebellion. She longed not for a satisfying revenge, but for the quickest end to the tormenting of her friends. And then it was she conceived the idea of the need for a human sacrifice to buy the salvation of women:

I lay like a log for some time. When I did recover a little, I got up and smashed out the remaining panes of my window, then lay down again until I was able to get out into the corridor. In my mind was the thought that some desperate protest must be made to put a stop to the hideous torture which was now being our lot. Therefore, as soon as I got out I climbed on to the railing, and threw myself out on to the wire-netting, a distance of between twenty and thirty feet. The idea in my mind was 'one big tragedy may save many others'; but the netting prevented any severe injury. The wardress in charge ran forward in horror. She tried to get me off the netting, and whistled for help. Three others came and tried their best to induce me to go into my cell. I refused.

After a time their suspicions were allayed, and the matron came through into the ward to visit some of the prisoners; while she was there the wardresses relaxed their watch, and I began to look again. I realized that my best means of carrying out my purpose was the iron staircase. When a good moment came, quite deliberately I walked upstairs and threw myself from the top, as I meant, on to the iron staircase. If I had been successful I should undoubtedly have been killed, as it was a clear drop of thirty to forty feet. But I caught once more on the edge of the netting. A wardress ran to me, expostulating, and called on two of my comrades to try and stop me. As she spoke I realized that there was only one chance left, and that was to hurl myself with the greatest force I could summon from the netting on to the staircase, a drop of about ten feet. I heard someone saying 'No surrender!' and threw myself forward on my head with all my might. I knew nothing more except a fearful thud on my head. When I recovered consciousness, it was to a sense of acute agony. Voices were buzzing around me; in the distance someone said, 'Fetch the doctor.' Someone tried to move me, and I called out, 'Oh, don't!' Then the doctor came and asked for me to be moved to a cell close by. They lifted me as gently as possible. He asked me to go to hospital, but I begged him to leave me there – which he did. I also managed to say, 'For heaven's sake, don't feed me, because I shall fight.'

That was a year ago. For twelve months she was brooding over this plan to close a bloody war by giving her body to death. We belittle her if we think that her great decision can have made that decision to die an easy one; her last months before death must have been a time of great agony. To a woman of such quick senses life must have been very dear, and the abandonment of it a horror which we, who are still alive and mean to remain so, who have not even had the pluck to unseat the Government and shake it into sense, cannot conceive. And this decision was made by a soul harried by a body whose state was such as would have killed the courage in most of us. For the harsh treatment to which she subjected herself was nothing to the treatment she received from the prison officials, and between the two her body was shattered:

To my amazement the doctors came to forcibly feed me that afternoon. The operation, throughout which I struggled, caused me such agony that I begged the three comrades who were released that afternoon to let friends know outside what was being done.

From that time on they fed me twice a day, in spite of the torture it caused me, until Thursday when, to our intense relief, they fed me only once. We all said that any food that could have been poured into us in a second operation could not possibly have done us the good that the relief from a second torture did.

Meantime nothing was being done to make my condition better. My head was dressed on Sunday. Nothing further was done to it. By the examination I knew that besides the two injuries to my head the seventh cervical vertebra was injured, and another at the base of my spine. They seemed very much worried about my right shoulder-blade. The sacrum bone was also injured, not to mention the many bruises all over my arms and back. All the vertebrae at the back of the head are very painful, and it is torture to turn.

From these injuries she never quite recovered. Till the day she died her spine still hurt her. Twelve months of misery of body and soul we inflicted on her by tolerance of this vile Government.

Many of the women in that funeral march were weeping; the sight of the broad arrows on her purple pall kept me from tears. Surely it was the most merciful thing that ever befell Emily Davison that her death, unlike her life, was unshadowed by prison walls. To the end the sunlight was on her face. Mr McKenna had no part in her sickroom; he paid no delicate deathbed attentions with the stomach-pump and nostril-tube. I was glad that for her executioner she had an unmalicious brute. But except for these kind circumstances of her death it was all grief.

When I came out of the memorial service where, in our desire to testify that the way of high passion which she had trodden was the only way, we had said and sung rather inadequate things over her coffin, I heard that Mrs Pankhurst had been re-arrested. And for a moment I was choked with rage at the ill-manners of it. Imagine a government arresting an opponent simply and solely to prevent her doing honour to the body of another opponent! But then I realized what it meant. Mrs Pankhurst was very ill, so ill that her nurse had tried to dissuade her from rising for the funeral, lest she should die on the way. And now she was taken back to Holloway and the hunger-strike. I felt a feeling that is worse than grief. It was the feeling that one has when one is very ill and has not slept all night. There comes an hour in the early morning when one realizes that one will not sleep again for a long, long time; perhaps never. So now it was not only that England had passed through a hot restless night of delirious deeds. But England has murdered sleep. Before us stretch the long, intolerable weeks during which they are going to murder Mrs Pankhurst. During that time we shall know no innocent rest, and surely some plague should fall upon us afterwards.

They have released her since. It must be for the last time. We dare not bear the double guilt of the death of Emily Davison and of Mrs Pankhurst. We must avoid it at the risk of turning the British Constitution upside down, at the risk of driving from the Cabinet 'the best-dressed man in Parliament', at the risk of breaking Mr Asquith's evil, obstinate heart. We must drop this masochist attitude of long-suffering, which is the mistake of the revolutionary movements, and show ourselves an angry England. We must have a demonstration in Trafalgar Square that will tell an astonished government that positively in the beginning of the twentieth century, in the centre of civilization, after seven years of Liberal government, there are still people who object to the murder of women. And when the Government absurdly asks: 'But what are we to do?' we must tell them that we prefer law-breakers to be at liberty; that if the women must burn grandstands they must; but that at any cost these wonderful law-breakers must go free, for they are the stuff of which England is built. And if the Government dislikes the resulting state of chaos it can give Votes for Women.

What a foe we have to fight! Can we hand Mrs Pankhurst over to that foe? This mishandling of women has its roots in horror. Doctors know that there is an obscene kind of madness that makes men torture women. Twenty-five years ago London was sick with fear because one such maniac crept through the dark alleys of Whitechapel mutilating and murdering unfortunate women. In those days people cursed him. They tried to hunt him out of his black hiding-place and make him pay for his crime. But today Jack the Ripper works free-handed from the honourable places of government: he sits on the

Front Bench at St Stephen's or in those vast public sepulchres of conscience in Whitehall, and works not in secret but through Home Office orders and scarlet-robed judges. Scotland Yard is at his service; the medical profession, up to the President of the Royal College of Surgeons, places its skill at his disposal, that his mutilations may be the more ingenious. And for his victims he no longer seeks the shameful women of mean streets. To him, before the dull eyes of the unprotesting world, fall the finest women of the land, the women of the most militant honour and the wisest courage. How times can change in a quarter of a century!

And the backing behind this Government! The *Manchester Guardian* whimpered evil of the dead last week; so party passion can turn fools to knaves. The unspeakable *Pall Mall Gazette*, whose pages in their technical excellence and spiritual nauseousness remind one of an efficiently managed sewage farm, had a vulgar leader with a comic title on the death of Emily Davison. The dreary mob of Pecksniffs and heavy-jowled stockbrokers that stand behind these papers! And poverty has made many allies for the perverted Government. Near King's Cross there was a horrible crowd that jeered at the hearse. Old men, that looked like wicked little boys, little boys that looked like wicked old men, lively young prostitutes with bare arms scrawled with tattooing, old women putrescent with sin. They cried out lovingly upon the name of one Jones, the King's jockey, for these were betting people. Again I was glad that Emily Davison was killed by a horse and not by the kind of person she was fighting with.

Now that she is laid to earth, will we break up the procession and melt into the wicked crowd? Or will we continue to follow in the hard path of tolerance and defence of a cause that is fighting under extraordinarily difficult and perplexing conditions, till her spirit, eased by our achievements, may rest in peace, all being won?

1913

ENGLISH SAGA

ARTHUR BRYANT

But what, puzzled men with long but hazy memories asked, had happened? Why had the soldier who had overcome so much failed after the peace to achieve those simple and elementary hopes for which the dead had died? The things he wanted in those far days in the trenches had seemed so reasonable, and for a rich country so easy. A tithe of the effort and cost which Britain had expended in defeating Germany could have made her a different land, offering good homes for all, ample pleasant places unsullied by the wastage of competitive industry, an assurance to every man of work in which he could take pleasure and pride and by which he could earn a modest but secure livelihood.

All over tortured Europe other men who had suffered and bled had asked the same things. They also had had their dream, conceived in an hour of blinding and agonizing revelation – Frenchmen and Italians; vanquished Russians, Germans and Austrians, Hungarians, Bulgarians and Turks; Serbs, Belgians, Romanians, Greeks, Jews, Poles and Czechs. They too had wanted, each in the form dictated by their racial and national pasts, the same elemental human satisfaction: the home of their own, the craft of their choice, the bit of land – status, security, creation and continuity. God who had made man in His own image had meant him to have these things, and out of the whirlwind of Verdun and Caporetto had spoken of them.

It was not to these that the returning soldiers, marching with set faces to demobilization across a broken Europe, returned. It was to frustration and disillusion: to hunger and enforced idleness, to untilled fields and empty factories. All they had suffered for their loved ones and country ended only in more suffering: not in a Christian and compassionate commonwealth but in a pigsty. The politicians in all countries had promised a land fit for heroes. But when the soldiers came home they found a world designed for stockbrokers and *rentiers* and civil servants. It was built not in the image of their apocalyptic dream but in that of the utilitarian labyrinth of the money-changers from which they had gone forth in 1914.

For industrial society as it had grown up in the past century, first in island Britain and then everywhere else, did not admit the fulfilment of the soldiers' need. *Laissez-faire* capitalism postulated a fluctuating reserve of labour and therefore unemployment, the power of the man with capital to hire and dismiss his workers as he chose and therefore insecurity; and the legal priority of usurious over equitable rights and therefore the accumulation of property in the hands of the few and its denial to everyone else. The men who had gone to battle to defend such a society were divided from it by a great chasm which they had crossed in agony, sweat and blood. But those who had to reconstruct a broken Europe – the political leaders, the industrialists, the clever thinkers and capitalists who had stayed at home – were still on the other side.

The only remedy these men of an older generation could see for the ruin around them was to rebuild the world they knew before the war. It never occurred to them that they were restoring the situation that had caused the war. The basis of their world was the overriding necessity of earning expanding profits. The test of every human enterprise in every country had increasingly come to be: will it make enough to meet the contractual demands of the initiating lender? The universal search of the profit-maker was a fruitful field for exploitation in some other country. The *desideratum* of every national policy was not whether it increased the actual wealth of a country – the crops, homes, amenities, health, happiness and character of its inhabitants – but whether it multiplied the returns of the men of money and of those to whom their money, seeking multiplication by usury, was advanced.

The success of the great British capitalists of the nineteenth century had blinded civilization to the essential difference between profits and real wealth. A rare combination of native character, vigour and inventiveness, geographical good fortune and historical opportunity had caused their experiment to succeed in its early stages beyond their wildest expectations. Britain became richer than any other nation had ever been before. But she also became poorer. Her soaring exports and accumulating investments were the products of the new economic individualism. So were the conditions of the early factory towns.

It was the paradox of the nineteenth century – an epoch in which Britain led the world – that the practice of a sturdy and often heroic individualism, which increased the potentialities of human wealth out of measure, unwittingly created social injustice and inhumanity on a scale formerly unknown to Christians. The economists were proved right in their contention that enlightened self-interest, unfettered by State control, could enrich men more quickly than any other means. Yet the human misery caused by its pursuit justified the prophets of a more ordered society who warned unheeding generations that profits created at the price of social health and contentment were illusory. In the long run they were not profits at all. For they had still to be paid for in the cumulative loss of working power sustained through inhuman conditions of life and labour and inferior breeding capacity. The flaw in *laissez-faire*, and in the entire system of accountancy to which it gave birth, was that it regarded man as a self-sufficient unit like a machine. It forgot that he grew. It failed to recognize that the human economic unit was the continuing society – nation, group or family – from which the individual derived his habits and instincts. It failed to perceive that the effect of undernourishment, bad housing, unemployment and social injustice was not confined to the immediate victims but was transmitted to his descendants. A business that only operated in one generation might profit from overworking and underpaying human beings. A nation could not. Yet there was no nation of any importance that did not follow Britain's example.

Those who set out so gaily along that glittering road of accumulation failed to see to what it led. They did not grasp the moral truth, hidden from the utilitarians, that greed always overreaches itself. By enthroning it as the motivating principle of all economic activity, they set society on a downward declivity. At first the profits accruing to a man of enterprise, who under such a system was encouraged to apply his entire energies to their pursuit, could be great. Operating in a community in which wholesale exploitation had not hitherto been permitted, he was able to command the vigour, contentment, health and character of its people without paying anything towards the cost of these commercial assets – the accumulated legacy of former ages of sane and virtuous living and the real wealth of a continuing society. But with each generation the margin of available profit diminishes until the day arrives when the society under exploitation consists of debilitated, inefficient and resentful human beings without property, social cohesion or religion. The seven good years of the capitalist's policy are presently consumed by the seven lean. The exploiter is driven to seek new fields to succeed those already used up. And in these fields rival exploiters encounter each other, narrowing profits still further.

The peacemakers who assembled in 1919 could not see the flaw in the system. They were not bad men: only uninspired and, for all their entourage of experts, ignorant. They had none of the knowledge of far humbler men whom their great limousines passed marching on the dusty roads around Paris. They had not shared the soldier's crucifixion and his blinding, revealing vision. They could not therefore conceive a new world. They could only speak in the language of an old. They thought in terms of maps, political frontiers, racial rights and creeds, above all in markets and fields of profits for their bankers and industrialists. With infinite pains they re-erected the structure not of a co-operative but of a competitive world. They never saw the simple truth that for four years had been flashed nightly across the sky above the trenches in which millions of men who had no conceivable personal quarrel lived troglodyte lives to slay one another in the slime: that a competitive world ends in a warring world.

The peacemakers not only strove to reconstruct an impracticable system: they unconsciously aggravated it. They not only set the profit-makers and usurers of all nations in renewed competition with one another, they intensified and embittered that competition. There was little that was vindictive about the political terms of Versailles. It was just that France should regain her stolen provinces, Italy, Romania and Serbia their natural frontiers, and Poland and Bohemia their independence. It was only common sense that Germany should be disarmed and the claws of the Prussian bully cut. But it was madness deliberately to reshape the frontiers of central Europe in order to ensure the bankruptcy of German, Austrian and Hungarian producers and enrich their rivals in the victor states. The British soldier in the trenches had fought only for one reason – to beat the Germans and teach them to keep their place. He had not endured that four years' agony in order to render future generations of workers poor and restless.

The German of 1919 was under no illusion as to who had won the war. He was cowed, humble and very hungry; he was fed up with imperialism and dreams of world conquest. He wanted to be what his ancestors had been before the Prussians had taught Teutons to dream of worldly domination and the financier and industrialist had made it seem a necessity – a home-loving, sentimental bourgeois smoking a pipe, swilling beer and imbibing music and philosophy. He had been taught his place.

There was no need, after thrashing him and taking his arms, to bankrupt him. It was suicidal, if a Germany was to remain part of Europe, to render it a financial cripple. As Maynard Keynes pointed out, during the half-century before the war Europe had become industrialized round the hard core of a manufacturing Germany. Instead of a continent of self-supporting agricultural states, manufacturing only for luxury, there had grown up an intensely complicated polity based on the industrialization of the more advanced communities and a grouping of the others as customers and growers of their foodstuffs and raw materials. It might have been far better had no such economic alignment ever taken place. But since it had, any rearrangement of political frontiers that ignored it was bound to unsettle the life of millions.

1940

THE CASE FOR THE MINERS

SIEGFRIED SASSOON

Something goes wrong with my synthetic brain
When I defend the Strikers and explain
My reasons for not blackguarding the Miners.
'What do you know?' exclaim my fellow-diners
(Peeling their plovers' eggs or lifting glasses
Of mellowed *Château Rentier* from the table),
'What do you know about the working classes?'

I strive to hold my own; but I'm unable
To state the case succinctly. Indistinctly
I mumble about World-Emancipation,
Standards of Living, Nationalization
Of Industry; until they get me tangled
In superficial details; goad me on
To unconvincing vagueness. When we've wrangled
From soup to savoury, my temper's gone.

'Why should a miner earn six pounds a week?
Leisure! They'd only spend it in a bar!
Standard of life! You'll never teach them Greek,
Or make them more contented than they are!'
That's how my port-flushed friends discuss the Strike.
And that's the reason why I shout and splutter.
And that's the reason why I'd almost like
To see them hawking matches in the gutter.

1921

MY COUNTRY RIGHT OR WRONG?

ARTHUR SCARGILL

Let me begin by taking issue with the title of this series. When I look at the history of Britain marked by centuries of ruling class greed and the exploitation of working people, I see an unfolding saga of hardship and struggle by those whose labour has always created this nation's wealth.

Against such a back cloth, I could never say: 'My country, right or wrong.' In a deeply divided class society such as this, the phrase 'my country' always had a hollow ring to the working-class child I was, and to the miner and trade unionist I grew into.

Today, with increasing numbers of British people disenfranchised by unemployment, homelessness and lack of training or educational opportunity, the phrase is even more meaningless.

What is 'my country' today? It is a nation nearing the brink of economic and social collapse. Its basic and manufacturing industries, starved of investment in an anarchic free market-place, have been all but destroyed. Unemployment continues to rise, with human consequences that must terrify anyone who has any social conscience at all.

Look at the poverty and physical fear in which old people live today. Look at the growing crisis of homelessness and what that has done to families and single people alike. Look at both inner-city and rural communities: the forms of decay are different, but the tense desperation they produce is the same.

Look at the levels of racist and sexual violence – shaming to any society that considers itself 'civilized'. Even the utterly biased and distorted mass media cannot hide the fact that – in an age which is capable of providing everybody with security, good health and peace of mind – despair and decay and degradation have this country firmly in their collective grip.

The education system to which most of Britain's children are tied is in chaos, with pupils and teachers alike denied essential support and resources. Our National Health Service, once an example to the rest of the world, is still being slashed to ribbons; hospital closures and chronic understaffing have now left hundreds of communities without access to emergency, casualty or diagnostic care.

Public transport networks are being rubbed out, condemning to ghettos millions of people who depend on bus and local train services as their lifelines to the world outside the streets or villages where they live.

That is 'my country' today, and it is no wonder that alienation is rampant among our youngsters. Who can have a sense of belonging in this kind of society? Who can identify with it, or have a sense of pride in it?

However, I can and do identify with the history of my class, and from the days of childhood have developed a vision of the way 'my country' should be: the way it must become if catastrophe is not to engulf us all. I want to participate in turning Britain into a nation whose every institution exists to serve *all* the people.

My vision is of a socialist Britain, in which people not only own but control the means of production, distribution and exchange – a society in which everybody, not just a privileged handful, is able to control his or her own destiny.

The lives of all human beings would be respected from birth. I do not believe in a society that cocoons people, but in one that provides a springboard on which a child can build energy, develop potential, gather strength and go from one achievement to another. Of course, this is only possible through collective involvement and organization.

Government would operate within a system of total accountability; a complete transformation, obviously, from today's red-taped Whitehall and the endless bureaucratic chambers and corridors of the EC.

The means of mass communication (press, television, radio) would also be held in common ownership – and not, as at present, in the stranglehold of a handful of multi-national pirates and state-controlled corporations which function as a poorly disguised Thought Police.

Resources would be properly planned, developed and used, beginning with the production/consumption of food and energy. The terrible waste we see today in terms of food production would be eliminated.

Energy resources would come from coal and alternative sources such as solar power. We would, of course, have completely phased out the terrifyingly uncontrollable nuclear industry.

In this transformed Britain, government and political energy would be spent not only on growth but on peace. As a committed internationalist, I know that peace in my country depends on peace throughout the world. In a socialist Britain, there would be no interest in war, or in weapons of mass destruction, or in maintaining bases to house those weapons.

These are but outlines of what I could proudly call 'my country'. It must be a society in which all citizens feel they have a place, and to which they want to contribute. I believe wholeheartedly that, far from being an elusive dream, 'my country' can – indeed must – become reality. I, for one, shall certainly keep fighting to achieve it.

1988

THE WOMAN WHO HANGS THIS MORNING

CASSANDRA

It's a fine day for haymaking. A fine day for fishing. A fine day for lolling in the sunshine. And if you feel that way – and I mourn to say that millions of you do – it's a fine day for a hanging.

If you read this before nine o'clock this morning, the last dreadful and obscene preparations for hanging Ruth Ellis will be moving up to their fierce and sickening climax. The public hangman and his assistant will have been slipped into the prison at about four o'clock yesterday afternoon.

There, from what is grotesquely called 'some vantage point' and unobserved by Ruth Ellis, they will have spied upon her when she was at exercise 'to form an impression of the physique of the prisoner'.

A bag of sand will have been filled to the same weight as the condemned woman and it will have been left hanging overnight to stretch the rope.

If you read this at nine o'clock then – short of a miracle – you and I and every man and woman in the land with head to think and heart to feel will, in full responsibility, blot this woman out.

The hands that place the white hood over her head will not be our hands. But the guilt – and guilt there is in all this abominable business – will belong to us as much as to the wretched executioner paid and trained to do the job in accordance with the savage public will.

If you read this after nine o'clock, the murderess, Ruth Ellis, will have gone.

278

The one thing that brings stature and dignity to mankind and raises us above the beasts of the field will have been denied her – pity and the hope of ultimate redemption.

The medical officer will go to the pit under the trap door to see that life is extinct. Then, in the barbarous wickedness of this ceremony, rejected by nearly all civilized peoples, the body will be left to hang for one hour.

If you read these words of mine at mid-day the grave will have been dug while there are no prisoners around and the Chaplain will have read the burial service after he and all of us have come so freshly from disobeying the Sixth Commandment which says thou shalt not kill.

The secrecy of it all shows that if compassion is not in us, then at least we still retain the dregs of shame. The medieval notice of execution will have been posted on the prison gates and the usual squalid handful of louts and rubbernecks who attend these legalized killings will have had their own private obscene delights.

Two Royal Commissions have protested against these horrible events. Every Home Secretary in recent years has testified to the agonies of his task, and the revulsion he has felt towards his duty. None has ever claimed that executions prevent murder.

Yet they go on and still Parliament has neither the resolve nor the conviction, nor the wit, nor the decency to put an end to these atrocious affairs.

When I write about capital punishment, as I have often done, I get some praise and usually more abuse. In this case I have been reviled as being 'a sucker for a pretty face.'

Well, I am a sucker for a pretty face. And I am a sucker for all human faces because I hope I am a sucker for all humanity, good or bad. But I prefer the face not to be lolling because of a judicially broken neck.

Yes, it is a fine day.

Oscar Wilde, when he was in Reading Gaol, spoke with melancholy of 'that little tent of blue which prisoners call the sky'.

THE TENT OF BLUE SHOULD BE DARK AND SAD AT THE THING WE HAVE DONE THIS DAY.

1955

HOW AN OLD GEYSER FELL ON HARD TIMES

BERNARD LEVIN

An elderly widowed lady of whom I am rather fond was notified some time ago that she was about to undergo the full horrors of conversion to Natural Gas. Resigning herself to a future of uncontrollably fluctuating gas-pressures, burnt saucepans and higher bills, she awaited the coming of the converters. The day dawned. Two men came; they converted her stove, her kitchen water-heater, her refrigerator and her gas fires. She also has, however, in her bathroom, a geyser of ancient design and dilapidated condition (I suppose we had better pause here for the one that goes 'Mornin' lady; 'ave you got an old geyser 'ere what won't work?' – 'Yes, 'e's just gone down to the Labour Exchange to draw the dole'), but which – mark these words, and mark them well – has operated adequately and served her well.

Obstinate in its faith, the geyser resisted conversion. The two gas men explained that it needed a device that they did not have with them, but which they would bring; meanwhile, the geyser was out of action. The lady bore her bathless state with as much fortitude as she could muster, and awaited their return.

They did not return, of course. Nor, of course, did she hear from anybody at all on the subject. So she telephoned the office from which the men had come; they had left a form with its address and telephone number. (It was the Conversion Report Centre, Oakington Road, London W9, telephone 349 3171, and I put these details in so that whoever is in what is laughably known as charge shall know exactly where the finger is pointing.) She explained that she had now been without a bath for a week, that a promise had been made and broken, and what was going to be done about it? The reply was that action would be taken. About a week later (nobody, of course, had told her anything at all in the interim) two more men turned up. They, too, tinkered with the geyser, they, too, said that it needed an extra device that they had not got with them; they, too, said that they would return with it; they, too, of course, did no such thing. Nor, of course, did anybody at all get in touch with her.

The lady in question, I will have you know, likes to bath regularly and often; moreover, she is not accustomed, or for that matter able, to take a bath in a kettle. So when another week had gone by, she telephoned the Gas Board. The office for the district in which she lives is North Thames Gas Board Area 5, telephone number 328 1717, address not given in the telephone book (I suppose they are afraid of violence from their customers, and well they might be). An official of the Gas Board came round (she cannot remember how long after her call, though she doubts if it was immediately, and so, by God, do I); he explained that the Gas Board and the conversion programme are independently run (if 'run' is the right word, and my own opinion is that it is most emphatically not the right word), but that he would inspect the geyser. He did so, told her that he knew exactly what was needed, and left with the memorable words, 'Leave it to me, Mrs Levin.' The reason he addressed her thus was that Levin is her name, and this seems as good a moment as any to reveal that the fact that it is the same name as mine is not a coincidence; she is my mother.

She did indeed leave it to him; she is a patient and trusting soul, and – rather more to the point – she had no option. He did not return, of course; nor, of course, did anybody get in touch with her. So she rang the Gas Board again. She was assured that action would be taken. It was: another man arrived (this made six she had actually seen, plus several more she had spoken to on the telephone). Had he, she asked, brought the necessary device? 'I have brought nothing,' he replied with candour; nor had he. (He also explained that he knew nothing of any extra and needed part.) He would, however, go back to the office and report the situation. He went; that was on Monday. Not long after he left an official (female) telephoned from the Gas Board to ask if he had been. Yes, said my mother, grinding her teeth, he had; but he had not brought the magic device, and had therefore gone away. In that case, said the official, I will see what the situation is, and ring you back and let you know. She didn't, of course, and at the time of writing this (Wednesday afternoon), my mother had heard nothing more from anybody.

I now want three things to happen. First, I want my mother's bathroom water-heater fixed, and at once. Second, I want a written apology to my mother to be sent from both the Natural Gas Conversion office and from the Gas Board.

That will satisfy my mother. But I also want a third thing on my own behalf; or rather, on behalf of the public in general, who have to put up with the kind of behaviour I have just described. I want a public answer to this question: what is wrong with a national organization which gives its customers not the service they pay for but, instead, incompetence and a string of broken promises?

Later:

The nation, I gather, is agog to know whether my mother is clean. This is not, I take it, a matter into which a well-bred nation would normally seek to inquire. But since I sang the saga of my mother's bathroom water-heater and the North Thames Gas Board, recounting how she was without hot water from her geyser for over three weeks, its normally copious supply being replaced only by a flow of broken promises from officials of the North Thames Gas Board, I have had virtually uncountable numbers of letters wishing to know whether my words have had the desired results.

All in good time. But first, about those letters in general. To begin with, their number exceeded, by a very considerable margin, those I have received on any single topic arising out of this column since I began writing it two and a half years ago. Next, in the overwhelming majority, the writer recounted experiences, at the hands of the North Thames Gas Board, that were undoubtedly at least as bad as, and in a substantial number of cases very much worse than, those undergone by my mother. Finally the pattern of behaviour on the part of North Thames Gas Board was the same in almost all the accounts: promises of action unfulfilled, and no co-ordination whatever between any two people in that organization, so that the men who supposedly come to fit a part which a previous visitor has declared necessary and promised will be sent, come without either the part or any knowledge of a previous visit or the conclusions formed by the previous visitor. (My mother had four sets of such visitors: one correspondent had nineteen.) Several sufferers, incidentally, seeing the advantage of being my mother, offered to adopt me; one asked if I would adopt *her.*

I am also informed by *The Times* Business News that the subject on which they regularly receive the largest number of letters is the North Thames Gas Board and its incompetence, though incompetence, to judge by my postbag on the subject, is too mild a word; the organization seems to be putrescent from top to bottom, its officials leaving letters unanswered, phone calls ignored, and customers offered nothing but false assurances of action.

Which brings me to the question of my mother and her bath. The first conclusion to be drawn from the affair is that top officials of the North Thames Gas Board read *The Times*. Not long after breakfast on the morning the article appeared, my mother's flat was filled from wall to wall with North Thames officials – eventually, at least seven. There were engineers, and fitters, and executives, and one man who, from my mother's account, appears to have been the apologizer. Anyway, just as the place was about to collapse from the weight of Gas Board men (some of them even arrived from outside, by ladder) they finished the job and left. My mother, exhausted by the weeks of battle, and no doubt in addition emotionally drained by the abrupt discovery that she was the owner of the most famous bathroom geyser in the world, immediately went away on holiday, pausing only to take a bath.

When she returned (she got her written apology, incidentally) she found that North Thames had, while doing the work, apparently installed a fascinating and novel system. Whenever she takes a bath, and much of the time now even when she does not, water pours out of the ceiling in the room next door. This, of course, enables her to offer a visitor, in addition to tea and cakes, an informal shower in the kitchen, but she cannot help feeling that the degree of informality in the arrangement is excessive, and the bucket she puts underneath does tend to fill rather quickly, besides adding little if anything to the kitchen's appearance. ('It seems,' she says – she is a woman long accustomed to seeing into the heart of a problem – 'that they must have knocked a hole in something.') Unless the Gas Board, feeling that it has done its final duty by the tribe of Levin, has now given up *The Times*, perhaps any senior official reading this might care to indicate to his colleagues that something in the nature of a return to square one is urgently needed.

1979

NOT WAVING
BUT DROWNING

Are memorable poems still being written in English? Yes, of course they are. Here are six personal favourites. First Kingsley Amis's wry 'Song of Experience'; next Philip Larkin's lament for the disappearing countryside beyond the town; then a piece of pure strawberries and cream from Laurie Lee. I'm publishing 'England's Glory' by Fleur Adcock because, born in New Zealand, she has such a precise grip on the North–South divide in England and puts it so elegantly. Next, the poem by Stevie Smith which contains the line most people remember best from all poetry written since the war: 'not waving but drowning'. Finally, 'Instead of a Poet' by Francis Hope, from his book of poetry with the same name. He was killed in the DC10 crash at Paris in 1974, aged thirty-five. A brilliant academic and fellow of All Souls, he was working for the Observer at the time. There were those who said he had not time to fulfil his promise, and no doubt this is true; but 'Instead of a Poet' is no bad legacy to leave, and many of us would settle for having written its haunting last two lines.

A SONG OF EXPERIENCE

KINGSLEY AMIS

A quiet start: the tavern, our small party,
    A dark-eyed traveller drinking on his own;
We asked him over when the talk turned hearty,
    And let him tell of women he had known.

He tried all colours, white and black and coffee;
    Though quite a few were chary, more were bold;
Some took it like the host, some like a toffee;
    The two or three who wept were soon consoled.

For seven long years his fancies were tormented
    By one he often wheedled, but in vain;
At last, oh Christ in heaven, she consented,
    And the next day he journeyed on again.

The inaccessible he laid a hand on,
    The heated he refreshed, the cold he warmed.
What Blake presaged, what Lawrence took a stand on,
    What Yeats locked up in fable, he performed.

And so he knew, where we can only fumble,
    Wildly in daydreams, vulgarly in art;
Miles past the point where all delusions crumble
    He found the female and the human heart.

Then love was velvet on a hand of iron
  That wrenched the panting lover from his aim;
Lion rose up as lamb and lamb as lion,
  Nausicaa and Circe were the same.

What counter-images, what cold abstraction
  Could start to quench that living element,
The flash of prophecy, the glare of action?
  – He drained his liquor, paid his score and went.

I saw him, brisk in May, in Juliet's weather,
  Hitch up the trousers of his long-tailed suit,
Polish his windscreen with a chamois-leather,
  And stow his case of samples in the boot.

1956

GOING, GOING

PHILIP LARKIN

I thought it would last my time –
The sense that, beyond the town,
There would always be fields and farms,
Where the village louts could climb
Such trees as were not cut down;
I knew there'd be false alarms

In the papers about old streets
And split-level shopping, but some
Have always been left so far;
And when the old part retreats
As the bleak high-risers come
We can always escape in the car.

Things are tougher than we are, just
As earth will always respond
However we mess it about;
Chuck filth in the sea, if you must:
The tides will be clean beyond.
– But what do I feel now? Doubt?

Or age, simply? The crowd
Is young in the M1 café;
Their kids are screaming for more –
More houses, more parking allowed,
More caravan sites, more pay.
On the Business Page, a score

Of spectacled grins approve
Some takeover bid that entails
Five per cent profit (and ten
Per cent more in the estuaries): move
Your works to the unspoilt dales
(Grey area grants)! And when

You try to get near the sea
In summer . . .
       It seems, just now,
To be happening so very fast;
Despite all the land left free
For the first time I feel somehow
That it isn't going to last,

That before I snuff it, the whole
Boiling will be bricked in
Except for the tourist parts –
First slum of Europe: a role
It won't be so hard to win,
With a cast of crooks and tarts.

And that will be England gone,
The shadows, the meadows, the lanes,
The guildhalls, the carved choirs.
There'll be books; it will linger on
In galleries; but all that remains
For us will be concrete and tyres.

Most things are never meant.
This won't be, most likely: but greeds
And garbage are too thick-strewn
To be swept up now, or invent
Excuses that make them all needs.
I just think it will happen, soon.

1974

286

HOME FROM ABROAD

LAURIE LEE

Far-fetched with tales of other worlds and ways,
My skin well-oiled with wines of the Levant,
I set my face into a filial smile
To greet the pale, domestic kiss of Kent.

But shall I never learn? That gawky girl,
Recalled so primly in my foreign thoughts,
Becomes again the green-haired queen of love
Whose wanton form dilates as it delights.

Her rolling tidal landscape floods the eye
And drowns Chianti in a dusky stream;
The flower-flecked grasses swim with simple horses,
The hedges choke with roses fat as cream.

So do I breathe the hayblown airs of home,
And watch the sea-green elms drip birds and shadows,
And as the twilight nets the plunging sun
My heart's keel slides to rest among the meadows.

1955

ENGLAND'S GLORY

FLEUR ADCOCK

Red-tipped, explosive, self-complete:
one you can strike on the coal-face, or
the sole of your boot. Not for the south, where
soft men with soft hands rub effete
brown-capped sticks on a toning strip
chequered with coffee-grounds, the only
match for the matches, and any lonely
stray (if they let them stray) picked up
from a table or found loose in a pocket
can't, without its container, flare
fire at a stroke: is not a purely self-contained ignition unit.

287

'Security' proclaims the craven
yellow box with its Noah's ark,
'Brymay' Special Safety's trade-mark
for southern consumption. That's all right, then:
bankers can take them home to Surrey
for their cigars, and scatter the odd
match-head, whether or not it's dead,
on their parquet floors, without the worry
of subsequent arson. Not like here
where a match is a man's match, an object
to be handled with as much respect
but as casually as a man's beer.

You can't mistake the England's Glory
box: its crimson, blue and white
front's a miniature banner, fit
for the Durham Miners' Gala, gaudy
enough to march ahead of a band.
Forget that placid ark: the vessel
this one's adorned with has two funnels
gushing fat blue smoke to the wind.
The side's of sandpaper. The back
label's functional, printed with either
holiday vouchers, a special offer
on World Cup tickets, or this month's joke.

Somewhere across England's broad
midriff, wanderingly drawn
from west to east, there exists a line
to the north of which the shops provide
(catering for a sudden switch
of taste) superior fried fish, runnier
yogurt, blouses cut for the fuller
northern figure; and the northern match.
Here England's Glory begins; through all
the vigorous north it reigns unrivalled
until its truce with Scottish Bluebell
round about Berwick and Carlisle.

1986

NOT WAVING BUT DROWNING

STEVIE SMITH

Nobody heard him, the dead man,
But still he lay moaning:
I was much further out than you thought
And not waving but drowning.

Poor chap, he always loved larking
And now he's dead
It must have been too cold for him his heart gave way,
They said.

Oh, no no no, it was too cold always
(Still the dead one lay moaning)
I was much too far out all my life
And not waving but drowning.

1957

INSTEAD OF A POET

FRANCIS HOPE

There were no dragons in his dreams,
  No armies wheeling in his sky.
  To his exact and conscious eye
The world remained the thing it seems.

The flat and documentary truth
  Clung to him like a nagging wife,
  Complaining of the wretched life
Her narrow vision gave them both.

But sometimes winter mornings brought –
  Frost-sharp, ice-clear – the feeling of
  A wider certainty of love
Colouring the outlines of his thought.

And foreign towns could sometimes chase
  Routine like clouds away, and yield
  Visions of otherness revealed
In the exactitudes of place.

At times like these, he cried aloud
  That not to be a poet is
  The worst of all our miseries,
That silence choked him like a shroud;

And scribbled lines like fallen hopes
On backs of tattered envelopes.

1965

ALL WHAT JAZZ

Let us end by celebrating England's greatest single asset, her marvellous language. Here are some short snatches of modern prose which show we still have writers who understand its beauty and power. The first is from Bitter Lemons *by Lawrence Durrell.*

These thoughts belong to Venice at dawn, seen from the deck of the ship which is to carry me down through the islands to Cyprus; a Venice wobbling in a thousand fresh-water reflections, cool as a jelly. It was as if some great master, stricken by dementia, had burst his whole colour-box against the sky to deafen the inner eye of the world. Cloud and water mixed into each other, dripping with colours, merging, overlapping, liquefying, with steeples and balconies and roofs floating in space, like the fragments of some stained-glass window seen through a dozen veils of rice-paper. Fragments of history touched with the colours of wine, tar, ochre, blood, fire-opal and ripening grain. The whole at the same time being rinsed softly back at the edges into a dawn sky as softly as circumspectly blue as a pigeon's egg.

Another assured member of the master class is William Golding. In this short passage from Lord of the Flies *he uses a deceptively simple prose to convey an instant impression of the tangible world. Note the sting in the tail.*

Somewhere over the darkened curve of the world the sun and moon were pulling; and the film of water on the earth planet was held, bulging slightly on one side while the solid core turned. The great wave of the tide moved further along the island and the water lifted. Softly, surrounded by a fringe of inquisitive bright creatures, itself a silver shape beneath the steadfast constellations, Simon's dead body moved out towards the open sea.

Is it the matter or manner which moves us in a fine stretch of writing? The two are probably impossible to untangle. In this extract from Doris Lessing's Summer Before the Dark *the sustained metaphor is electrifying, but so is the power with which it is put across.*

. . . what a remarkable thing it was, this room full of people, animals rather, all looking in one direction, at other dressed-up animals lifted up to perform on a stage, animals covered with cloth and bits of fur, ornamented with stones, their faces and claws painted with colour. Everyone had just finished eating animal of some kind; and the furs that were everywhere, despite the warm evening, were from animals that had lived and played and fornicated in forests and fields, and everyone's foot-covering was of animal skin, and their hair – no, one had to come back to this again, it was impossible not to – their hair was the worst; mats and caps and manes and wigs of hair, crimped and curled and flattered and lengthened and shortened and manipulated, hair dyed all colours, and scented and greased and lacquered. It was a room full of animals, dogs and cats and wolves and foxes that had got on their hind legs and put ribbons on themselves and brushed their fur. . . .

And here is a passage from The Collector *by John Fowles in which, as one critic observed, prose becomes graffiti.*

I hate God. I hate whatever made this world, I hate whatever made the human race. . . .

If there is a God he's a great loathsome spider in the darkness.

He *cannot be good.*

This pain, this terrible seeing-through that is in me now. It wasn't necessary. It is all pain, and it buys nothing.

Gives birth to nothing.

All in vain. All wasted.

The older the world becomes, the more obvious it is. The bomb and the tortures in Algeria and the starving babies in the Congo.

It gets bigger and darker.

More and more suffering for more and more. And more and more in vain.

It's as if the lights have fused. I'm here in the black truth.

God is impotent. He can't love us. He hates us because he can't love us.

All the meanness and the selfishness and the lies.

People won't admit it, they're too busy grabbing to see that the lights have fused. They can't see the darkness and the spider-face beyond and the great web of it all. That there's always this if you scratch at the surface of happiness and goodness.

The black and the black and the black.

Travel writer Freya Stark, famed for her intrepid odysseys, is in a more domestic and reflective mood in this description of her grandmother:

She always had a book in her hand and she was never busy; she would put it down and her arms would open to enclose any human being, but particularly a child, who needed a refuge there; what she gave was affection pure and simple, deliberately free from wear and tear of understanding or advice. She did this because she believed in affection as the panacea for all the evil in the world, and the essence of this simple love has wound itself in my memory with her scent of eau-de-cologne, and her blonde lace, and the wide silk folds and bits of warm satin that made up the black friendly labyrinth of her gowns. There one nestled for hours while she told stories. The book of Genesis, myths of Greece, the Siegfried Sagas, the Seven Kings of Rome, Tasso, Dante, Goethe, came to me in this good way, not arid noises from a mechanical cavern, or black and white deserts of print, but warm with the person of the teller, modulated with the inflections of a voice that meant safety and kindness, so that the childhood of the world merged with my own and lies there entranced in the same afternoon light that melted into twilight, and gradually dimmed the ivory face and left the voice almost alone to call up pageant after pageant, while one fondled the small hands, so soft and old, whose rings had taken the shape of the fingers and lost their lustre through more than half a century of wear.

Another travel writer of the first rank is Patrick Leigh Fermor. His prose is sometimes too purple for some people; but not, I think, in this delicious description of cavorting dolphins from his Mani.

. . . a school of dolphins was gambolling half a mile further out to sea. They seemed to have spotted us at the same moment, for in a second, half a dozen were tearing their way towards us, all surfacing in the same parabola, and plunging together as though they were in some invisible harness. Soon they were careering alongside and round the bows and under the bowsprit, glittering mussel-blue on top, fading at the sides through gun-metal dune-like markings to pure white, streamlined and gleaming from their elegant beaks to the clean-cut flukes of their tails. They were beautiful abstractions of speed, energy, power and ecstasy leaping out of the water and plunging and spiralling and vanishing like swift shadows, each soon to materialize again and sail into the air in another great loop so fast that they seemed to draw the sea after them and shake it off in mid-air, to plunge forward again tearing two great frothing bow-waves with their beaks; diving down again, falling behind and criss-crossing under the keel and deviating and returning. Sometimes they flung themselves out of the sea with the insane abandon, in reverse, of a suicide from a skyscraper; up, up, until they hung poised in mid-air shaking in a muscular convulsion from beak to tail as though resolved to abandon their element for ever. But gravity, as though hauling on an oblique fishing-line, dragged them forward and down again into their rifled and bubbling green tunnels. The headlong speed through the water filled the air with a noise of rending and searing. Each leap into the air called forth a chorus of gasps, each plunge a sigh.

Not all writers of good English prose are household names. Here is an extract from Michael Lindsay's Mindsprung.

He liked London. He liked the polychromic garishness, the unconvincing-of its cement and plate-glass lushness. He liked the skyscrapers that had sprung up everywhere, distant and incongruous but as perfect in their detail of windows and aerials as if they had been giant toys in the next street. He liked the jet-liners, alien invaders with their gem-like splendour, slowly banking above the acres of shabby terraces, and the sky sunset-pink at midnight, and the ozone whiff of nipple-punctuated T-shirt fronts, swaying bums like scaled-up peaches, pub forecourt sunlight glinting on the sheen of small hairs on the tanned forearms of other blokes' girls. But still he seemed to be waiting for something to happen.

For lucidity and balance, it would be hard to better this meditation on marriage from the elegant pen of Anthony Powell in Casanova's Chinese Restaurant.

To think at all objectively about one's own marriage is impossible, while a balanced view of other people's marriage is almost equally hard to achieve with so much information available, so little to be believed. Objectivity is not, of course, everything in writing; but even casting objectivity aside, the difficulties of presenting marriage are inordinate. Its forms are at once so varied, yet so constant, providing a kaleidoscope, the colours of which are always changing, always the same. The moods of a love affair, the contradictions of friendship, the jealousy of business partners, the fellow feeling of opposed commanders in total war, these are all in their way to be charted. Marriage, partaking of such – and a thousand more – dual antagonisms and participations, finally defies definition.

Not every poet writes beautiful prose; but one who does is Peter Levi. Here he evokes the stony spirit of Greece in this extract from The Hill of Kronos.

They were rough to the hand, an encrusted, starlit, greyish assembly. They reared up very high. I have seen them by storm light in the winter when they were blazing greyish-white shapes, and by snowlight, when they were greenish-black and dripping. I saw them next morning, as the sky turned grey and then blue, and the shadowed mountains shared the transformations of the columns. Bassai is half a temple, half a mountain cairn. When it was found it was a vast cairn of stones, and at night it still belongs to wolves and foxes, although there are no wolves left so far south. Nikitas was as impressed as I was by the columns at that hour. We wandered about staring and feeling our way. The donkey grazing was the only noise.

Finally, a passage from All What Jazz, *by Philip Larkin, which squeezes the barrier between prose and poetry wafer-thin.*

My readers . . . Sometimes I wonder whether they really exist. Truly they are remarkably tolerant, manifesting themselves only by the occasional query as to where they can buy records: just once or twice I have been clobbered by a Miles Davis fan, or taken to task by the press agent of a visiting celebrity. Sometimes I imagine them, sullen fleshy inarticulate men, stockbrokers, sellers of goods, living in thirty-year-old detached houses among the golf courses of outer London, husbands of ageing and bitter wives they first seduced to Artie Shaw's 'Begin the Beguine' or The Squadronaires' 'The Nearness of You'; fathers of cold-eyed lascivious daughters on the pill, to whom Ramsay Macdonald is coeval with Rameses II, and cannabis-smoking jeans-and-bearded Stuart-haired sons whose oriental contempt for 'bread' is equalled only by their insatiable demand for it; men in whom a pile of scratched coverless 78s in the attic can awaken memories of vomiting blindly from small Tudor windows to Muggsy Spanier's 'Sister Kate', or winding up a gramophone in a punt to play Armstrong's 'Body and Soul'; men whose first coronary is coming like Christmas; who drift, loaded helplessly with commitments and obligations and necessary observances, into the darkening avenues of age and incapacity deserted by everything that once made life sweet. These I have tried to remind of the excitement of jazz, and tell where it may still be found.

BREAD AND BUTTER LETTER

A book like this with many moods and tastes is best nourished by help from many hands and I was particularly fortunate to be able to call on so many. First, I must thank my fellow-writers for so generously sending me their nominations. By some weird rule of literary life, their letters came back in broadly inverse relation to the calls on their time, with the busiest man among us replying by return of post; but all their ideas were equally welcome and many have been adopted. My warmest thanks, then, to Bernard Levin, Keith Waterhouse, George Bull and David Hughes for their sterling support. Former colleagues on *The Sunday Times Magazine* were equally prodigal in their help, and I am grateful, not for the first time, to Peter Crookston, Meriel McCooey, David Robson and David Sylvester for marking my card so well.

Once again I must thank my daughter Amanda Smith, who not only researched with her usual energy, but also enlisted the help of many friends in the quest. In this way I was able to call on the taste and experience of a younger generation, thus lending the book a fizz it could not otherwise have had. Carey Perloff and Candida Lacey helped with American names; Vicky Licorish suggested West Indian and Deborah Mabbett New Zealand writers; David Akerman offered a wide variety of ideas ranging from Arthur Scargill to the *Aeropagitica*; John Davies suggested Baldwin, Simon Wilson contributed Simone de Beauvoir and Gareth Price added Akenfield. A variety of names were put forward by Julian Gorham, Michael Hatt, Caroline Knight, Chris Macrae, and Caroline Larrington. To each and every one, my warmest thanks.

June Primmer at the English Tourist Board, Paul Anderson at *Tribune*, and Jane Thomas at the *New Statesman* all gave cheerful help; and I am particularly grateful yet again to the friendly staffs at the Westminster City Libraries, the London Library, and the British Film Institute Library.

None of this would have happened without the fertilising mind of Colin Webb, managing director of Pavilion Books, who suggested the book to me. To him my thanks once more. Margaret Nairne and Jillie Norrey dealt with the daunting flow of copy at Pavilion Books with dispatch; and Steve Dobell edited the text with his usual care. Finally, a special word of thanks to our designers, John Gorham and Tom Sawyer, who made the book such a pleasure to read and to hold.

ACKNOWLEDGEMENTS

'The English People', an extract from *The Collected Essays, Journalism and Works of George Orwell* (1968) by Sonia Brownell Orwell, reprinted by permission of The Estate of the late Sonia Brownell Orwell and Secker and Warburg Limited; the speech 'On England' from *On England and Other Addresses* (1926) by Stanley Baldwin MP is reprinted by permission of Lord Baldwin of Bewdley; 'The Present – Notes on the English Character', an extract from *Abinger Harvest* (1936) by E. M. Forster, reprinted by permission of Edward Arnold; 'A Letter to My Fellow Countrymen', by John Osborne (1961), an extract from *Tribune 40: The First Forty Years Of A Socialist Newspaper* (1977) reprinted by permission of Quartet Books Ltd © 1977 Tribune Publications Ltd; an extract from *The Old Country* (1978) by Alan Bennett reprinted by permission of Faber and Faber Ltd; 'Anglo-Saxon Attitudes', an extract from *This England* (1968) from the New Statesman reprinted by permission of Unwin Hyman Ltd; the extract 'Kingsley Amis' from *Brief Lives,* copyright © 1982 by Alan Watkins, reprinted by permission of Hamish Hamilton Ltd; the essay 'Lewis Carroll' from *Forewords and Afterwords* (1943) by W. H. Auden reprinted by permission of Faber and Faber Ltd; 'James Woodforde', an extract from *The Common Reader* (1932) by Virginia Woolf reprinted by permission of the Estate of Virginia Woolf and the Hogarth Press; the extract 'Stanley Parker' from *He That Plays King: A View of the Theatre* (1950) by Kenneth Tynan is reprinted by permission of Mrs Kathleen Tynan; the extracts from 'Valentine's Day Messages' 1988 are reprinted by permission of The Observer and The Sunday Times; *Attack* (1919) by Siegfried Sassoon is reprinted by permission of George Sassoon; the excerpt from *This Happy Breed* (1943) by Noel Coward is reprinted by permission of Methuen London; 'World ain't wot it used to be', an extract from *Leslie Baily's BBC Scrapbook volume 2* (1918–1934) (1937) by Leslie Baily is reprinted by permission of Unwin Hyman Ltd; the poem *The White Cliffs* (1941) by Alice Duer Miller is reprinted by permission of Methuen and Co.; 'Aftermyth of War' from *The Complete Beyond The Fringe* (1963) by Alan Bennett, Peter Cook, Jonathan Miller, Dudley Moore is reprinted by permission of Methuen London; the extract from *I Saw Two Englands* (1942) by H. V. Morton is reprinted by permission of Violet Morton; the extract from *London War Notes 1937–1945* (1972) by Mollie Panter-Downes is reprinted by permission of Longman Group Limited; 'On Style', an extract from *On The Art Of Writing* (1895) by Sir Arthur Quiller-Couch, is reprinted by permission of the Cambridge University Press; 'The Mysterious English', an extract from *Unpopular Opinions* (1946) by Dorothy L. Sayers is reprinted by permission of Victor Gollancz Ltd; 'The English Language', an extract from *The Collected Essays, Journalism and Works of George Orwell* (1968) by Sonia Brownell Orwell is reprinted by permission of The Estate of the late Sonia Brownell Orwell and Secker and Warburg Limited; *The Plain Style in English Prose* (1984) by Sir William Rees-Mogg is reprinted by permission of Sir William Rees-Mogg; extracts from the Book of Common Prayer of 1662, the rights of which are vested in the Crown in perpetuity within the United Kingdom, are reproduced by permission of Eyre and Spottiswoode Publishers, Her Majesty's Printers, London; *The Time Machine* (1895) by H. G. Wells is reprinted by permission of William Heinemann Ltd; 'La Clé des Chants', an extract from *The Unquiet Grave A Word Cycle by Palinurus* (1944) by Cyril Connolly is reprinted by permission of Hamish Hamilton Ltd; the extract 'The Young Wife's Tale' from *Jolly Super* (1971) by Jilly Cooper is reprinted by permission of Methuen London; an extract from *The Young Visiters* (1919) by Daisy Ashford is reprinted by permission from The Estate of the Author and Chatto and Windus; 'The Second Philosopher's Song' from *The Collected Poetry Of Aldous Huxley* (1920) is reprinted by permission of Mrs Laura Huxley and Chatto and Windus; the extract 'Tum's Column' from *The Best of Nathaniel Gubbins* (1978) is reprinted by permission of Blond and Briggs, Beaverbrook Newspapers Ltd; 'The Great Sermon Handicap' from *The Inimitable Jeeves* (1953) is reprinted by permission of Century Hutchinson Publishing Group Ltd; the extract 'How Long, O Lord . . . ?' from *Waterhouse At Large* (1986) by Keith Waterhouse is reprinted by permission of Michael Joseph Ltd; the song 'Mad Dogs and Englishmen (1931) from *The Lyrics*, written and composed by Noel Coward is reprinted here by permission of the Estate of the late Noel Coward and Methuen London; the extract from 'The Pub and the People' from *The Tom Harrisson Mass-Observation Archive* (1943) is reprinted by permission of Century Hutchinson Publishing Group Limited; the extract 'In Defence of English Cooking' from *The Collected Essays, Journalism and Works of George Orwell* (1968) by Sonia Brownell Orwell is reprinted by permission of The Estate of the late Sonia Brownell Orwell and Secker and Warburg Ltd; the extract 'The Preface to the first Good Food Guide' from *The Good Food Guide* (1951) is reprinted by permission of the Consumers' Association; the extract 'Love is Dead' from *First and Last Loves* (1952) by John Betjeman is reprinted by permission of John Murray (Publishers) Ltd; the piece 'Cottage Industry, from *The Original Michael Frayn* (1966) © The Observer 1966, is reprinted by permission of Elaine Greene Ltd; *Akenfield* (1969) by Ronald Blythe is reprinted by permission of the author and Viking Books; the extract 'Soft Landing' from *Falling Towards England: Unreliable Memoirs II* (1985) by Clive James is reprinted by permission of the author and Jonathan Cape Ltd; the extract 'School Life' from *Finding A Voice* (1978) by Amrit Wilson is reprinted by permission of Virago Press; an extract from *The Prime Of Life* (1962) by Simone de Beauvoir is reprinted by permission of George Weidenfeld and Nicolson Ltd; an extract from *Look Back In Anger* (1956) by John Osborne is reprinted by permission of Faber and Faber Ltd; an extract from *Forty Years On* (1969) by Alan Bennett is reprinted by permission of Faber and Faber Ltd; the extract 'Hammond in Command' from *Walter Hammond* (1962) by Ronald Mason is reprinted by permission of the author; an extract from *England, Their England* (1933) by A. G. MacDonnell is reprinted by permission of Macmillan, London and Basingstoke; 'Test

Match at Lord's' from *To Whom It May Concern: Poems 1952–57* (1955) by Alan Ross is reprinted by permission of the author; an extract from *The Art of Coarse Rugby* (1960) by Michael Green is reprinted by permission of the author and Century Hutchinson Publishing Group Ltd.; an extract from *Reynard the Fox* (1919) by John Masefield is reprinted by permission of the Society of Authors as the literary representative of the estate of John Masefield; an extract from *Nigger at Eton* (1972) by Dillibe Onyearma is reprinted by permission of Leslie Frewin; an extract from *Sinister Street* (1914) by Compton Mackenzie reprinted by permission of Macdonald and Co.; an extract from *Summoned by Bells* (1960) by John Betjeman is reprinted by permission of John Murray (Publishers) Ltd.; the extract 'Drinking' from *The Essays, Articles and Reviews of Evelyn Waugh* (1963) edited by Professor Davit Gallagher © 1983 The Estate of Laura Waugh reprinted by permission of A. D. Peters & Co. Ltd.; the extract 'Palette for 1927. Autumn' from *Previous Convictions* copyright © 1958 by Cyril Connolly reprinted by permission of Deborah Rogers Ltd.; the extract 'Mr Oakroyd Leaves Home' from *The Good Companions* (1929) by J. B. Priestley reprinted by permission of A. D. Peters & Co. Ltd.; an extract from 'Autumn Journal' from *The Collected Poems of Louis MacNeice* (1939) by Louis MacNeice reprinted by permission of Faber and Faber Ltd.; the extract 'The Life of Emily Davison' from *The Young Rebecca* (1982) edited by Jane Marcus reprinted by permission of A. D. Peters & Co. Ltd.; and extract from *The English Saga* (1940) by Arthur Bryant reprinted by permission of Collins Publishers; the poem *The Case for the Miners* (1921) by Siegfried Sassoon reprinted by permission of George Sassoon; 'My Country Right or Wrong' (1988) by Arthur Scargill is reprinted by permission of the *Telegraph Sunday Magazine*; the piece *The Woman Who Hangs This Morning* (1955) by Cassandra © Daily Mirror reprinted by permission of the Daily Mirror; the piece 'How an old geyser fell on hard times' from *Taking Sides* (1979) by Bernard Levin reprinted by permission of the author; the poem 'A Song of Experience' from *Collected Poems 1944–79* (1956) by Kingsley Amis © 1956 Kingsley Amis, reprinted by permission of Jonathan Clowes Ltd., London on behalf of Kingsley Amis; the poem 'Going, Going' from *High Windows* (1974) by Philip Larkin reprinted by permission of Faber and Faber Ltd.; the poem 'Home from Abroad' from *My Many-Coated Man* (1955) by Laurie Lee reprinted by permission of Andre Deutsch Ltd.; the poem 'England's Glory' © Fleur Adcock 1986, reprinted from *The Incident Book* by Fleur Adcock (1986) by permission of Oxford University Press; the poem 'Not Waving but Drowning' from *The Collected Poems of Stevie Smith* (Penguin Modern Classics) (1957) reprinted by permission of James MacGibbon; 'Instead of a Poet' (1965) by Francis Hope reprinted by permission of The Bodley Head; an extract from *Bitter Lemons* (1957) by Lawrence Durrell reprinted by permission of Faber and Faber Ltd.; an extract from *Lord of the Flies* (1954) by William Golding reprinted by permission of Faber and Faber Ltd., an extract from *Summer Before the Dark* (1973) by Doris Lessing reprinted by permission of the author; an extract from *The Collector* (1963) by John Fowles is reprinted by permission of Anthony Sheil Associates Ltd; an extract from *Grandmother* (1950) by Freya Stark reprinted by permission of John Murray (Publishers) Ltd.; an extract from *Mani* (1958) by Patrick Leigh Fermor reprinted by permission of John Murray (Publishers) Ltd.; an extract from *The Hill of Kronos* by Peter Levi is reprinted by permission of Collins Publishers; an extract from *All What Jazz* by Philip Larkin reprinted by permission of Faber and Faber Ltd.

Every effort has been made to trace the holders of copyright material used in this anthology. We apologise for any omissions in this respect, and on notification we undertake to make the appropriate acknowledgement in subsequent editions.

INDEX OF AUTHORS AND TITLES